COMMUNITY DEVELOPMENT IN THEORY AND PRACTICE

AN INTERNATIONAL READER

Community Development in Theory and Practice

An International Reader

Edited by

Gary Craig, Keith Popple and Mae Shaw

SPOKESMAN

First published in 2008 by Spokesman
5 Churchill Park
Nottingham
NG4 2HF
Phone 0115 9708381
elfeuro@compuserve.com
www.spokesmanbooks.com

© Spokesman

ISBN 978 0 85124 730 4
A CIP Catalogue is available from the British Library.

CONTENTS

Editorial Foreword

Gary Craig, Keith Popple and Mae Shaw

The Community Development Journal *(CDJ)*, which is probably the widest-read and certainly the most prestigious international journal focusing on community development, was established in 1966. It emerged at a time when many of those then practising community development in the UK had had experience – in some cases very many years of experience – of working in British colonies, as community development officers, extension workers and so on. On their return to the UK they discovered that British social welfare was primarily focused on the casework approach with its 'emphasis on confidentiality, professional detachment and a clinical relationship towards the individual client'. (Dickinson 1973) In response, they wanted to see if it was possible to introduce and adapt the community development approaches used in the colonies to the UK scene.

This led to the production of various Newsletters and Bulletins, including the *Community Development Bulletin* which was the forerunner to the *CDJ* and produced through the Institute of Education, University of London. The first editor of the *CDJ* was Peter du Sautoy, previously Director of Social Welfare and Community Development in Ghana, and at the time a lecturer in Fundamental Education and Community Development at the University of Manchester. Although he edited and handled the business affairs of the journal from his home, the Oxford University Press had been persuaded by Sautoy and the board of distinguished writers, including Reg Batten, to publish the *CDJ*.

In the past 40+ years, the *CDJ* has gone from strength to strength, reaching a wider and wider audience (at least in terms of the range of countries in which it is read and about which it has published articles), continuing to be published by Oxford University Press, and edited by a succession of editors from both academic and practice backgrounds but, compared with most journals, relatively few in number. The Editorial Board is probably now more dominated by academic interests than hitherto, but it is supported by a wide-ranging International Editorial Board from many parts of the world. This International Board provides a conduit to practice, theory and news from many parts of the world with which the *CDJ* might otherwise have had a rather tenuous and haphazard connection.

In 2006, the Board received a proposal from us for this edited Reader and enthusiastically supported it, providing a small grant to cover development costs and to subsidise the price so that the book could be more available to those on relatively low incomes. Oxford University Press also encouraged us to proceed with the project and seek an appropriate publisher. This we have done.

Despite the temptations to do so in this age of league tables, this collection of just under thirty articles should not **necessarily** be seen as the 'best' of the *CDJ* (not that we think it would in any case be possible to identify what the 'best' would be). What we have drawn together here is, we think, a collection of articles which are representative of the time when they were written, of the different countries and contexts in the world where community development is **practised** and/or written about, and of the changing nature of community development itself. Thus, in making a choice for this book, **which is necessarily limited by considerations of size and cost,** we were faced with exactly the same dilemma which faced **successive** editors of the *CDJ*, issue by issue: how to select a range of articles which met a quality threshold (even if, in some cases, considerable editorial help was required to get the article over that threshold!), which was representative of time and place, and which also had a cutting edge in terms of theory or practice or taking community development theory or practice into new territories.

Over the 40+ years of the *CDJ*, something like 1000 articles have been published in the Journal. A further 2000-3000 were rejected for a variety of reasons, Some were not relevant to the *CDJ*'s interests; some were simply very badly written or unclear; many added little to our thinking; in the case of one or two countries, we received a substantial number of papers over the years which appeared to have been written from the same template with only the names of key players or places changed to give a suggestion of novelty. From this 1000 published articles we have chosen just under thirty articles.

The basis of our choice was this: first, we wanted to ensure that as many parts of the world, with their different political, cultural and socio-economic contexts, could be represented; within this collection you will therefore find chapters from every corner of the world. Secondly, we wanted to be able to include a selection which took the reader steadily through the life of the *CDJ* – and therefore, we would argue – of the life of community development itself. Thus there are papers from all of the decades from 1966 to the present. These are also, as Marjorie Mayo notes in her preamble, grouped within a threefold structure, covering the period from the 1960s to the late 1970s, when community development was reinventing its identity from a colonial past to a largely urban and western context; the 1980s and early 1990s, when community development positioned itself largely in opposition to the state; and the last 15 years, where the social and political context for community development has been dominated by the growth of social movements but also where it has had to cope with the pressures of privatisation and marketisation of welfare as a whole. This is a crude categorisation but helps the reader, we hope, to understand the context within which the papers were written. Thirdly, we wanted to reflect the practice of community development within differing contexts: from a government or local government base, with specific populations, in relationship to differing welfare sectors such as health, housing, employment, and so on. Fourthly, we wanted to ensure there was an adequate selection of articles focusing on theory: we believe that community development theory receives far too little attention – too many community workers continue to stare exclusively at the gutter rather than at the stars. And fifthly, and finally, we wanted to ensure that important social divisions were represented in our selection. Here we were less successful: whilst we have articles which focus on gender and 'race', we have none which focus on disability; this simply reflects the fact that the *CDJ* has had very few articles written about this territory.

The consequence of this framework is that we had to make some very difficult decisions indeed: articles which we all wanted to see again in print on the basis of some factors were excluded by others simply because the latter met some alternative but unavoidable criteria. Another consequence is that some of the articles appear, also unavoidably, completely dated. Of course they were written in another time and that is precisely why they are important: because they show how community development has adapted over time, how it struggled to create an identity and then, having more or less done so (although disputes continue about the way values and theory are interpreted in practice – as you would expect from a practice which is inherently political), to defend that identity against the encroachment of virtually every other political and policy current which has attempted to rebrand itself as 'community something-or-other'; and how both practice and theory have become more subtle over time. Some articles were very short in their original form and thus are reproduced more or less verbatim; others were much longer and have thus had to be edited substantially.

The practice of community development aligns itself clearly with the democratic project. At a time when campaigns to 'spread democracy' are, at the very least questionable because of their hidden economic agendas, verging on forms of political, cultural and economic imperialism, it is worth reminding ourselves that the task of community development is essentially about giving an effective voice to those many groups and interests whose voices are rarely heard in a world – east or west, north or south – characterised by vast disparities of power, income and wealth, so that the needs of those who are most disadvantaged, can be articulated and met. We hope this collection, from a fascinating range of perspectives, can contribute further to strengthening that now-global project. Community development workers are, by and large, not the most avid of writers about their work and we make no apology for reproducing work which has appeared in print before. Many of the articles will, in any case, be new to very many readers.

We are grateful to the *CDJ* Editorial Board, and to Oxford University Press for their support; to Professor Marjorie Mayo for her incisive and characteristically thoughtful preamble; and to all the authors of the articles included within this collection. We were not able to contact every one of them to obtain written permission, despite our best efforts, but we are confident they would be more than pleased to be associated with this project. Some, of course, have died since their original article was written and we hope this provides an appropriate tribute to their particular contributions.

Finally we would like to thank Spokesman for their confidence in the Reader and for assisting us through its publication. Viv Edwards, at the University of Edinburgh, was enormously helpful with transcription typing, as was the Moray House Library for access to their CDJ archive.

For further information about the *CDJ* contact
Christopher.miller@uwe.ac.uk

For further information about this collection, contact
G.Craig@hull.ac.uk

References
Dickinson, A. (1973) Guest editorial: on the approach to this journal, *Community Development Journal*, **8** (2), 58-59

Community Development, Contestations, Continuities and Change

Marjorie Mayo

As a student, I recall being given the lesson that there were no lessons to be learnt from history, closely followed by Marx' famous dictum: that history does indeed repeat itself – but the first time as tragedy, the second time as farce. So this chapter starts with a note of caution. On the one hand, lessons may be learned from a critical reading of the history of community development over the past forty years, it will be suggested. There are parallels and continuities, recurring theoretical debates and re-emergent practice dilemmas. But so are there discontinuities, in diverse contexts, over time. Both need to be unpacked, before attempting to explore their contemporary relevance.

Community development has been and continues to be a contested field, characterised by varying definitions and competing theoretical perspectives, aims and objectives. This introduction starts by identifying examples of continuing debates within and around the definitions and purposes of community development, together with recurrent issues and dilemmas for practice. Having identified examples of continuities, it moves on to explore key differences and discontinuities, over time. The context for community development in the late 1960s and early 1970s differed significantly from the context from the mid-1970s and early 1980s, just as that differed from the 1990s and beyond. These contexts are reflected in the organisation of this book as a whole. Marx also famously remarked that men (and women) make their own history, but not in circumstances of their own choosing. The contexts within which community development workers operate differ, impacting upon their range of choices, offering varying opportunities and challenges. These differing contexts set the framework for the evaluation of differing community development strategies, together with their potential relevance for contemporary contexts in the first decade of the twenty-first century.

Community development: contested definitions and competing perspectives

The definition of 'community' itself has been problematic enough, let alone the consequent definitions of 'community development'. Even by the mid- to late 1960s, when the *Community Development Journal* was first published, 94 definitions of community had been identified, leading the sociologist Margaret Stacey to doubt whether the concept referred to any useful abstraction at all. (Stacey 1969) Community development has been and continues to be similarly contested.

Rather than engage with these varying definitions here, the point to emphasise is simply this, that these terms have been and continue to be used in widely differing ways. As Biddle (1966) argued, way back in the 1960s, 'Two enthusiasts for Community Development, in conversation, will often discover that they are talking about quite different experiences, even though they both lay claim to the admired title'. In his discussion of Key Words, Raymond Williams (1976) suggested that virtually any concept of significance was or had been the subject of contestation, which at least puts community development in good company.

These problems of definition raise further questions in their turn. First, it raises Stacey's question as to whether a term so inherently fuzzy refers to any useful abstraction at all. Parallel questions continue to be posed in contemporary contexts, when terms such as community participation and community empowerment are similarly applied as 'spray-on effects', meaning all things to all people and so perhaps meaning nothing to anybody in particular. The term 'participation', for example, has been identified with at least four different approaches in varying ways over time. (Hickey and Mohun 2004)

The term community development may still carry warmly persuasive connotations, promising alternatives to the self-absorption and the alienation accompanying contemporary capitalism, as Richard Sennett (1976) has suggested, promising islands of 'homely and cosy tranquillity in a sea of turbulence and inhospitality' in Bauman's explanation of current preoccupations with the vision of community. (Bauman 2000) But how might the term be carry varying connotations in practice, masking fundamentally differing perspectives and agendas? Along with community and youth work, community development has a long history, dating back to the nineteenth century, in Britain and elsewhere. Charitable impulses can be identified on the part of sponsors along with progressive impulses for social justice and social change. But so can less disinterested motives. The development of youth and community work in Britain, for example, was at least partly concerned to civilise 'the barbarians' (i.e. working class youth) promoting fitness so that working class youth could 'shoot and drill and "scout"' – as Baden-Powell, the founder of the Boy Scouts at the beginning of the twentieth century went on to argue 'we must all be bricks in the wall of that great edifice – the British Empire ... fortifying the wall of Empire'. (quoted in Springhall 1977)

The point of these quotations is absolutely not to suggest that the early history of community and youth work was entirely related to the requirements of Empire or simply to patronise the poor, let alone that there were no progressive aspects to its history. On the contrary, the point is precisely to emphasise again that this has long been a contested field and continues to be. (Craig 2007) Community and youth work has been promoted, along with community development more generally, to service imperial agendas, managing social change in the interests of the powerful. And they have been promoted to facilitate self-help in order to legitimise reductions in service provision, shifting responsibilities from the public sector to the voluntary/non-governmental (NGO) and community sectors. But so, at the same time but in parallel spheres of action, have they been promoted for alternative agendas, to facilitate solidarity and critical understanding, building progressive movements for social development and indeed for social justice.

As the following section will suggest in more detail, these competing agendas have emerged in varying guises, over the past four decades, just as relations between the global North and the global South have taken differing forms, from the last days of Empire to the challenges of contemporary globalisation. Before exploring these differing contexts over time, however, there are a number of other common threads to be recorded. These illustrate some of the ways in which issues and dilemmas can emerge and re-emerge over time, with powerful parallels as well as significant differences.

Continuing debates and dilemmas for community development in practice

Alongside competing definitions and perspectives there have, in addition, been continuing debates about the relevance of theory and its relations with practice. In periods of rapid change and uncertainty the importance of theory has been particularly emphasised, the need for clear strategic thinking, in order to identify emerging spaces and new opportunities for effective practice. Conversely, the relevance of theory for practice has also been the subject of debate. To what extent have particular theoretical approaches, including radical approaches, posed unattainable challenges for practice? Or to what extent has theory actually informed or even been consistent with practice – how far do we actually do what we say we do – uncomfortable questions which have arisen from research in varying contexts over time. Theory has been valued as a guide for strengthening effective practice. But community development debates have also been characterised by anti-theory, anti-intellectual strands, alongside varying forms of populism. (Hickey and Mohun 2004) Many community workers have preferred to fix their eyes on the gutters, rather than on the stars, to concentrate on everyday issues rather than think strategically about how to effect change.

There would seem to be connections here with continuing debates about professionalism and continuing dilemmas about professionalisation. Community development has always been characterised by considerable ambivalence about these issues. Challenging hide-bound bureaucratic procedures and top-down approaches to development, community workers have emphasised the importance of more holistic, bottom-up approaches, focusing upon participation and inclusiveness, working in inter-disciplinary ways across professional boundaries. Attempts to regularise community and youth work, community education and development training and professional development have met with resistance, typified as strategies for state control. In the current context of increasing managerialism, regulation by log frames and ever more tightly defined targets, the prospect of further regulation may provoke correspondingly increasing anxieties. Professionalisation has, in addition, been criticised as representing the professional self-interest of an exclusive elite, aiming to promote increasing credentialism to exclude others, including unpaid activists and volunteers in the very communities in question.

Being a 'jack of all trades', the generalist development worker promoting service integration, has always, however, had its own limitations, too. In the current context, with the contemporary emphasis upon working across professional boundaries in partnerships, community development's particular ethos and values risk dilution, reduced to a set of aspirations about participation, tagged on to a range of professional job descriptions, with the community worker in charge of a tool kit of technical fixes to ensure that the 'consultation' target box can be ticked. (Banks *et al.* 2003)

There are links here with continuing debates about process versus outcome, dilemmas for practitioners attempting to balance the importance of promoting sustainable development and regeneration processes for the longer-term, with the need to meet more immediate targets in the here and now. Here too, there are recurrent questions about the balances to be struck, just as there are continuing debates about the balances to be struck between working to meet bottom-up priorities as against top-down dictates or indeed to meet wider social needs. The Non-Directive Approach (see Batten, Chapter 5 this volume) typified the former position in past debates just as the Directive Approach typified the latter. In practice, the reality has proved more complex, of course, as debates on the ethics of community development in the context of diversity and difference have illustrated. Community development statements of values, as set out, for example, by the International Association for Community Development,[1] clearly enshrine commitments to the promotion of equality of opportunities and respect for diversity within as well as between communities, alongside the values of democracy, social inclusion and human rights. The Non-Directive Approach would not be acceptable, then, as a justification for condoning racism, sexism or indeed any other form of discrimination against oppressed or otherwise disadvantaged groups. This is arguably an extreme case. The choices to be made – between intervention and non-intervention – remain problematic in so many circumstances, however, posing continuing dilemmas for workers as they attempt to balance the competing needs and priorities of differing interests and groups within and between communities. There are inherent tensions here, with differing theoretical perspectives on the balances to be struck between the claims of identity, identity politics and locality versus the interests of solidarity, building progressive alliances within and between communities and wider movements for social justice, both locally and beyond. (Mayo 2000)

This brings the discussion to the issue of conflict more generally. There have been and continue to be debates on this topic within and around community development. Broadly there would seem to be two aspects here. The first concerns the use of conflict tactics as a tool for practice, a contentious issue that has emerged at various points and localities over time.

The second and more fundamental aspect concerns the extent to which community development has been based upon social theories that emphasise consensus. Pluralist approaches, in particular, start from the common interests that underpin communities and societies, more generally, whatever the apparent differences, in terms of whose voices tend to be most effectively heard. From this perspective, the community development worker's job is to ensure that everyone is enabled to participate so that different voices can indeed be heard.

This approach stands in contrast with structural conflict approaches, approaches based upon the view that communities and societies are underpinned by fundamental conflicts of interests. From this perspective the community development worker's job is to enable those with less power to recognise the sources of these underlying inequalities so that they can make informed decisions about whether and how to develop strategies for change, building alliances with others, in the cause of greater social justice. Differing positions on the extent to which communities and societies are underpinned by consensus or conflicts of interest relate then to differing perspectives on community development and its goals more generally.

There are, in addition, related debates about the sources of power and the focus for challenge and change, both locally and beyond, internationally. To what extent might community development strategies need to focus upon the state and its structures and agents, providing key services for development/ regeneration (or not as the case may be)? Or alternatively, to what extent might community development strategies need to focus upon issues relating to the *market*, and/ or strengthening civil society in relation to the *market* as well as to the *state*? There have been shifts of emphasis here, mirroring to some extent, perhaps, the shifting relationships between civil society, the market and the state, in the context of increasing globalisation, shifts that relate to the different periods to be identified in the following section.

The differing contexts for community development

Any attempt to divide history into particular periods of time is potentially problematic. So much depends upon which aspects of history are to be the key focus – community development in this case – but other socio-economic, political and cultural factors clearly impinge. This book divides the relevant periods as follows but it has to be recognised that these periods shade into one another and that the process of change is not usually marked by critical fault lines.

- 'Re-inventing British Community Development: the postcolonial legacy'
- 'Community Work and the State'; and
- 'The Impact of social movements in a globalising world'

'Re-inventing British community development –
the post-colonial legacy':
the context from the mid to late 1960s

The *Community Development Journal* began publication in a period of rapid change, the implications of which were only beginning to emerge, and which gained increasing recognition as the 1960s unfolded. Internationally, the beginning of the 1960s was a period of some optimism, perhaps, in the context of post-war reconstruction and development. Social development was on the agenda (more or less) along with economic development, especially rural development, including the need to address problems associated with rural-urban migration. There was, in addition, some increasing awareness of the importance of addressing equalities issues, including women's inclusion in education and welfare programmes (even if so many initiatives still focused upon women's traditional domestic roles with little recognition of their roles as farmers/ producers and less still recognition of the case for challenging gender inequalities more fundamentally). Most importantly, decolonisation was in process, following Indian independence in 1948, marking the beginning of the end (albeit a long drawn-out process for some) of empire for a number of former colonial powers.

Community development had already been identified as relevant in the post-war context. As the then Secretary of State for the Colonies had opined, Mass Education (the fore-runner to community development) was a 'movement designed to promote better living for the whole community, with the active participation of and, if possible, on the initiative of, the community'. (quoted in Mass Education Bulletin 1949) Mass Education, and then community development programmes, were to promote social development. And they were to promote 'political development', meaning, in the contemporary context of the Cold War, winning hearts and minds, keeping the newly-independent Commonwealth and other states safe from communism – economically as well as politically integrated within the frameworks of Northern agendas. In the event, of course, community education and development programmes contributed to strengthening movements for colonial freedom, as in the case of the Gold Coast (now Ghana). But community development programmes were also promoted as part of counter-insurgency strategies (Walters 1951) – far more dubious strategies that included the emergency 'resettlement' (i.e. forced removals) of some half a million people in 'community development' villages in what was then Malaya.

By the mid- to late 1960s, however, these Northern agendas were coming in for increasing criticism. In Britain and other Northern states, the first optimism of the post-war reconstruction period was giving way to growing awareness of the problems that remained. Unemployment began to rise as the economy was slowing down, in Britain, whilst industrial restructuring had disproportionately serious effects upon the older industrial areas. Meanwhile cracks were increasing apparent in the British Welfare State, as services were seen to be failing to meet growing demands. And racism was a growing problem, as migrants who had been encouraged to come from the former colonies (to fill the least attractive job vacancies that had been hard to fill during the post-war boom years) were blamed and subjected to discrimination, in the competition for jobs and affordable housing. This was the context for the launch of the first British major governmental programme to promote community development at home in British cities, the Community Development Programme (announced in 1968 in part to address the '"race" relations' problem in inner cities); 'the Empire Strikes Back', as Stuart Hall alternatively described the impact of the colonial past, reverberating in Britain more generally at this time. (Centre for Contemporary Cultural Studies 1992)

There were parallels as well as differences in the United States, with the launch of community development programmes in the mid-1960s, to tackle the increasingly evident problems of poverty through the so-called 'War on Poverty'. In the USA, there were, in addition, powerful challenges to the problems of racial discrimination, as the Civil Rights Movement campaigned for racial equality. Community development programmes had of course, existed in the past, in varying contexts, but there was renewed impetus for action at the federal level at this period. Like Britain, only more so, the USA was also increasingly concerned to promote community development abroad, to win hearts and minds, in the context of the Cold War. Vietnam was a case in particular (Brokensha and Hodge quoted in Mayo 1975), a case that became the subject of major controversy within community development debates, as well as becoming the subject of contestation and social mobilisation more generally.

By the mid- to late 1960s, then, community development was being re-discovered and promoted in the North, just as it was being promoted in the South, for varying reasons, including reasons associated with the Cold War and with the agendas of the great powers including the former imperial (and neo-colonial) powers. This was a period of dynamism and challenge. (Fisher 1994) There were mobilisations for Civil Rights and there were mobilisations against the war in Vietnam, mobilisations that spread, internationally, along with international mobilisations of student movements in many Western countries. There were fundamental criticisms of US foreign policy, just as there were fundamental criticisms of domestic policies, and fundamental criticisms of the roles of key professionals working within the public services, as structural analyses of the underlying causes of poverty and social disadvantage were being developed.

Community work and the state: from the 1960s into the 1970s

This background context is key to an understanding of debates within community development at this period. There were challenges to government programmes in the North, (such as the structural analyses developed by participants in the British Community Development Programme: CDP 1976) just as there were challenges to international programmes, including those promoted by the USA. The state, (including the local state), was the target of much criticism, along with state officials and welfare professionals, although the private sector came in for criticism too, as the costs of industrial change – deindustrialisation, urban dereliction, disinvestment and unemployment – were off-loaded onto particular communities, in the interests of private profitability. And there was increasing interest in building alliances across the divides between communities and workplaces, community action and industrial action. (see Bryant: Chapter Four this volume)

Meanwhile counter-cultural movements posed alternative visions for the future. Former student activists and student activists took new ideas into differing fields including community activism, a phenomenon that can be identified across a range of different contexts, both North and South. Similarly, feminists began to raise issues about gender and the importance of challenging gender inequality within development in general and community development more specifically (although there were time-lags, here, within community development debates, with less explicit focus upon gender until later in the 1970s, in Britain).

In particular, the work of Paulo Freire, the Brazilian educator, made increasing impact internationally, during this period. (Freire 1972) His approach to education for the development of critical consciousness provided theoretical insights as well as practical tools for those concerned with community education and development. Freire's work was, in addition, seminal in the development of participatory approaches and participatory research more generally.

The mid to late 1970s to the late 1980s

In summary, this was a period of uncertainty and change – but in very different directions. Although the oil crisis in the first part of the 1970s was not the sole cause, this symbolised the beginnings of increasing economic pressures, internationally. With mounting economic concerns about profitability, international agencies and governments began to demonstrate growing interest in alternative strategies, strategies that began to shift the balance between sectors. Disillusion with big state-led development projects was accompanied by increasingly vocal arguments for rolling back the state to make way for the private sector. The market would provide, and the benefits would 'trickle down' to the poor and the poorest, or so it was argued. Britain experienced one of the earlier examples of what later came to be known as structural adjustment in the mid-1970s, when public expenditure, and consequent public service cuts, were imposed as conditions for International Monetary Fund (IMF) support. By the end of the 1970s, retrenchment gathered momentum with the election of the Thatcher government in the UK, Margaret Thatcher and Ronald Reagan (and their imitators elsewhere in the world later on), between them coming to symbolise the triumph of neo-liberalism, rolling back the state, in order to give the private market freer rein.

The 1980s have been described as a 'lost decade' in terms of development. Neo-liberalism was predominant, internationally, as international agencies such as the World Bank and the IMF promoted the 'Washington Consensus' of free market economics, promoted via structural adjustment – the enforcement of neo-liberal strategies as conditions for loans, as so many countries found themselves deeper and deeper in debt. These were challenging times for community development. Margaret Thatcher herself once famously commented that there was no such thing as society, only individuals and their families, rational producer and consumers in the market economy maximising their own self-interest. Community development was hardly a priority here. The British Community Development Projects had already been wound down in the mid-1970s, by government and local government not wanting to hear their analysis of structural conflict. This seemed like the beginning of the end indeed for community development.

The reality was more complex and contradictory, however. Even in Britain, community development survived in particular spaces (if sometimes under other guises) whether supported by local authorities prepared to challenge the dominant view or whether presented in terms of promoting local economic development. (Craig *et al.* 1984) Whilst the market was to rule, with the individual consumer as sovereign, there was, in addition, some recognition of a continuing role for the voluntary/NGO sector, if only to promote self-help, filling some of the gaps that emerged as public services suffered retrenchment. Community development debates from this period illustrate considerable heart-searching, as to the balances to be struck and the compromises which should or should not be made here, keeping services going – but at the risk of letting the public sector off the hook, legitimising cuts and down-playing the voluntary/NGO sector's advocacy and campaigning roles.

Meanwhile, spaces were creatively taken in a range of other contexts too. This was also a period of advance in the development of theories and practices of participatory development, theories and practices that were to have increasing influence, North as well as South. And gender issues were being actively debated in the context of development (Young 1993) just as were equality issues more generally (including the rights and needs of people with disabilities).

Despite the challenges, this was also a period of great creativity, as participatory approaches were being developed in a range of contexts in the global South, including participatory approaches to support popular mobilisations against authoritarian governments and top-down approaches to development. PRIA, the organisation promoting participatory research in Asia was launched in 1982, for instance, a key organisation with now a twenty five-year track record of promoting participation and empowerment. Drawing upon the work of Freire, Bud Hall and other adult educators, PRIA has built international links, building alliances based upon the view that knowledge is power – the prerequisite to effective empowerment and participation, and predicated upon a rights-based approach to development.

In summary then, this was a contradictory period, with significant advances despite the challenges of the Reagan/Thatcher years of rampant neo-liberalism. More strategic approaches were required, to find the spaces for community development for progressive social change agendas in this contradictory context – and these were beginning to emerge. Advocacy and campaigning were developing around global issues as well as local issues by the beginning of the 1990s and there was increasing recognition of the importance of participation as a human right.

'The impact of social movements in a globalising world': the 1990s and beyond

Being so much closer, this latter period is perhaps less in need of summary. In brief, the following factors would seem to have particular relevance for community development. The end of the Cold War, symbolised by the fall of the Berlin Wall, was hailed by some on the political right as marking the end of history, with the global triumph of western-style democracy. (Fukayama 1992) Democratisation has certainly been promoted, not only in Eastern and Central Europe but also in a number of Southern contexts, as former military dictatorships came to an end. To support democratisation, a range of strategies have been developed to strengthen civil society, including strategies to promote decentralisation and community participation via community development[1]. Community development would seem to have been rediscovered.

The reality, however, would seem to be considerably more complex – as the supposed 'New World Order' began to seem more like the 'New World Disorder'. As the human costs of neo-liberal policies became more evident, with protests against the effects of structural adjustment programmes, for example, there were policy adjustments. 'A human face' was to soften the effects for the poor and the poorest, women and children and other vulnerable groups, encouraging self-help initiatives into the bargain. Involving the poor in participatory planning processes would add legitimacy, too, perhaps – illustrating, once again, increasing scope for community development together with some of community development's inherent dilemmas on this score. (Craig and Mayo 1995)

Meanwhile, democratisation was being imposed by force – an increasingly evident contradiction in contexts such as Afghanistan and, more recently, Iraq. And transnational corporations have been continuing to identify opportunities for profit, including opportunities for profit in situations of conflict and post-conflict reconstruction. Are we witnessing the so-called 'End of History' or simply the triumph of global capitalism?

Here again, the reality would seem considerably more complex. 'Globalisation' (to use yet another contested term) has also been associated with increasing ease of communication via the internet, just as there have been expanding opportunities for advocacy and campaigning internationally as well as locally. Of course these have not been one-way processes. Despite global mobilisations against the war in Iraq, the war went ahead, fuelling disillusion – widening the so-called democratic deficit in western democracies and fanning the flames of violence on either side (attacks on civil liberties, for example as well as attacks by terrorists). (Tarrow 2005) But there have been major mobilisations with some potential for building movements for social justice, rights-based approaches to development, advocating for an end to unpayable debt, campaigning for trade justice and for the right to education and to health care, including rights for women and for all oppressed groups. (Mayo 2005) The Millennium Development Goals and campaigns such as Jubilee 2000 have provided particular foci for these campaigns, including campaigns on environmental issues, increasingly evidently key for sustainable development.

In summary then, the current context can be characterised in terms of increasing complexity and growing challenges for community development, but with new spaces for linking the local with the global, as the basis for building potentially powerful and sustainable movements for change. (Edwards and Gaventa 2001)

Potential lessons for community development today?

This Introduction began by suggesting that learning from history can be a hazardous business. There are intriguing parallels to be drawn, as particular issues and practice dilemmas re-emerge in different contexts over time, debates about the role of community development in the context of multi- service teams, for example, differences of view about professionalisation in the context of increasing marketisation, and dilemmas around the promotion of self-help and community participation in the context of 'decentralisation' programmes defined by centrally-imposed targets. Such parallels may be intriguing, but potentially misleading if taken out of context.

Perhaps the key lesson may be the lesson that has already been drawn – the lesson about the importance of strategic thinking, in the face of increasing complexity, strategic thinking about perspectives and long-term goals and strategic thinking about ways of identifying the spaces for creative practice in the context of globalisation. Global advocacy and campaigning would seem to be most effective when soundly rooted in local constituencies, communities, trade union organisations and their allies in civil society, relating global issues to local priorities. Community development has continuing relevance, I would argue. And community development workers can continue to make significant contributions as reflexive practitioners in the current context, when drawing upon the lessons to be learned from their own experiences of practice, to strengthen the roots of sustainable movements for social change and social justice.

References

Banks, S., Henderson, P. and Butcher, H. (2003) *Managing Community Practice*, Bristol: Policy Press.

Bauman, Z. (2000) Liquid Modernity, Cambridge: Polity Press.

Biddle, W. (1966) 'The fuzziness in definition of community development', *Community Development Journal*, No 2: 5-12.

Brokensha, D. and Hodge, P. (1969) *Community Development: An Interpretation*, New York: Chandler.

CDP (1976) *Gilding the Ghetto*, London: Community Development Project.

Centre for Contemporary Cultural Studies (1992) *The Empire Strikes Back: Race and Racism in 70s Britain*, London: Routledge.

Craig, G. (2007) 'Something old, something new....' *Critical Social Policy*, Vol. 38, No 3, August: 335-359.

Craig, G., Derricourt, N. and Loney, M. (1984) *Community work and the State*, London: Routledge Kegan Paul.

Craig, G. and Mayo, M. (1995) *Community Empowerment*, London: Zed Books.

Edwards, M. and Gaventa, J. (2001) *Global Citizen Action*, London: Earthscan.

Fisher, R. (1994) *Let the People Decide*, New York: Twayne Publishers.

Freire, P. (1972) *Pedagogy of the Oppressed*, Harmondsworth: Penguin.

Fukayama, F. (1992) *The End of History: The Last Man*, London: Hamish Hamilton.

Hickey, S. and Mohun, G. (2004) 'Towards participation as transformation: critical themes and challenges' in Hickey, S. and Mohun, G. (2004) *Participation: From Tyranny to Transformation?*, London: Zed Books: 3-24.

Mass Education Bulletin (a precursor to the *Community Development Journal*), 1948 issue.

Mayo, M. (1975) 'Community development: a radical alternative?' in Brake, M. and Bailey, R. (1975) *Radical Social Work*, London: Edward Arnold.

Mayo, M. (2000) *Cultures, Communities, Identities*, Basingstoke: Palgrave.

Mayo, M. (2005) *Global Citizens*, London: Zed.

Sennett, R. (1976) The Fall of the Public Man, New York and London: W.W. Norton.

Springhall, J. (1977) *Youth, Empire and Society*, London: Croom Helm.

Stacey, M. (1969) 'The myth of community studies', *British Journal of Sociology*, 20.2: 134-147.

Tarrow, S. (2005) *The New Transnational Activism,* Cambridge: Cambridge University Press.

Walters, O. (1951) 'Emergency settlement and community development' in *Community Development Bulletin*, 1. 3, December 1951: 1-8

Williams, R. (1976) *Keywords*, London: Croom Helm.

Young, K. (1993) *Planning Development with Women*, London: Macmillan.

Notes
1. See www.iacdglobal.org for the Budapest Declaration.

Marjorie Mayo is Professor in Community Development at Goldsmith's College, London and a long-standing member of the *CDJ* Editorial Board. She has worked in the community sector as well as in local government and with central government (in the national Community Development Project) and has experience of working internationally.

1

Community Development in Britain?

Peter du Sautoy

Last year I met an Australian University Lecturer, who gives courses in community development, who said that after four months in Britain he had not yet come across any real examples of 'community development' as internationally understood. He had, however, met excellent examples of community social work, which tended to be erroneously described as community development. Perhaps, however, there are some small schemes of genuine community development of the 'project' type – unheralded and unsung?

I am greatly concerned, therefore, that any attempts to introduce 'community development' into this country[1] should not either (a) be too attached to existing vested interests in allied fields, such as adult education or social work or (b) range so widely into every field dealing with community affairs that we shall (i) distort a term which is beginning to have a more precise significance internationally, as a result of considerable effort of definition, and (ii) become out of step with international thinking and an emerging consensus of view. It should be remembered that there is much very useful work in the development of communities which is *not* community development in the more precise current use of the term – and a certain amount of work called 'community development' which also isn't.

I accordingly suggest that those in Britain who are interested in seeing the growth of 'community development' should *firstly,* agree to adhere to the definition of community development used for working purposes by the U.N. (U.N. Economic and Social Council 1956) (which, according to the U.N., would cover programmes in about 70 countries) and therefore not allow anything which does not fall within that definition to be called community development; and *secondly,* study the growth of the use of the term 'community development' which now covers a wide variety of different processes in the U.S.A., in order to avoid similar confusions here.

Biddle (1964a) shows the penalty of popularity in the use of the term and how its use grew from a number of different sources – each, I feel, a little unwilling to relinquish its main starting base and to look at 'community development' as a subject in its own right. Biddle has also made a plea for regarding community development as an 'open-ended' or 'non-terminal' process. (Biddle 1964b) He points out the problems arising in the U.S.A. from a historical identification with (a) 'underdeveloped countries', (b) rural life, (c) planning for local improvement and (d) identification with social conflict. In this country one could see problems arising from undue identification with social work, adult education or town planning. Indeed the paper submitted by the U.K. delegation to an international conference in S.E. Asia (Economic Commission for Asia and the Far East, 1963) does not claim to have a co-ordinated community development programme (as in India or Ghana) but sows the seeds of one growing separately in various activities in what are at present regarded as different but allied fields.

I think that those concerned must face up to the fact that in many countries today, community development is now regarded as a subject or activity in its own right, with its own specially-trained professional practitioners. I have tried to make this point concisely in my own writing. (Du Sautoy 1963) It has borrowed from other subjects (as so many modern specialities have) and now consists in the application of a balanced mixture of certain philosophies and techniques to a number of diverse development problems. However, the introduction of a new multi-purpose approach into a system of specialized and compartmentalized training and administration presents a number of problems – particularly since, as has been pointed out more than once (see in particular Sanders 1958), the term 'community development' is used to denote both a philosophy of approach and a programme of action. Its practice also falls within the dual categories of 'communication' and 'co-ordination'.

Are we in the highly complex social and administrative structure of Britain ever *really* going to get a co-ordinated community development *programme* as understood elsewhere? It will, however, be felt that we ought to start *somewhere*. (Ross 1955)

To my way of thinking, the most promising areas are in those of urban renewal (as in the U.S.A.), new towns (which are tending to appoint 'community development' or 'social development' officers), and areas of immigrants. But this still leaves out most of Britain. Moreover, the co-ordinating techniques of community development flourish better in a more centralized administration system. In Britain 'community development' activity would probably have to be undertaken at the level of the larger local government units – with a concomitant unevenness of approach – unless the new Regional

Advisory Councils can be persuaded to take it up.

One is also up against professional and institutional divisions. In Ghana, over ten years ago, a 'general purpose' social worker was successfully developed as being better than the compartmentalized social worker so common in Britain. (see du Sautoy 1955) In a Leader in the *Guardian* of 28ᵗʰ April, 1965 I saw that Professor Titmuss's suggestion of multi-purpose social workers here was characterized as 'radical'. Will existing workers allow themselves to be concentrated and co-ordinated here, as real community development demands?

However, most pioneer community development programmes have started with an 'entering wedge' of activity – in developing countries through self-help building, adult literacy or agricultural extension. What might be the best 'entering wedge' basis for a conscious introduction of community development principles (even if one cannot have an all-out community development programme)? I see some signs that health workers in Britain are beginning to see some of the possibilities in the community development approach – perhaps stimulated through talk of 'community care' (which certainly is *not* yet community development as internationally understood) and through existing experience of a general practitioner approach to ordinary people. The growth of the term 'ekistics' is also indicative of the interests of the architects and town planners in something very akin to community development.

However, where 'community development' is used only to indicate a philosophy of approach, all services concerned in 'nation-building' in relation to people need to co-operate in understanding what it is about and in what way co-ordination of effort might be achieved. Perhaps a few pilot projects in (a) holding conferences about community development for councillors and officials followed by training courses and (b) field co-ordination in an action project on community development lines in some progressive local authority areas, might be convincing starts. Indeed, I think that the more training in the *communication* aspects of community development (which may lead to greater co-operation in other ways) needs to be given as a 'core' course in all the training of the wide variety of professions whose members are dealing with *people*. In addition, much more needs to be done to draw the attention of councillors, administrators and planners generally to the existence of community development (the letters C.D. still stand more for civil defence in the minds of many people in Britain than for community development).

This is done in countries like India, Ghana, Venezuela, the Philippines and Greece. Are we too 'superior' to do the same? One could call such gatherings 'conferences' or 'workshops' rather than 'seminars' or 'courses' if one wanted to avoid offending the dignity of the influential – but they should, at least, be made *aware* of community development as a possible approach to some British community problems.

Finally, I do not think that community development will progress very far in Britain until people are prepared to regard it as something in its own right – and not as a useful appendage or tool for other subjects – for which special training or study of an 'open-ended' kind is needed. We are already behind many other countries in looking at this newly formalized approach to communication and human relations in developing administration – and I greatly fear that we may be in danger of producing some form of 'community organization' in the purely social field, of calling it 'community development', and then of being surprised that we continue to be out of step with other countries which have accepted a different understanding of the term on an international basis.

References

Biddle, W. (1964a) *Currents in Community Development in the U.S.A.* Columbia: University of Missouri.

Biddle, W. (1964b). *The C.D. Bulletin of the U.S. Board of Presbyterian Missions*, October.

du Sautoy, P. (1955). 'The all-purpose social worker in the Gold Coast', *Social Service*, Summer.

du Sautoy, P. (1963) 'A Guide to the Administrator on the Principles of Community Development' *Journal of Local Administration Overseas*, October.

du Sautoy, P. (1964) 'Health and Social Services in Relation to Community Development', Paper delivered to the Salford meeting of the Royal Society of Health, December.

Economic Commission for Asia and the Far East (1963) Report of the Asian Seminar on Urban Community Development, January.

Ross, M. (1955) *Community Organization: Theory and Principles.* New York: Harper, esp. p. 5.

Sanders, I. (1958) *The Community.* U.S.A.: Ronald Press.

U.N. Economic and Social Council (1956) *20th Report of the Admin. Committee on Co-ordination*, New York: United Nations.

Waller, F. and du, Sautoy, P. (1961) 'C.D. and Adult Education in Urban Areas', *International Review of Community Development*, No. 8.

Notes

1. It should be remembered that the title 'community development' appears to have been invented in this country but for export only. It is now much better understood overseas than here.

Peter du Sautoy is editor of the *Community Development Journal:* Vol. 1 No. 1 (1966): 54-56.

2

Social Welfare and Its Place
in Developing Africa

Malcolm J. Brown

Much of the African Continent is on the move and is in a hurry. After centuries of little change a new sense of urgency is felt as the undeveloped nations seek to make up some of the leeway with the more developed countries of the world. Great emphasis is placed upon economic planning and planning agencies of governments are assuming an importance and a control over other agencies of government, hitherto unknown.

As nations construct long-range development plans to cater for the overall development of the many aspects of human activity, there are, for the social worker, disconcerting indications that the development of social welfare programmes are not keeping pace with other national developments. Further, that some developing countries are actually spending proportionately less on social welfare activities, as other development programmes are moving forward.

This situation stems largely from the fact that the authority for the allocation of resources among the many competing demands lies with economic planning agencies and that social welfare departments are unable to convince these agencies of the necessity for a constant or increasing proportion of government revenue to be allocated to social welfare.

Economic planners usually base their objections to social welfare receiving a more realistic share of a nation's wealth around three main areas. These are:

(a) with so little money and so much that needs to be done with it, it is pointless to use up scarce resources upon unproductive and undeserving sections of the community;

(b) it is sensible to wait until a country is developed economically before embarking upon comprehensive social welfare services; and;

(c) social welfare services are unnecessary in Africa because traditionally African peoples always look after one another when there is a human need or suffering and that the provision of social welfare services will actually do harm because they will cause the breakdown of this good and traditional institution of caring for one another.

Certainly there are elements of truth in all of these arguments but also they contain certain flaws and misconceptions that warrant closer investigation.

First, most governments would agree that economic development is not wanted for its own sake but only in order that its citizens can have a fuller, happier or more satisfying life; and that governments are concerned with developing all of their citizens to the fullest potential of which they are capable. To label individuals or sections of a community then as unproductive or undeserving is to make a value judgement that few of us are in a position to do. Certainly, economically, a blind, uneducated man will always be less productive than a brilliant, young, sighted engineer. But to give every opportunity to the latter to advance in his career but to provide no resources for the blind member of the society, is to lose sight of the fact that our real goal is a better life for all citizens and not economic development of itself. Economic development is one way of achieving our goal – but the provision of homes and sheltered employment for the blind is another.

To label people as undeserving is even more difficult to justify. We do not blame a child if he responds in an anti-social way to the treatment of unloving, cruel and neglectful parents. We tend to say that there are no delinquent children, only delinquent parents. Yet if we do not blame the child who has never been taught how to behave properly and has never received the love that is essential for his normal emotional development, how can we logically blame him as an adult, for not behaving in a responsible way? Or how are we justified in condemning an ex-prisoner for committing a further offence if nothing was done better to equip him for a reasonable life, during his years in prison? Rather than label as unproductive or undeserving certain sectors of the community and ignore them or give them but a cursory attention in our development plans, do we need to include all citizens in our planning and, through the provision of social welfare services, help them to become more productive and more deserving; and, in accordance with our main aim, give them, too, the opportunity of a better life.

Turning now to the second main argument, in reality few nations can never afford social welfare. Demands for resources invariably exceed supply and social welfare programmes would fare very badly indeed if they only got what was left. Yet in another and in a very real sense, very few nations can afford not to have a social welfare programme. For, to say – let us first concentrate on economic development and provide social welfare services later when we can afford them – can be likened to the father of the house who concentrated all of his efforts in obtaining economic security for his family. He worked hard himself, often long into the night and sent his wife out to work that she might supplement his income. He never had time to play with his children and hardly gave them any love or affection because he saw so little of them. When the great day came that he had been working for for so long and he was not economically secure, he turned to his family to provide them with all the other necessities for a good and full life, but he was too late. Governments too, cannot afford to say – let us make this five-year plan solely an economic one and social welfare can go into the next. For, 'too late', says the old man rejected by his own children. 'Too late' says the delinquent youth and 'Too late' says the neglected child.

But if we concentrate on alleviating social problems there will be nothing left for economic growth and we shall be worse off than before – the argument goes on. This of course is true; a developing country cannot possibly meet all social needs. What it can do however is to allocate a proportion of its budget for social welfare and ensure that this proportion is maintained as overall government expenditure increases and not rely on the faint hope that one day in the future, social welfare services can be afforded.

Finally, economic development invariably means a degree of industrialisation and movement from rural to urban areas. The changes that the individual is required to undergo are many and substantial yet we are inclined to assume automatically that he will maintain his traditional attitudes to those who seek his help. The African in transition is likely to be working for wages instead of producing his own requirements and will be obliged to pay money for the things that he needs. He will be in an inter-tribal situation, constantly coming up against cultures and customs at variance with his own. He will pay rent for his accommodation instead of building his own home and will buy his vegetables instead of growing them. A whole range of attractive goods will be on show before him and working in order to buy life's luxuries will become meaningful to him for the very first time. Caring for one's less-fortunate fellow men when it is merely a matter of enlarging the village home and sharing the fruits of the garden is one thing but it is a different matter altogether when this compassionate act involves paying extra money to rent larger quarters (when rents are already at a premium) and continually paying hard cash to feed one's relatives and tribal associates who are in need. This is not to deny that many Africans continue to do just this but neither can we deny the fact that for many, the cost of maintaining this particular tribal tradition is becoming too great a price to pay when there is so much else to do with one's earnings. Nearly all African countries report a breakdown (at varying rates of disintegration) in traditional ways of caring for others. In some tribes even aged parents are being neglected – a situation totally unheard of just a few years ago. In the light of this new reality situation we are unjustified in assuming that all is well and that the African – even in transition – will continue to look after his own. This does not only apply to material assistance but also in ways of relating to one another and in dealing with human situations. Here is an example:

> Mr. and Mrs. Boka came to the social worker and complained that their 14-year old daughter was leading an immoral life in an urban town 200 miles away. In response to the worker's questions they explained that they had come to the town 10 years ago and had tried to show their daughter the way to behave in accordance with the customs of their tribe. The daughter however had taken little notice of them and had been influenced by the unsatisfactory behaviour of girls living in the same street. The Bokas then explained that they had sent her back to the village to be disciplined by her grandmother – adding, with some surprise, that she had run away from the grandmother. The social worker asked what they planned to do now and they replied that they had done everything they knew and that there was nothing more that they could do.

This family was clearly overwhelmed by their urban situation. In the village their daughter would probably have been obedient to them. Failing this, certainly being sent to be disciplined by the grandmother would have had the desired effect. The traditional ways of handling this family problem however were of no effect in the urban situation and there were simply no further tribal resources to call upon.

This case is not used in an attempt to illustrate the need for keeping people in their rural areas or to try to turn back the clock, but it does suggest that familiar ways of dealing with situations are often of no avail to the emerging family and that we have a clear responsibility to provide the social welfare services that are needed to take over where tribal methods can go no further. In this particular case the government had provided social workers to help families in towns deal with their problems created by the transition from rural to urban life.

To suggest that social welfare will break down existing ways of helping those in need is generally to miss the mark. What welfare services attempt to do is to support existing and traditional ways of helping those in need but to take from the situation the extreme or intolerable burden imposed by the urban or traditional situation. For example, it may be customary for a man to care for his brother's children in the event of the latter's death. In the village this may be a reasonable means of dealing with these needy children. The cost of carrying out this practice in the city however may be too much for this uncle. In the absence of a social welfare programme he may neglect the children, return them to the village without ensuring that they will be properly cared for by someone else, or demand that the State take responsibility for them. Inadequate services may result in the children being placed in an institution, thus breaking up the tribal tradition for this family. Adequate services would help and support the uncle in caring for the children himself and thus maintain tribal ways of caring for children – but lessening the impossible financial burden imposed upon the uncle. Many other examples could be given with regard to the aged, the sick and the unemployed.

While economic planning is of the utmost importance, it is important too that the wholeness of man should be catered for and that economic growth should never be allowed to become a nation's goal – but only a means to achieve its goal. A decision always needs to be taken as to how much of governmental expenditure should be set aside for those in need of help of a social welfare nature There is never enough to meet all needs so this decision must, of necessity, be taken arbitrarily. It has often been suggested that developed nations help the developing ones to the extent of 5% of their budget. Few consider that this figure is too high. Equally, this 5% might be a reasonable figure for the developing nations of Africa to allocate from their own budgets through social welfare programmes, for those who will directly benefit least from economic growth – that all might share the fruits of good government and economic progress.

Malcolm J. Brown: Vol. 3 No. 3 (1968): 139-142.

3
Whither Community Development in Canada?

Jim Lotz

Introduction

In April 1968 a group of people met in the Ontario Institute for Studies in Education in Toronto. They came from as far west as Alberta and as far east as Newfoundland. The group included university professors studying culture brokers, adult educators, social workers involved with 'hippies', film makers, people working with so-called unemployables. This National Workshop on Community Development Teaching and Research[1] brought together a number of people who had one thing in common. Each had first-hand contact with poverty and disadvantaged peoples. Each had experienced and become sensitized to the needs of others – and to their own needs. Each accepted the need for change in social, economic and political spheres, but was unsure as to how to bring about change in an evolutionary manner. Each rejected a revolutionary approach to change while remaining aware that this option was one that was being actively considered in parts of the country. Each wanted to work for effective action, and each had rejected the concept of community development as a simple panacea to solve all the ills of people.

If some voices expressed doubt and concern about the ways of bringing about change in Canada, there were other surer and more strident tones to be heard in the land. The following statement is typical of young radicals in Canada. It is only unusual in that it appeared in the alumni magazine of one of Canada's oldest and most traditional universities.

> *With reference to Canada and the United States, we see American society as one in contradiction, in structural conflict and social class antagonism, not as a monolithic unity. The blacks, the poor of all races, the students, and hopefully in the future, the working-class, represent genuine oppositionist social forces in the American system, and we side with and work in common with these movements – the oppositionist and radical movements, the other pole of the contradiction of a society in structural antagonism. We have common interests and therefore see ourselves developing a common outlook and strategy for the purpose of defeating the ruling classes of the United States and Canada. While we recognise the fact of American imperialist*

control, we focus not upon developing independent capitalist nation-states, but upon developing an international revolutionary student and working-class movement.

And let me remind you that the future of this continent lies not with the corrupted politicians, corporate chieftains or lifeless bureaucrats who now control the organs of national power, nor, for that matter, with their intellectual flunkies and apologists in the universities, but rather with today's generation of revolutionary youth.(Gray 1968)

Canada's community development dilemma

It is impossible, not to say presumptuous, for one person to discuss community development in Canada. Elsewhere, I have expressed my own biases about community development. (Lotz 1967) Canada is such a vast country with so many diverse aspects that it is difficult to find out what is going on in community development, let alone generalize about it. At one time, when the term was much in vogue, any human-focused programme was called community development in Canada.

Each person – and perhaps whole structures and nations – may have to go through the process that the French call the *prise de conscience*. At first sight, human problems seem simple and the fond belief arises that all that is needed is a little money, some goodwill, a spirit of co-operation, and a few weeks and the problems will be solved. Slowly but surely, the immensity of human problems becomes apparent. The enormous complexity of peoples and places becomes clear and the first thought of the would-be community developer is to flee or to put the lid on things and claim that the problem has disappeared or been solved. Then there is the slow realization that something can be done to improve the human condition, but that community development is not something that starts and goes straight to a successful conclusion, in a mechanical manner. The process is rather discursive, meandering, untidy and with a lot of loose ends, sudden discoveries, changes, failures and new problems replacing the old ones. In short, community development is like life itself, a constant attempt to keep aspirations and achievements within sight of each other. The community developer who stays with the problem and the people seems to be moving up a spiral. At times it seems as if everyone is back where they started, but at each turn, everyone should be at a higher level of abstraction, in theoretical terms, and in a better position to solve their own problems in their own way, in practical terms.

The process of community development is complicated in Canada by the fact that the country got a late start. Each nation needs an awareness of the real dimensions of its socio-economic problems before it can begin to tackle them. And it also needs a 'critical mass' of developers before things can happen. Community development in any nation will reflect the country's ethos. There has been a tendency in the past to see community development as a universal process involving 'co-ordination of effort' and 'self-help'. If the community development process over the past twenty years has demonstrated anything it is that such abstract terms only become concrete realities within a specific framework of operational limitations and possibilities. The egalitarianism of the modern era that assumes that all parts of the world are the same and that all people are equally endowed has given way to a realization that every place is unique, as is every human being.

In Canada, the paradox of development is amply demonstrated. Development implies a process of comparison, and this is made easy and instantaneous in the era of mass electronic media. Canadians compare the standard of living in one part of the country with that in another part of the nation, or in the United States, and feel a strange disquiet. Many feel they are missing something. At the same time, they want to be different – to retain their traditional values, culture and life styles as a sort of mooring post. The dilemma is demonstrated by Canada's Indians. They have become vociferous in recent years – they want more control over their own affairs and a life style similar to that of other Canadians (good housing, good jobs, etc). At the same time they want to retain their traditional culture and to build on it so that they can pass from the past to the future with the minimum amount of disruption and social cost. 'Red Power' advocates the abolition of the Department of the Indian Affairs and Northern Development; other Indians teach their children the traditional languages.

In Canada, the old and the new run together. The operational limits of Canada are staggering. The country is the second largest in the world, but the population numbers only 20,000,000. Most of this population crowds along the U.S. border. Canadians have a public image of a northern people living in a rough, rugged and difficult land occupied mainly by Mounties, Indians and Eskimos. The private image is one of a timorous, post-colonial people dominated by an English tradition in social matters and by American influences in economic matters. Canada suffers from an immense technological gap, and also from cultural lag. The country needs the highest level of science and technology. In the past there has been a tendency to imitate, unthinkingly, American or European models in mechanical things. Houses, cities, cars, clothes all show these influences. As the nation searches for its identity, a vigorous attempt is being made to discover and to utilize the past and to blend it with the best of the present. This is not an easy task. The problem of the application of science and technology to improving living conditions comes down to 'human problems' and human responses.

Although the country is extremely wealthy on a national basis, there are significant pockets of poverty. About 20% of the population has been designated as living below the poverty lines. (Economic Council of Canada 1968) The poverty is regional – the Maritimes, the Interlake Region of Manitoba, the Gaspé, the northern parts of the provinces – and it also exists more among certain groups than others. Older people, people on pensions and fixed incomes, the Indians, the Eskimos, the unskilled can all be classified as poor by Canadian standards. Inflationary trends in the economy diminish the purchasing power of everyone's dollar and this makes life difficult for people who have limited possibilities for increasing their incomes.

The welfare dilemma

Canada is well into the welfare state era. The country inherited, or adopted, British ideas about social justice and the necessity for providing pensions, family allowances and other transfer payments that would ensure every citizen a minimal standard of living. No one starves in Canada, although quite a few go hungry or suffer from an inadequate diet.

There is some temptation to see community development as a souped-up form of social welfare. In Canada, it soon becomes obvious that social problems are well looked after. In a study carried out by the Canadian Research Centre for Anthropology in a low income area in Ottawa, it was found that if a need arose, there were a large number of agencies that could help. (Gelineau 1968) These agencies frequently operated in an unco-ordinated way, and there were people who did not know about forms of assistance or did not like social agencies. But there is little need to duplicate the excellent work being done by these agencies, as has happened in the United States. Everyone wants co-ordination, but no-one wants to be co-ordinated. It would appear, in Ottawa, that social agencies are willing to pool their resources and to focus around a family or a community. Interest is being expressed in Neighbourhood Centres as a focus for the efforts of social agencies.

One effective way of providing co-ordination seems to be to establish a 'central place' where data and information on the resources for problem-solving are available to all. The free dissemination of knowledge and information to all comers is a quiet and effective aid to community development. But there is a need to go beyond this passive function. One of the Canadian Research Centre for Anthropology's Research Associates, Thomas Haley, has been effective in working with young people and others who came to him because they do not wish to have contact with established agencies. In any community there are people who do not fit into established categories and whose problems do not directly fall under one agency. If community development is seen as a human-focused approach to social and economic problems, it is necessary to deal with individuals who are often difficult to handle for a variety of reasons. Such people resent being treated as a means to the ends of others, and frequently develop strategies for manipulating agencies and individuals. The myth still persists in Canada that the poor, the Indians, the Eskimos and others are inherently noble, and that all that is needed is a little kindness so that they can achieve middle-class respectability. This attitude has been attacked by Valentine. (1968) The life of all groups and cultures has its own standards and its own integrity. Moral indignation about the real or alleged shortcomings of a group or a person is no substitute for a search for means of improving their lot in terms that are acceptable to them.

Stereotyping groups or individuals prevents a realistic approach to problem-solving. One paradox in community development is that it involves dealing with groups or 'communities' and at the same time means working with individuals whose problems and approaches to life may or may not be characteristic of a larger number of people. Community development must be a scientific process, and the first question should be 'What is the problem?'. On the identification of the problem will depend the identification of possible solutions. In community development, it is necessary to ask 'Whose problem are we talking about?'. Too often, in social agencies, it is the problem of the agency rather than of the client that causes difficulty. Lack of co-ordination within and between agencies, bureaucratization, and dependence for financial support upon conservative elements in the population who still believe social problems can be handled on the basis of charity, prevent a prompt response to human needs that are changing rapidly. This is less a dilemma of social agencies – and of social workers – than of western society at this time.

The welfare state approach tends to put people into a hammock that keeps them at a certain level of existence. Dependency is created and sustained, and the cost of simply keeping people alive rises year by year. The refusal to recognise the fact that most people do not wish to live a life of dependency, 'on welfare', coupled with the belief that poverty is mainly an individual and not a social problem, persists in Canada. The problems of the poor are seen as poor people's problems – as if they are not related to national, regional, community and individual realities. All the evidence indicates that people would rather make their own mistakes, and learn from them, than have mistakes made for them by those who claim to be experts. There is still not wide recognition that development is a risky business. The lack of professionalisation that bothers some community development workers can be an asset. In an era when knowledge is increasing so rapidly and its content changing so radically, even the best trained professional will have difficulty keeping up with things. Our basic concepts about the social, economic and political dynamics of our world are changing so rapidly that flexibility is needed by all those working with people. And the learning process will necessarily involve mistakes.

The need for springboards

A realistic approach to community development takes into account the frailties of people – and this includes community developers. Utopian thinking and blindness to the difficulties that come with working with real people rather than with abstract beings has been one weakness of community development in the past. In Canada, the dimensions of the 'people problem' are becoming clearer each day. Accurate data is replacing guesswork; a realistic understanding of operational limits is taking the place of vague rhetorical statements about the nature of the country.

Canada is a federal state with a large number of government agencies operating at the national, provincial, regional and municipal levels. In theory, the civil service is supposed to work for people. In practice, it is often the other way round. There is abundant evidence that the era when government agencies could do no wrong and could command the obedience of all is at an end. Bureaucracies do not seem to be able to change quickly enough to meet the needs they were set up to deal with. There is a tendency to condemn bureaucracies while failing to realize that the people in these bureaucracies are also 'victims'. The bureaucracies – originally established to protect people from arbitrary actions by those in power – are becoming less and less relevant. (Blau 1956) In the post-industrial era, knowledge forms the basis of wealth and power; it is a person's capacity to adapt and change and learn that is important, not his ability to do one job in one way in one place. (Bell 1967)

Post-industrial society demands and involves a high level of science and technology, a constant recycling of people so that they retain the capacity to change their minds and their jobs as fresh opportunities appear. Education then becomes a life-long pursuit of personal development, instead of a series of pills taken at intervals. Again, the paradox appears in Canada. There is a need in the country to change rapidly and to develop human potential very quickly. But how can this be done? Every time a person turns round s/he bumps into some government agency charged with doing a job, but seemingly unable to do that job quickly enough or to the satisfaction of its clients. People 'get mad' at government without understanding its operational limitations. The time and energy of agencies is taken up with dashing around and putting out fires. Governments in a welfare state act on an egalitarian basis – if one person gets something, then everyone must get it. The dilemma arises that development must be built around equality and also leave scope for individual and group excellence. (Gardner 1961) But how can this be done?

The development process involves controlling the enormous release of human energy that comes with mechanization and modernization. The machine frees man, although it can enslave him. The machine makes life easier – and also more complicated. People are faced with a number of choices as to what to do with their surplus time, money, energy. Ends suddenly become important. In Canada there has been a great deal of talk about ends (Canada is creating a 'just society' whose dimensions are vague at this time) but little discussion of means. The development process involves the creation of new 'resources' (more food, more local autonomy) and the redistribution of existing resources. But if the cake of resources is seen as a fixed one, for which all must fight for a larger share, then chaos can result. If efforts are combined to create a larger and more efficient cake through the use of science and technology, and if, at the same time, genuine efforts are made to ensure that everyone has access to the new resources, development can move from an acquisitive, selfish, materialistic process where everyone tries to grab as much as they can, to a pursuit of mutual interests from which all benefit.

One tradition has already developed in Canada: social animation. The method has been described by two of its chief practitioners in Canada. (Beaucage 1967) It involves creating an awareness of what people's problems really are, followed by a discussion of possible ways of solving these problems. By the use of the media and information teams, people in an area are brought face-to-face with the reality of their world. Social animation is a dynamic approach to problem-solving that increasingly is being used in Canada.

The Canadian choice

Canada still has some choice in the way social, economic and political problems are solved. All the processes of the modern world – industrialization, urbanization, rationalization, secularization – are beginning to affect the country. Canadians, generally speaking, prefer an evolutionary and humanistic approach to change. But the inability of existing structures to channel the energy being generated in the country is causing some concern. There is no dispute about goals, but it is the timing that causes concern. Expectations are rising daily.

There exists, throughout Canada, an informal network of people and groups who are working towards improving the human condition. These people see their role as aiding others to identify and solve their problems – not solving problems for people. Anything that does not assist people to get more money, power and responsibility is frankly a waste of time in development. Development is about power and money and it is foolish to see it in vague social terms alone.

Canada has a chance to combine the social technology of her traditional peoples and the mechanical technology of the west within a human and realistic framework. Such a synthesis might open new vistas for western people and for traditional peoples. A mutual quest and a sharing of benefits would replace the present exploitive and manipulative relationship that exists between the 'haves' and the 'have nots'. This split can be seen in Canada, especially in the North. The extent to which Canada is able to manage the tensions of development will be an indication of the contribution that the country can make to the theory and practice of community development.

Conclusion

This article has presented some highlights of the philosophy and action involved in community development in Canada. At the 1968 Toronto conference, some priorities were listed for action. These included the following:

● better theoretical models for action and the development of a coherent body of theory are needed. The implications of social indicators (Bauer 1966) need to be discussed;

● a Canadian curriculum for community development is needed. What are Canada's problems and how can they be tackled in a Canadian context? The whole question of training for community development needs to be re-examined;

● a need was recognised to sensitize government agencies to the problems and promise of community development for solving socio-economic problems; and

● there still does not exist in Canada any central clearing house for community development or a method of linking together scattered groups and individuals working throughout the country.

Canada is still a frontier country where the known interacts with the unknown. Community development is still a frontier discipline where all must tread warily and work in an experimental manner. In Canada, the real and the ideal, the medium and the message come together. A small number of people are working towards the emergence of a new kind of society built around the needs of real people. And this group welcomes help in their self-help efforts, from wherever it may come.

References

Bauer, R.A. (1966) *Social Indicators*, Cambridge, Mass: M.I.T. Press.

Beaucage, J. (1967) 'La Participation', *Anthropologica*, 9 (2): 61-64.

Bell, D. (1967) 'Notes on the Post-Industrial Society', *Public Interest*, 7 and 8, Winter-Spring.

Blau, P.M. (1956) *Bureaucracy in Modern Society*, New York: Random House.

Economic Council of Canada (1968) 'The Problem of Poverty', in *The Challenge of Growth and Change*, Fifth Annual Review, September.

Gardner, J.W. (1961) *Excellence. Can We be Equal and Excellent Too?* New York and Evanston: Harper Colophon Books.

Gelineau, P. (1968) *The Lower Town Project; L'Étude de la Basse Ville*, Ottawa: Canadian Research Centre for Anthropology.

Gray, S. (1968) 'Student Radicalism. An American Import?', *McGill News*, Nov.: 22.

Lotz, J. (1967) 'Is Community Development Necessary?', *Anthropoligica*, 9 (2): 3-14. (Special Issue on Community Development in Canada).

Valentine, C. (1968) *Culture and Poverty,* Chicago: University of Chicago Press.

Notes

1. Ontario Institute for Studies in Education, Department of Adult Education, National Workshop of Community Development Teaching and Research (April, 1968).

2. In the summer of 1968, the Canadian Research Centre for Anthropology ran a Drop-in Centre in Ottawa's Lower Town.

Jim Lotz, Vol. 4 (1969): 61-67.

4

Linking Community and Industrial Action

Richard Bryant

Community and economic organization are often treated as two distinct and separate worlds in the literature on community work. This separation tends to be a particular characteristic of the thinking about community work in advanced industrial societies. In Britain the influential and best selling report of the Gulbenkian Foundation, *Community Work and Social Change* (The Calouste Gulbenkian Foundation 1968) – contains hardly a mention of the impact of economic organization upon patterns of community life, or any serious assessment of how economic forces may shape and condition the roles of professional community workers. Yet in many parts of Britain, especially the major industrial conurbations, community workers are confronted daily with the social repercussions of economic organization. Issues related to declining industries, unemployment, poverty and low wages cannot be ignored by front-line community workers in the same myopic way they have been by theorists.

The failure to relate community work to the economic framework also prevents any systematic consideration of how community and industrial action can be linked, as part of any overall strategy for promoting social change. At the present time in Britain we find little attention being paid to how community groups may engage in direct forms of economic activity or how relationships might be established between organizations which are active in community and industrial settings. There are many precedents for these types of links and relationships being created: the utopian community movement, with its central emphasis on integrated economic and community activity, attempts to organize unions to represent the unemployed and welfare claimants, links between trade unions and tenants associations, the Co-operative movement and consumer protection groups.

This article will briefly attempt to examine one strand in the complex interplay between community and industrial action – the relationship between community groups and trade unions. Historically, trade unions have formed one of the few organized channels for the representation and promotion of working class interests in Britain. Today many professional community workers are employed in helping to develop community organizations in areas which have predominantly working class populations. Thus it would seem important to examine some of the links which can exist between these two forms of organization and to identify the problems which might be involved in attempting to forge closer relationships between them.

Community organizations and trade unions

There are a number of possible links which can exist between community organizations and trade unions:

Interlocking membership
At the very basic level of individual participation it is not unusual to find people who have a dual involvement in community organizations and trade unions. A number of studies of British housing estates have recorded the prominent position which active trade unionists can hold in local tenants' or residents' associations (for example, Mitchell and Lupton 1954). It has also been frequently noted that organizational experience and expertise gained in an industrial setting can help equip trade union members for leadership roles within community settings. Knowledge of committee procedures, experience of organizing collective union activities and negotiating with managements, can be vital assets in the formation and development of community organizations. For some activists, participation in community life forms a direct extension of their union work and the dual involvement in industrial and community organizations is an expression of a wider class or political consciousness:

> If you're going to fight the boss for a wage increase it seems logical that you should now resist the landlord trying to take it back off you. Otherwise there's a lot of wasted energy ... but there's more to it than just being trade unionists. Because invariably active trade unionists are probably active out of a sort of class consciousness and the same consciousness can find its expression in a tenants' association. So you have the two coming together (Liddell and Bryant forthcoming).

However, the 'active', political, conscious trade unionist may not be representative of a wider trade union membership. Many trade union members have a more passive involvement in their organizations and do not make regular and direct connections between their work and community situations. It should also be noted that, as far as the formation of an activist role is concerned, the relationship between work and community settings is not always a one-way process. Although the work situation can be considered as the dominant focus for developing political and organizational experience, an involvement in collective community action can, for some people, lead to a wider involvement in other spheres. For instance, the experience of working with a tenants' association may lead a previously passive trade unionist to develop a new involvement in his work situation. Of course, for some groups in the population, especially retired people and housewives, the community setting forms the only or the major arena for participation open to them.

It would be deceptive to assume that interlocking membership occurs in all areas with the same degree of intensity. In some areas, few residents may be members of trade unions and as a consequence the likelihood of finding people with a dual involvement is likely to be slight. This is often the situation in areas which have a high concentration of people living in poverty and where there is a tradition of employment in low wage industries which have weak trade unions. Coates and Silburn (1970) in their study of the poverty-stricken St. Ann's district of Nottingham reported that only 18% of the area's breadwinners were members of trade unions. This compared, at the time, with a national figure of around 50% for the male working-class population. The lack of union membership in areas like St. Ann's may be interpreted, in part, as a critical comment on the failure of the trade union movement to organize effectively amongst the poor and the low paid.

Collective issue-centred action
Collective actions which mobilize community organizations and trade unions around issues of common concern provide the clearest demonstration of the links which can exist. A recent review, by Moorehouse, Wilson and Chamberlain (1972) of four major rent strikes in Britain, provides some examples of industrial action, taken in support of community protests over rent increases in both the private and public sectors of housing. The rent strikes occurred in Glasgow (1915), the Clyde (1921-26), St. Pancras, London (1959-61) and East London (1968-70). The industrial support varied from official union action to unofficial initiatives taken by individual trade unionists, shop stewards and groups of workers. The action taken

embraced a variety of strategies: sympathetic strike action, threats of strike action, participation in tenant demonstrations, support for evicted tenants, offers of financial assistance and assistance in printing literature and compiling information. As the authors of the review point out, it is significant that the clearest link between community and industrial action, over the issue of rent protests, has tended to be in 'occupational communities', that is areas which have a close economic dependency upon one or two major industries and where group associations formed in the work situation carry over into the community setting.

Friends at work are likely to be neighbours on the local housing estate. Wages and rents are common concerns which directly cut across the two settings. This type of close social and economic integration, which is characteristic of many industrial areas in the North of England, South Wales and Scotland, can be contrasted with some areas in the Midlands and South East of England which have a more complex and diversified occupational structure. In these areas the residents of a housing estate may work in a number of different workplaces and be members of a wide range of trade unions and work associations. At times of community crisis, the mobilization of industrial support becomes more problematic and demands the creation of inter-workplace links as well as joint action between unions and community organizations.

The same type of comment can be applied to the reverse situation, when community groups mobilize in support of industrial action which is focused on a wage dispute or a threat to employment opportunities in a major industry. In an occupational community, a crisis in a major industry is often a community-wide crisis, affecting not only the local workforce but the entire fabric of social, religious and commercial life. The famous 'work-in' at the Upper Clyde Shipbuilders (1971/72) was a classic example of a crisis in an occupational community. A government decision to close the shipyards on the Clyde directly threatened some six thousand jobs, in an area which already had an unemployment rate of well above the national average. In the town most affected, Clydebank, the shipyards provided the second largest source of local employment. The work-in organized by the shop stewards committee received widespread support from local community groups and many other organizations which were not directly involved in the shipbuilding industry (for an example of the response by social workers in the area see Challoner and McLaughlan 1971). A similar, if less publicized, mobilization of community support occurred in mining areas during the national strike of the miners' union in 1972.

Obviously this type of direct community response is more problematic in areas which have a great diversification of industry and employment opportunities. But it would be too simple to conclude from this that the objective social and economic conditions for collective issue-centred action are unique or specific to occupational communities or that we can only expect to find this action occurring in the traditional working class areas of regions like the West of Scotland. Such a view assumes that other more fortunate areas are somehow immune from the impact of shifts and changes in the market economy. For instance, a recession in the motor car industry or a redeployment of American investment in the British sector of this industry could plunge many towns in the Midlands and South-East of England into crisis situations which might be comparable to those experienced in the more traditional occupational communities.

Trade union sponsorship of community programmes
So far we have only looked at the links which can exist at the rather fragmentary levels of interlocking membership and issue-centred action. A third possible link involves a more formal and planned relationship, the direct sponsorship of community action programmes by trade unions. These programmes could have a particular potential and relevance in severely deprived areas, where few union-community links exist and the residents lack any political bargaining power. Direct trade union intervention in these areas could embrace such activities as recruitment campaigns amongst low-paid workers, the establishing of local inter-union bases to support the development of community organizations and the appointment of full-time organizers to link community groups and local Trades Councils. Coates and Silburn (1970. esp. Ch. 10) see this type of involvement as being a necessary part of the trade union movement's campaign against poverty and low pay. The precedent they cite for these community initiatives is taken from American experience – the attempts by the Teamsters' and Automobile Workers' Union to establish 'Neighbourhood Unions' in ghetto areas. The very fact that Coates and Silburn have to turn to American trade unions for a precedent is a clear indication of the current absence of these programmes in the British situation. Indeed, some critics of the British trade union movement would seriously

question the credibility of proposals which urge direct union involvement in areas of poverty and deprivation. Members of the independent Claimant Unions – organizations which seek to represent the interests of the unemployment and welfare claimants – have been particularly prominent in articulating this view. They argue that the trade unions have abdicated their political responsibilities for the poor and that groups in poverty must organize themselves and should not expect any assistance from the established unions (see for example Jordan 1973). A number of well-known community organizers have shared this critical perspective. These include the late Saul Alinsky, and Cesar Chavez the organizer of the famous Californian grape strike. Over twenty years ago Alinsky wrote the following about American labour unions – his words echo some of the current criticisms of British trade unions:

> Labour thinks and acts as does big business. This alliance between organized labour and organized industry has reached the point where in essence it is a working partnership ... the leaders are committed to the idea that the welfare of their organization is contingent upon the welfare of industry or capitalism. (Alinsky 1946: 80)

These criticisms raise some fundamental questions about the relationship between organized labour and the poor in industrial societies, questions which bring into play different political ideologies and social experiences as well as conflicting interpretations of the recent record of trade unions in relation to the poor and the low-paid. The author of this article shares some of the reservations expressed by the critics of the trade unions and is in complete agreement with them over their insistence that the creation of organizations representing the poor – like the creation of many early trade unions in Britain – should be built around the self-organization of the poor. But at the same time it should be clearly recognized that the separation of organized labour from the poor or 'pauper class' – a separation which is suggested in a very deterministic way by some of the critics – could, in the long term, prove socially and politically negative for the poor themselves. A strategy of rigid separation, whether expressed in ideological or organizational terms, might function to reinforce the social isolation of the poor in society and cut them off from a number of potential sources of assistance, including that from local union branches and groups of trade unionists.

The central problem is one which should be familiar to any

community worker – how to develop new independent organizations within an overall framework of co-operation with established organizations. The pitfalls are numerous. At one extreme there is patronage and control by established organizations, at the other extreme the possibility of independence but social and political isolation. The attempt to forge links between community organizations and trade unions may not avoid these dangers, but at least it seeks to challenge the assumption that we should accept existing divisions and arrangements as being beyond change.

References

Alinsky, S.D. (1946) *Reveille for Radicals*, Chicago: University of Chicago Press.

Challoner, B. and McLaughlan, J. (1971) 'Unemployment: Urgent Concern for the Social Implications'. *Social Work Today*, September.

Coates, K. and Silburn, R. (1970) *Poverty: The Forgotten Englishman*, Harmondsworth: Penguin Books.

Jordan, B. (1973) *Paupers: The Making of the New Claiming Class*, London: Routledge and Kegan Paul.

Lewis, N. (1970) 'Slave Labourers in the Vineyard' *Sunday Times Magazine*, February 1st.

Liddell, H. and Bryant, R. (forthcoming). 'A Local View of Community Work' In: *New Developments in Community Work*, London: Routledge and Kegan Paul.

Mitchell, D.G. and Lupton, T., (1954) 'The Liverpool Estate' In: Mitchell, P. *et al.., Neighbourhood and Community*, Liverpool: The University of Liverpool Press.

Moorhouse, B., Wilson, M., Chamberlain, C. (1972) 'Rent Strikes – Direct Action and the Working Class' In: R. Miliband, and J. Saville (eds.) *The Socialist Register*, London: Merlin Press.

The Calouste Gulbenkian Foundation (1968) *Community Work and Social Change*, Harlow: Longmans.

Richard Bryant is Lecturer in Social Administration and Social Work at the University of Glasgow: Vol. 9 No. 1, (1974): 28-32.

5

The Major Issues and Future Direction of Community Development

T. R. Batten

As I look back over my years of research, study and fieldwork, my overall feeling is one of sadness that so much community development effort has, on the whole, resulted in relatively so little actual betterment and more especially for the poor and underprivileged people who need betterment most. I know, of course, that powerful minorities in every country often succeed in influencing development policies in their own interests at the expense of the mass of ordinary people, and I accept that as a fact of life we have to live with. What concerns me much more is that the well-intentioned efforts of so many planners, administrators and field workers who really want to promote betterment have, on the whole, so often fallen so far short of realising their full potential. To give but two examples: in India great dissatisfaction was expressed at the 1969 National Seminar on Panchayati Raj 'that the social and economic benefits (of rural development) have flown to the more affluent sections of the rural communities ... The benefits it was expected to confer on the weaker and underprivileged sections of the rural population have not materialised in many cases'. (Rao 1969; Brown 1970; Muthia 1970; Thornton 1970) Again, although the Basic Democracies Works Programme in East Pakistan has resulted in great physical improvements in drainage, flood control and transportation, it has also been heavily criticized as having mainly benefited the larger landowners, widened the pre-existing gap between the rich and the poor, enlarged the number of landless labourers and worsened their condition. (Sobhan 1968)

Overall development objectives are necessary

Such examples could be multiplied indefinitely, which suggests that something is seriously wrong here. Basically, I believe, it is because each social and economic development agency, and there are many, pursues its own objectives with its own selected clientele and too readily assumes that by achieving such objectives it contributes its share to overall betterment. What is much needed, but in practice lacking, is any common agreed and overall purpose for development to which every

55

agency aims to contribute and by which it continually assesses the results of its work. It seems to me that the current situation is well summed up by one student of development who writes: 'At the moment we are in an impasse. Recent theories of development ... have certainly defined the problem areas, and very well too. But they have left the problem or problems largely unsolved, especially the problem of *what* constitutes development and how it is to be attained.' (Nettl 1968)

Betterment, especially of the poor

Here, I think, I need to make my own standpoint clear. The basic position from which I start is that every development objective, or target, or activity should desirably contribute to betterment of people. If this is accepted, it follows that no development objective, or target, or activity should be regarded as an end in itself but only as a means which needs to be rigorously and continuously assessed, and if necessary modified, in order to ensure that it really does contribute to people's betterment, and more especially, perhaps, to the betterment of the poor and underprivileged people who need it most. To promote betterment in this sense should be the overall purpose of every development agency and every development worker.

The promotion of environmental change

Next, I feel I should try to define this overall betterment purpose rather more precisely. This is difficult to do in only a few sentences but I would say that achievement of this purpose involves promoting changes of two quite different kinds: one, changes for the better in people's local, regional or national environments; and the other, changes for the better in people themselves. Changes of the first type are usually detailed as development objectives or targets on every development agency's programme. They include provision of services and amenities that people are seen to need, for example schools, clinics, community centres and reading rooms, and the servicing of groups such as co-operatives, women's groups and youth groups. The problem here is to ensure that the people for whom such amenities or services are provided really do value them, use them and benefit from them in the way that was intended.

The promotion of change in people

Changes of the second type occur, for example, as people become more open-minded to change; more self-reliant; more willing to act responsibly in implementing their own decisions for themselves; more skilled in organizing and planning how best to achieve what they have decided on; more concerned to promote the welfare of people other than themselves; and more willing to work together for the common good. The problem here is to find the agencies which really are purposefully working to promote changes in people of the kind I have described. True, there are social groupwork agencies and casework agencies, but these are almost entirely concerned with individuals in special need, such as delinquents, problem-families and the like. Most other agencies are much more concerned with providing people with specific amenities, facilities and services than with just how, in fact, what they provide and how they provide it will promote the development of people in the sense I define it.

The community development
approach to development

However, community development agencies do claim to work purposefully for both kinds of betterment. The relevant concept, of course, is to be found in the felt-wants theory. According to this theory, it is during the process of people thinking, discussing, and deciding on what they really want, and then planning, organising and acting together to implement the decisions they have reached that, at one and the same time, they both develop more fully their potentialities as people *and* promote changes for the better in the environment in which they live. And, indeed, it has been proved many times that by stimulating people to discuss, decide and work to meet their own felt-wants, a skilled development worker can promote both aspects of the overall development purpose at the same time.

In the late 1940s, when this community development way of working was first introduced by government officers in rural areas of Asia and Africa, its immediate results were impressive: and many politicians and high-ranking government officers regarded it as a breakthrough. Indeed, one I know was so impressed that he talked of 'the mystique' of community development almost as if he regarded it as magic. But, as we all know, it has not lived up to its earlier promise, and for two main reasons. One is that people cannot want possibilities that they do not know exist, and the more backward they are the less able they are to formulate ideas for their own betterment. Yet it is the things they do not know about, and therefore do not want, that are usually key objectives in extension agencies' programmes. The second reason is that many of the things that people do want, often do not fit in at all well with the requirements of national and regional development programmes.

The two limitations are both so fundamental that even the keenest protagonists of community development have acknowledged them. Thus Albert Mayer when writing on 'felt-needs' comments: 'After the early introductory stage, the question of Felt Need becomes more complex. The people on the plane of formulation tend to run out of them temporarily ... the second stage is the "induced felt need", i.e. the felt need resulting from the interaction of the people and the agency. The dogma is of course that we democratically keep following the people's wishes, but I think this is naïve.' (quoted in Dunham 1960)

Again, to quote Julia Henderson: 'If there is to be any general impact of community development on economic development – for example, if there is to be a real connection with the national plans – then there does have to be an educated and persuaded need. (International Society for Community Development 1967)

The development of more directive, imposed approaches

These comments draw attention to the very real limitations of the existing felt-wants concept, but if we take at their face value Albert Mayer's comment that it is 'naive' to keep following the people's wishes, and Julia Henderson's that there has to be 'an educated and persuaded need', where do they lead us? I suggest that they lead us – and in fact have led us – to a very blurred image of ourselves in which we say we believe in encouraging people to think and decide for themselves, but in practice spend a great deal of time in trying to get them to accept and act on what we other people have already decided for them. What then becomes of our goal of developing people by involving them in thinking and deciding for themselves? To my mind, this is the basic issue which faces would-be community developers today. Indeed, until it is resolved, the term 'community development' has lost all real meaning.

The need for a non-directive approach

But is the felt-wants theory really quite as restricted in its application as the comments I have quoted suggest? As this theory is currently stated, I think the answer must be 'yes'. But I also believe that the theory can be expanded in a way that frees it from its existing limitations and which opens up a very wide field of potential application. For this to happen, the key requirement is that the expanded concept must demonstrably be able to produce better results than the traditional extension method of persuasion – not only in promoting growth in people, *but also – and from the technical extension agencies' point of view more particularly – in enabling them to achieve their specific technical development objectives.*

Here, I can only present you with the barest outline of my elaboration of this theory. I start by making two general statements, the full implications of which are too often ignored in extension work practice. They are:

1. that whenever a development 'authority' or agency has no effective means of forcing people to accept an innovation, the power to decide whether to adopt it or not (i.e., the *effective authority*) rests with the people; and

2. that no suggested innovation is effectively 'good' however important it may seem to the agency which sponsors it, unless ways can be found of getting people to implement it and *go on implementing it*.

Final decisions must rest with the people

Therefore in all this area, and it is a wide one, the final decisions are made by the people, however backward and ignorant they may sometimes appear to be. This leads us on to the really basic issue, which is how best to ensure, as far as humanly possible, that the people will accept and make beneficial use of each suggested innovation that really will contribute to betterment for them. Is it to try to persuade people into accepting the innovations that the agency thinks will turn out well for them? Or is it to encourage and help them realistically to assess both the advantages *and* disadvantages of any such innovation before deciding whether it really has a favourable balance of advantage for themselves?

Proposed innovations must satisfy criteria

Let us note first that lasting success in getting people to adopt any particular innovation depends on whether it satisfies certain basic criteria. These are:

1. it must be technically sound: that is, it must produce the advantage aimed at when people apply it in their own locality;

2. this advantage must be functionally related either to some existing want or to something the people learn to want;

3. it must be locally practicable in terms of the materials and skills available; and

4. the people must feel that the advantage they have gained by adopting the innovation outweighs *for them* any disadvantages it may also involve for them.

How well does the commonly-adopted persuasive approach fit in with these requirements? I see this as essentially a *directive* kind of approach since the aim of the workers who use it is to 'sell' their pre-determined programme objectives to people rather than to get them thoroughly to consider each proposed innovation – both its merits *and* demerits – for themselves. Thus the key technique of persuasion is to present an idea as attractively as possible by highlighting, demonstrating and emphasising only its advantages. It can be summed up as 'Trust us. Do this. This is why it well be good for you'.

Outcome will follow accordingly

Whether persuasion succeeds or fails depends on whether the innovation, as decided on and presented to the people in any particular place, fully satisfies each of the criteria I have just mentioned. If it does, then very often persuasion can produce excellent results. If it doesn't, then it will fail, and the most common cause of failure is that the advantage of the innovation, however real, is more than outweighed, in the people's minds, by disadvantages which the agency has not foreseen. In all such cases one of three results will follow: either,

1. if the people are aware of any such disadvantages and feel secure enough to say so, they will reject the idea outright; or
2. if they are too polite or feel too insecure to say so, they will appear to accept the innovation at the time, but then do nothing about it; or
3. if they are not initially aware of any disadvantages, they will accept the innovation and try to implement it, but reject it later when the disadvantages become apparent. (Batten 1957: 10-12 and Ch. 5) (A rejection of this kind can be particularly damaging since it tends to make people generally mistrustful of the agency's desire and competence to help them).

Why is the directive approach so widely used?

Such adverse reactions are quite common when extension work is based on the advantage concept rather than the balance of advantage concept, so why is the persuasive approach still so widely used? One reason, I think, is that most development agencies do not continually and rigorously evaluate their work, and more especially the causes of their failures. Thus they do not learn the lessons these could teach. Another reason is that they are not aware of any really viable alternative: especially as, with some justification, they tend to mistrust the capacity of ordinary people to reach sound conclusions on the basis of their own unaided thinking. Hence, most agencies continue to rely on persuasion and, if they fail, they attribute such failures to the ignorance, incompetence or apathy of people with whom they work.

The directive approach is often unrealistic

This is a negative and unprofitable reaction. It is true that very many people, and more especially those under-educated and under-privileged people who are the main concern of most development agencies, are not all that well-practised in systematic and objective thinking. It is true that they lack many of the ideas, and much of the knowledge, that they need in order to reach soundly-based decisions about what they ought to do for their own good. It is also true that often they have not even thought out their own purposes at all clearly.

But this does not mean that extension agencies are being realistic when they therefore resort to persuasion, for to do so is to ignore three basic facts. The first of these facts is that the people will decide anyway; that what they decide will in the end be the product of their own thinking; and that all the agency can do is try to ensure that they think as soundly as possible in the light of all the facts. The second is that by trying to persuade, i.e., by using the advantage concept instead of the balance of advantage concept, the agency is trying to restrict the scope of people's thinking at the risk of promoting unrealistic thinking. And the third is that a development worker who has been trained to help people think can contribute a great deal to raise the level of their thinking. Such thinking can turn vague dissatisfaction into a clear awareness of certain needs; awareness of a need into wanting some specific kind of change; and wanting some specific kind of change into readiness to take some clearly defined action in order to bring it about.

Key characteristics of the non-directive approach

What then are the key characteristics of the alternative approach? It is for the worker to get people to look critically at any idea he is suggesting: both in order to get them to assess the full extent of all its potential advantages for them; and equally, on the other hand, to identify any disadvantages they think might also be involved. Then if they do foresee any disadvantages, to promote realistic discussion in the light of all the available facts in order to get the people to think out whether, and if so just how, any such disadvantages can be avoided or reduced.

The worker's purpose throughout is to help people come to an informed and therefore realistic decision. Thus, he does not want them to accept an idea, however well-intentioned, unless and until they are sure it has a favourable *balance of advantage* for them. It is this approach which I call *non-directive* in order to distinguish it clearly from the other. I regret very much having to use such a negative sounding word to describe such a positive role. It is, perhaps, significant that although the English language contains many words, such as lead, guide, persuade, sell, direct, manipulate, enforce and threaten, which one can use to indicate directive action, it does not contain any one positive word solely indicative of the non-directive role of helping people to think clearly and systematically in the light of all the available facts in order to reach a really sound decision on matters which can vitally affect them.

It is by stimulating and encouraging people to test this agency's ideas for innovation in the light of their own local knowledge of what is really practicable and acceptable for them that the extension worker can best ensure that his agency's ideas for innovation really get tailored to fit. And as they do get tailored to fit, so in effect, the worker has created in people new felt-wants. And if, in the end, no way can be found of getting some ideas to fit, then surely, it is better that they should be rejected, for what, after all, is the development purpose if it is not to promote betterment? And here it is worth noting that when an extension worker, by working in this way, really involves people in a process of thinking and deciding for themselves, so also he is actively helping them to develop more fully their own potentialities as people: and thus, like the community development felt-wants worker, he promotes both aspects of the overall development purpose at one and the same time.

So far, I have dealt only with the applicability of this *non-directive approach* to the work development agencies do in order to promote their own specific programme objectives. But can we assume either that it is not needed, or that it is already effectively applied in our own traditional field of work in relation to people's existing felt-wants? Indeed, we cannot, for in fact the rural areas of Africa and Asia, to mention only two continents, are bespattered with the relics of such projects as, for example, feeder roads, community centres, reading rooms, and even wells which people said were their felt-wants but which either they started but did not complete; or, if they did complete them, have since found it too much trouble to use and maintain. Such results are largely avoidable and should be avoided. They do not add up to betterment of any kind. They leave people dissatisfied and disillusioned, both with themselves and with the agencies which encouraged them. They breed apathy.

The fact is that it is temptingly easy for a community development worker to take what people say is their felt-want at its face value – and all the more tempting if what they say they want is what the development planners want them to want. He then has every incentive to get them started on a project to add to his list when he reports: unless, that is, he aims to promote real betterment and has been trained in the skill of helping people to think.

The functions of a community worker

Here I can indicate only in bare outline the worker's functions when he adopts this non-directive role (sec Batten 1969 for full discussion). In brief, he aims to do two things:

1. to help people to think in a more orderly, systematic and logical manner than they would otherwise do. He achieves this mainly by asking unloaded questions which are designed, *inter alia*

   a) to ensure that the people he is working with really are agreed about just what need, or want, or problem they are aiming to discuss;

   b) to ensure that the people base their thinking on facts rather than assumptions about facts;

   c) to ensure that they consider both the pros and cons of each and every alternative open to them rather than restricting themselves to considering only one; and

   d) to help them avoid getting involved in unproductive argument (He does this by suggesting that they all concentrate on listing and assessing both the merits *and* demerits of each of their conflicting viewpoints rather than on some arguing for one viewpoint and some for another. What he does *not* do is to show himself in favour of one viewpoint rather than another, for he would then get involved in the argument himself. It is only by remaining impartial that he can hope to promote objectivity in the discussion).

2. to ensure as far as humanly possible that the people are in possession of all the relevant facts. He achieves this:

   a) by asking questions which draw people's attention to their need to get at all the relevant facts; and then

   b) encouraging people to contribute the relevant local facts for themselves; and

   c) by contributing relevant non-local facts, but not opinions, himself.

This non-directive approach to working with people derives from basic community development theory, but elaborates and expands it. It elaborates it in the sense that it clarifies and defines the positive role and functions of a worker who aims to help people to think, decide, plan, organise and act to promote their own betterment for themselves: and in the process to help them develop more fully their potentialities as people. It expands it by providing the field workers of the specialist extension departments with a viable alternative to their traditional persuasive role – an alternative which not only provides them with a more effective way of realistically achieving their target goals, but which also, at one and the same time, contributes to the wider development goal of promoting growth in people.

The issues I have so far discussed – the first, whether underlying all development activities there is, *or* should be, one overall development purpose, and if so whether it should include both development of people's environment and development of the people themselves; and the second, whether adoption of the non-directive approach as I have defined it would enable each and every agency and each and every one of its field workers to contribute to both aspects of it – these are both key issues in the sense that *whether* they are decided, and if so *how* they are decided, will determine the future direction, not only of community development, but of the whole field of development activity of which community development is a part.

The barrier of specialized, professionalized, departmentalized community development

The major barrier, as I see it, to the resolution of these two issues in a way that could potentially maximise the contribution to overall betterment of every worker of every agency is the present trend towards the specialization, professionalization, and departmentalization of community development. Community development's core concept of working *with* people rather than *for* them – of helping them to think and decide realistically for themselves rather than, often unrealistically, attempting to think and decide for them, is I feel, much bigger than any one specialization, profession or department. It is potentially applicable to the work that every specialist agency does with people, and as such should be part of each specialised agency's professionalism. This had profound implications for the organisation, content and method of training which we, as would-be professional community development educators and trainers have, as yet, barely perceived. As we perceive them, if we do, so perhaps we shall see more clearly the full scope and nature of the professionalism to which we aspire.

References

Batten, T.R. (1957) *Communities and Their Development*, Oxford University Press.

Batten, T.R. (1967) *The Non-Directive Approach in Group and Community Work*, Oxford University Press.

Brown, L.R. (1970) *Seeds of Change: The Green Revolution and Development in the 70's*, Pall Mall Press.

Dunham, A. (1960) 'The Outlook for Community Development: An International Symposium', *International Review of Community Development*, No. 5: 44.

International Society for Community Development (1967) Report on Symposium, *'The Outlook for Community Development'*, held during The International Conference of Social Work, in Washington, D.C., September 8, 1966, New York: 18-24.

Muthia, C. (1970) 'Green Revolution: Some Implications', *Kurukshetra*, 19 (6).

Nettl, J.P. (1968) 'Strategies in the Study of Political Development', in C. Leys (ed.) *Politics and Change in Developing Countries: Studies in the Theory and Practice of Development*, Cambridge University Press.

Rao, C.H.V. (1969) 'Panchayat Raj: Retrospect and Prospect', *Kurukshetra*, 18 (3): 3-4.

Sobhan, R. (1968) *Basic Democracies Programme and Rural Development in East Pakistan*, Bureau of Economic Research, University of Dacca.

Thornton, D.S. (1970) 'Silent Revolution in Agriculture: 3 Economic and Social Aspects', *Progress*, LIV (1): 21-25.

T.R. Batten, previously Reader in Community Development Studies at the University of London, and now a Community Development Consultant, is Chairman of the Editorial Advisory Board of this Journal: Vol. 9 No. 2 (1974): 96-103.

6

Looking Ahead:
Community Work in the 1980s

Paul Waddington

Introduction

The ambitious task of this paper is to look ahead and attempt to clarify the future of community work. The paper begins with an analysis of the contemporary condition of community work set in its immediate historical context. This analysis serves to illustrate some signposts to the future and explores some of the possible pathways towards which these might lead and along which community work seems likely to travel over the next decade. It is as well to remember that the 1980s begin next year whilst the next quinquennial review of the state of community work will fall due in 1984!

For reasons of clarity as well as brevity, I offer only one view of the future of community work. This makes it a highly subjective and no doubt simplistic statement, but the paper will have served its purpose if it triggers a reaction in readers which stimulates the construction of alternative scenarios and perspectives. In trying to avoid indulgence in pure fantasy, the analysis of the future has been grounded in an understanding of the present situation, thus providing a rudimentary triangulation from which to attempt the survey of the unknown territory. This gives what is a relatively short paper a very broad scope indeed and necessitates an impressionistic and broad-brush treatment which may sometimes seem insensitive to fine detail.

The paper falls into four sections, dealing in turn with: the immediate past; the present; a scenario for the future; and some implications of this, with particular reference to methodology and professionalisation. Reduced to its essence, the paper develops an argument along these general lines:

● that community work in the U.K. is essentially the product of the last decade; that its development over that period should be seen not merely as a chronicle of 'internal' events but also as a reflection of the political history of society at large;

● that at the present, community workers are collectively exhibiting a significant degree of uncertainty and anxiety about the role and future of community work activity, i.e. there is a crisis of belief, and

66

community work can be said, yet again, to be at the crossroads;

● that the future destiny of community work, like its present and past, will be inextricably bound up with that of the state; and the crisis of community work can only be resolved through personal and collective clarifications of that relationship; and

● that there will continue to be different positions within community work on the nature of this relationship, which suggests the possible future widening of divisions within community work, especially around issues of professionalisation.

The last decade

Contemporary community work in the United Kingdom is essentially the product of the last decade. 1968, as the climax of a period of substantial social and political upheaval, seems to have left a lasting inheritance in the continuing searches, on the one hand, for new forms of social and political expression and, on the other, for new forms of social and political control. Of course, within a longer-term and broader perspective, it has to be recognised that the origins of community work go back much farther than the somewhat arbitrary date of 1968, whilst it also must be observed that the recent expansion of community work in this country reflects an extensive borrowing from overseas experience, especially in colonial areas and in North America. Indeed, on the former point, many interesting parallels can be drawn between the events of the last decade and the period of expanded working class political activity at the end of the nineteenth century which laid the foundations of the present labour movement.

Then, as now, the inspiration for pressures for social change came from a range of different quarters and sentiments which represented an uneasy blend, as Perlman and Gurin (1972) put it in relation to the United States:

> Compassion for victims of misfortune, anger at injustice, and fear of unrest have impelled people throughout this country's history to turn their thoughts and energies to our social problems. Whether compassion, anger, or fear predominated has depended on the state of knowledge and beliefs concerning social problems and on the interests and ideologies of those who sought to resolve the problems.

The explosive growth of community work and action and its subsequent history over the last decade can be seen as the product of two contradictory sets of forces working reciprocally or dialectically over time and reflecting changing patterns of political relationships in society as a whole:

1. pressures for change from below represented by the growth of self-help, pressure group and 'urban protest' movements in a multiplicity of forms; and
2. pressures for change from above, reflecting the growing needs of the state and of the dominant political interests.

The history of community work over the decade and its changing fortunes and moods can be traced to the changing relationship between these two sets of forces, and the early period of romantic optimism amongst community workers generally can be contrasted with a later period of uneasiness and increasing pessimism. In the early 1970s, the rapid growth of residents' groups and other forms of grass roots organisations and the apparent success of 'stop the bulldozer campaigns' and other struggles helped to promote a massive confidence in the pragmatic tactics of neighbourhood organisation. The political analysis of most community workers basically reflected a gut reaction against bureaucracy and a rather unspecific idealism which owed rather more to the ideals of the 'alternative society' than to the thinking of the New Left.

But as the decade has progressed and the sense of national crisis has deepened, we have seen the State, from tentative beginnings, increasingly involved in the regulation and management of community work. (Dearlove 1974) There has been a process of progressive institutionalisation and incorporation of community work, in the 'voluntary' sector as well as within statutory organisations. This advance in direct state involvement has latterly been accompanied by a significant waning of community action nationally. Following the general lines of Bridges' (1975) analysis, the different stages which can be identified in the relationship of the State to community work over the decade represent a shift from pragmatic, ad hoc responses to the adoption of community work as an urban buffering or mediation function, and now increasingly to the formal incorporation of community work as a necessary instrument of contemporary urban management. This shift can be seen in the increasingly sophisticated usage of tools for 'repressive tolerance' via the control of funding arrangements and the sort of structural relationships which are being evolved in the Inner City Partnership Programmes. The decade has evidently been a period of learning for government institutions; the future of community work is now assured in one sense at least because the State has found that it needs it! (Cockburn 1977)

Looking back over the last decade, it can be seen retrospectively that the time around 1974 was a watershed and that events like the 'cuts campaign' and the peak of the Community Development Projects (CDPs) spanned a time of transition. Before then, community workers attacked the Welfare State, after it we tried to defend it. Events since 1968 have savaged the early optimism of community workers and it is the changing needs of the State that are increasingly becoming dominant in the construction and development of community work rather than the needs of grass roots organisations and the working class.

The last few years have seen an intensive search by some community workers for theoretical understandings that adequately explain this evolving situation, and there has been a general sharpening of political perspectives. In general, however, community workers seem much more uncertain about their practice than they were five years ago and there appears to be some loss of corporate sense of direction. There is certainly less confidence about the ultimate capacity of community work to fulfil its aims and perhaps a sense of a dream lost in the failure thus far of community work to build a major popular movement. The CDPs fulfilled a prophetic function in plugging community work's yawning theoretical and ideological cavities with a 'structural perspective', at least for a time. But after the ending of the CDPs, many community workers have found it difficult to operationalise or apply the theory to their own practice, partly because the material produced by the Projects have tended to be longer on analysis than on applications.

The present predicament

The picture of community work that is presented here, hopefully not too melodramatically, is one of some contemporary disarray. The development of more effective practice theories is necessary if community work is to be capable of responding more adequately to demands made on it from its environment, both in the present and into the future. The most important single lesson to be derived from the hard lessons of recent years is the fact that a community work which seriously addresses issues requiring social change and reform is going to need a strategy which can be sustained into the medium and longer-term. Such a strategy will need to be much more sophisticated than the pragmatic opportunism or simplistic conflict tactics that seemed adequate in the early 1970s. Before identification of future directions can seriously begin, however, community work needs to be located in a broader social and political analysis.

Whether we recognise it or not, it appears to be the case that we are living through a period of profound change, a period of transition from one era of relative stability to, perhaps, another. If we had such a thing as an oscillograph capable of measuring social change and uncertainty, it would undoubtedly have been recording some alarming swings during the last five years, in marked contrast to the relatively more gentle ups and downs it would have registered during the previous twenty-five years.

The developing crisis of the western economies, which gathered pace in the 1960s and culminated in the depression which began in 1974/75 and still continues, seems to have produced major and apparently permanent shifts in the political economy. We have witnessed the end of the post-war era with its confident expectation of steady growth and full employment and its consensual faith that social democracy and liberal reformism offered an adequate framework for the solution of all important social problems – and that era has undoubtedly gone forever.

Put in this broader context, it becomes clear that the disarray within community work discussed earlier is a reflection of a much more general crisis of the whole ideology of social democracy. As David Donnison (1979), a champion of the virtues of social democracy over an extended period, was moved to say in a recent article:

> Social democratic ideology is itself in disarray, and a larger political and philosophical reappraisal will be needed before anyone can launch a sustained movement for social reform of the sort we have seen over the last generation and more, or develop the body of knowledge such a movement will call for.

It has to be recognised that, for all its anti-establishmentarianism in its period of rapid growth in the early 1970s, mainstream community work was essentially a product of the social democratic ethos. In practice, community work fed off the annual surplus of a growing economy and was part of a system of public sector redistribution to disadvantage and marginal groups, a form of 'kitty bargaining' which helped to give substance to the claims of pluralist politics. The progressive adoption of community work by the State has – amongst other reasons – followed recognition of its value as a tool to reinforce a flagging belief in social democracy, especially amongst economically marginal groups. (Corrigan, unpublished)

Unfortunately, the capacity to finance the continuation of the process of social reform which is necessary (however marginal its practical effects may sometimes be) if belief in social democracy is to be sustained by the working class, has been largely undermined by the Government's political strategy of massively shifting resource allocation from personal, social and collective consumption (on, for example, housing and the social services) to the making of profits in the private sector – profits which it hopes one day will be translated into greater industrial investment and into the creation of new employment opportunities. It was this previous capacity of the state to finance the process of social reform, in relation to for example the provision of new and improved housing, which provided the 'baits' which were the essential stimulus for community action. And it is quite simply the withdrawal of such baits that has been a major cause of the falling off of levels of community action and the disorientation of many community workers. The plain fact is that many community work activities, as we originally conceived them, have simply lost their point. Our current predicament is that we are no longer collectively quite sure of what we are trying to do or of how to do it.

The broader political shifts described above have taken place against the background of a continuing crisis of legitimisation of the state within the capitalist social democratic framework.[1] This crisis again is reflected in most of our social and political institutions, including the political parties, the trade union movement and also the professions, especially those which are more closely tied in to the state apparatus, such as social and community work.

As community workers we need to make strenuous efforts to come to terms with this type of broader social analysis of the context in which we are working and with its implications for our practice before we can seriously begin 'to make sense of community work', and give clearer shape to our aspirations for its more effective practice in the future. The sheer difficulty of doing this has to be recognised, especially for workers in hard-pressed agencies with limited resources and support, and this appears to be an area in which a substantial improvement of resource availability for in-service educational and training support is badly needed. Without this support, many workers will be forced to retreat from the task of making sense of community work, with unfortunate results which have been to some extent in evidence recently. One manifestation of this is an increasing impatience with 'theory', a wish to get back to the concrete realities of practice and to get the lid back on after the events of recent years. Another and often related manifestation is a growing intolerance of the innate value pluralism of community work – as captured in the typologies of, for example, Rothman (1970) and Bryant (1976) – a characteristic which has not only been a source of much vitality but which seems essential in a professional activity committed to ideals like that of self-determination.

A scenario for the future

As will have been clear from the foregoing analysis, I believe that the process of institutionalisation and incorporation of community work will continue into the future and that coming to terms with the inevitability of this will provide a major challenge to community workers. The process can be responded to in a variety of ways, of course, and will provide a range of opportunities for practice, according to different ideological perspectives and other considerations. Obviously, it is difficult to regard the process without misgivings and it will be vigorously resisted in many quarters, but then again it need not be regarded as necessarily leading to the establishment of an entirely watertight system of community control to which the only legitimate response by 'good' community workers should be suicide or despair. There will continue to be spaces for conscientious and radical community work, but workers who seek them will increasingly need to think and plan much more rigorously and strategically than has tended to be the case in the past to be sure of finding and keeping those spaces.

The last decade has been a period of learning for the interests that sponsor and manage community work and provide the resources which are necessary for its maintenance and expansion. One of the results of this learning process is that the days of the open-ended job description have virtually gone. The belief that community work, after a short-lived boom, is now a contracting industry seems unfounded, however, as a cursory perusal of current job advertisement columns would demonstrate. As well as jobs which are specifically described as community or neighbourhood work, the word 'community' is attached to an increasing number of posts in social work, education, health, housing and so on. The explanation for this arises out of the fact that the recent trend within the state apparatus, especially local government, towards a rationalisation which has mirrored that of private industry has been accompanied by the selective incorporation of aspects of community work. The reasons for this have been the needs to strengthen organisational capacities to monitor environments and manage inter-agency relationships, to underpin shifts in resource allocation within a fixed envelope and to engage the structurally unemployed.

The scenario for the future of community work that follows is presented in a somewhat stark way in order to provide an uncompromised basis for discussion and reaction. Too many variables would have to be taken into account to present alternatives, even if sufficient space was available to make this possible. Any vision of the possible situation in 1984 must start with the economy. Although the initial reaction of the Government and sponsoring agencies and of the establishment generally to CDP's economic analysis of the problems of the project areas[2] was that these problems only represented a cyclical hiccup, it is now generally recognised by most reasonably impartial observers that the problems of the economy are in fact structural and that these will continue to be manifested in structural unemployment for a considerable period (i.e. for the foreseeable future). Despite the claims being made for the microprocessor that it will initiate a new Jerusalem, it seems more likely that its effect on employment in industry and commerce will be to merely reinforce the long-established processes of industrial centralisation and rationalisation which have already created mass unemployment and effectively de-skilled large sections of the population. This is especially the case amongst the working class sections of the population and in the so-called 'deprived areas' in which community workers predominantly operate.

It seems a fair bet that any government in the immediate future which values political consent and seeks to operate within the broad social democratic consensus which has characterised much of the lat twenty years will be forced to continue with the strategy of 'make-work', in one variant or another. This will be unlikely to be in the form it took in the 1960s and early 1970s with the expansion of formal employment in the public sector and will probably be an extension of the Manpower Services Commission's supposedly temporary palliatives. This may take on some longer-term aspects with the creation of 'new careers' for the poor and for those made redundant, along the lines of the American poverty programmes. Potential vehicles already exist in the form of the Inner City Partnership Programmes (ICPPs) and the Urban Programme.

Notwithstanding these possible developments, it also seems likely that severe constraints will continue to operate on resource allocation to the major social services and housing. The search for cheaper methods of service delivery will result in a strengthening of what Corrigan (unpublished) has described as the 'state community strategy' and in increasing emphasis on 'community caring', the usage of volunteers and, again, the creation of new careers for para-professionals to service an otherwise diluted and cheaper system. The concept of 'positive discrimination' will be used, as it is already, to legitimise a shift of resource within a fixed or declining cake, from one area or sector of need to another, thus eroding even further the principle of 'universality' which has been a central part of the ideology of the Welfare State since Beveridge. This type of thinking appears already to provide most of the intellectual basis for schemes like the ICPPs.

This scenario, assuming it is at all credible to the reader, has obvious and profoundly serious implications for the communities and sections of the population with which community workers predominantly work. Conditions in many already stressed areas will continue to worsen whilst at the same time many of the mainstream remedial social services will also be deteriorating. Amongst some sections of the population (like young blacks) and in some areas (like Kirkby), those who have jobs seem likely to become the exception rather than the rule.

The role of community work?

What will be the role allocated by state and quasi-state organisations to community workers and allied workers in related fields within this new picture? People called 'community workers' or something similar will be paid to service and in many ways create this new system. It will be their task to manage the multiplicity of new groups and organisations which will have to be brought into being to engage the long-term structurally unemployed and to provide the new community-based social services. An increasing part of their work will involve the professional supervision of a new tier of para-professional, sub-professional and non-professional volunteer workers. The new community workers will act as the outreach agents, the eyes and ears, of the corporately managed major established institutions in helping them better to monitor their environments and manage geed-back and to handle increasingly complex inter-organisational relationships. The larger existing quasi-statutory and quasi-voluntary organisations, like the Councils of Voluntary Service and Community Relations Councils, which already act as mediating organisations, will be strengthened and new organisations will be created where necessary to fulfil similar functions. In the establishment of this new system, increasing use will be made of staff secondment by statutory to voluntary organisations as an alternative to the direct funding of new posts by the supplicant bodies. The new community workers will spend an increasing part of their work in deskbound activities and will do less direct fieldwork with clients. They will be more involved in management, in making policy, and in controlling budgets and resource allocation. Looked at overall, their work would assume a shape which might better be described as 'community organisation and social planning', as it is called in the United States, than as 'community work' in the sense in which the term has traditionally been used in the UK.

It would be simplistic to suppose that the new system could be operated in a monolithic line-management way and its inevitable contradictions will provide locations for new forms of struggle. Alongside the quest for control from the centre, there will also be struggles for control from the periphery and the grassroots. Many organisations will struggle to maintain maximum autonomy. Alongside more domesticated organisations will be the countervailing influence of other new and more challenging organisations like workers' cooperatives, black and feminist consciousness groups, resource centres and other organisational forms which may grow out of debates within the labour movement.

How will community workers respond to this new future? The short answer is variously, just as they always have in the past. Ultimately, the ways in which workers respond will depend on personal and collective clarifications of the relationship between community work and the State. Put very crudely, it depends on whether the worker regards the State as the neutral referee who holds the ring, or as the committee of the ruling class, or as a battleground for struggle between class forces. Since any theory of the State must inevitably reflect also a theory of society, another way of looking at this is in terms of the two broad categories of theories of change quoted by Rein (1970):

> There are those that accept social conditions as a constraint and conclude that change must start with the individual ... By contrast, other theories treat external conditions as the targets of change, rather than as constraints. Their argument is that man cannot change until the world he lives in is transformed.

So far as community work is concerned, it will depend on whether the individual sees his or her work as primarily aimed at helping people to cope with reality, or with helping people to change that reality.

Different pathways towards the future of community work will arise out of differing approaches to the broader political crisis which was analysed in the preceding section of this paper. Within a broader context in which the state, and therefore society, is caught inextricably on the horns of the dilemma there described, a situation redolent with contradictions and potential social conflict, should the future of community work be regarded primarily as either:

(i) a tool which reinforces the ability of those who govern to manage the economic and political crisis more smoothly and effectively in order to guide the shop of state to smoother waters (and therefore in Freire's [1972] terms as a tool for domestication) or as:

(ii) a tool which reinforces the ability of those who are politically and economically marginal to engage more effectively in political struggles through concentrating strategically on the contradictions within the system at a time of crisis (and therefore in Freire's terms as a tool for liberation)?

It would fall most obviously to the 'professionalists'[3] – those who tend to place most stress on the technical aspects of community work and who mainly adhere to consensual/pluralist models of society – to make the new scenario for 1984 work as smoothly as possible. They will find many attractive new perches within the new system. But what positions will the other broad camp within community work take up – the radical dissenters? These are the workers who regard community work as essentially part of a broader social movement for change and who see its aims as inextricably linked with the major social and political issues of the day.

There are a number of different horses in this second stable, with several cross-variants. There are the Marxist structural analysts, seeking to develop a practice which connects together 'community' struggles with struggles at the point of production; looking for alliances and aiming perhaps to build a new political movement. There are the Libertarian Socialists, more anarchic and perhaps sceptical of the possibilities for change presented by large organisations and movements; committed to politicisation at the grassroots level and to the development of alternative organisational forms like cooperatives. The other main group are those who are into Person Consciousness, emphasising the fact that 'the person is political'; superimposing (usually) onto a class analysis, an analysis which emphasises the sector of reproduction and the importance of sexual divisions (feminist groups) or the importance of questions of race and ethnicity (black groups); and concerned with the raising of consciousness as the basis for developing struggles and campaigns.

What will this variegated group of radical dissenters do within the scenario for 1984? They will need to look for the relatively autonomous spaces in the new system – the 'nooks and crannies' as they are often referred to – and to seek out the subversible areas, identifying and working on the contradictions. They will find ways of disrupting the progressive routinisation of the system's operation which will tend to be the consequence of increasing institutionalisation, by generating counter-organisations – like, for example, the new Resources Centres – which have the capacity to develop the materials and provide the resources which are needed to support more broadly based campaigns and to foster the development of alliances between different progressive interests. And above all, they will need the strategy and the stamina for a continuing struggle.

Implications for methodology and professionalisation

It remains to examine some implications of the scenario for the development of the practical skills and understandings which will be needed and to consider the implications for professionalism.

More effective community work will require closer attention to the relationship between method and purpose. It could be argued that whilst some earlier views of community work over-emphasised questions of method and virtually excluded questions of purpose, other more recent views have over-emphasised purpose and neglected methods. The absolute necessity for community workers to develop strategies has already been noted – and an effective strategy could be regarded as the product of the effective union of method with purpose. This concept of community work as an informal educational process arising out of dialogue, social action and reflection, as in Freire's (1972) practice of freedom, seems to take the debate about the relationship between method and purpose a significant step forward.[4]

Increasing recognition of the innately political nature of most community work, regardless of the worker's stated ideology, will necessitate the strengthening of skills in political analysis and interaction. Specht (1975) was fully justified in his criticisms of the neglect of organisational awareness and analysis in community work in this country because, beyond much contemporary rhetoric about accountability, lies the fact that:

> The needs and problems of the community are not funnelled and defined directly between the practitioner and the community segment to which he is related; instead, needs are defined and shaped by the constitution and goals of the employing agency. ... Whatever the practitioner's activity, he is guided by the structure, aims and operating procedures of the organisation that pays the bills. (Zald 1970)

The development of skills in political analysis will need to promote not only understanding of employing bodies but of the whole organisational environment within which action strategies will operate.

Finally, some remarks on the thorny question of professionalisation. In the future, community work will move substantially towards fuller professionalisation because that is the corollary of institutionalisation and incorporation. The decision of the Association of Community Workers in 1973 to voluntarily reverse what is regarded as the normal process of professionalisation (Cox and Derricourt 1975) can be seen in retrospect as a way of temporarily ducking the issues involved rather than of permanently resolving them, given the considerable ambivalence towards professionalisation which is to be found in community work circles. When it was realised that the field had been left open to others and the quasi-statutory Central Council for Education and Training in Social Work began to move into the space, this forced an attempt at a pre-emptive reaction which has led to the creation of the Federation of Community Work Training Groups, another half-way house.

It is impossible to discuss the future of professionalisation of community work without making reference to social work. Changes in community work along the lines previously discussed will be paralleled by changes in social work as well as in other closely related areas like youth work, community education and housing management. Major changes in methods of delivery of social work services seem inevitable in the near-future as a growing recognition of the obsolescence of traditional theories of social work is accompanied by pressure to develop more cost-effective methods. In this context, the invention of the 'integrated approach' to social work, which painlessly incorporates community work into generic social work as one of a number of neatly nested levels of intervention, is the answer to the maiden's prayer of the social work manager and of many education and training institutions. Despite the antagonism which many community workers may feel towards this theory, the logic of resource allocation by sponsoring bodies and of educational and training policies suggests that mainstream community work and social work will draw increasingly closer together in the future. Indeed, an eventual merger can be predicted, with some asset stripping along the way, thus establishing a new generic grouping which will be closer to the pattern of practice in the United States and in other parts of Europe.

Community workers will respond to this process of professionalisation in differing ways, reflecting the different ethical and ideological trajectories which they are following. Returning to Specht's (1975) dichotomy, those whose primary interest in community work is as a professional activity will naturally grow into the integrated approach as the new 'managerialist' ideology. Those whose primary interest in community work is as part of a social movement and who have developed 'critical' ideologies will be less comfortable. The legitimacy of a profession has been said to lie in the acceptance of its claims to mastery of method (that is to say, a technology), not in its expertness in determining ends, since the later is supposedly the function of the political process, at least within a democratic society. (Rein and Marris 1968) The kernel of what is truly innovative, challenging and radical in community work is inimical to professionalisation. Some aspects of this kernel will find ways to survive within an increasingly established profession, where they will be reflected in the establishment of radical splinter groups and in trade unionisation as well as in other ways. Others may drift away from community work and cease to recognise the title. The seeds of a possible new grouping lie in recent developments within the broad field of adult education.

Conclusion

Looking ahead is never easy and this paper includes many crude generalisations and inadequately-argued assertions. It is hoped, however, that for all its limitations it will have some value in helping to sharpen debate about the future of community work in the 1980s. Although the picture of the future may seem to some readers to be a disheartening one, there is much about contemporary community work that gives grounds for optimism. There are significant areas of innovation and new developments in thinking and practice and much too will come from stoically plugging away at essential work at a time when the struggles seem so much harder than they did a few years ago. The considerable fund of idealism within community work is in the process of being tempered by realism and what will eventually emerge will be much stronger.

References

Bridges, L. (1975). 'The Ministry of Internal Security British Urban Social Policy 1968-74', *Race and Class*, XVI, 4.

Bryant, R. (1976) ' Crossing the Boundaries of Social Work'. *Community Care*, 29.9.76.

Cockburn, C. (1977) *The Local State*. London: Pluto Press.

Corrigan, P., (unpublished). *The Community Strategy, State Policy and Class Struggle 1966-76*. Unpublished conference paper.

Cox, D.J. and Derricourt, N.J. (1975) 'The De-Professionalisation of Community Work'. In: D. Jones and M. Mayo (eds) *Community Work Two*. London: Routledge and Kegan Paul.

Dearlove, J. (1974) 'The Control of Change and the Regulation of Community Action.' In: D. Jones and M. Mayo (eds) *Community Work One*. Routledge and Kegan Paul.

Donnison, D. (1979) 'Training for Social Work'. *Social Work Today*, 10(24).

Freire, P. (1972) *Pedagogy of the Oppressed*. Harmondsworth: Penguin.

Kraushaar, R. 1979. ' Policy Without Protest: the Dilemma of Organising for Change in Britain'. *C.E.S. Urban Change and Conflict Conference Papers*.

National C.D.P. (1977) *The Costs of Industrial Change*, London: CDPIIU.

Perlman, R. and Gurin, A. (1972) *Community Organisation and Social Planning*. Chichester: John Wiley and Sons.

Rein, M. (1970) 'Social Work in Search of a Radical Profession'. *Social Work*, 15(2), April.

Rein, M. and Marris, P. (1968) 'Poverty and the Community Planners' Mandate'. In: B.J. Frieden and R. Morris (eds) *Urban Planning and Social Policy*. New York: Basic Books.

Rothman, J. (1970) 'Three Models of Community Organisation Practice.' In: F. Cox *et al.* (eds) *Strategies of Community Organisation*. Ithaca: Peacock Press.

Specht, H. (1975) *Community Development in the U.K.* Association of Community Workers.

Thomas, D. (1977) Chapter 13. In: N. McCaugham (ed.) *Group Work: Learning and Practice*. National Institute Social Services Library.

Zald, M.N. (1970) 'Organisations as Polities: An Analysis of Community Organisation Agencies.' In: F. Cox *et al. op. cit.*

Notes

1. See Kraushaar (1979) for a discussion of this.
2. As later expressed in National C.D.P. (1977) and in early studies by individual local projects and on an inter-project basis out of which this analysis grew.
3. The profession/social movements dichotomy is derived from Specht (1975).
4. See Thomas (1977).

Paul Waddington is Lecturer at Birmingham Polytechnic. Vol. 14 No. 3 (1979): 224-234.

7

Participation in Development in North-East Brazil

Peter Oakley

Introduction

In many current Third World rural development initiatives, 'participation' of rural people themselves – in the process of development in decision-making, planning and execution – is frequently stressed. Efforts are made to define the term 'participation', a concept which remains diffuse. Commonly, however, the concept is used in the context of the need to encourage people to respond to development programmes established by others for their benefit.

Participation is essentially a political act: the ideological context of any process of participation cannot be ignored. In any programmes which include 'participation as a basic objective, it is important to ask *who* is to participate and on *what* terms, *why* the participation of the people is sought and *how* they are to participate'. (Migdal 1977: 210-221) Invariably, participation is sought by an outside agent which determines its nature, its content and the conditions under which it is to be enjoyed by local people. Such is the practice of most participatory exercises directed, for example, by conventional community development or rural animation programmes. Both these latter methodologies stress people's participation as an important goal. Yet essentially both induce participation from outside in a pre-determined manner. (Meister 1972) The demands of the existing politico-administrative structure of government development policies are also critical in determining the nature of participation offered.

This case study recounts efforts in the past 15 years in N.E. Brazil to identify an appropriate methodology for the participation of the people themselves in the process of development. I argue that the work can be characterised as a movement and trace the evolution of a continual process of research and development to identify such a methodology. The movement is little structured with no formal basis. Its most prominent features include the following:

(i) It is wholly a non-government activity. It involves consistent efforts of voluntary agencies, the Roman Catholic church and a myriad of local

82

groups. An informal network of communication exists between the many agencies and groups, with the Church Parish structure playing a pivotal role, under the loose co-ordination of *FASE* (an indigenous voluntary agency) whose servicing and supporting role is vital.[1]

(ii) Following the early period, when it was somewhat paternalistic in nature and methodologically immature, the movement has come to emphasize *non-formal* educational processes to achieve the objective of participation. This process is, however, seen as an *end* in itself, not as a means to an end, which is conventional community development practice.

(iii) in developing a relevant methodology, it emphasises the need to prepare people to tackle the *structural* and *institutional* problems of N.E. Brazil, and not merely problems relating to the region's physical attributes. The basic condition of *dependence* under which most people in the region live, their *marginality* and the *oppression* they suffer, are the key problems which the people must be prepared to tackle. These three conditions are symptomatic of a 'culture of silence'. (Freire 1972)

(iv) It is essentially a *dynamic* process which seeks to change the *status quo* by focusing on factors (dependence, marginality and oppression) which help maintain it.

I deal briefly with the initial years of this movement (1960-1970), then outline the latter years and, more particularly, the process of participative education.

Brazil's north-east region

North-East Brazil (the states of Maranhao, Piaui, Ceara, Rio Grande do Norte, Paraiba, Pernambuco, Alagoas, Sergipe and Bahia) has been described as a 'country within a country' (Robock, 1966). It covers an area of 598,000 square miles (18 percent of Brazil's total area) with a population estimated in 1976 at approx. 33 million, about one-third of Brazil's population. The region (*zona de mata*) comprises the transitional zone (*agreste*), the semi-arid interior (*serato*), periodically affected by drought, and the westerly fringe bordering upon the Amazon basin. Sixty per cent of the region's population is rural, major cash crops being sugar and cotton and the staples beans, corn, cassava and rice. In the coastal region, plantation agriculture is extensively practised; in the transitional zone, small-holding (*minifundia*) dominates whilst in the massive semi-arid interior large-holding (*latifundia*) is the basic tenurial arrangement. (Hirschman 1965:19-25)

Most of the population gains its livelihood from the land. However, access to this basic resource is unequal. Apart from the predominance of small-holdings in the transitional region, good arable land is largely controlled by big landowners. On the coast, vast sugar plantations dominate, the rural labour force having little power or influence. In the transitional region the plots are so small and institutionalized support so totally lacking, that a viable existence is difficult. For the north-eastern peasant his patron (*patrao*) is the key figure in his world of social relations. E. de Kadt (1970: 17-18) has summarised this relationship as follows:

> The peasant's patron is the landowner on whose land he squats or with whom he has a sharecropping arrangement, or the merchant on whom he depends for the sale of his crop. The patron must protect the peasant from hostile outsiders (such as government officials) and come to his aid in the case of unexpected setbacks resulting from natural or economic causes. As most peasants still live at very near subsistence level, little is needed to force them to petition the patron for such a special favour. Other, more usual, 'favours' include the granting of a piece of land on which to plant subsistence crops, or that of allowing the peasant to buy necessities on credit between harvests – a doubtful privilege, which effectively binds the peasant to the patron in debt peonage.

This patron-client relationship is particularly dominant in the coastal region. Even in the transitional region it is the patron who provides the support, the credit and the necessary resources for agriculture. The system breeds the 'culture of silence'. The peasant exists on society's periphery with little access to resources, no participation and no voice in the region's development. Drought, hunger and misery are words synonymous with Brazil's North-East. (de Castro 1952; Gallet 1972)

Until early in this century, the North-East received scant attention from the Brazilian Federal Government. Sugar and cotton reigned supreme and there were few Federal Government efforts at regional development. A severe and disastrous drought – the region's great scourge – in 1877-79, aroused Government concern, finally translating into the establishment of a Federal Drought Control Agency in 1909. Successive drought periods in 1931-32, 1951-53, and 1958-59 then led to the creation of a powerful Federal Agency, the Superintendency for the Development of the North-East (SUDENE) in 1960. Since that date, direction of the North-East's capital development has been controversially in that Agency's hands.

The speed with which SUDENE was eventually established was also largely in response to a mood of latent protest within the region's rural population. In 1955, braving intimidation, the peasant labour force on a plantation in Pernambuco state, banded together to achieve modest aims, such as to set up a fund for a schoolteacher's salary, form a vegetable growers' co-operative and campaign for protection guaranteed by the Federal constitution. This incipient movement sought the services of a quick-witted lawyer – Francisco Juliao – whose inspired direction prompted a wide-spread peasant protest movement. The Peasant Leagues were born, whose activities were limited to two basic objectives: the abolition of the *'cambao'* (literally the 'yoke' or the ties of bondage between the master and worker) and opposition to any increase in land rents. The Peasant Leagues movement spread rapidly during the years 1955-1960, appealing especially to tenants and small-holders, but also at a later date to the sugar-estate workers. The left-wing Government of President Goulart (1961-1964) went with the tide, legalized rural trade unions and, in 1963, supported a strike by 200,000 peasants in support of new laws regarding labour conditions and remuneration. Inevitably, the 1964 coup d'etat brought swift retribution. The government-sponsored unions and the Leagues were repressed and landowners gained their vengeance. It is in this context that we now examine the process of community development in the North-East. (Leeds 1965; Juliao 1972; Pearse 1975)

The early years 1960-1967

The Catholic Church was in the vanguard of efforts in the early 1960s to involve local people in the region's development. It can be argued that this Church concern was largely a direct result of the emergence of the Peasant Leagues and fears of some form of extreme left-wing control of the incipient peasant movement. Church-inspired bodies began a vigorous campaign to win rural peasants' allegiance. The 'movement' was *ad hoc* in nature with little co-ordinated action. It was, however, the first initiative of what was to grow into a more influential and far reaching church-inspired social action movement.

In these early years, the movement was essentially paternalistic. The principal activities included:

(a) the formation of rural trade unions within the framework established under Brazilian Law;

(b) the training of local leaders, and;

(c) the diffusion of Catholic social doctrine.

These activities had little methodological basis, and there was no co-ordination between the various church-inspired bodies. Activities were undertaken either by the parishes or by the organizations concerned, with little support and few professional staff.

The first attempt to provide some methodological basis for these early initiatives came from MEB (*Movimento de Educacao de Base –* Community Level Education Movement). This was established by the Brazilian Bishops' National Confederation in 1961 to expand the experience of radio schools – used for educational purposes – in several Dioceses to other parts of the North-East. It should also be seen in the context of the church's response to political agitation in the North-East in the early 1960s. (de Kadt 1970) The basic unit of organization was the *system* which was made up of the MEB team, the peasants and the village level workers (*monitores*). The basic function of a *system* was literacy training via the radio, although as *systems* became established, a wider process of community development emerged.

The number of MEB *systems* rose from 11 in 1961 to 59 in 1963, but declined to 37 in 1966 as a result of the 1964 coup. The village level worker was the essential cog in the MEB machine, and as the Movement developed, he came to be seen less as an auxiliary teacher, more as a community leader. Similarly the Movement's self-image underwent a change, from an emphasis upon literacy to a greater stress on peasant organization. In 1963 the systems began to move away from broadcasts and radio classes as their main concern, becoming more concerned with preparing peasants for trade union participation. Training sessions and group discussions became important parts of the *system's* work and non-directive techniques were introduced. It was during this period that the concept of *concientizacao* (concientization or 'awareness' creation) first emerged in the vocabulary of the North-East. Peasants attended training sessions organized by the MEB monitor, whose main task was seen as follows:

> To supply data which will make it possible for the trainee (peasant) to verify his personal responsibility and his role of agent in history. This will enable him to choose between either accepting the existing situation, or attacking at the roots the unjust and inhuman set-up under which he is suffering.'
> (de Kadt 1970: 127-130)

The MEB approach was the first attempt to bring methodological rigour to this movement, seeking to prepare the peasant to participate in the development process. In the context of North-East Brazil at that time, the approach was radical, progressively laying emphasis upon non-formal educational techniques, as opposed to physical improvement projects. MEB's importance was that not only did it help establish an informal non-governmental development structure but also greatly expanded the movement's influence. Its approach at the community level, however, was still methodologically undeveloped, depending too much on the monitor and an ill-defined process of consciousness-raising. The repression following the 1964 coup severely restricted MEB's activities and this particular period of radical catholic social action was temporarily blunted.

FASE and community creativity (1967-1972)

The first attempt to provide a rigorous methodological basis for the movement in the North-East was provided by FASE. An indigenous voluntary agency, in the late 1960s FASE gradually assumed a central role providing methodological support for the many local associations, community and parish groups working in the North-East. During this period FASE itself had 3 offices in the North-East and was responsible for training hundreds of local non-government community-level workers. This training represented the first efforts to bring some cohesion to a previously disparate movement and provide a common methodological approach to the process involving the peasants in development.

The basis of this FASE approach was community creativity (*criatividade communitaria*). It employed a rather simplistic systems analysis and divided the community or social system into 15 component sub-systems such as education, family, health, communication and religion. The process involved, essentially an exercise in group dynamics, could be best understood as a series of stages:

Contact with rural community ⟶ Structuring of the group on community (geographic) lines ⟶ Group Leadership Training ⟶ Community Creativity

The component sub-systems would form the basis of group discussion, which would 'analyse' the particular sub-system, identify community problems within the sub-system and, accordingly, prepare a course of action to tackle the problems related to that sub-system. This approach dominated the activities of the movement until the early 1970s. Even a massive government rural development project adopted its methodology. The approach, whilst it must be seen as a first initiative in the field, suffered severe limitations:

(i) It was theoretically simplistic and poorly thought-out. It also proved somewhat difficult to articulate comprehensively to community level workers;

(ii) It was extremely rigid and compartmentalized in its understanding of sub-systems within a social system, and took no account of inter-relationships or linkages;

(iii) It led to a proliferation of innumerable *ad hoc* physical community projects. It seemed unable, however, to identify or tackle these community problems *whose cause lay outside the community*. In this respect it was sometimes uncharitably referred to as the 'aspirin' approach;

(iv) It caused an increasing dissatisfaction with the community – defined geographically and localistically – *as an adequate social unit for development*. It exposed the need for a more functional, as opposed to territorial, approach to the determination of this unit.

These latter two criticisms were crucial to furthering the development of an appropriate methodology and were responsible for a redefinition of the FASE approach and for the emergence of the concept of participative education.

Concientization

The concept of concientization is elaborated in the works of Paulo Freire, who was born, studied and taught in North-East Brazil. As noted, concientization first appeared in the vocabulary of the North-East in the late 1960s and was widely adopted by many local and church groups. The term loosely referred to a process of non-formal education which aimed at an 'awakening of peasant consciousness', but was employed with little methodological rigour. For many, the community creativity approach was seen as essentially a process of concientization, the term becoming a characteristic of most community-based development efforts. Its influence on the evolution of the concept of participative education was significant. (Smith 1976)

Participative education

Dissatisfaction with the community creativity approach, whose inadequacies were clearly apparent, gave rise to a period of intense research and development to improve the methodological basis of the movement's community work. As observed earlier, dissatisfaction was largely based upon community creativity's use of the *community* as the social unit for development and with the palliative nature of that approach's effects. There was also need for a more dynamic model for guiding the process of participation in development. The two main issues to emerge from this period of reconsideration were:

(a) The formation of common interest groups, as opposed to spatial communities, as the social units for development. Although it was not clearly established by what criteria these groups would be defined, in the rural areas the relationship to the land became the dominant criterion.

(b) The emphasis upon participative education as a process, having a definable objective, with the process considered to be an end in itself, not just as a means to an end. In this context any small projects of physical improvement were considered as the means to achieving this end.

The following could be considered as a definition of this process of participative education:

> The creation of groups (or communities) able to diagnose and analyse their own problems, to decide upon collective action and to carry out such action to deal with these problems, independent of outside influence. (Oakley and James 1976: 23)

The process consists of *five* basic concepts: (a) critical faculty, (b) participation, (c) organization, (d) solidarity, (e) articulation. The process of participative education, therefore, is directed towards creating and nurturing these concepts within a group, which should result in a state of autonomy on the part of the group. As these *five* concepts are fundamental to the process, we look separately at each.

(a) **Critical Faculty**: This concerns the development within the individual and the group of an awareness of 'reality', which is defined in terms of group interest vis-à-vis other groups or sections of society. This 'reality' could be expressed, for instance, as follows:

(i) the group's access to and security of resources i.e. land

(ii) the group's position in the local marketing/commercial structure.

The creation of critical faculty enables the group to analyse its situation in terms of its 'reality' and eventually to propose a course of action to change this 'reality'. It involves several stages:

(i) problem defining;

(ii) deciding where the causes of the problem lie;

(iii) prescribing courses of action to deal with the problems; and

(iv) realization that action is possible to tackle these causes.

Stage (i) is concerned essentially with the definition of 'reality'.

(Berger *et al.*1974) This stage, however, depends fundamentally on *who* is defining the 'reality', concepts used in problem formation and who is ranking the priorities of the problems. If this initial stage is achieved by the group itself (with outside personnel assuming a passive role) then the process could be seen as *participative* education. If, however, outside personnel are active in 'reality' definition, then the validity of the participation is open to question.

(b) **Participation:** This concerns not only actual membership of a group but, more importantly, the active participation of group members in terms of decision-making, planning and execution of agreed action. An important aspect is the initial stage of participation (i.e. group membership) which is according to pre-determined economic criteria i.e. land-holding size, position in marketing structure, etc.

(c) **Organization:** Initially, group organization is a function of an external agency (FASE). This initial stage evolves into the internal structuring of the group in terms of group control over organization, group leadership and decision – making.

(d) **Solidarity:** An initial stage of co-operation within the group leads, over time, to a sense of group solidarity. Group behaviour becomes co-operative, and *not* competitive, individualistic or subject to external domination. Group solidarity is an essential pre-requisite to tacking problems whose root causes lie outside the community; it then extends to solidarity with similar groups.

(e) **Articulation:** There could be two basic interpretations of this concept:
(i) the taking of action by the group to tackle problems whose causes lie outside the group;
(ii) the process of diffusion i.e. the establishing of contact with similar interest groups inside and beyond the region.

An important way of understanding the functioning of these concepts is to see them as *processes* occurring over time i.e. *organization* as a characteristic of the group does not occur instantaneously but develops over a period of time.

This shows the theoretical content of the concept of participative education. It is now important to understand how the concept functions in practice and it is in this respect that difficulties are encountered. The concept is still essentially at the stage of research and development, and it is difficult clearly to understand its practice. During the course of field visits to local FASE teams, which were applying the methodology in the field, attempts were made to define the process more clearly. The starting point was the emphasis upon participative education as a *process*. Simply defined, the process had a starting point (the selection of the target audience) and an end (the autonomy of the group).

It was suggested that it might be possible to understand the process in terms of recognizable *stages*. The work of FASE teams with local groups over a period of time was reviewed and incidents, actions, activities and general group development were examined to determine whether it would be possible to identify particular stages in the evolution of the group towards its ultimate objective. In this respect the five critical concepts were employed in terms of their presence as characteristic of any particular stage. In other words the achieving of one or other of the critical concepts was a prerequisite for the group being at a particular stage.

Illustrative examples

Of the field teams visited, two provide illustrations of the team's understanding of the process of participative education.

(a) *Garanhuns, Pernambuco State*
FASE had established a team in this area and over a period of five years from 1971 extended its work to a dozen groups. Garanhuns is located in the transitional region of North-East Brazil where small-holdings dominate. The FASE team had begun its work in this region using the community creativity approach, but since 1974 has increasingly adopted the participative education approach. The team functioned, however, in a highly experimental manner.

A review of the Garanhuns team's work with its group over a period of six years and an understanding (as articulated by team members) of the stages through which the groups had evolved, produced the following understanding of the process of participative education:
SELECTION OF TARGET AUDIENCE
      ⟶ FORMATION OF COMMON INTEREST GROUPS
         ⟶ ACTION *INSIDE* GROUP
           ⟶ ACTION *OUTSIDE* GROUP
             ⟶ AUTONOMY OF GROUP

The selection of the Target Audience is largely a function of the geographical location of the FASE office and a broadly-defined purpose to work with the rural poor. The groups are largely defined in terms of their relation to the land, being principally constituted by small peasant proprietors with title to between 2-5 hectares of land. There was little evidence that group selection had been rigorously determined although actual group composition, in economic terms, appeared homogeneous. The particular feature of this understanding process is the distinction between action *inside* and action *outside* the group. If we consider the stages of development of the critical concepts, action *within* the group covers that period when internal organization is beginning to evolve, initial membership leads to increasing participation and early co-operation begins to cause a sense of solidarity among group members. Action *outside* the group reflects the taking of action as a group in relation to other groups within the immediate economic and social system i.e. action to intervene in the marketing process or to petition local government. The taking of action *outside* the group over time eventually leads to the independent action of the group, which is the ultimate objective of the process. Of the twelve groups with which the FASE Garanhuns team had been associated, one was considered by the team as being now largely independent of FASE and three at the stage of consistent action *outside* the group.

(b) *Fortaleza, Ceara State*

The work of the FASE team based in Fortazela covered several locations within the state. The area where the team's work was more developed was in the Curu Valley, 120 kms to the east of the state capital. The Curu Valley is located in the northernmost part of the semi-arid interior region. During the period 1974-1976 the FASE team worked directly with 165 rural families from four different communities. The majority of these families were small peasant landowners, although there was also a significant number of tenant farmers and sharecroppers. This aspect is particularly interesting in that the FASE team determined its group principally in spatial terms. It worked basically with groups in four communities and the groups included both small landowners and tenants. Its groups were effectively locally-defined communities and were considered to be economically homogeneous.

Methodologically, the Fortaleza team was from the beginning more sophisticated than other FASE teams visited. The basis of its work with the four communities was a non-formal educational approach and it defined its long-term objectives as:

(a) the establishment of autonomous communities capable of directing their own affairs; and

(b) the establishment of inter-community relations within the region.

With these objectives in mind the team presented the following as the process which guided its work with the four Curu communities:

Stage	Participation	Organization	Solidarity	Articulation
1 Dependent on F.A.S.E.	Immediate Personal	Meetings Paternal leadership	Solidarity as expressed individually	Articulation between individuals
2	Group interest enlarging to community interest	Systematic meetings Planning of action Questioning of old leadership structurer	Economic base for solidarity at local level	Inter-group articulation at local level
3	Inter- communal Regional	Organization structure New leadership Power	Economic base for solidarity at regional level	Articulation between different areas
4	Class Interest	Participation in class organization	Mobilization on political, economic and social lines	Articulation between class organizations and between other organizations
Independent of F.A.S.E.	CRITICAL FACULTY			

The Fortaleza FASE team's understanding of the process interestingly differs from the understanding of their Garanhun colleagues. The concept of Articulation is strictly defined in terms of diffusion and inter-community contact. Most noticeably, the concept of Critical Faculty is considered as indicating the achievement of the other concepts and an indispensable characteristic of an autonomous group. In early 1976, the team had undertaken a major evaluation of its work to date in the Curu area and this evaluation study was largely responsible for their articulation of the process which guided their work. The evaluation generally revealed that the few communities with which the team worked could be located, in terms of the stages of the process, between stages two and three. Internal community organization had developed, community solidarity was seen to be evolving and the four communities had already established contact between themselves and were extending this contact to communitics not yet formally supported by FASE. The communities were still, however, essentially at the stage of action *within* the community and still dependent upon the FASE team to maintain the momentum of the participative process.

Change agent

The essential person in the participative education process is the change agent who initially directs, then later accompanies it. These agents are referred to as local level agents (*agentes de base*) or agents of intervention (*agentes de intervencao*). In view of the non-material objectives established by the participative education process, the skills required of such agents must reflect the tasks to be undertaken. The important characteristics of these agents include:

(a) *skills* – the emphasis is placed on communication, articulation and powers of observation and interpretation. Critical ability is important, with a general political awareness and sensitivity;

(b) *functions* – the basic function of the agent changes over time from one of *direct intervention* in the work of the groups to one of *indirect support*. The agent's role is to direct and guide the educational process and, importantly, to help organize the functioning of the groups;

(c) *training* – emphasis upon training in the social sciences and, in view of the sophisticated nature of the FASE methodology, agents have normally had some form of higher education.

FASE teams work in both urban and rural areas in Brazil. Whilst emphasis upon staff composition is on educationalists and social scientists, each team normally also has an agricultural technician member. The objectives of FASE's work is *not* to seek to satisfy the technical and other services requirements of the groups, but to prepare the groups to seek and demand such services for themselves from government sources which typically neglect the small farmer. As groups achieve a sense of unity and purpose, so they undertake projects of a productive nature with the assistance of available government resources. Without the educational process, such groups are never formed and its members rarely benefit from government development efforts.

Conclusions

The search for a relevant methodology to facilitate the participation of rural people in the development process in North-East Brazil is still very much at the stage of research and development. It is not difficult to be critical, especially in terms of the lack of a rigorous definition for some of the concepts employed. Similarly we are still very much at the stage of generalized interpretations of the process, as articulated by its field practitioners. These interpretations reveal a fascinating potential for this approach to participation, but they have yet to be supported by hard empirical evidence of the validity of the interpretations at the group level. Furthermore, the relevance of the methodology, in terms of the dynamics of Brazilian society, needs to be more carefully documented and a more detailed analysis of the functioning of the methodology in different socio-economic contexts in the North-East would be useful. Finally, the process of group formation, which is crucial to the whole process of participative education, must be critically monitored and more definitive criteria established for group membership.

It is expected that the movement will continue as a loosely co-ordinated non-government effort, under the general direction of FASE. In the past few years, non-government agencies have come into conflict on more than one occasion with the Brazilian Government and its personnel have been harassed and even imprisoned. Such conflict is inevitable. The development of Brazil is wholly a top-down process with unfounded faith that the benefits will 'trickle-down' to rural peasants. Officially, the peasant is not being asked to participate in this development. Privately, he is beginning to demand this participation as an inalienable right.

References

Berger P. (1974) *The Pyramids of Sacrifice*, Harmondsworth: Penguin, esp. Ch. 4.
de Castro J. (1952) *Geography of Hunger*, Boston.
de Kadt E. (1970) *Catholic Radicals in Brazil*, Oxford: Oxford University Press.
Freire, P (1972) *Pedagogy of the Oppressed*, Harmondsworth, Penguin.
Gallet P. (1972) *Freedom to Starve*, Harmondsworth: Penguin.
Hirschman A. (1965) *Journey Towards Progress*, New York: Doubleday.
Juliao F. (1972) *Cambao – The Yoke*, Harmondsworth: Penguin.
Leeds A. (1965) 'Brazil and the Myth of Francisco Juliao' in J. Maier Praeger (ed.) *Politics of Change in Latin America*: 190-207.

Meister A. (1972) 'Characteristics of Community Development and Rural Animation in Africa' *International Review of Community Development*, 27-25: 75-132.

Migdal J.S. (1977) *Peasants, Politics and Revolution*, New Hartford: Princeton University Press.

Oakley P. and James P. (1976) *Evaluation of Participative Education Projects in N.E. Brazil*, Oxford: Oxfam.

Pearse A. (1975) *The Latin American Peasant*, London: Frank Cass.

Robock S. (1966) *Brazil's Developing Northeast*, Washington: The Brook Institute.

Smith W.A. (1976) *The meaning of concientizacao, the goal of Paulo Freire's pedagogy*, Boston: University of Massachusetts.

Notes

1. Federacao de Orgaos para Assistencial Social e Educacional (Federation of Organizations of Social and Educational Assistance – FASE) was established in 1962 as an indigenous counterpart to Catholic Relief Services (CRS), Brazil. Its first office was in Rio, but within a decade it had established regional offices in Sao Paulo, Porto Alegre, Recife and Belem. Each of these regional offices established a series of subsidiary offices. FASE's basic objective is to assist the development of marginalized rural and urban communities.

Peter Oakley is a lecturer in the Agricultural Extension and Rural Development Centre, University of Reading: Vol. 15 No. 1 (1980): 10-22.

8

Community Action
and Anti-Poverty Strategies:
Some Transatlantic Comparisons

Martin Loney

Scale

The 1960s saw the development of innovative approaches to the problems of poverty and area deprivation in Canada, the USA and Britain. Frequently comparisons have been made between the American War on Poverty and the British Urban Programme though the scale of the two is markedly different. When the British Urban Programme was announced in 1968, annual federal expenditure on the American Office of Economic Opportunity had passed three billion dollars. (Plotnick and Skidmore 1975) In Britain Demuth (1977) has calculated that between 1966 and 1975 the British Government spent a total of only £121,000,000 on programmes to combat educational disadvantage and urban deprivation.

Political commitment

The American programmes were launched with Presidential backing. Johnson called on the congress to support 'a national war on poverty. Our object total victory'. (Clark and Hopkins 1969: 2) The war on poverty was based on the earlier programmes developed under the auspices of the President's Committee on Juvenile Delinquency (PCJD) which had themselves been carefully assessed and monitored. These programmes had an explicit commitment to using social action to achieve significant social change. Clark and Hopkins (1969: 6) argued that the PCJD recognised that 'a serious programme of community social action (which) would necessarily involve political confrontation and the possibility of abrasive conflict between those forces seeking fundamental changes and those forces required to resist such changes'. This aspect may not have been as clear to those who backed the subsequent War on Poverty but, as we will argue, it remained an important element in the American programme, in marked contrast to the ideas behind the British programme.

In Canada Prime Minister Trudeau committed his government to

'The Just Society', citizen participation became a government priority, the Opportunities for Youth programme and the Company of Youth Canadians financed innovative social change projects. (Loney 1977)

In Britain, Prime Minister Wilson announced an Urban Programme on May 1st, 1968, but while the American War on Poverty had its roots deep in the Kennedy era and the liberal and intellectual wings of the Democratic Party, a senior Labour Cabinet Minister commented that the difficulty of Wilson's proposal had been 'to make any practical sense of this idea'. (Crossman 1977) Wilson's Birmingham speech followed soon after Enoch Powell had forecast 'rivers of blood' in British cities as a consequence of the growing size of the black population. Conceived in haste, borne in confusion, the urban programme had neither the financial resources nor the political commitment of the American and Canadian programmes.

Models and strategies

The Community Development Projects (CDPs), the main community action component of the British Programme, were initiated in the Children's Department of the Home Office where Joan Cooper was concerned to find a community dimension to social work since, as she argued in a contemporary paper, '...highly skilled treatment with the individual is wasted if he is returned to a disordered community which could offer little support'. (Cooper 1969) The model on which they were based was one of social pathology: 'The true purpose of the exercise, and the true field of application of the lessons learned in the feasibility study (i.e. in the first project)', was to discover how better to enable people with many problems to use the helping services creatively and not just as permanent forms of external support or a permanent patter of future organisation. (Interdepartmental Working Party C.D.A. 1968) Specht (1976) has challenged the view that the CDPs were based on a social pathology explanation of poverty, but as has been argued elsewhere the evidence does not support his claim. (Loney 1978) The target population were those who 'through ill-fortune or personal inadequacy suffer from a multitude of inter-related problems and deprivations which cannot be resolved by uncoordinated support from a series of separately organised services.' (C.D.A. 1968) Community action was seen as a means of 'reaching a minority of the population suffering from multi-deprivation and of enabling them to function more autonomously. (C.D.A. 1968)

The sweeping objectives of the American programmes were absent. In the words of one U.K. Cabinet Minister the objective was to see how 'a community can pull itself up by its own bootstraps', and clearly seen as self-help and not radical social change. (Crossman 1977) The American programmes stressed the importance of creating relatively independent centres for community mobilisation. Many of those involved recognised that the central dilemma of the programme was 'that it simultaneously demanded the mobilisation of the people of a depressed community for social action and social change, and sought to finance such programmes through federal and local funds'. (Clark and Hopkins 1969: 5) In contrast the British CDPs were deliberately placed under the control of the relevant local authority. The intent was to minimise independence, not to facilitate the kind of conflicts seen as a *sine qua non* of success by many of the American War on Poverty supporters.

When the British projects were launched Holman argued that local authority control would neutralise their impact and force the community workers to rely on a consensual strategy: 'as institutionalised bodies, like local authorities, will not countenance conflict, the community development project is unlikely to promote radical improvement'. (Holman 1969) This view was shared by other academics. Smith and Anderson (1972) argued that the kind of participation which it was envisaged that people in the local project areas would have 'is effective in contributing to the control of social problems but is not effective at the level at which the social structures giving support and meaning to these problems can be radically questioned.

Practice

In the light of these arguments the subsequent development of the CDPs was all the more remarkable. Far from remaining firmly locked in the clammy embrace of the local authorities, local projects engaged in radical action and produced an analysis of the urban crisis, and of persistent poverty and inequality, far more trenchant than that attempted in the more free-wheeling American projects.

We have already referred to the weak political base of the British Urban Programmes. Many Labour MPs saw it as little more than another piece of political chicanery: an attempt to create the illusion of action without the necessity of significant government expenditure. Michael Meacher, then a backbench MP, noted that the annual cost of the urban programme then stood at a mere 0.1% of the total expenditure on social services. (Meacher 1974)

Programme assumptions

Similar Conceptions of the Nature of the Problem

Both the British and American programmes assumed the existence of a cycle of poverty. This was summarised by the Council of Economic Advisors in their 1964 Report to the President: 'Poverty breeds poverty. A poor individual or family has a high possibility of staying poor. Low incomes carry with them higher risks of illness, limitations on mobility, limited access to education, information and training. Poor parents cannot give their children the opportunities for better health and education needed to improve their lot, lack of motivation, hope and incentive is a more subtle but no less powerful barrier than lack of financial means ... the cruel legacy of poverty is passed from generation to generation'. (Economic Report to the President 1964) The British version found its way into the Press Release which announced the setting up of the CDPs: 'An example of the vicious circle in which such families could be trapped is; ill-health/financial difficulties/children suffering from deprivation/consequent delinquency/inability of the children to adjust to adult life/unstable marriages/emotional problems/ill-health/the cycle begins again'.

The Conception Challenged

In fact there was ample evidence in both countries to challenge this conventional wisdom. Harrington, whose book, *The Other America*, played a major role in turning poverty into a significant social issue in the United States was arguing, in the early years of the war, that what was required was a major shift in government policies, in particular a commitment to full employment. (see Moynihan 1969) This focus on the national and structural characteristics of poverty was shared by other critics. Gladwin in a book on poverty published in 1967 argued: 'The social reforms necessary to make poverty avoidable and remediable must embrace a larger part of our society than just the poor alone ... These reforms must furthermore reallocate power and above all money and the power that flows from money, within our society ... else the poor will remain forever poor'. (Gladwin 1967) Rainwater argued that since poverty was primarily a relative concept it could only be significantly affected through redistributive measures by 'a radical shift in the national income distribution in the direction of greater income equality for the lower half of the population'. (Rainwater 1969) Baran and Sweezy (1966), two noted American Marxists, argued succinctly 'capitalism everywhere generates wealth at one pole and poverty at the other'.

Social pathology arguments, however, are attractive in that they locate the problem within the sphere of the individual, rather than constituting a critique of the social order. Indeed, surely the justice of the social order is reflected in its concern to reform these unfortunates. Structural remedies not only threaten the existing distribution of rewards, they are also expensive. Miller (1976: 168) has argued that the most important factor shaping the character of the War on Poverty was 'President Johnson's political unwillingness to have it contain an expensive public employment programme for the unemployed and an expanded transfer programme for those out of the labour market'.

In the United Kingdom the argument for a fundamental shift in resources had long been popular among the left wing of the ruling Labour Party, and had a variety of academic supporters. Indeed the architects of the CDPs were well aware of the argument that the experimental small project approach was irrelevant to combating poverty. The principle civil servant behind the project, Derek Morrell, told an Anglo-American conference of Experiments in Social Policy and their Evaluation: 'the prime object of government was to maximise the total supply of welfare ... (and) to produce a more equitable distribution of welfare. Inevitably there was a conflict between these two aims ... Some might take the view that only a socialist solution could reconcile the two, but this basis was not open to the conference'. (Halsey 1969) Halsey, in a revised version of a paper presented to the same conference recognised that the CDPs 'afford no serious opportunity of experimenting with alternative forms of the hypothesis that the abolition of poverty is possible by large-scale redistribution of national resources'. (Halsey 1974)

It would be wrong to believe that the acceptance of explanations of poverty which sought to explain its persistence in terms of the characteristics of the poor was the result of either erroneous research or accident. Rather the approach had much to commend it to governments uninterested in any radical change in policies. In fact the relationship between social science and policy is opportunistic, there is little consensus amongst social scientists and as Miller argues, 'policy-markers are always in the business of selecting the social science findings which fit their policies'. (Miller 1976: 138)

Community action was a logical corollary of the programmes, for if the poor were apathetic or held deviant values, which prevented them from achieving success in the mainstream of society, then mobilisation, particularly under the guidance of properly socialised outsiders could help to create new values and aspirations. The logic of the argument also demanded explanations of how the mainstream institutions had tolerated the immiseration and isolation of the poor. This was provided in both countries in the critique of the inability of social services at the local level to offer a coordinated approach to problems. In addition, it was argued, many agencies were simply not offering services appropriate to the needs of the poor. Community action which encouraged the poor to articulate their needs and press for reform would improve the effectiveness of social science.

In America community action was also supported, as I will argue, by more radical supporters of the War of Poverty for quite different reasons.

Differences in approach

Independent Frameworks for Local Projects
The American and British programmes laid down substantially different frameworks within which community action would operate. Initially, the American government intended to allow the local projects a substantial amount of independence. Federal funding of local community action agencies under the Community Action Programme (CAP) of the 1964 Economic Opportunity Act, was seen as an essential guarantee of the ability of projects to challenge local institutional inertia and conservatism. Levitan (1969a: 4) notes that through CAP 'the distribution of Federal funds could ignore established political boundaries and elected public officials'. This provision subsequently gave rise to considerable political conflict. In 1965 the US Conference of Mayors accused Kennedy's brother-in-law, Sargent Shriver, the head of the Office of Economic Opportunity, of 'fostering class struggle'. (Marris and Rein 1974: 3-11) Three years later an amendment, moved by Congresswoman Green, popularly known as the 'bosses and boll-weevills' amendment gave the city government the right to take over the independent community action agencies running programmes in their cities.

The early American emphasis on independent community action reflected a tolerance, at this stage, of conflict strategies. One writer who worked in the Johnson administration and helped to prepare the Economic Opportunity Act described the CAP provisions thus: 'community action was fervently anti-establishment: schools, employment services, welfare agencies, city hall, were all part of an 'establishment' or 'system' which served 'the disadvantaged' by referring them from one 'helping service' to another without ever really understanding or challenging the 'culture of poverty' and with no real ability to move families out of poverty'. (Donovan 1967) Even Republican Senator Javits was moved in the early days to declare himself 'sympathetic [to] social action programmes like rent strikes, civil rights protests, marches on Washington'. (Marris and Rein 1974: 271)

There were a significant group of planners who remained involved in the OEO who viewed community action in relatively sophisticated political terms and who saw poverty in terms of the blocked opportunities of the poor. The intellectual antecedents of this group are to be found in the work of Cloward and Ohlin and the Mobilisation for Youth Project in New York. (Cloward and Ohlin 1960; see also Marris and Rein 1974) It is unlikely that their conception of community action was understood by those who voted the Economic Opportunity Bill through. Levitan (*op.cit.* 66) argues that most 'Administrative spokesmen were quite innocent of CAP's meaning'. Nonetheless, a significant difference between the American and British programmes was the absence of any comparable conception of community action amongst those who designed and administered the CDPs. In Britain such ideas were held at the grass-roots and by some of the outside recruits to the centre, but they were unknown to the civil servants and politicians in charge.

In Britain, where central government historically had much greater control over local government and financed the bulk of local spending, the new programmes were deliberately designed to ensure local government cooperation and control. Urban aid money which was available to selected voluntary groups, as well as direct to local governments, could only be granted with the approval of the relevant local authority, which had the final veto since it was required to provide 25% of the funds. The Community Development Projects were established in twelve areas after the approval of the local authority had been obtained. The local authority had the power to hire the staff and to terminate the project – a power exercised on no less than three occasions.

Independence of projects in practice

In spite of this the British projects acted with a great deal more independence than their American counterparts. Under CAP local projects were to be 'developed, conducted and administered with the maximum feasible participation of residents of the areas and members of the groups served'. (quoted in Levitan 1969a: 66) In practice participation by the poor was frequently token and the independence of the local agencies from the traditional welfare establishment was largely illusory. By 1966 the OEO had made agreements in fifteen cities to clear all CAP grants through the city hall. (Levitan 1969b) In a study of the operation of CAP, Rose (1972) found that 'the social service strategy underlay approximately 94% (329 out of 350) of all the programmes, while the income producing strategy underlay slightly less than 3% (or ten out of the 350 programmes) and the institutional change strategy – the logically derived or expected outcome – underlay only *slightly more than* 3% (11 out of 350) of all Community Action Programmes conducted in the twenty cities in 1964-66' (emphasis in the original; another study came to a similar conclusion, Clark and Hopkins 1969). In spite of the presence in the American programme of a group of senior planners and bureaucrats who saw radical implications in the Community Action Programme, in practice these implications were largely neutralised. Rose concludes: 'the professionals from both the education and welfare fields prove to be politically accomplished as well as durable, for they were able to capture over 92% of the monies to be used in reforming their 'establishments''. (Rose 1972)

Radicalism

The radical image of the American projects which alarmed both congress and the Mayors is not substantiated by an analysis of their practice. Tom Wolfe's account of the OEO in San Francisco no doubt captures an element of both the confusion and mutual chicanery which characterised interactions between the black poor and their would-be-saviours, but reality was usually more mundane. (Wolfe 1971) Marris and Rein (1974: 315) conclude that 'probably no more than 1% of OEO's funds were devoted in any way to the organisation of the poor.

If we take these conclusions as indicative of the radical impact of the American programme then it stands in marked contrast to the experience of the British Community Development Project. In Britain all of the projects rejected the original social pathology assumptions arguing that: 'problems of multi-deprivation have to be redefined and re-interpreted in terms of structural constraint rather than psychological motivation, external rather than internal factors'. (CDP Information and Intelligence Unit 1973) The focus on the social pathology of the poor, of the target areas, was replaced by a concentration on the societal factors creating and sustaining disadvantage.

Five years after the projects were established they were arguing: 'The cure for poverty is not to be sought simply in marginal government policies nor in self-help by the 'poor' but through the development of working class action and pressure from the widest possible front'. (CDP Information and Intelligence Unit 1975) Some project workers went further and the influential Political Economy Collective which had considerable support amongst local project workers state bluntly: 'It is realised that without the complete overthrow of capitalism and the establishment of socialism there can be no lasting solution ... What socialist community workers are about is the development of working class politics, in the context of an understanding that the problems of working class areas are directly related to capitalism. (CDP Political Economic Collective 1976)

At the local level the projects varied in the tactics they adopted and in their level of commitment to the philosophies articulated at the national level. Some, notably the Oldham, Upper Afan and Liverpool Projects were only peripherally involved in the national activities and concentrated their efforts at the local level, where they operated within a broadly pluralist framework, but this group were in a minority. Most of the projects sought to transform the radical critique developed at a national level into community work practice in the neighbourhood, linked to a national dimension, though this was by no means a straightforward task. The radical community workers confronted problems as formidable as any other group which seeks fundamental social change. Some clear indications of what the radical critique meant in terms of local action did emerge. In particular the community workers sought to relocate the focus of their practice and to encompass both community and work place issues. Most local projects directed a large part of their effort into employment issues. (Corkey and Craig 1978) In addition the projects increasingly sought to relate local action to national issues. Corkey and Craig argued that: 'the basic assumption' which by late 1974, informed most CDP work was that local action 'has to be complemented by action at a wider, even a national, level.' In part the CDP National Reports were written with this end in mind. (see for example CDP 1977)

The last of the local CDPs closed in 1978 but the community work strategy developed by the radical projects continues to be reflected in contemporary British projects. In Newcastle the West End Resource Centre, successor to the Benwell CDP, is playing an important role in fighting the planned closure of Vickers Engineering Works. In London former CDP staff are active in the Joint Docklands' Action Group, which provides research and administrative support to community and trade union groups, concerned to prevent speculative development in the Docklands area and press for industrial regeneration and housing improvements. National action is pursued through groups such as the Inner City Alliance which brings together a variety of local community projects to press for more effective government intervention in the inner city.

The British community action programme was placed firmly under the control of the relevant local government. It was designed and established by a group of conservative administrators who were little influenced by the more radical strands within the American Poverty Programmes. The Labour politicians who backed the development of the CDPs shared the social pathology perspective. When Richard Crossman, a senior Cabinet Minister in the Wilson Government involved with the establishment of the CDPs, described the project objectives in a deprived area as to 'access the problem of how such a community can pull itself up by its own boot straps ... The team must then get down to the job of seeing that the community tackles it itself,' (Crossman 1977), it was clearly no part of his intention that community action would lead to demands for more government resources and major shifts in government policy. Yet, in spite of the administrative constraints placed on the programme and its conservative parentage, the conclusions were markedly at variance with conventional wisdom.

Contrasting political cultures

The more free-wheeling American Community Action Programme failed to initiate any similar development; radical criticism remained peripheral to the programme, though wherever it did occur it aroused strong reaction from the local politicians and ultimately from Congress.[1] This difference must be understood in the context of the contrasting political cultures of the two countries. Radicalism in the United States is frequently seen as synonymous with a militant pluralism and the pursuit of the rights of the underdog (Akinsky's approach reflects this, see: Akinsky 1969, 1972). In Britain the principle source of radical ideas lies in one or other variant of socialism. In the United States a combination of economic success, McCarthyism, Soviet repression in Eastern Europe and the ideological legacy of the frontier spirit has succeeded in marginalising socialism and frequently equating it, in popular consciousness, with illiberal anti-democratic tendencies.

In Britain the local CDP activists found people, in the project neighbourhood, who already had a sophisticated critique of area decline and a belief in an egalitarian solution to the problems of the disadvantaged, emanating from the election of a genuinely socialist government. The radical politicisation of many local project workers took place through a combination of interaction with local problems and the availability of explanations which located the sources of these problems in the operations of a market economy, dominated by the interests of capital. Socialist critiques were propagated both by local activists and by key figures in the CDPs, who subsequently came together in the Political Economy Collective.

Socialism, as an ideology, enjoys significant legitimisation in British working class areas through the trade unions and the Labour Party. While any analysis of the performance of recent Labour Governments would hardly substantiate the proposition that their policies were even remotely socialist, they are so described by the popular press, often in order to discredit them, and by Labour Ministers, in order to justify themselves to the party rank and file. From the point of view of socialist community workers the situation has both strengths and weaknesses. While it is relatively easy to propagate socialist ideas, without being dismissed as dangerously subversive, it is more difficult to develop strategies which result in a confrontation with those who claim the historic mantle of the socialist movement – the Labour Party. This can be illustrated by the experience of the North Tyneside CDP which, in mounting a campaign against the housing policies of the Labour Government and the local Labour Council, found its ability to build a significant local movement hampered by the fact that loyalty to the Labour Party deterred many from militant action. The project final report notes that, for one trade union representative on the Campaign Committee, 'there was an unwillingness to do anything which had the potential of being embarrassing to the local council'. Some members were reluctant about 'rocking the boat, when a Labour administration was in power'. (North Tyneside CDP 1978)

Nonetheless, the relative acceptability of socialist ideas was markedly higher than in the United States.

In a recent debate about community organising, in the Mission Hill area of Boston, the question of why the organisers had not advocated a socialist approach was raised: 'Often this is because we fear losing our neighbours' friendship when we don't really know how they feel. For instance, *The Good News*, the Mission Hill community newspaper: '… Many times the editorial collective, who have strong roots in the community, have discussed the possibility of a socialist editorial position, but the collective members have rejected this opinion because they expected a conservative reaction'. (Waitzken 1978) Such a reaction would not be probable in a similar district in Britain.

What I am suggesting is that we can only fully understand the political direction taken by community action by viewing it dialectically in terms of the relationship between the community worker, the neighbourhood and the wider political culture. Radical community workers may accelerate local politicisation but they do so within limits laid down by historical and social factors extraneous to a particular project. From this perspective it is no accident that many of the most imaginative developments in community work have taken place where political debate and conflict has been most vigorous – notably for example, in Italy. (Jagi, Muller and Schnid 1977)

Conclusion

The Socialist Trend in Community Work
The experience of community action in American and Britain obviously had implications for community work practice in both countries. In Britain the dominant tendency in contemporary community work is socialist. The consensual assumptions which underlay the work of earlier community work writers (for example, Batten and Batten 1967; Leaper 1968) are largely absent from current work (see for example, Curno 1978; Dungate *et al.* 1979). The intellectual heirs of the consensualist tradition adopt a more technocratic mode seeking to scientise community work, focussing on such questions as evaluation, management structures, social planning and the appropriate use of outside consultants (for example, Briscoe and Thomas 1977; Thomas 1978). The professional ethos which Specht urged British community workers to adopt as 'a potentially strong basis for legitimacy', (Specht 1976), has been rejected by the principal community work body, the Association of Community Workers.

In the United States the literature continues to be dominated by the social planning school (for example Cox *et al.* 1974). Recently, however, there have been indications of a shift into a more class-based approach. Perlman (1976), in a survey of community action in the US, argued: 'One can foresee a link-up between the grassroots network and the more progressive elements of the Labour movement which have shown themselves to be forces for social and economic change'.

The continuing economic recession on both sides of the Atlantic makes radical approaches increasingly attractive, for it is clear that the conventional wisdom of the past cannot provide either a satisfactory explanation of, or a solution to, the current crisis. The view that a continued growth in national prosperity would provide the resources and flexibility to tackle social problems, which underlay the War of Poverty, has lost its currency. In contrast, governments in both Britain and America seek a solution to the current crisis in public sector cutbacks and measures to restrain wages (for a USA/UK comparison, see Miller 1978). Two consequences of this are rising unemployment and accelerating inner-city decline.

Official sympathy for the poor and disadvantaged has been replaced by attacks on welfare spending, which, it is claimed, undermines the work ethic and produces consistent abuse of available benefits. Miller summarised the new ideology in America, in terms particularly apposite to Britain's Conservative Government: 'A renewed emphasis on individual consumption and corporate profit is being offered. Lower corporate taxation, less regulation of business, short expansions to prevent the building up of inflationary pressures, less spent on education and welfare … The result, I think will be greater poverty and inequality, deterioration of public services, the constriction of attention in social policy only to aspects of social problems bearing immediately on productivity …' (Miller 1976: 168)

Shift to Right in Government
It is not my intention to argue that the shift to the right in government policy will inexorably lead to growing radical and socialist protest at the grassroots. It is clear that amongst the working class and poor there are those who are attracted by the clichés of the new right, but just as the break-up of the Keynesian welfare state consensus leads to the pursuit of right-wing policies in government, so the ideological vacuum which has opened up provides space for socialist critiques and solutions. The policies advocated by the new

right will increase unemployment and encourage the operation of precisely those market forces which lead to urban decline. Only redistributive measures, active government intervention and full support for local cooperatively-managed initiatives could reverse this process. This was the logic of the CDP argument and there is every reason to expect the argument to become not only more pertinent to the American situation but also more widely accepted amongst American community activists.

References

Alinsky, S. (1969) *Reveille for Radicals*. New York: Vintage Books.

Alinsky, S. (1972) *Rules for Radicals*. New York: Vintage Books.

Baran, P. and Sweezy, P. (1966) *Monopoly Capital*. Monthly Review Press: 286.

Batten, T.R. and Batten, M. (1967) *The Non-Directive Approach in Group and Community Work*. Oxford: Oxford University Press.

Briscoe, C. and Thomas D. (eds) (1977) *Community Work: Learning and Supervision*. London: George Allan and Unwin. Particularly chapters 1, 2 and 3.

C.D.A. (1968a) *Draft Report to Ministers*. Home Office Internal Paper (12).

C.D.A. (1968b) *Second Draft Report to Ministers*. Home Office Internal Paper (13).

CDP Inter-Project Report (1973) CDP Information and Intelligence Unit, pp 8.

CDP Political Economic Collective (1976) *Community Work or Class Politics?* London: 6-7.

CDP (1977) *Gilding the Ghetto*. London: CDPIIU.

Clark, K. and Hopkins, J. (1969) *A Relevant War Against Poverty*. New York: Harper and Row.

Cloward, R. and Ohlin, L. (1960) *Delinquency and Opportunity: A Theory of Delinquent Gangs*. New York: Free Press.

Cooper, J. (1969) 'Social Disadvantage and Social Help' In: *Approved Schools Gazette*, March.

Corkey, D. and Craig, G. (1978a) 'CDP: Community Work or Class Politics?' In: P. Curno (ed.) *Political Issues and Community Work*. London: Routledge and Kegan Paul.

Cox, F.M. *et al.* (1974) *Strategies of Community Organisation*. Itasca, Illinois: F.E. Peacock.

Crossman, R.H.S. (1977) *The Diaries of a Cabinet Minister*, Vol. 3. London: Cape, Hamish Hamilton.

Curno, P. (ed.) (1978) *op. cit.*

Demuth, L. (1977) *Government Initiatives on Urban Deprivation*. London: Runnymede Trust.

Donovan, J.C. (1967) *The Politics of Poverty*. Western Publishing.

Dungate, M. *et al.* (1979) *Collective Action*. London: Community Projects Foundation and Association of Community Workers.

Economic Report of the President (1964) Washington D.C.: US. Government Printing Office.

Gladwin, T. (1967) *Poverty U.S.A*. Little, Brown and Co.

Halsey, A.H. (1969) 'Government Against Poverty'. In: *Experiment in Social Policy and their Evaluation*. Report of an Anglo-American Conference, Ditchley Park. London: Home Office.

Halsey, A.H. (1974) 'Government Against Poverty in School and Community'. In: D. Wedderburn (ed.) *Poverty, Inequality and Class Structure* Cambridge: Cambridge University Press.

Holman, R. (1969) 'The Wrong Poverty Programme'. *New Society*, 20th March:444.

Interdepartmental Working Party, C.D.A. (1968) Third Meeting, Internal Paper, Home Office.

Jagi, M., Muller, R. and Schnid, A. (1977) *Red Bologna*. London: Writers and Readers Cooperative.

Leaper, R.A.B. (1968) *Community Work*. London: National Council for Social Services.

Levitan, S.A. (1969a) The Community Action Programme: A Strategy to Fight Poverty. *The Annals of the American Academy of Political and Social Science*. 385.

Levitan, S.A. (1969b) *Great Society's Poor Law: A New Approach to Poverty*. The John Hopkins Press.

Loney, M.A. (1977). 'A Political Economy of Citizen Participation.' In: L. Panitch (ed.) *The Canadian State: Political Economy and Political Power*. Toronto: University of Toronto Press.

Loney, M.A. (1978) 'C.D.P.s: The End of a New Beginning'. *Community Care*, 22nd March.

Marris, P. and Rein, M. (1974a) *Dilemmas of Social Reform*. 2nd edn. Harmondsworth: Penguin.

Meacher, M. (1974) 'The Politics of Positive Discrimination.' In: H. Glennerster and S. Hatch (eds.) *Positive Discrimination and Inequality*. Fabian Research Series, 314.

Miller, S.M. (1976) 'The Political Economy of Social Problems: From the Sixties to the Seventies' *Social Problems*, 24 (1).

Miller, S.M. (1978) 'The Recapitalization of Capitalism' *International Journal of Urban and Regional Research*, 2 (2).

Moynihan, D. (1969) *Maximum Feasibility Misunderstanding*. New York: Free Press.

North Tyneside CDP (1978) *Organising for Change in a Working Class Area*. Final Report, 3. Newcastle-on-Tyne Polytechnic.

Perlman, J.E. (1976) 'Grassrooting the System'. *Social Policy*, 7 (2): 20.

Plotnick, R.D. and Skidmore, F. (1975) *Progress Against Poverty, A Review of the 1964-74 decade*. Academic Press.

Rainwater, L. (1969) 'The Problem of Lower-Class Culture and Poverty – War Strategy.' In: D. Moynihan (ed.) *On Understanding Poverty*. New York: Basic Books.

Rose, S. (1972) *The Betrayal of the Poor: The Transformation of Community Action*. Schenkman.

Smith, L. and Anderson, B. (1972) 'Political Participation Through Community Action.' In: G. Parry (ed.) *Participation in Politics*. Manchester: Manchester University Press.

Specht, H. (1976) *The Community Development Project*. London: National Institute for Social Work, Paper No.2.

Thomas, D. (1978) 'Community Work, Social Change and Social Planning.' In: P. Curno (ed.) *Political Issues and Community Work*. London: Routledge and Kegan Paul.

Waitzkin, H. (1978) ' Dilemmas of Community Organising: Mission Hill in Boston, A Reply.' *Social Policy*, 9: 152.

Wolfe, T. (1971) *Radical Chic and Mau-Mauing The Flak-Catchers*. New York: Bantam Books.

Notes

1. In 1967, spurred on by increasing local controversy, Congress excluded OEO staff from a pay increase awarded to federal employees (Marris and Rein, 1974e).

Martin Loney is a Lecturer in Social Policy at the Open University, Milton Keynes: Vol. 15 No. 2 (1980): 91-103.

9

Reviewing the Direction of Community Development in Singapore

S. Vasoo

Introduction

Community development in Singapore has undergone significant changes since 1959, and these changes have come about as a result of conscious efforts by the Government to build a more cohesive community comprising people of various ethnic origins such as Chinese, Malays and Indians. Because of the diverse linguistic and cultural backgrounds of these people, the Government has always felt it would be vital to set clear policy directions to enhance the social and economic integration of the population (now standing at 2.5 million). In the social field, the Government has initiated many grassroots organisations such as Community Centres (CCs), Citizens' Consultative Committees (CCCs) and Residents' Committees (RCs). These organisations promote community development, aimed at the mobilisation of mass support, the provision of opportunities for political participation, and the promotion of more community cohesiveness and mutual help among people living in the urban neighbourhoods. Besides the Government's initiatives in promoting community development, the voluntary sector also plays a supplementary role through a number of social services agencies. This role is limited in comparison with the Government's, and its attempts have been concentrated on the pioneering of community development projects which help to facilitate the growth of community self-help groups, particularly in public housing estates of various New Towns.

This article will attempt to review the direction of community development in Singapore since the British colonial administration period (i.e. specifically from 1950 to 1958) and up until recently (i.e. 1981).

The beginnings of community development

The beginnings of community development in Singapore can be traced back to the early 1950s when the Social Welfare Department was charged with the responsibility of initiating community development. The-then colonial administration saw the relevance in

113

this aspect of work because:

> *there was already a high degree of development in Singapore and there existed a highly integrated society with definite racial, social and political and co-operative groups.* (Social Welfare Department Annual Report 1952: 33)

At the same time, the pattern and nature of community development was felt to be somewhat different in undeveloped areas of Singapore. The colonial administrators saw that in order to assist the co-ordination of this work, it was necessary to establish a Standing Committee for Community Development. (*Ibid.* : 33-4) The function of this Committee was primarily advisory, and involved in the co-ordination of various civic organisations. As noted succinctly in the same Report

> *Its main work will be to foster in all areas of Singapore the growth of responsible bodies which can take their full part in initiation, planning and carrying out of the many aspects of betterment work that are now developing.* (*Ibid.*)

Birth of community centres

The interest in promoting community development or what is sometimes termed 'community work', by the colonial administrators, led the Department of Social Welfare to usher in the birth of a number of community centres, of which a few grew out of children's centres. The success of such centres enabled the Social Welfare Department to take more concrete steps to deploy funds to build the so-called 'model' community centres (CCs). Between 1953-1956, more than a dozen CCs were established in suburban and rural areas. These centres provided a place for local residents to meet their social and recreational needs and more specifically to disseminate colonial government policies and information. Also, the centres' hidden function, not obvious then, was to identify local opinions relevant to the colonial administrators in reshaping policies which were not well-received by the people.

On the whole, one could rightly conclude that during the 1950s, community centres were not seriously promoting community development but were established with an intention to gauge the extent of anti-colonial sentiments amongst the local population. If any activities were undertaken, they were mainly centred around the promotion of indoor recreational programmes. The community centres during that period adopted a 'boys' club mentality' and hence acted as a sanctuary for a small group of youngsters to socialise. Their functions remained parochial and it was not until 1959 that their entire management was overhauled. This sweeping change came about because of the need to build up rapport between the common people and newly-elected political leaders from the People's Action Party (PAP).

It was only after Singapore attained internal self-government in 1959 that the work of community centres was reshaped and decisions regarding the introduction of community development techniques were centralised. As a result of this, more concrete actions were undertaken by Government, one of which was the establishment in July 1960 of the People's Association (PA), a statutory body, to co-ordinate the work of community centres. The PA is managed by a board of management comprising both elected and appointed members, including representatives of social organisations which are corporate members of PA, top civil servants, and leading politicians holding important portfolios. All policy matters pertaining to PA are deliberated by the Board and those policies which are endorsed are implemented by senior administrators of PA down to the community centres' management committees (CCMCs). The CCMCs are made up of members nominated from among the informal grass-roots leaders in the community. This being the case, it provides the Government with an additional channel to communicate with ordinary citizens. Almost all CCMCs have members who are of different ethnic origins and such an ethnic diversity in the membership of the CCMCs is closely maintained by the Government through its policies of selection on the assumption that a heterogenous ethnic composition in the CCMCs would enable the authorities better to achieve its racial integration and community building policies.

The CCMCs have two major functions; the management of the routine activities of the CCs and fundraising to meet operational costs. Although it is necessary for the CCMCs to concentrate efforts in these two areas, there are other equally important management functions which should not be neglected. The most pressing of these seem to be: reviewing their programmes to see if they are meeting the changing needs of residents living in the neighbourhood; encouraging the growth of self-help groups among children, youths or adults; and setting up more volunteer groups to initiate services in the neighbourhoods that are not within their precincts. In order for them to steer away from their concentration on these traditional management functions, it will be necessary for them to encourage residents with organisational and management skills to be involved so that they can still remain as viable as they were in the 1960s. The need is crucial to involve more residents with professional backgrounds, who generally abstain from the activities of the CCs because of their scepticism about being associated with party politics. It is indeed vital to attract more professionals as they have the expertise to contribute to the social betterment of the various neighbourhoods in Singapore.

The growth of the number of CCs during the 1960s and 1970s inevitably precipitated the need for more staff to manage them. Concomitantly, training of large numbers of personnel became urgent and as a result, the National Youth Leadership Training Institute was formed to provide community work and leadership training to organising and assistant organising secretaries. These two categories of personnel work with the CCMCs, some well-known local leaders and residents to organise various community development programmes for people living in the neighbourhoods. They are responsible for implementing the many activities of the CCs.

The 1960s and 1970s saw a growth of the People's Association style of community development, distinguished from the style adopted by community workers trained in social work and employed by the voluntary sector. The People's Association type of community development is rather centralised and 'community centre-based' in its approach. The programmes are organised at the CC level for the people who are interested in them. Some direct efforts are undertaken to decentralize programmes into the neighbourhoods of the CCs, but the reaching-out concept does not form an integral part of the strategies that can make a community development impact in community. However, it must be stated that the People's Association through its various CCs still carry out a prominent role in local attempts to develop community participation in meeting neighbourhood needs.

Further enlargement of the base
for community development

The Government, besides establishing community centres in different parts of Singapore, has also taken steps to initiate parallel organisations to penetrate further into the grass-roots. This move is the most recent development in the community development scene in

Singapore and the underlying reason for such a massive effort by the Government to stimulate participation of people in community affairs is perhaps to enlarge the base for community development. At the same time, it appears that the Government, through such a concentrated effort, would like to close the gap between the governing elites and the governed, prevent the bureaucracy at the local level from being inflexible, promote better understanding and acceptance of important policy issues, and identify and recruit people with organisational skills to revitalize government-supported grass-roots organisations in a constituency.

The Government's increased interest in grass-roots organisations came about when it recognised that the rapid relocation of people into public high rise estates (a result of its housing programmes) has not promoted cohesive communities and community identity. This is due, as Goh states, to the fact that;

> *many of these estates are new and their residents have moved in only recently from other parts of Singapore. They have to grow new roots in a new environment, know neighbours, make new friends. If they are left alone, new housing estates will take a long time before they become a friendly, throbbing community bustling with life and activities. Maybe never.* (in Tong 1980: 13)

Public housing estates have become a notable feature of the landscape of Singapore, constructed by the Housing and Development Board (HDB), and the Government's plan to provide decent homes to many Singaporean families earning below $3500 has been successful. About 65% of the population are already housed in the public housing schemes. In a move to hasten the process of community bonding, the Government established the Citizens' Consultative Committees (CCCs) in 1965 and subsequently in 1978, the Residents' Committees (RCs) to further complement the work of the CCCs and to reach out to most residents. These two elaborately organised grass-roots organisations are formed with an intention to promote community development within the neighbourhoods. They have acted as intermediary organisations whose membership comprises residents with some local standing in community affairs or with connections with a number of voluntary organisations such as clan association, merchants' organisation and trade union. Most of them are constituency-based and the number of members in each varies from constituency to constituency.

Besides the CCCs' mediatory role, they run a number of programmes on a constituency-wide basis. Campaigns which are of importance to the Government and which have an educational value to the ordinary citizens, are undertaken. Campaigns such as anti-crime, tree-planting, physical fitness, health, family planning and courtesy, are scheduled during different times of the year and the CCCs assist in organising them in their respective constituencies. The effects of these campaigns have been significant and have created positive social attitudes in the area. Other than the launching of various campaigns, the CCCs also make recommendations to the Government to improve the facilities in the neighbourhoods. As members of the CCCs are drawn from the informal leaders within and outside the constituencies, some of them have, with the support of local residents, acquired the role of mediators between them and the Government.

The community development roles of these intermediary leaders were more significant in the 1960s and 1970s because they were dealing with the 'bread and butter issues' prevalent at that time, faced by ordinary citizens ignorant about how to seek redress to their problems. In the 1980s, the leadership roles of the CCCs will be subjected to close scrutiny by a more demanding younger generation who are well-educated and resourceful, particularly in their abilities to solve the more complex problems of the urban high rise environment of Singapore. Whether they will continue to play an important role remains to be seen.

The Residents' Committees (RCs) are the most recent grass-roots organisations introduced by the Government in various public housing estates of Singapore's New Towns. A number of underlying reasons could account for the Government's enthusiasm to establish RCs. First, the HDB is beginning to give more attention to its social management role as it recognises that the prevention of physical deterioration of public housing and the solutions to some problems faced by residents can best be tackled by encouraging the residents to be involved in solving problems. (*Straits Times* 2 February 1979) Secondly, CCs and CCCs are limited in their effectiveness to gauge the opinions of residents and mobilise them to participate in community programmes. Therefore, a more sensitive infra-structure is required to assess and respond to the changing needs of residents living in the public housing estates. Thirdly, as more residents with better educational levels live in the public housing estates, they would be expected to be more articulate and motivated to partake in the decision-making processes affecting their neighbourhoods and the wider community.

The objectives of the RCs are primarily to promote neighbourliness among residents; provide a more effective channel of communication between the residents and the various government authorities or departments; ensure better maintenance of the physical conditions in the housing estates; enhance better social order and security; and encourage mutual assistance among residents. State objectives are broad and all-embracing; and in essence they are aimed at the promotion of community development at neighbourhood level. However, realisation of these objectives depends heavily on the socio-political orientation of the people nominated into the leadership of the RCs. Probably, people with high deference values which includes such characteristics as high civic consciousness, high neighbourhood activism, less self-centredness, and high devotion to community service, in the leadership of the RCs, are more likely to help the RCs' objectives to be realised. At this juncture, no in-depth analyses of the leadership profiles of the RCs' members have been undertaken and it would be premature to forecast the type of leaders suitable for these organisations.

At the moment, it appears that the community development strategies adopted by the RCs are more service-delivery focused but there seems to be great potential for more resident-focused work which will encourage a higher degree of citizen participation. With greater emphasis on resident-focused work, the RCs can eventually help to facilitate the growth of small self-help or interest groups among residents to deal with problems arising as a result of urban high-rise living.

Community development by the voluntary sector

Only after 1969 did there appear to be evidence of some interest in the voluntary sector to contribute directly to the growth of community development in Singapore. From this point, community workers were employed to carry out community development projects, including several in the New Towns. In the pioneering years, this group of community workers, together with some concerned Christians and church groups took an active role in promoting projects in a few selected urban public housing estates.

The first three community development projects, the Jurong Industrial Mission Project (JIMP), the Bukit Ho Swee Community Service Project and the Toa Payoh Community Development Project were established in 1969. The objectives of these Projects were more or less similar and were first, to encourage local residents to solve problems relevant to their neighbourhoods, secondly to develop leadership and skills among residents to deal with their needs, and thirdly, to encourage residents to form self-help groups in meeting their social, cultural and recreational needs.

Since the inception of the Bukit Ho Swee Project, many children and young persons have been encouraged to be involved in the various activities, such as the children's clubs which organise outings, outdoor camps, tuition, excursions and concerts, and the youth clubs which concentrate on vocational guidance, literacy education, excursions, outdoor camps, leadership training, and voluntary service work. So far, all the programmes undertaken tend to focus on the personal needs of small groups of children or young persons and the programmes provided are supposedly to assist them in their socialisation and person growth. A tentative assessment suggests that the Project has not achieved its community development objectives, as the groups involved are still dependent on the community workers of the Project to plan programmes for them.

The Toa Payoh Community Development Project came into existence as a result of the work of priests attached to the Methodist and Roman Catholic churches in Toa Payoh New Town and community workers providing service for the less privileged sector in the New Town. The main service so far has been remedial education for school children because it was found at the beginning of the Project that many of the families in the low-income group were concerned about the educational under-achievement of their children. Parents of the children who were in need of remedial education programmes were organised as a group by the community workers to assist in the recruitment of voluntary trained teachers living in the community. As a result of this exercise, an action group comprising both the parents and the voluntary teachers was formed to manage the remedial education programme which has become the life of the Project. Since 1973, no new area of growth in community development has been recorded by the Project because the remedial education programme appeared to have consumed most of its available resources of finance and manpower.

JIMP was started by a group of concerned Christians and community workers with the support of the Jurong Christian Church in 1969. The prime motivation of those associated with JIMP at that time was to promote urban industrial mission work aimed at assisting young workers and residents to integrate better in the Jurong industrial setting, designed as one of the largest industrial zones of Singapore. JIMP, in its earlier stages of development, (1969-73), concentrated on organising residents living in the working class neighbourhood of Jurong to request better services from the various government departments, especially those dealing with education, health, environment and management of estates. In 1974, JIMP shifted its emphasis from working with residents in the working class neighbourhood to young workers employed in some of the factories operating in Jurong. This change of focus was accidental, because at that time there happened to be more demands from the young workers on the Project to advise them in their negotiations with employers for improvements in working conditions. Aside from the change in JIMP's client group, it adopted in totality the Alinsky model[1] for solving problems faced both by the residents living in the working class neighbourhood and the young workers. The adoption of this model of intervention in JIMP's work led to its failure to take roots in the Jurong community.

In the early years since the inception of the three Projects, each developed its own ways to entrench itself in the community. The community workers attached to these Projects devised differing strategies and these had subsequent consequences on the life-span of the Projects. JIMP, which concentrated on confrontational strategies in community problem-solving, ceased to exist when it failed to gain the co-operation of various power groups within the community, and because of the lack of funds to support its work. In the case of the Bukit Ho Swee Community Service Project and the Toa Payoh Community Development Projects, they managed to find their roots in the respective localities. The community workers in these two Projects used collaborative strategies in community problem-solving, and in doing so, they were able to bring different groups in the community together.

Since the initiation of the three early Community Development Projects, community workers, subsequently employed in a number of other voluntary agencies, began to make more serious attempts to promote community development through their agencies in the public housing estates which had been established rapidly by the HDB. The increase in the number of housing estates and the realisation that some people needed to be supported in their adjustments to life in the high-rise environment, have contributed directly or indirectly to an increase in interest among local community workers to influence voluntary agencies to embark on community development projects.

Community development approaches

The major approach towards community development both by Government and voluntary sector seems to concentrate on the provision of services to consumers whether they be clients or citizens living in the locality where the agencies operate. It has become apparent that very little effort has been directed towards the encouragement of citizen or consumer participation which can in the long run motivate the beneficiaries of the services to undertake self-help projects in meeting their needs. In essence, it can be stated that the emphasis in community development by the respective sectors is 'service delivery focus' rather than 'resident-focus'. (Briscoe 1981) It may be interesting to examine some of the underlying reasons leading to this situation.

First, community workers and the local leaders involved in community development are uncertain about the approaches most applicable to the local context. They all have attempted to try the following approaches:

a) *Locality Development approach*
This approach presupposes that 'community changes may be pursued optimally through broad participation of a wide spectrum of people at the local community level in goal determination and action.'

b) *Social Planning approach*
This encompasses a 'technical process of problem-solving with regard to substantive social problems such as delinquency, housing and mental health. The emphasis of this approach is planned change through research and rational planning.'

c) *Social action approach*
This is based on a presupposition of 'a disadvantaged segment of the population that needs to be organised, perhaps in alliance with others, in order to make demands on the larger community for increased resources or treatment in accordance with social justice and democracy.' (Rothman 1974)

All the above approaches have been applied with minimal

consideration as to their applicability to the field context. More often than not, an approach is applied haphazardly without being given sufficient time to assess its consequences on the community. Secondly, many community workers are engaged by voluntary agencies which have been established to provide services to specific client groups such as children, youth, aged and families. As a result of this, the service orientation of these agencies is directed towards clients who are identified to have social problems and to be in need of remedial assistance. The services of the voluntary agencies delivered in this way do not in the long run make any relevant impact on the wider community where the agencies operate.

Thirdly, most efforts in local community development by the voluntary and government sectors seem to concentrate on 'service delivery focus'. This is because the staff find it easier either to exercise control over the types of programmes their organisations offer to the community or curtail programmes which are not attractive to the potential consumers. Besides this, the attitudes prevalent amongst the providers and controllers of the resources, particularly those in the voluntary sector, also influence the way the service is provided.

Fourthly, although programmes are essential in enhancing community development, these are unfortunately developed for their own sake and serve as ends rather than as means to encourage local people's participation. This perspective is overzealously guarded by community workers and local leaders and as such, they measure the success of their work by the number of programmes implemented and not by assessing the extent to which people involved in the programmes are capable of initiating actions on their own to meet community needs.

Finally, the lack of discussion and exchanges of information on progress of community development among community workers as well as local leaders contributes to a stalemate situation and a strong desire in community workers to maintain that 'service delivery focus' is the most practical approach in community development even though this may not necessarily be the case. Confusion about the precise nature of 'community development' has also inhibited the development of practice.

The essence of community development

The term 'community development' is often misunderstood by those who preach it and wrongly applied by those who practise it. This is so because the term is itself elusive and open to many subjective interpretations by those involved directly or indirectly in community development whether they be community workers, politicians, social and welfare agency administrators, local leaders or concerned citizens. Frequently, the term is visualised by those involved as an activity directed towards organising services or programmes for people living in a specific community and not as a planned process to encourage people living in a specific community themselves to initiate services or programmes to meet their felt needs. Community development should be primarily concerned with two essential elements which should be emphasised strongly. It entails the encouragement of:

> *the participation by people themselves in efforts to improve their level of living with as much reliance as possible on their own initiative, and the provision of technical and other services in ways which encourage initiative, self-help and mutual help and make these more effective.* (Report of the United Nations Seminar on Community Development and Social Welfare in Urban Areas 1959: 5)

In short, community development should in the long run encourage people to become more self-reliant in social and economic pursuits and be more participative in improving their communities.

Conclusion

Community development in Singapore appears to have been influenced by various social and political factors during the period under review. In the colonial administration period, community development programmes were undertaken with extreme caution and were more inclined to a non-interventionist stance. This stance was adopted because it was presumed that a more concerted effort to promote community development would have unintended consequences for the colonial administration. The main concern was that it would kindle the fire of anti-colonialism which was surfacing during that time.

After attainment of internal self-rule and then independence, the Government saw an urgent necessity to play an interventionist role in promoting community development through various government-sponsored grass-roots organisations. More resources in terms of staff, finance and facilities have been and are being channelled into community development programmes in the various neighbourhoods. In fact, government interest to induce the growth of grass-root organisations has been very significant over the last 20 years and this emphasis reflects a need to provide an organised channel for citizen involvement in community affairs. The issue which rises from such an interventionist role by Government is whether these grass-root organisations, induced and supported by governmental efforts, will provide the culture for the development of indigenous leadership.

The voluntary sector's role in community development has remained supplementary and it is unlikely to grow significantly. It should therefore concentrate on an educational role, pioneering community projects which could be used in demonstrating to those involved in community development the use of appropriate effective local approaches. Meanwhile, the continued and widespread use of the 'service delivery focus' approach may in the long run stifle citizen initiatives in community development; consequently, citizens may be socialised to assume less responsibilities in neighbourhood affairs. Therefore, it is crucial for community development agencies, both public and voluntary, to encourage local citizens to be involved in promoting activities which are relevant to their own interests.

References

Briscoe, C. (1981) 'Community Work in Social Service Departments', in Henderson, P. and Thomas, D.N. (eds.) *Readings in Community Work*, London: Allen and Unwin: 171-175.

Rothman, J. (1974) 'Three Models of Community Organisation Practice', in Cox, F., Rothman, J. and Tropman, L. (eds.) *Strategies of Community Organisation*, Itasca: F.E. Peacock: 22-38.

Social Welfare Department (1952), *Annual Report*, Social Welfare Department: Singapore.

Tong, G.C. (1980) *Eunos Crescent RC Seminar Souvenir Programme*, Singapore.

United Nations (1959) *Report of the United Nations Seminar on Community Development and Social Welfare in Urban Areas*, Geneva: United Nations.

Notes

1. The Alinsky model prescribes a conflict approach to problem-solving based on the view that the disadvantaged or the deprived sectors of the community, if organised, can have the power to influence the resource-holders to meet their needs. For a further understanding of this model, the reader is referred to the work, Alinsky, S.S. (1971) *Rules for Radicals: A Practical Primer for Realistic Radicals*, New York: Random House.

Dr Vasoo teaches in the Department of Social Work, National University of Singapore, Vol. 19, No. 1: 7-19.

10

From Social Welfare to Community Development: Maori Policy and the Department of Maori Affairs in New Zealand

Augie J. Fleras

Introduction

The Department of Maori Affairs is one of the oldest Departments of State in New Zealand having endured in one form or another since 1840. At one time, the Offices associated with Native affairs were limited in size and gradually restricted to the administration of Maori land title. But, following the creation of the social welfare division in 1944, the Department evolved into a bureaucracy of formidable proportions. Of the many functions assigned to it, the Department was responsible for solving 'the Maori problem' in a fashion consistent with the prevailing ideology of assimilation. As a result of this directive, the social welfare division expanded to the point where it consumed much of the Department's commitment and expenditure. But recently, in response to external pressure, the Department has undergone a shift in image, style and philosophy while a decentralisation in the administration of social services has brought about a significant realignment in the Department's relationship with its increasingly assertive clients.

Here, I examine innovations in Maori policy administration, with particular emphasis on the emergence of a community development philosophy. The paper is divided into three sections. The first part provides the necessary background for contextualising these administrative changes. Events related to the evolution of the Department from a minor caretaker body to a large scale welfare agency of increasingly diminished value are discussed. The second part looks at why the Department experienced a dramatic reversal in philosophy, structure and style after 1977. I shall argue that the eventual emergence of a 'Tu Tangata' ('stance of the people') policy followed by subsequent reforms in Departmental organisation, was indicative of a move towards fulfilment of community development principles. The third and final section briefly summarises both the political acceptance of Tu Tangata and, also, Maori reaction to administrative innovations within the Department.

126

The emergence of a social welfare philosophy

A commitment to assimilation has historically characterised the New Zealand Government's policy towards the indigenous Maori. As policy, assimilation sought to eradicate the cultural basis of Maori society and to Europeanise them as quickly as possible into the mainstream. During the 1950s, the concept of integration began to replace assimilation as official policy without, however, making a substantial difference in Government treatment of the Maori. (Hunn Report 1960; Hunn and Booth 1962) Notwithstanding surface differences in approach, the collective aim of these policies focused on the creation of an egalitarian society, united under a single government and common set of laws, in which distinctions of class and race were deemed irrelevant. (Ward 1974; Adams 1977)

To assist in the Europeanisation of the Maori, various Offices for managing Native affairs were instituted. Ostensibly, their role revolved around the need to protect, civilise and amalgamate the Maori into the social and political order. In practice, these Offices did not take an active role in assisting the Maori since responsibility for Maori welfare was widely regarded as outside the scope of Government activity. Instead, most of their energy was expended in matters pertaining to the sale of Maori land to satisfy the demands of land-hungry settlers. This state of indifference and neglect persisted, with minor exceptions, until well into the twentieth century.

In 1935, the first Labour government came to power on the platform of universal justice and equality. (Orange 1977) Maori, in particular, were singled out for treatment because rather than disappearing, as predicted, they had shown a remarkable tenacity for survival. But those who survived were hopelessly behind the *pakeha* (European) in terms of social and economic standing. Many Maoris lived in rural isolation amidst conditions of poverty, disease and drunkenness. Worse still, the Depression had undermined the rural foundation of their existence, throwing them off the farms and onto the relief rolls. (Love 1977) Alarmed at the prospect of exacerbating the nation's economic crisis, the Labour Party acknowledged the need for Government intervention in Maori affairs. State resources were ploughed into Maori land development schemes while public funds were set aside for improvements in Maori housing. Of major note, the recently-reorganised Department of Maori Affairs assumed responsibility for these programs of rehabilitation. Later, in 1944, the Department's social welfare division was established to assist those

Maori who had sought employment in war-related industries. From then on, the rapid growth of social welfare following the Second World War coincided with the massive urban migration of the Maori, many of whom, it appeared, experienced difficulty in coping with the demands of a new environment. The combination of overcrowded housing, juvenile delinquency and grinding poverty emerged as Maori problems that could not be easily ignored. Accordingly, the Department reinforced its welfarist activity in an effort to remove those obstacles which it perceived as interfering with economic progress and cultural absorption of the Maori people.

To sum up, then, it is evident that circumstances arising from events related to the Second World War and the Great Depression contributed to a political awareness of Government responsibility to assist the Maori. (Hanson 1980) A new ideology of 'more government' arose to replace the earlier philosophy of laissez-faire which had dominated government thinking in the nineteenth century but which was no longer acceptable in the light of Maori indigency. With public acceptance of the need for State intervention in Maori affairs, the impetus was provided to entrench the Department's social welfare section and bring about a massive increase in its scope and sophistication. But, unfortunately for the Maori, the enlargement of the Department did not lead to a parallel increase in their socio-economic status. According to statistics from the late 1970s, Maori were more likely than the general population to end up underemployed, poorly-educated, imprisoned, or impoverished. (National Party on Maori Affairs 1981) Frustrated and angry over their subordinate status in New Zealand society, Maori became increasingly militant during the 1970s. The Government, in turn, responded to these protests by re-appraising the validity of an assimilationist Maori policy and the role of the Maori Affairs Department in servicing Maori needs.

Towards community development

In 1977, the Minister of Maori Affairs commissioned a review of his Department's material assets and future prospects. The authors of the subsequent report, Puketapu and Haber-Thomas (1977) found the Department lacking in many respects. The rapid growth of its social welfare division had created a paternalistic, centralised bureaucracy removed from the clients it was expected to serve. Clients were viewed as passive, hapless victims whose primary function related to their role as consumers of services designed for their benefit by faceless experts. Solutions to Maori problems were left in the hands of professionals who stipulated what was best for the Maori, stifling local initiative in the process. Programmes were formulated in private boardrooms and imposed upon the population with little consultation over objectives or means. (Puketapu 1982) Under such conditions, the gap between the Maori and Department began to widen as the Department drifted along, a law unto itself, with a distinctive logic and rationale often at odds with the aspirations of the target group. Consequently, unless the Department could justify its existence, control expenditures and improve overall effectiveness, the Government had little choice but to dismantle the organisation, phase out its operations and transfer the remaining functions to existing Departments of State. Later that year Puketapu, himself a Maori and career bureaucrat, was appointed Secretary for Maori Affairs to try and restore the Department's 'image, vitality and accessibility' (Puketapu 1981) without sacrificing its operational efficiency in the process.

Immediately, he set about to reform the Department along the lines of a 'people-oriented, people-managed agency'. (Department memo, Puketapu 1982) Positive steps were initiated to upgrade its tattered image as 'Big Brother', and to dispel any misunderstanding regarding Departmental objectives. Puketapu went out to the people and fronted up to them: what did they want? And what could the Department do to help? He prodded senior officials to search for imaginative solutions that concurrently respected Maori cultural values as well as budgetary limitations imposed on the Department. In the end, he unveiled a new policy which established a consistent framework for the attainment of Maori self-determination. Tu Tangata, as the policy came to be called, sought to:

> *promote people in a way that recognises their talents and resources both as individuals and as a group. And in a way that will ensure their fullest development for the advance of Maori communities – and the common good of New Zealand.*
> (Department of Maori Affairs 1980)

The Department of Maori Affairs paper focused on the social and economic advancement of the Maori as Maori. It attempted to institute measures whereby the Maori would enjoy the best of both worlds – socioeconomic equality with the *pakeha* on the one hand, and retention of their cultural identity, language and land on the other. Maori youth and community development were singled out as priority items under this policy. Shortly thereafter, the Department was reformed from top to bottom to logically complete the administrative implications of the paper

As part of its new image, the Department rejected its former attachment to a welfare ideology with its negative emphasis on crisis intervention, handouts and band-aid solutions. In its place, a community development strategy appeared that emphasised promotion, action-oriented local projects and community involvement in the planning and implementation of policy and programs. The term 'welfare' was expunged from Departmental vocabulary and replaced with the more affective referent 'community'. When the social welfare division was closed down, social workers were transferred to other Departments of State or reclassified as community workers. Much of the welfare caseload was placed on the shoulders of Maori voluntary organisations or redirected to the appropriate Government agency, a move endorsed by Puketapu in his review of the Department in 1977. Finally, to avoid any distortions inherent in focusing on the negative, the Maori were promoted, not as a problem for the Government to solve, but as a source of untapped energy, which, if handled properly, enhanced the well-being of all New Zealanders. (Department Memo January 1981)

The concept of community development emerged as the cornerstone of Puketapu's Tu Tangata philosophy. The term itself was not clearly defined (Hayes 1981: Constantino-David 1982 for discussions on the uses and abuses of this concept), except in reference to the 'development of the Maori people and their resources'. (Department Memo July 1981) By inference, however, this orientation to community development sought to reverse the image of the Maori as passive and incapable of helping themselves to help themselves. The local community was encouraged to become involved in the planning of priorities and programs on the assumption that local solutions to local problems were more acceptable and more effective than solutions devised through the infusion either of more experts or more funding. The Department's community officers, while providing the backup support for these community-based programs, were instructed to minimise their say in the direction or pace of these projects. This decision lay in the hands of the local community who collaborated with Departmental officials to arrive at a common goal, complementing each others' strengths and avoiding unnecessary overlap. Finally, programmes were directed at the elimination of the source of the problem, not merely at treating its effects. Prevention, not treatment, became the motto as the Department envisaged long-term solutions to recurrent problems through the utilisation of all resources and resourcefulness available to the community. In brief, the Department's community development philosophy superseded its earlier 'top-down' approach to community services with one that advocated a 'bottom-up' participatory strategy, commensurate with the implications of Tu Tangata. (see also New Zealand Council of Social Services Report 1978)

Likewise, in terms of style, the Department underwent a number of sweeping changes to accommodate this shift towards a community development philosophy. I indicated earlier that the Department was commonly perceived as a *pakeha*-based institution where the presence of Maori was perceived as irrelevant towards satisfactory completion of the job. But, upon his appointment, Puketapu looked to rectify this situation by imparting a Maori presence to the Department. *Pakeha* welfare officers were taken out of the field and posted elsewhere, preferably outside of the Department. For replacements, an effort was made to recruit Maori personalities from all walks of life: entertainers, artists, community leaders and former gang members were seconded into service, not on the basis of their academic credentials, but for their ability to project a Maori image, to relate to the Maori people and to sell the Department's Tu Tangata programmes.

In addition to redefining the grounds for employment, Puketapu tried to Maorify the Department in other ways. He instructed his senior officers to think and to speak Maori and to use Maori protocol whenever possible. He also exhorted them to search deep inside for that creative energy (*wairua*) with which to carry out their assigned mission. Together, their combined spiritual forces would permeate the Department with the ethos of Maoritanga (the essence of Maori), and revolutionise its operational style from within.

It was also imperative for the image-conscious Puketapu to devise a new means of interaction between his field officers and the members of the Maori community. In the past, field officers carried out their duties in a manner consistent with the expectations of the social welfare model. They responded to situations which they felt warranted their attention. Members of the community were portrayed as victims requiring constant control or supervision. The officers, themselves, were organised on a 'line' type of operation consistent with a hierarchical division of labour and bureaucratic rationality. But under Tu Tangata, a novel kind of community administration emerged which, by inverting the bureaucratic pyramid, approached the ideal of community participation in the delivery of social services. These *kokiri* administration units (*kokiri* means to advance) operated on the principle that Maori community officers were more effective when deployed in daily interaction among their intended clients. Accordingly, each *kokiri* team consisted of three community officers permanently stationed in the field and commissioned to respond quickly to the demands of a locally-recruited, corporate management committee which itemised monthly priorities for the unit. These officers were expected to use their mobility to focus on concrete problems related mostly to Maori youth at schools, at work and in courts. Their accessibility and roving style ensured an awareness of Maori sensibilities for as one *kokiri* officer said to me in late 1982:

> *Kokiri units work in a Maori way. There is no rushing around, fixed to a schedule, but an attempt to get to know the community, talk to the people, let them know community officers are around if needed. We like to think of ourselves as liaison between the Department and the people.*

It should be evident that *kokiri* units exemplify the Department's preference for community development over social welfare, teamwork over individual casework and prevention over 'patch-up'. Maori field officers no longer regard themselves as experts; instead, they see their role in terms of partners, catalysts and consultants. As catalyst, *kokiri* units are in the promotion business. They aim to stimulate the creation of self-help projects by applying those resources available within the community, the Government or the private sector to focus in on problem areas. As partner, *kokiri* units work alongside members of the community and engage the assistance of the voluntary sector to co-produce local programmes. Financial aid (in the form of 'seeding money') and moral support are provided to get a project started and see it through to completion. Finally, *kokiri* units serve as consultants to advise both Government agencies and members of the Maori public on a recommended course of action.

In sum, the Department of Maori Affairs has witnessed a series of far-reaching reforms in its philosophy (community development) and style (decentralisation in planning and delivery of services). Having rejected the 'stand-over' tactics of the past, the Department now perceives itself as one of the components in the total mix of people's efforts to stand tall (Tu Tangata) and to advance with confidence into the future. (Department Memo, January 1981) It hopes to invert the bureaucratic pyramid and replace the traditional approach to Maori affairs with one that emphasises cooperation (*kotahitanga*), sensitivity (*aroha*) and Maori self-determination (*Mana Maori Motuhake*). The inception of a distinctive style of community administration would appear to vindicate the Department's desire to redefine its relationship with the Maori as 'partner and working mate'. (Puketapu 1981)

Reaction and response to recent developments

The Tu Tangata philosophy has been in existence for about five years. To date, response and reaction to the new policy has been positive although sectors of the Maori population have expressed a degree of indifference and, in some cases, scepticism and hostility. On the positive side, numerous programmes have appeared under the umbrella of Tu Tangata which reflect the desire of the community to take control over its cultural and economic destiny. Included in this list are homework centres for Maori secondary pupils, vocational and trade training projects for school leavers, and rural cottage industries. Of these, few have captured the public's imagination to such an extent as the Department-inspired 'Te Kohanga Reo' program (Maori Language Nests). These Maori preschool centres, based on the principles of *whanau* (Maori extended family values) and conducted entirely in Maori, typify the Department's commitment to produce bilingual, bicultural children comfortable in both Maori and *pakeha* worlds.

At the other end of the spectrum, a wide cross-section of Maori, from activists to local leaders, are critical of the Department's motives in coddling up to the Maori. They regard the consultation process as a 'sham' which serves to 'rubber stamp' decisions already taken in private. Others, including the Public Service Commission, are upset at the Department's intent to eliminate its social welfare division and to service Maoridom 'on the cheap', through enlistment of an already over-worked voluntary corps. Moreover, not all is well within the Department. There, the swiftness of reorganisation has left a number of officials confused over what is expected of them. In light of this mix of positive and negative responses, it should be interesting to see whether the promise of community development will result in an authentic devolution of power or, simply, in a redistribution of the workload.

Non-Maori reaction to recent developments has been overwhelmingly positive. The Government in power, the National Party (Conservative), has endorsed Tu Tangata and community development as the basis of its Maori policy (National Party on Maori Affairs 1981):

The philosophy [of Tu Tangata] is one of growth, independence and cultural identity. This goes to the heart of National Party philosophy. Maori people have the resources which are greatly under-utilised and the National Party believes that the Tu Tangata philosophy is ensuring that these resources are being used for the greater good of the Maori and for the nation as a whole.

Clearly, the principles underlying Tu Tangata and community development are consistent with the Party's neo-conservative philosophy of 'less government'. This is politically understandable since circumstances ranging from Maori assertiveness to excessive welfare expenditures have inspired Party strategies to accept the far-reaching proposals of Tu Tangata as a matter of political expediency and economic survival. After nearly 50 years of uninterrupted expansion in state services, the Government has had to acknowledge that the maintenance costs of financing these services have escalated to alarming proportions. (Economic Monitoring Group 1978; New Zealand Planning Council 1979) The virtual cessation of economic growth since 1973, combined with high levels of unemployment, ruinous rates of inflation and a massive imbalance of payments have compelled the Government to reconsider state spending especially in health and welfare which reputedly consumed nearly one-third of the Government's budget. Yet, despite the vast sums expended, the high cost of Government intervention in the delivery of social services has not had the intended effect of improving Maori performance at school or in the labour force. If anything, the Maori as a group are falling further behind the general population in terms of most economic indicators. To add to injury, the serious decline of Maori cultural heritage, especially among the growing legions of disaffected urban youth is viewed with dismay by Maori leaders who point to the failure of Government intervention to deliver the goods as promised. Thus, in an attempt (1) to trim the cost of Government spending on the Maori, (2) to reduce Maori dependency on Government service and (3) to pacify Maori pressure for increased self-determination, the National Party has endorsed the Department's effort to stimulate local initiative, self-sufficiency and voluntary self-help. Whether or not the

Government, in conjunction with the Department of Maori Affairs, is successful in transforming the rhetoric of community development into an ongoing reality remains to be seen.

Conclusion

This article has tried to recount the progression of Maori policy administration from one based on the principles of dependency and social welfare to one grounded in the philosophy of self-determination and community development. The impetus for this shift is attributable, in part, to Maori demands for self-determination and, in part, to the inability of the State to sustain its former levels of social spending. Widespread enthusiasm over Tu Tangata and acceptance of its administration implications are indicative of the appeal of the community development philosophy in serving the vested interests of the Maori, the Government and the Department of Maori Affairs.

References

Adams, P. (1977) *Fatal Necessity: British Intervention in New Zealand, 1830-1837*. Auckland: Auckland University Press/Oxford University Press.

Constantino-David, K. (1982) 'Issues in Community Organisation', *Community Development Journal*, 17: 190-201.

Department of Maori Affairs (1980) *Tu Tangata, Stance of the People*. Unpublished report.

Economic Monitoring Group, New Zealand Planning Council (1978) *Economic Trends and Policies*, Report No. 1, Wellington: Government Printer.

Hanson, E. (1980) *The Politics of Social Security: The 1938 Act and Some Later Developments*, Auckland: Auckland University Press/Oxford University Press.

Hayes, S.E. (1981) 'The Uses and Abuses of Community Development, A General Account', *Community Development Journal*, 16: 221-227.

Hunn, J.K. (1960) *Report on the Department of Maori Affairs*, Wellington: Government Printer.

Hunn, J.K. and Booth, J.M. (1962) 'The Integration of Maori and Pakeha in New Zealand', *Study Paper*, No. 1, Wellington: Department of Maori Affairs.

Love, R.H.N. (1977) *Policies of Frustration: the Growth of Maori Politics, The Ratana/Labour Era*. Unpublished Ph.D. Thesis. Political Science Department, Victoria University of Wellington: Wellington.

National Party on Maori Affairs (1981) *Maori Affairs, Position Paper*, Unpublished report, Research Unit Reference 81/39.

New Zealand Planning Council (1979) *The Welfare State? Social Policies in the 1980s*, Report No. 12, Wellington: Government Printer.

New Zealand Council of Social Services (1978) *Sharing Social Responsibility*, Wellington: Government Printer.

Orange, C. (1977) *A Kind of Equality: Labour and the Maori People, 1935-1949*. Unpublished MA Thesis, History Department, University of Auckland: Auckland.

Puketapu, I.P. (1981) *The Rogue*, Unpublished Paper delivered to the Indigenous Peoples International Conference, December, Wellington, New Zealand.

Puketapu, I.P. and Haber-Thomas, P. (1977) The Community Services, Report of the State Service Commission Review on the Department of Maori Affairs, Wellington: Government Printer.

Ward, A. (1974) *A Show of Justice, Racial Amalgamation in Nineteenth Century New Zealand*, Canberra: Oxford University Press/Auckland University Press.

Also consulted were various memoranda, letters, circulars and unpublished papers housed in the library and archives at the Department of Maori Affairs, Head Office, Wellington, New Zealand.

Augie Fleras is Assistant Professor, Department of Anthropology in the University of Waterloo, Ontario, Canada: Vol. 19 No. 1 (1984): 32-39.

11

Confronting Gender, Poverty and Powerlessness: An Orientation Programme for and by Rural Change Agents

Sundari Ravindran

Introduction

Even as seminars and conferences, articles and studies are engaged in a seemingly endless debate on how women can be 'integrated' into development, attempts are being made quietly but relentlessly by women from the most exploited sections of society in many parts of the world, to define their own priorities and to change their conditions of existence. This article describes one such attempt by a group of rural women belonging to the untouchable 'Paraiya' caste in S. India to initiate and build an organisation of their own and to help women in their communities organise themselves to stand up for their rights and to challenge their oppression.

Evolution from literacy to health action

Rural Women's Social Education Centre (RUWSEC) in Chingleput, S. India was initiated in 1981 by a group of ten women who belonged to the villages of Chingleput, and the author. They had come together because of involvement in a nation-wide literacy campaign in which the ten village women worked as literacy teachers in their respective villages. The experiences gained as a result of their participation in this programme, brought a profound change in their lives. They not only realised their own worth and potential but also felt committed to the task of working with other women in their communities to facilitate the women's own realisation of their power and potential to work together to change their exploited situation. This was the motivating force behind the formation of RUWSEC.

The main focus of RUWSEC's work has been activities and issues related to women and health. The women who initiated the organisation had learnt from their own experiences that understanding the normal functions of their bodies gave them a sense of power and control over their lives and the confidence to challenge things around them. Health was also an important concern for

137

women since it was they who customarily shouldered the responsibility of caring for the sick.

Ten women 'animators' began work in their villages carrying out health-care, health education and working towards building a women's organisation in those villages. The approach of the animators was to help women understand their own and/or communities' health problems and participate in their own healing rather than act as Messiahs who could cure all illnesses.

Women met once a week with the animators to learn and discuss health-related problems, at the women's centre – a small hut much like their own humble homes. There were also meetings, discussion sessions, role-plays and street theatre through which women began to participate in a process of developing a critical awareness of the society in which they lived. These activities helped in the consolidation of women's groups in all the villages during the course of two years, and women's *sanghams* or associations were formed. These *sanghams* have become well-known for their active involvement in village problems and health issues. To mention just a few examples, their immediate action in the face of an epidemic of measles saved the lives of several children; and their organised effort to get officials to take drought relief measures during a severe drought in 1983 won them the support of both the women and the men. As a result, there were requests from several villages in the neighbourhood for the setting up of women's centres, and the animators decided to extend their work to five more villages.

They visited the five villages, and requested a community meeting to be called in each. They explained their work and requested the community to nominate their own animators. The animators thus nominated were young women between the age of nineteen and twenty-five. Three of them were married women with children. They were introduced to the work and philosophy of RUWSEC through a six-day orientation programme organised by the senior animators.

The orientation workshop

Building confidence through sharing experiences
The six-day workshop was divided into four major sections. At the outset the first section consisted of an entire day spent helping participants to feel at ease and to gain enough confidence to be able to actively participate in the activities of the days to follow. The second section consisted of reflecting on the position of women in society and

the third of understanding the double burden of being poor and a woman. The fourth section consisted of discussions on the inter-relationship of poverty, powerlessness and disease so as to be able to tackle the issue as a whole, particularly through health education which would give them greater control over their bodies, and through organising for better living conditions and greater power in decision-making at all levels.

The training programme began with a brief introduction by two animators about the organisation and its work during the past years. The first animators described their role as animators and shared some of their experiences and the difficulties they had faced. As women who were daring to venture into new vistas, they had come under criticism from the traditional male leaders in the community. It was for men to tackle village problems, wasn't it? They and the village women who had been interested in starting women's *sandhams* had often been ridiculed: 'When four turbans (men) get together some work of importance is done. When four plaits (women) get together, what could you expect but chaos?' they had said. But things were beginning to change, though very gradually. At least many women in the communities were becoming involved. One of the speakers asked the trainees not to feel inadequate or afraid, and recalled how she had felt in her first such training. She reassured them, saying that if she could learn and change to be the assertive and confident person she was today, she did not see why the same was not possible for them. After this introduction, the objectives and programme plan were explained.

Participatory training techniques
The introduction of participants was done through a game in which the group was paired off in twos and after ten minutes spent getting to know each other, each participant introduced her partner to the larger group. The trainees expressed their great relief at not having to talk about themselves or in front of a large group right away.

This was followed by another game designed to stimulate discussion on the problems encountered by groups when trying to function democratically and as a collective. The participants, in groups of five, had to simulate a situation of decision-making in an emergency situation of a rising tide which would sweep away their hut in about ten minutes. They had to decide which household articles to take along. At the end of five minutes the group had to announce their decisions, and more importantly, describe how they arrived at them.

It became clear that collective decision-making is no easy task. Some participants described how 'collective' decision-making in their groups had meant one person making up her mind and merely asking the others if they agreed with her. The others had been too timid to contradict her and besides, time was short. This led to the question as to whether those who failed to participate and chose instead to be on-lookers were not to be blamed equally. This was a difficult issue to resolve, but finally it was agreed that when members of a group are not on an equal footing – in this case, some were more experienced than others – it was the responsibility of the former to ensure that they did not intimidate the participation of the others, even if it meant deliberately underplaying their own opinions.

Another problem encountered in the game had been that of arriving at a consensus when all participants were adamant about their stand. It called for maturity and self-assurance. One of the animators recommended the women not to feel threatened when their view was challenged but to co-operate to come to a consensus decision for the benefit of the whole group. From working together in a group, participants went on to the next activity, that of public speaking for two minutes on a given topic. It must be mentioned that not only had none of the trainees ever done public speaking before, they had been brought up to be quiet and withdrawn, never assertive and never to have an opinion of their own let alone to state it in public. The women were very nervous, they despaired, they were sure they could never do it. When at last they did do it, it was for them a great leap forward.

By the end of the first day all the trainees who had begun by being reticent and very unwilling to speak up, seemed to have broken out of their shells. They were at ease with the senior animators, and were addressing them as *akka* (older sister). The first basic theme of the programme – reflecting on the status of women in society – was introduced at this juncture.

Reflecting on women's position in society
Seven popular proverbs about women in vogue in their villages were written on different strips of paper and each strip was torn into two halves so that each half had part of a proverb. The following were the proverbs discussed:

'Father of five daughters, even if he is a king, will be reduced to a pauper.' (This refers to the custom of giving dowries and presents at and after marriage throughout the daughter's life.)

'Does the day dawn with a hen crowing?' (Do women do anything of importance?)

'If you trust a woman, you will be stranded on the streets.'

'It is woman who caused the fall of Indra (King of Gods) and Chandra (the moon God).'

'A girl who has attained puberty should be given away in marriage, be it to a *chakkiliya*.' (*Chakkiliya* is a caste that works with leather and is considered lowest of the low).

The participants were no strangers to these proverbs; in fact, they said, such proverbs were constantly hurled at them to keep them in their place. They expressed anger at the way women were degraded in the proverbs and treated as useless, untrustworthy and scheming. This initiated a spontaneous exchange by the women of how voiceless they were in their own households. The exchange was charged with emotion, and at the same time an awakening as to how similar their plights were. One of the women had to put an end to her fascination for books after her marriage since it was only a lazy woman who whiled away her time reading, according to popular conception. Another, who had been married at thirteen and had borne seven children before she was twenty-five, told of how she seemed to have forgotten who she was. She, as a person with desires and aspirations, did not exist in the eyes of her husband and in-laws. But she had been 'bright' in school, and had wanted to be a teacher – only to have to stop schooling after sixth grade. Many animators already working in RUWSEC described the constant pressure on them not to appear too independent or too opinionated and having to contend with rumours of their being women of loose morals since they moved around several villages all by themselves.

This activity had set in motion a process of reflection about rural women's lives, beginning from their own experiences. The conversations and discussions which ensued all evening and late into the night, was evidence that they were totally absorbed in it. The next morning began with small group discussions around two stories of rural women's lives. The first, of a newly-married woman's problems in her joint family, and the second, a similar story from China before the revolution. The story from China was a revelation of how universal the oppression of women was. In the first story, Sita, the main character finds herself treated as nothing but an additional hand to work for the family into which she has newly entered as daughter-in-law. Strict codes of conduct are laid down for her by her mother-in-law, and she does not even have the possibility to talk to her husband freely. In the second story, Golden Flower, a newly-married young woman in rural China is in an identical situation, slaving all day in the house and in the farm, never a moment for herself, and with no freedom to relate to her husband.

The first story posed questions as to how a woman could react in a similar situation, and all the women eagerly participated in suggesting solutions. The woman could persuade her husband to set up house separately – or alternatively, she could live alone, but for that she would need regular employment. In the latter case, she would need a lot of support from other women, which was considered often difficult to come by. That was because a woman who supports another who had dared to break the rules of society is herself in danger of being labelled immoral. This was why other women were afraid to support her. But should we not, it was suggested, try to break away from this vicious circle at some point? The participants agreed, and the session ended on a hopeful note – of trying to change rather than comply.

In the next session, participants worked in three groups, each group analysing respectively, the image of women in popular fiction, films and in film songs. They did this by taking one or two concrete examples and going over in detail how the subjugation of women is reinforced by their media-image.

Creating new attitudes of self-value
The third day of the workshop was designed to help the women to focus on traditional attitudes held by themselves and by society regarding women's social and sexual roles. It began with the presentation of a case-study of a rural woman's life by narration combined with drama.

The story was about Meenu, the daughter of poor peasant *harijan* parents. She went to school for two years, and at the age of eight stayed back to help with household tasks and to take care of her younger brother and sister while her mother worked in the fields. At thirteen she attained puberty. The occasion was celebrated with the customary rituals, beginning with her physical isolation for five days since she was 'unclean'. She was shocked and confused. In the days that followed more restrictions were imposed on her. She could not leave home after dark, she could not talk to boys or even come out of the house if men other than her family members were present. She was filled with fear and contempt for her new state, but got no advice from anyone about the facts of life. She began to see why they said it was a curse to be born a woman, especially when every month for the rest of her life she was going to be treated as 'untouchable' during her periods.

At sixteen, Meenu was married to a young man from a neighbouring village. Before she knew what, she was pregnant. Her life followed in a drab rhythm thereafter – work, more work, pregnancies, childbirths, miscarriages, deaths of children – everything happening without her will or consent, without her being able to control or change anything.

The case study struck a familiar chord in all the trainees. Meenu's story was not very different from their own. Even those of them who were married and had children had had no idea of conception except that it was related in some way to copulation. They had no idea about the processes of pregnancy and childbirth. All they knew was that it was a messy business, and that they would not wish even their enemies to be born women.

The rest of the day till late in the night was spent going through the Tamil version of 'Child-Birth Picture Book' which RUWSEC had produced. This dealt in detail with the reproductive system, puberty, conception, normal pregnancy and childbirth. Myths surrounding menstruation and childbirth were brought up by the trainees and many hours were spent discussing and arguing about them. The poverty conditions of women which prevented adequate care following pregnancy were also discussed, through a narration of personal experiences by participants. The trainees said later that this was one of the most meaningful sessions, and expressed deep appreciation for the opportunity to talk about the issues for the first time and to clarify their many doubts with other women.

Identifying oppressive attitudes and structures in society
The fourth day aimed at presenting the exploitation of women in the context of an unjust society and arriving at an understanding of what poor, rural, *harijan* women are up against in their struggle for equality and justice. This was done mainly through games and stories that stimulated discussion and led participants to narrate from their own experiences the injustices in their own lives.

The first was a game called 'The Unequal Race'. Participants divided into two groups, the rich and the poor. Each person was the head of a family and received a set of 6 cards; one was an asset card detailing any assets the person had. The other five cards denoted important events in a family's life cycle. Beginning with given assets they had to go through important events in the family's life-cycle – like the birth of a child, education of children, finding them employment, arranging for their marriage, etc. which entailed spending a certain amount of money. At the end, the assets that remained with each person in both the groups were calculated. The point was to stimulate discussion regarding some of the popular misconceptions as to why some people are poor, like laziness, lack of thrift, ignorance and wasteful spending for marriages.

Following this, two fables were enacted. One was about a lone goose who dared to challenge the authority of a fox in a society where foxes occupied all important positions – in the police force, judiciary, and the political sphere. She lost her battle and fell prey to the foxes. The second was the story of the wolf and the lamb. This time however, the lamb gathered together all the sheep and lambs, and together they succeeded in ejecting the wolf from the forest.

Next was a board game similar to Monopoly but different in that it had true-to-life rules – some people were more equal than others. Two of the players were landlords and the others were wage labourers, in a village situation. The landlords began with ten times more cash than the labourers, and already also owned 25% of the property on the game board when the game began. The last activity of the day was a skit enacted by the senior animators, about a poor *harijan* woman called Valli.

Valli was a poor *harijan* woman who eked out a living doing agricultural wage labour. Her husband was also a wage labourer. Valli was tricked by the landlord for whom she worked into meeting him at mid-day when he was alone in his house and was raped by him. When she got back to the fields to resume her work for the afternoon, she heard that her husband had been caught drinking water from the well of the upper caste people. All the important landlords of the village had assembled, and Valli's husband tied to a tree, was awaiting their verdict for the 'crime' he had committed – 'polluting' the well. The landlord who raped Valli was also among them. Beside herself in rage, Valli rushed in front of the man and shouted aloud whether he did not get polluted by raping a *harijan* woman? The 'untouchable bitch' and her husband were punished by a boycott by the landowners against hiring them for work.

Reflections of the participants on the day's activities summed up the concerns of poor *harijan* women. They had seen how women were exploited by society, but more important, that society itself was divided into the rich and the poor, the powerful and the powerless, the exploiters and the exploited. Exploitation of women could not be seen in isolation from this. Women like Valli – the majority of women in their community were in a similar position – had to face all the disadvantages of being poor, powerless and women. The importance was realised of women getting together to fight injustices, and to oppose anyone who trampled on their rights, be it men or women.

The socio-economic and political causes of disease
In the fifth and the sixth days of the training, trainees analyzed the inter-relationship of poverty, powerlessness and disease, and discussed how they visualised their future role as animators who would help women organise themselves around health issues – thus claiming their rights to 'health' in the larger sense of the word. The theme was introduced with narration of the story of Murugan, a village boy who died of tetanus. Participants then had to go over each line of the story and identify all the different reasons that led to his death. For example, Murugan's foot was pricked by a thorn when he was grazing cattle. Why? Because he wore no shoes, he was too poor. Why was he too poor? Further, he had not been vaccinated against tetanus. Why? Because the team from the health centre could not get to his village, there were no roads. Why didn't they make the effort, and why were there no roads? and so on. The discussion lasted all day, and participants made up a poster depicting the medical, social, economic and political causes of Murugan's death. The success of the exercise may be judged from the fact that the physician who assists the training team had been present at this session, and he said that it was for him a significant learning experience. He had never stopped to consider all those 'whys' before.

Later in the evening the trainees volunteered to enact a role play about how the poor were often treated by the health care system. The message of the play was that villagers were apprehensive of going to hospitals because they were treated as dumb and stupid people with no minds of their own, and with no rationale behind their decisions except ignorance. In fact they have well-considered reasons for what they do. For example, when villagers refuse vaccination it may be because they fear getting fever and thereby the loss of a day's wages.

If they are not regular in their visits to the doctor this may be because they did not have the money for bus fares. There was seen to be the need for a radical change in the attitudes and priorities of the prevalent health-care system and its functionaries.

Following the role-play and discussion, a paper entitled 'A post-mortem of our health-care system' was read and discussed. It dealt with the lop-sided prioritics of the health-care system and how women – and especially poor women – suffered most because of this. Women need medical attention not only when they are ill, but also during pregnancy and childbirth. The consumer-oriented health-care delivery system deprives them of care when they need it most since it serves only *those who approach it*. The poor women are often preoccupied in their battle for survival and have neither the time nor the money to go to even the primary health centres. They are dependent on doctors for birth-control advice. The over-burdened free family-planning clinics advise use of intra-uterine devices (IUDs) or administer pills without sparing a thought for side effects. Village women who undergo sterilisation in hospitals are often sent home without any advice whatsoever regarding further care, and the result was that many women did not even change their bandages for several days, causing infection and pus-formation. Most of what the paper said was based on the animators' experiences in the past years in the villages. The trainees added their own personal experiences to the paper, and the basis seemed to have been laid for deducing how *not* to work as health workers.

Examining the role of animators
The next task was to discuss how the animators perceived their role, given their two-fold concern of improving the health status of the community and improving the overall conditions of the life and status of women. Their reflections were interesting. In the present state of affairs, it was seen that on the one hand society functioned in such a way that some people profited at the cost of many, while the rich grew richer, and the poor grew poorer. Poverty and powerlessness were the cause of most disease, so how could one work for better health without tackling the root causes? Hospitals and health centres were seen to have a very limited role in this context, especially considering the lopsided priorities of the health system where preventive health gets little attention, and those most in need of medical attention are unable to get it. The animators saw their role as comprising curative

health (for which they were to undergo further training), health education which aimed at identifying all the causes of disease, not only the medical ones, and organisation in order to eradicate all these causes.

They drew up a list of ways in which their health work would be different from that of the existing health personnel. They would visit people at their homes at the latter's convenience, talk to them about preventive measures, mobilise action against diseases, treat patients as people with ability to understand their own diseases and participate in their own healing. They would respect the wisdom and experience of the people, treat rich and poor alike, use local home remedies as far as possible, and be prepared to take all necessary steps and risks to strike at the root causes of disease.

The main focus would be women and children's health problems, and they would involve women in learning about symptoms and treatment of diseases while at the same time discussing what were the causes. Malnutrition for instance, may not be possible to eliminate without organising for higher wages for the work they do. They would also have to deal with the status of women, since it was their double oppression as women and as poor that was causing most of their diseases.

The trainees had been introduced during the evenings to some of the ways in which ideas could be communicated and discussion stimulated. Street theatre based on rural women's life stories, role plays and problem dramas that portrayed women's problems and provoked discussion on how to change the situation, songs that told of their lives and struggles, and simulation games were all ways in which a beginning had been made to involve women in the process of reflecting about their lives and questioning what they had often taken for granted. The senior animators explained how this usually led on to the formation of *sanghams* to act collectively on some priority needs such as drinking water or higher wages. However, the point was not to push for *sanghams* before the women felt the need for it, and could genuinely use them for their own voice as vehicles for their participation. In some villages, they reported, it may perhaps be possible for *sanghams* to emerge. Their approach was to wait and try to understand local circumstances instead of blindly setting up an organisation from above. That was not their purpose, they said, nor should 'high-handedness' be their style of work. The programme ended with an evaluation by the trainees and by the other animators who had each led a training session. The trainees then returned home to begin to work.

Conclusion

The promotion of grass-roots women's organisations has come to be recognised as an important step towards the improvement of women's status. However, most often there is a 'top-down' approach to setting up grass-roots organisations which are seen merely as vehicles to carry out established programmes. This can be self-defeating. This is not to deny the need for any external input but it is essential to create conditions which can facilitate the emergence of women's own groups at the local level. What is needed is assistance and guidance when called for, without being directive or dominating.

The animators of RUWSEC, after two years of training in administration, accounting and management, and in conducting training programmes, are today in charge themselves of all their activities, and have ventured to further build and expand their organisation. This article stands testimony to their tremendous potential, and is a pointer to the untapped potential of women inherent both in our countryside and shanty towns and in the rest of the world, which when unleashed and channelled could change the world.

Sundari Ravindran, development economist, has worked as an adult educator and initiated rural development programmes in Tamil Nadu, South India: Vol. 20 No. 3 (1985): 213-221.

12

Ideology: The Bridge between Theory and Practice

Jennifer Sayer

Community work has long been characterised by a multiplicity of theoretical perspectives, and ideological principles, leading to a confused understanding of the field of practice, and of the role and tasks of the workers. Frustration with this situation led me to study the personal perspective of a number of workers employed in different contexts, with a view to identifying the impact of that perspective on their activities. Through this research (Sayer 1985), I began to identify much more clearly the nature of the gap between theory and practice and particularly the fact that we do not have an understanding of community work which reflects practitioners' experience. I would like to explore how I began to identify ideology as the bridging mechanism through which we can both explain and redevelop practice and identify the nature of the process in which we are all involved.

The nature of the gap

As community work theory has developed, it has increasingly relied on a structuralist perspective, within a sociological analysis. This theory implies practice which has organisational change as its target, even at the cost of individual development goals. On the other hand, practitioners frequently operate on an interpersonal level, and are trained on courses which teach those skills within a psychological and individualised framework e.g. groupwork is often taught using an interactionist, or therapeutic underpinning, with a client group orientation and treatment goals. A community worker may well have to rearticulate her skills into a theoretical perspective which has learning at its base, issues as an orientation, and action against an outside influence as its goal. Little wonder she identifies a gap between theory and practice!

A complementary aspect to this gap between sociological analysis and interpersonal practice is the gap between the urgency and immediacy of the task/issue faced by the community, and the need for growth within individuals who have to learn how to tackle this issue

149

collectively. We often teach people how to organise, without recognising the level of personal growth required to enable them to undertake new roles. Then we complain about apathy when they fail to become involved.

The tension between action and process goals, also identifies a third aspect of the gap – the time perspective. Practitioners are often faced with the daily impact of lives structured by poverty and inequality. This pulls them strongly towards instant problem-solving action. When there is a fire, one tends not to sit down and discuss the process whereby we can prevent fires – we get out of the building! If practitioners are also using a structural analysis as a framework for their activities, they may get depressed, and feel inept, inadequate and hopeless, because there is no way of seeing how their immediate helping contributes to long-term social change.

Finally, and less obviously related to the theory and practice debate, is the influence of the employing organisation. It was evident in my study, that whilst practitioners used theory to explain their work and perhaps to set goals, the agency often determined the key organising concept, e.g. workers in education agencies tend to use learning as the basis for a discussion of practice, whilst social workers tended to use 'support' or 'care'. Thus anything which might be called a discrete body of community work theory tends to be watered down and confused by the agency discourse. This process is reinforced by the fact that most full-time workers still have their origins in other forms of professional training (only two out of 33 workers interviewed in my study had been on a course specifically for community workers).

Thus the community worker is in a situation where she has a theoretical analysis drawn from other disciplines, a working context almost certainly using an analysis with a different basis, and a community which has an immediate need for a response. Small wonder we have difficulty in identifying a coherent framework for practice. As I explored the subject of ideology with practitioners, I became convinced that therein lay some of the answers to our search for an understanding of community work which relates to the complexity of being involved in it.

Identifying the field of practice

Current community work models can be seen to be based on learning, action or resource development. Whilst they all may operate within a certain set of principles, there often seems to be little obvious link between them. Community work tends to end up trying to be all things to all people, particularly as we have tried to use the adjective 'community' as the integrating concept. An understanding of the theory of ideology, and of the perspective of Antonio Gramsci (particularly as seen by Mouffe 1981) in particular, led me to recognise a different focus for describing the work, which bridged, for me, the gap between individual and collective, institutional and personal change.

Three specific aspects of this particular theory seemed to me to have particular relevance to community work. First, ideology is seen as being created and recreated through social practices in order to hold society together (Gramsci talks of it as 'cement'). It 'does not descend from above, nor does it emanate from below. It is rather the result of complex forms of negotiation between various groups on specific sites'. (Gramsci 1981) It is not something which happens merely in people's heads (i.e. the way they think about the world) but is manifested in practices, both informal and institutional. Thus the way we see family life, and behave within the concept, is created by institutions, the legal framework, by informal relationships between people, and by cultural influences such as media images. We have to 'speak through' the ideologies which are active in society; 'we formulate our intentions within ideology'. (Hall 1981: 31-2)

It should be evident that if a society has an extremely powerful economic and political elite, controlling all the mechanisms whereby ideology is created, then that society will get set in concrete (hegemony in Gramsci's terms). For change to occur (either in the nature of the hegemony, or in the 'cementing' ideology), then work has to be done on both institutional practices, and on the informal practices in civil society. This latter concept is of significance to community work because it actively recognises and uses every-day life in the process of change. It challenges us to recognise our contribution to that every-day life and to realise that by our very existence at the boundary between informal and institutional practices we are involved in ideological development whether we like it or not. Thus a neighbourhood-based family centre set up on principles of power-sharing and involvement may in fact inadvertently reinforce traditional female roles through its activities (e.g. *mother* and toddler groups). Similarly a youth centre claiming to be non-ideological may well reinforce the principle of competition, and sex-role stereo-typing through the way it runs its leisure activities.

We are challenged therefore to examine and evaluate not only *what* we do, but *how* we do it.

In order to do this, we need to identify the nature of the *content* of ideology, as this should define our field of practice. Hall defines ideology as 'those images, concepts, and premises which provide frameworks through which we represent, interpret, understand and "make sense" of some aspect of social existence'. (Hall 1981) It does not consist of isolated statements and separate concepts. The different elements are brought together (in Hall's language, articulated into) 'a distinctive set or chain of meanings': a discourse. (*Ibid.*) 'How we see ourselves and our social relations matters, because it *enters into and informs our actions and practices*' (*Ibid.*) (my emphasis). Thus the way a worker makes sense of the concept 'family' will condition her response to practices which demonstrate another discourse about 'family'. If a small child looks me in the eye and tells me 'women don't work', I am inclined to respond as a feminist!

The combination of the concept of civil society, and of discourse has exciting implications for community work. First, it raises the significance of interpersonal practices to something more than an area for individual development. Secondly, it identifies the significance of the term 'community', as a place where informal and institutional practices meet, at one and the same time, beyond the merely personal or the merely political. It is the site of intersecting discourses. If I continue to use family as an example, the elements of role, structure and societal function of the family are currently in question in Britain. The intersecting discourses include feminist (the family as the site of oppression of women); economic (the family as a basis for developing a healthy and productive work-force); child-rearing (the family as a basis for security and growth); Christian (the family as God's plan for humanity); social work (the family as the basis for caring) and so on. The practices related to these discourses will have significant effects on personal relationships, and ultimately on how society as a whole uses the concept 'family' (which might for example, result in an alternative distribution of welfare benefits). Community workers' intervening within the informal practices about family, will be contributing to the re-articulation of such elements as 'parent', 'mother', 'child-rearing' and so on. These elements are the sphere of change, and the reason for being involved, not simply that there are needs in families on a particular patch.

Thus the definition of 'community' is no longer one of locality, or organisation, but one of multiplicity of discourses which may or may not be articulated into the current hegemony of the State (or pre-revolution). Community work is part of the process of creating expansive hegemony. (Mouffe 1981: 223-224) Its significance lies in its place in civil society in the area of consent creation, where the battle for people's minds is at its most crucial (hence the popular idea of 'community' as 'public opinion'). It will not create radical change in itself, but is part of the mass of interrelating micro-practices which create thinking about social life.

The redevelopment of practice

Having established the nature of the process into which the practitioners are intervening, however, the trainer has to define the characteristics of these practitioners and what they need to be able to do. How does the concept of ideology at work through the creation and recreation of discourse redevelop our ideas about practice?

First, workers need to be aware of current ideological issues in society, and of the nature of the discourses being transformed. They have to ask:

a) Into which ideological field am I entering? Which elements are the target of practice? (e.g. patient or community care in a health setting, tenant in housing etc.)

b) Into which ideological perspective am I articulating my work and why? (e.g. Christian, feminist, anarchist, educator, etc.). What limitations and advantages does this perspective have? How do these relate to the discourses being employed by the people and institutions with whom I work?

c) Where are the points of potential alliance and confrontation?

Secondly, the workers have to be able to promote active, conscious involvement in rearticulating these elements through practices. Involvement in this sense does not mean a token involvement in organisational structures as they exist or are promoted by the dominant groups. It means involvement in the thinking behind those structures, and in redeveloping related procedures and behaviours, both individual and collective. One worker in my research (a man) described how he had needed to learn to recognise and respect the informal organisation between women in a block of flats, in order to understand why formal organisations were so alienating to women, and *not necessarily more effective*. In order to create change, he had to rearticulate the meaning of 'organise' and 'committee' so that the women were no longer rendered powerless, nor forced to learn to operate in the dominant frame of reference.

A third necessary skill, is that of being able to use activity to negotiate and transform ideology: a re-articulation into the new system via practices. In the example used above, the concept 'organised' had to be translated from 'a group of people with a task to do who have a chairman, treasurer and secretary, and who share out the work' to 'a network of people with a common interest, who communicate informally, make decisions collectively, and allocate work to people with the talent to do it, with roles as appropriate'. This relates ultimately to a cooperative as opposed to a competitive discourse, and may ultimately challenge, for example, the criteria used for establishing which groups receive funding.

Thus a practitioner has to be able to work simultaneously at several levels (individuals, groups, organisational and institutional) whilst being able to relate all the work into the specific ideological field within which they are operating. They have to be clear about their own position, the potential contribution of the work in which they are engaged, and about the 'ideological axioms structuring methods'. (Lanning 1980) Otherwise they will not be able to recognise their contribution to the change process and/or may further oppress rather than liberate:

> *Action without reflection is performance within ideology, not participation in exposing and recreating it.* (Freire 1972: 41)

They have to be able to answer three questions:
a) Does this work lead to any group's hegemony? Whose hegemony does it challenge?
b) Does it reinforce existing forces (such as prevailing attitudes to learning in education systems for example) and do I agree with those?
c) What sort of change will my activity stimulate, not only in who holds the power, but in the way in which power is exerted?

These three points illustrate that a community worker is not someone who merely acts like a motor mechanic, assessing, taking action, and curing the problem. She is one who in addition, recognises the contribution made by the intervention to the specific process of re-articulation in which the project is engaged. She can build from small activity to small activity on a dialectical model of reflection and action, using ideology as the mediating mechanism for herself and others.

Building the bridge

a) *Between a sociological analysis (the structures) and interpersonal practice (the people).*

Earlier I identified that we have as yet done little to develop a real concept of the practice which integrates with sociological analysis and explanation of our work. We have begun to explore particular perspectives, and their implications, but are still somewhat entrapped in a psychologising methodology. Somehow trainers have to bring together the analysis and the everyday practice, and it is the concept of discourse which can facilitate this. For example, one group of my students asked if they could discuss the application of community work to drug addiction. They had already examined the 'toolkit' of the occupation, and at some of the underlying concepts, but were still looking at it as the third social work method, and on drug addicts as the people with the problem. They were assuming a consensus view on addiction.

Our first step was to locate the contradiction within which they perceived addiction (in this case, normal – deviant). We then identified the different discourses which would be around, and how they would be manifested in practices, e.g. 'All drug addicts are bad influences, and should be locked up!' 'That could be my daughter – how can I help?' 'Everyone should be free to choose their lifestyle whatever the consequences'. We then examined how and where we all placed ourselves within the discourse and why; what kind of shifts in discourses we would personally like to see; and how those shifts were likely to relate to agency and various community discourses. We then identified the range of interventions into institutions and informal practices which might contribute to changing those discourse, and which would be relevant to community work practitioners, as opposed to others, and why.

The implications of using this method were threefold. First, the students finally grasped the difference between community work, and work in the community. Secondly, we engaged together in a joint exploration of personal and professional attitudes and an examination of related practices, which was a mutual process i.e. it changed the role relationship between trainer and student.

Thirdly, the students were able to link their macro-behaviour towards addicts as part of the macro-analysis of societies' discourse about addiction. In other words, they had built the bridge between theory and practice.

b) *Building the bridge between short-term action and long-term goals*
Community workers have long been wary of the pathologising tendency of much work with individuals. This has meant that workers have often been inadequately trained in the recognition of the use of conversations as part of the process of changing discourse. To continue the example of drug users; as a youth worker, I was involved within the contradiction of self-awareness and growth – self-destruction. Whilst on the one hand, I was working with individuals, using conversations, incident, groups to shift one discourse from 'drugs are the in-thing for finding yourself' (manifesting itself for example in one young man putting LSD in his friend's beer so that he would 'get free') to 'drugs can help you find yourself, but they have certain hazards, and there are alternatives'. Training needs to teach us how to use the micro-practice in order to help people move from partial penetrations (Willis 1977) to fuller comprehension of what is happening to them. This means a much higher concentration on detailed analysis of practice, either using video or role play, or feedback after action in reality. Role-playing from within specific discourses can be particularly useful. What would you identify, for example, as specific elements in the discourses about drugs currently in use today? I would suggest we could recognise 'control', 'punishment', 'prevention', 'cure', 'social acceptance and personal freedom' (particularly if you include alcohol), 'economic gain' and 'economic consequences' (of unemployment etc.). The training group can role-play from within these discourses (at one stage, I fell only too easily into a 'controlling policeman!'). Through the interaction, we can identify the practical implications, the potential changes, and the work necessary before the advent of a project. This process trains people in a new understanding of listening – not to the apparent authentic statements of individuals, but to their ideological origins. It also trains people to recognise the mechanisms whereby the ground is 'seeded' for change through dialogue, and that this is a reciprocal process between all involved, including the worker. Most important of all, it helps workers relate short-term behaviours to long-term goals.

c.) *Bridging the gap between involvement and objectivity*
It should be apparent that this idea of working on ideology in society challenges the concept of professional objectivity. Workers in my study identified the reciprocal nature of the work, and how their own personal perspective changed through their involvement. Recent

work by socialists and feminists (see e.g. Dixon *et al.* 1982; Smith 1983) has also highlighted the need for us to understand how practice is mediated through personal standpoint. In training terms, this means a different approach to curriculum development, particularly in relation to identifying potential learning within a specific piece of work. This work on ideology also changes our approach to what is usually termed 'values'. We can no longer examine them as things which stand in the way of a truly objective diagnosis and treatment. We have to see our personal standpoint as an essential part of the change process, and our own experience of structuring meaning into our lives as crucial to being able to help others do the same. For trainers, this means that we have to examine the ideology which is being transmitted through our training method. We need also to have experienced changes in our personal standpoint, and the re-articulation of our practices into a different discourse. This actually implies that there should be in existence not training courses, but training groups through which people examine their ideology through practice and vice versa. The trainer's expertise would lie first in 'ideological analysis', secondly in questioning and searching for implications, and enabling the group to develop its own capacity to do so. The groups would be specifically aimed at empowerment – enabling people to have control over their own work. Recent involvement I have had in helping projects develop their community work perspective suggests that this process can indeed strengthen the workers' framework for action and clarify how they want to contribute and why.

I have tried to illustrate in this article how a specific understanding of ideology as the field of practice in community work adds a dimension to training, and builds a bridge between theory and practice. I am conscious that much of what I have said is not new, merely described in a different way. I am convinced that we have to keep reflecting and re-articulating as I believe that we have to make sense of the real nature of the process called community work. Otherwise we will continue to work within simplistic polarisations of individual-collective, personal-political, radical-conservative, whilst others are busy incorporating 'community' into their own discourse, and determining the nature of relevant training.

Much work needs to be done, particularly in understanding the activities of community work practitioners. It is perhaps through combining training and research that we could eventually bring together a collective understanding of what it takes to be involved as a worker in the complexities which make up every day life at the local level. We could also become clearer about our own potential contribution to the process of social change, and development, both as individuals and as an occupation.

References

Dixon, G., Johnson, C., Leigh, S. and Turnbull, N. (1982) 'Feminist Perspectives and Practices' In Craig, G., Derricourt, N. and Loney, M. (eds) *Community Work and the State*. London: Routledge Kegan Paul: 59-72.

Freire, P. (1972) *Pedogogy of the Oppressed*, London: Penguin Books.

Gramsci, A. (1981) 'Class, Culture and Hegemony' in Bennett, T., Martin, G., Mercer, C. and Woollacott, J., *Culture, Ideology and Social Process*, London; Batsford.

Hall, S. (1981) 'The Whites of Their Eyes: Racist Ideologies and the Media' In Bridges, G. and Brunt, R. (eds.) *Silver Linings*, London: Communist University of East London.

Lanning, A. (1980) *Ideology, Methodology and Technology: What Relevance for Community Work Practice?* Talking Point No. 16. London: Association of Community Workers.

Mouffe, C. (1981) 'Hegemony and Ideology in Gramsci' In Bennett, T., *et. al.* op. cit.

Sayer, J. (1985) *How Does the Ideology of the Worker Affect the Community Work Process?* Unpublished M. Phil. Thesis, Lancaster University.

Smith, J. (1983) 'Possibilities for a Socialist Community Work Practice' In Henderson, P. and Thomas, D.N., *Readings in Community Work*, London: N.I.S.W.

Willis, P.E. (1977) *How Working Class Kids Get Working Class Jobs*, Hants: Saxon House.

Jennifer Sayer is Senior Lecturer in Community Work, School of Community Studies, Lancashire Polytechnic, U.K.: Vol. 21 No. 4 (1986):. 294-303.

13

Community Groups in Quebec: From Radical Action to Voluntarism for the State?

Jean Panet-Raymond

Is community development growing 'soft' or is it growing wiser? This is a question one has to ask as community groups have changed their practices since the supposedly radical 1970s. (Baldock 1977; Vass 1979) Are these apparently 'soft' practices dictated by 'survival tactics' in a context of tight public funding or do they reflect a change in the political context? Adaptability is an essential quality of community development but it can also lead to a rejection of important objectives. This article proposes to show some of the 'new' practices of community groups of Quebec, especially in their relation with the state. In trying to understand these changes, a few factors must be put in context. It is hoped that the case of Quebec will add to the debate on possible perspectives for community groups elsewhere. But first it will be useful to briefly describe some of the political context of Quebec in which these groups developed.

Community development in Quebec

Community groups, as we know them today, really came about in the mid-1960s with the influence of the American War on Poverty and a few Christian and socialist ideologies from French intellectuals. These influences came amidst the 'Quiet Revolution' of Quebec (1960-1966) which saw the birth of the modern welfare state. The Province of Quebec (or State of Quebec as most French speaking Quebeccers now call it) had been kept in the dark by a very autocratic conservative and repressive government, heralding itself as the protector of language (French) and religion (Catholic) in the WASP (White Anglo-Saxon Protestant)-dominated Canadian Confederation. The state reforms brought about by the Liberal government from 1960 to 1966 were dramatic, especially in the fields of education and health (jointly funded by the federal government). Public sector employees massively unionised and obtained the right to strike in 1965. Major organisational and ideological changes were seen in the flourishing labour movement:

it broadened its base and it moved from a very corporatist stand to a more left-wing position, espousing a class analysis of society.

The first community organisations came about in two quite different settings. First, in inner city Montreal, groups started asking for more play areas, health services and housing. They also fought brutal urban renewal policies coming from local, provincial and federal governments (joint funding). Secondly, action developed in the rural villages of Gaspésie, six hundred miles east of Montreal, where the provincial government, again with federal funding, had a massive economic development plan. In both cases governments initiated a certain form of community organisation in order to get people to participate in a predetermined plan. People quite quickly saw through this ploy and set up pressure groups that started using much stronger campaigning strategies (massive demonstrations, squatting, occupying ministers' offices). By 1968, it was clear to most groups that they had to get political power if they wanted their pressure tactics to get results. Thus followed the radicalisation of groups. But in the wake of repression brought about by the War Measures Act used during the 'October Crisis' to search out the members of the FLQ (Front de Libération du Québec), more than 500 activists were arrested without warrants. These events contributed greatly to the understanding of the state as a repressive class apparatus.

But then, both provincial and federal governments followed in a very different way to subdue radical organisations. They made massive funding available for job creation schemes for self-help projects. Community groups 'flourished', some lasting only the length of funding (six to twelve months). Marxist-Leninist groups began appearing, in the search for a clear political line. They tried (and often succeeded) to take control of unions and community groups in the mid-1970s. This was against a background of the social services reform started in 1973 (strongly based on the British Seebohm Report 1968), that was supposed to create a network of Local Community Services Centres (health and social services) based on prevention, citizen participation and community development. Again, some groups got on the bandwagon of accessible resources while others boycotted any collaboration with the state apparatus. Cuts started in the late 1970s as the economic crisis made its impact on the Welfare State. It is ironic that it is under the 1976 social democratic Parti Québecois (P.Q.) government that the cuts in government spending had to begin, as in Britain with the Labour Party. Many activists had supported the P.Q. and wanted to give it a running chance. Others saw it as just another bourgeois government to be fought. The question of the independence of Quebec (which was the P.Q.'s main objective) also created problems within groups: the right to self-determination was opposed to the need to unite the working class within all of Canada. All during the late 1970s, groups were plagued by internal political struggles that left many scars. It pushed some into populism and localism, and it even killed certain organisations.

What lessons were learned from these political and strategic debates? Did a new pragmatic socialism evolve or did the winds of Thatcherism take over in Quebec as in many other western countries? How can we explain the changes in the strategies and the activities of many community groups?

A new political, economic and social context

The present reorganisation of capital has created very difficult situations, if only by means of a very high level of unemployment and inflation. It has disrupted social classes, habits, values and the concept of salaried work. The precariousness of work has particularly hit the young, women and older persons. Thatcherism has created a climate of insecurity, of lost illusions, even of despair for many. It has forced a growing number of people to readjust their ambitions and plans. This has influenced community groups. They have attracted and accepted a number of people out of jobs, wanting to do 'volunteer' work, rather than 'militant' work as in the 1970s.

The increase in economic problems has been translated into social needs while the state is cutting those very social services and benefits it should increase. This crisis of the Welfare State is reflected itself in community groups. While the 1970s were marked by enormous demands on the state, the 1980s have seen new relations develop. This is for two reasons. First, the P.Q. government created or enhanced a number of public bodies demanded by groups (Rent Control Commission, Day Care Office, Handicapped Office, Office for Consumer Protection, Women's Status Council, Youth Secretariat, etc.). Secondly, it showed its willingness to cut down drastically on public spending. The 'new right' Liberal government elected in December 1985 wants to continue slashing budgets and privatise many of the state apparatuses. Community groups are caught off-balance. The state apparatuses exist but they don't really correspond to people's expectations and needs. Increased bureaucracy has diluted the content of reforms gained by community groups. So groups are caught in the difficult situation of using 'old' demands that tend to go stale as rallying cries. They must innovate. Meanwhile the state has innovated with its rhetoric on partnership, self-help and volunteer work in the community. Politicians and technocrats are taking a new line:

> *One of the major priorities of my government will be a complete revision of social programmes in order to save as much money as possible. One way of meeting that objective is to encourage the voluntary sector to participate more in the implementation of social programmes. Volunteer work is the most efficient method of work in Canada ...* (Mulroney 1983)
>
> *Ordinary individuals have more potential, abilities and interest to support and help themselves than the Welfare State approach presumed...We must first and foremost aim at supporting those informal networks where they exist and develop them where they don't.* (Ouellet, 1983)[1]

So the message is clear from Thatcher and Reagan to Mulroney: the state must opt out in favour of a partnership with community groups or the private sector. But on what conditions? This is where the British Barclay Report's (1982) proposal of developing a 'community approach' is being used as a rationale for dismantling the state apparatus. Private entrepreneurship, natural self-help networks and even the extended family are put forth as more efficient (cheaper) options to highly bureaucratised public services. That is the issue confronting community groups. Are groups finally getting the sought-after recognition or are they getting incorporated as a cheap option? We know the 'natural tendency for the state to control whatever it funds. Groups already experience the constraints of a certain dependence toward the state's funding. They also have become more bureaucratic, professionalized and specialised, in order to comply with state functioning. Funding has become a time-consuming straightjacket that forces groups to define activities in such ways as to fit state priorities. Added to these constraints, private funders are forcing groups to get registered as charitable organisations. As in Britain, the Ministry of Revenue has tightened its guidelines for charitable groups, forbidding any 'political' work. In those terms, can one talk of recognition? Or is it incorporation? Groups will have to make a choice between subsidised partnership in voluntary work and unfunded radical community action.

In this difficult dilemma, the organised labour movement could offer some support and there is a fairly recent tradition of reciprocal support and coalitions between unions and community groups.[2] But trade unions are also caught in the crisis of the economy and the state. Effective cuts in all public sector spending, and closures in big industries have cut their numbers and made recruitment difficult. Privatisation through sub-contracting has changed the rules of the game. The precariousness of employment has brought about an army of part-time, short-term, 'disposable' labour which is very difficult to organise. Unions are concerned with their own struggle to survive, while searching for 'a new political strategy'. The uncertainty among unions in both private and public sector has weakened their bargaining power. This, it seems, has favoured a more equal partnership with community groups who do not share similar short-term interests. Users of health and social services and 'competing' community or voluntary organisations are in a better position towards traditionally strong and arrogant unions. This new context has helped create a National Coalition against cuts in health and social services. Only the test of time will tell if this coalition can last longer than those of the past. It seems the class interests are often put aside by short-term corporatist interests and suspicions.

Another important factor is the appearance of new issues, and new groups that cut across class distinctions. Actually these 'new clienteles' are also the result of an artificial division, socially constructed by government programmes: the young jobless, the unemployed, women victims of violence, the elderly, physically or mentally handicapped, etc. These people have always existed of course but they have become the subjects of new priorities for the state, and this has entailed the mushrooming of corresponding groups and activities: youth centres, drop-in centres for young jobless, homes for women victims of violence, employment training schemes for the young, centres for refugees. Many of these activities actually respond to government policies and implement them through low-cost service contracts with the state. Among these 'service groups' there are also many that are set up as local economic development enterprises, especially in small towns or rural areas depending on a single industry that is closing down. Though they don't necessarily resemble the American community development corporations they are seen as typifying the self-help ideology the state is trying to promote. (Twelvetrees 1986)

Of course running parallel to these factors is the community approach touted by all with so many different and mystifying meanings: community centres, community social work, community youth workers, community probation, community corporations and even community police. But in using the community rationale, the state is opting out of a collective responsibility, attacking the concept of universality, of democratic rights and putting the burden of social costs on individuals and the family. This inevitably means that women are forced to go back to roles they had started to relinquish, with difficulty, during the 1970s. (Croft 1986) The community carers, the volunteers, the homemakers are generally women, and they will become the precarious and exploited workers, hired by entrepreneurs contracting with the state. The state is closing up institutions and 'dumping' on to families and communities 'their' elderly, and 'their' handicapped. Community groups are therefore being touted as alternatives to institutions, but with very little financial support. The ideology of community which is promoted also confuses issues and covers up the reality of a more centralised and controlling state, however less interventionist it might want to look.

New practices and new relations with the state

The new political context, and the existence of numerous self-help, service and economic development groups has forced 'traditional', more class-based groups and unions to a more open and pragmatic approach in dealing with each other and with the state. The perennial dilemma remains however: subsidised (albeit poorly) partnership or unsubsidised autonomy. Survival through marriage or poverty through celibacy!

Thus there is a tendency for groups to concentrate more on economics than ideology. Bread and butter issues, here and now, occupy groups more than ideological warfare and the search for the 'just' political line. The great ideological debates have been replaced by meetings or technicalities: how to prepare a meeting with a government official, how to prepare a media interview, etc. The demands of some groups illustrate this. Tenants' associations are asking for more public housing (which is not new) and support for the co-ops, but not for a general rent freeze and end to private use of housing for profit. The Regroupement Autonome des Jeunes (RAJ) (which is meant to sound like 'rage' in French), created in 1983, wants more welfare money for the single under-thirty year olds without discrimination. Women want more money for women victims of violence (short-term residential care). These examples show a will to reach very concrete and immediate needs of people, but also a fairly limited ability to organise long-term demands for basic rights. Groups try to get the realistic 'winnable' gains (which is a good community action principle).

An immediate consequence of this type of practice is the setting up of short-term coalitions on specific issues. Groups unite for a struggle with a 'light' organisation. This is a coalition in the true sense of the word, with a single focus, that lets in a variety of groups, even with possible ideological differences. Heavy super-organisations have often floundered because of the time spent in building them, tripping over details and losing sight of their objective. Alliances with leisure groups, church, public service centres and even local politicians are seen in neighbourhoods and towns where it would never have been possible in the 1970s. These tactical alliances are created to fight zoning laws, to demand public housing, to stop the construction of a motorway, to preserve a historical building from demolition or to fight pornography. Compromise is not a dirty word any more, and groups are willing to broaden their 'natural' base in order to win demands. One must recognise the positive aspect of this new pragmatism, but also question the weakness, in the long run, of the absence of a clear political perspective. There is a risk of activism multiplying small gains that are not used to forge structural change. One cannot help but think back to the early beginnings of community organisation.

Another new practice that is not really new but comes back on a regular cycle is the emphasis on a quality service, efficient, competent and … professional. Mobilisation and campaigning are not necessarily opposed to service, as they were often in all groups working with claimants (unemployed, tenants, consumers). Focus is put on answering urgent and immediate needs, which is easier than organising the masses. It is also the importance put on knowledge and expertise, which goes against the idea of democratising knowledge as a tool of the privileged. The very competence groups develop permits them to play into the state's objectives of cutting its costs and sub-contracting services to able 'community groups'. The state wins on all counts: cutting costs, gaining control, subduing potential revolt, creating jobs 'in the community', working in partnership and so on.

All this has brought about new relations with the state. Conflict is giving way to a cautious dialogue in many cases. Is this a simple tactic, evolving ideology or straightforward common sense? Probably a bit of all those things. But one thing is certain: the number of talking and coordinating forums between state, industry, unions and community is multiplying. Even among groups there is a tendency to shy away from formal national federation organisations in favour of local or regional networks. The networks are loosely-structured, based on concrete exchange and sharing of resources in specific fields of interests. One has to wonder if this is a remnant of the community control movement popular in the USA at one time (Altshuler 1970) or of traditional community organisation à la Murray Ross. (1967)

Conclusion

What can we make of all these changes? Has community development gone 'soft' or to the right? Has militant work been replaced by voluntarism to serve the state's interests and pay for the reorganisation of capital? There is definitely a move away from dogmatic leftism towards the right in many groups, old and new, and they are playing into the state's game. But, as Dylan sang 'the times they are a-changin'…and you don't have to be a weatherman to know which way the wind blows'. The wind is not blowing the way it was in the 1960s, but it may also be a time to re-evaluate tactics and strategies. Without being able to talk about a resurgence, there are some new practices that can at least serve notice to fixed ways of doing things and dealing with the state. The odds are not favourable. Community groups should be able to adapt to changing situations and institutionalisation will not give them that ability nor the power to influence events.

But community development is not just a question of adapting style and image. It should still be geared to defending the exploited and oppressed and changing the social, ideological and political structures that perpetuate those oppressions. A serious analysis must ensure that any action corresponds to those goals. And groups must maintain solidarities and alliances, however light or simple, in order to support each other against the state, whether using it (through funding) or not. In front of the state's push for partnership in voluntary work and cheap labour, groups must not sink into localism and isolation. Time will tell if these 'new practices' become a simple voluntarism, as an instrument of state policy, or if they can muster up new mobilisations of the oppressed, while using different ways and means. The open-minded and frank forums and coalitions of community groups and trade unions is certainly a good omen.

References

Altshuler, A. (1970) *Community Control*, New York: Pegasus.

Baldock, P. (1977) 'Why Community Action? The Historical Origins of the Radical Trend in British Community Work', *Community Development Journal*, 12(2).

Barclay Report (1982) *Social Workers, their Roles and Tasks*, London: Bedford Square Press.

Croft, S. (1986) 'Women, caring and the recasting of need – a feminist reappraisal', *Critical Social Policy*, 6(1): 23-39.

Mulroney, B. (1983) Prime Minister of Canada in an address to the Conservative Party Congress, 10th June.

Ouellet, H. (1983) *Social services in Quebec: reflexion on the '80s*. Federation of Local Community Services Centres of Quebec, October, (in French).

Ross, M. (1967) *Community Organisation*, (2nd edn.), London: Harper and Row.

Seebohm, F. (1968) *Report of the Committee on Local Authority and Allied Personal Social Services*, London: HMSO.

Twelvetrees, A.(1986) 'Lessons from American – Corporation Clues', *Community Care*, May 15.

Vass, A. (1979) 'The Myth of a Radical Trend in British Community Work: A Comparison of Statutory and Voluntary Projects', *Community Development Journal*, 14(1).

Notes

1. This Federation is comparable to the British Association of Directors of Social Services.
2. One of the three big union federations in Quebec, the Confederation of National Trade Unions (CSN), published a Manifesto in 1968, advocating work on the 'second front', meaning issues dealing with reproduction, outside the workplace. It also clearly put forth the case for socialism and independence for Quebec. The latter position has been that of most of the labour movement's leadership.

Jean Panet-Raymond teaches in the Ecole de Service Sociale, Université de Montréal, Canada: Vol. 22 No. 4 (1987): 281-286.

14

Street and State in Community Work: Some Developments from the Past 20 Years

Ad Raspe

Debates on the nature and function of community work go much further back than the past 20 years. Nevertheless, the existence and the growth of community work in Holland is closely connected with the past two decades; that is to say, equated with the introduction of community work as a professional area of work. On the one hand, community work tends to be considered as the fruit of the democratisation movement of the 1960s, a professional translation of influence by citizens. But government also stimulated the provision of community work in its initial period, and, sometimes more and sometimes less, controlled that community work. For community work, *'state'* and *'street'* act as two magnetic poles, so to speak.

The 1960s: crisis in democracy

During the 1960s, 'participation' and 'fundamental democratisation' (Egas 1970) were undoubtedly key concepts. Peper (1972) argued that community work appears to draw its task from the crisis in democracy. There was a large gap between the authorities and the people; planning took place while the people concerned remained uninvolved. It was Peper's opinion that the function of participation was to get popular agreement with the democratic system. A title of a NIMO-publication strikingly indicated the period: 'The distance between citizens and their local authorities.' (NIMO brochure No. 15) The core problem is seen as the relationship between government and citizens. But where did community work stand in this problematic relationship?

In 1971 the results of a NIMO survey, based on the way in which 46 community workers spent their time, were published and entitled *Conception of Function: Fulfilment of the Function by Community Workers.* The fact that community workers often wrote reports on behalf of the authorities, showed that community work was *'state'* rather than *'street'*. Community workers only incidentally functioned as spokespersons for the people (or groups of people). There was hardly any time left for 'social action', which was the central issue in those days. Most community workers looked upon social action as the last resort, after all other attempts to come to an agreement had been shipwrecked. A little more than half of the projects they dealt with concerned material matters such as a building or other facility. The remaining part concerned 'immaterial matters' like the creation of workgroups or committees.

The survey mentioned, moreover, that community work was trying to gain influence in urban renewal and rehabilitation, even though the results were still modest: 'The attempt to gain influence in those government policies and decisions, and to do this with the people themselves, remains a challenge in community work'. This way of doing community work, dating from the 1960s, was indicated by terms such as 'committee-community work', or 'bowtie-community work'.

In the very same period, however, action groups and various social movements mushroomed. Initially, existing community work did not know what to do with this phenomenon. To many people, it came as a surprise. In the second edition of their handbook *Community Work as a Social-agogic Method*, Van Tienen/Zwanikken (1972) mentioned 'social action' for the first time. The authors were confronted with the problem of the rapid developments that had occurred in the field of community work. Although they did not reject social action, they commented on it in a negative way and even compared it with left-wing terrorism: 'Social action as a remedy is worse than the disease it has to pass off through debate, boycott, hostage-taking, refusal of military service, squatting, bombing-raid, occupation and imprisonment'. But impulses from these social movements were gradually permeating vested interests in community work.

Later, in 1981, Paul Kuypers characterised this early community work as 'started in a period when there were not yet any fundamental social ruptures. It was a limited completion of the traditional techniques of control ...'. When the times of gradualness were over, community work was moved by the revolution of consciousness at the end of the 1960s and the beginning of the 1970s; it stretched its own image of itself in order to be able to join the scene of the intensifying societal contrasts and contradictions. (Kuypers 1981)

The 1970s: power play

Instead of the vague stimulation of participation for the benefit of recreational needs and facilities, some of this work was essentially modest. The more radical strand of community workers defined their work as organising the unorganised and supporting the neighbourhood organisations in question around (re)distribution of resources, e.g. building on behalf of the neighbourhood. The next step was that groups of neighbourhood residents really wanted to run the community agency themselves, and individual community workers often stimulated them to do so. In many cases, the field was associated with struggle, protest and conflict. Urban renewal was high on the list. The 1975 NIMO inquiry *Community Work in Urban Situations* (Raspe and van Els 1976) – an analysis of 498 projects – showed that well over a quarter of these projects related to renovation, redevelopment, maintenance, re-housing, rehabilitation and preservation.

Nowadays, the 1970s are often seen as the hectic years of community work, the heyday of oppositional practices, with the local authorities and their services as the opponent. This was only partially the case. In the analysis of the 498 projects, it emerged that the role of the local authority was positively evaluated in 100 projects and negatively in 90 projects. So, the authorities were not necessarily scapegoats in every situation. In this same inquiry, 90 community workers commented on statements about the relationship between the people and local government. Forty five per cent of these community workers agreed with the statement that 'one should unconditionally be on the people's side'; 63% thought that it was 'necessary to talk both the residents' and the local authorities' language'. And, according to a narrow majority of 54%, it was 'quite necessary to take the plans of the local authorities with respect to problem-solving into account'. These community workers seemed to have a considerable amount of 'government' in their blood.

In 1985, de Kleyn (1985) assessed the results of some thirteen neighbourhood action projects in the 1970s. He evaluated them according to the theory of the community process. His inquiry again showed how much the success or failure of neighbourhood organisations were related to the involvement of both *'street'* and *'state'*. The acquisition of material results and external support, the mobilisation of the neighbourhood, tenacity, the presence of key personalities, were the most important factors for the success of a neighbourhood action. The involvement of the government was directly or indirectly important too, for example in financial matters, and in the presence of a subsidised institutional structure.

Around about the middle of the 1970s, community work received criticism coming from an unexpected corner. The new magazine

Marge became the representative of social movements and Wolf Beck (1977) published his controversial article 'Promotion of interests by self-organisation: community work from illusion to concrete utopia'. Beck's article produced another pressure for the re-evaluation of community work. Beck used the terms 'Institutionalism' and 'incorporation' (*verstatelijking*). It would be, he argued, 'endlessly naïve to think that welfare work would be able to support the rising action groups, neighbourhood committees and the like' – a sharp reproach in the direction of community work, which was thought to be part of the street itself but which was not to be declined as partner.

The 1980s: new bridge-heads?

In the course of time community work did develop to some extent from 'intermediary' into an 'instrument in the hands of resident groups'. The new Platform Community Work, a loose organisation of local community work organisations, used this credo when it was started in 1980. Resident groups gave their instructions/demands to community work. Although this did not remove the ambiguous position of community work, the intention became much clearer. According to this perspective, community work was active in the area between '*street*' and '*state*' and considered itself the extension of resident and interest groups.

The following were judged as key priorities:
- serving resident groups and helping them to work on their collective interests and problems in their conditions of living;
- giving the necessary information to residents' groups in order for them to have an influence on decisions that concern them; and
- the organisation and building of resident/neighbourhood organisations.

The organisation and supervision of residents in processes of participation concerning welfare planning, town and country planning, and other policy sectors, were considered less important: 38% of the agencies considered this as characteristic. Community work now addressed itself to the '*street*' rather than to the '*state*'.

Other research showed that local authorities acknowledged the new view of community work as an 'instrument in the hand of residents' groups'. According to the agencies interviewed, the credo was rejected in only ten out of fifty municipalities. Now, in the mid-1980s, more attention is paid to the differences between groups in the neighbourhood. The neighbourhood is described as a myth. But it is not the fact that the neighbourhood shows so many differences that is a problem for community work or the proof that neighbourhoods no longer exist. The problem is rather how to act in this situation.

The detailed study of the fight against the establishment of the opera house in 'De Pijp' in Amsterdam illustrates, for example, the groups who were constantly claiming the so-called 'neighbourhood mandate'. Who is able to negotiate on behalf of the neighbourhood and act as representative of resident groups? (Blom and Beck 1980) This issue is often used by the defensive authorities as a counter-argument – is the neighbourhood organisation actually representative?

A fragmentation of interests is taking place at the level of the neighbourhood. Social-geographical circles – once an important source for community work – comment that the neighbourhood is 'a mosaic of separate life-styles': independent young people of 18-30, single parent, settled 30-40 year olds, families and old people. (Gastelaars 1985)

Community work occupies itself with not just merely territorial matters and therefore a sort of 'ideology of representativity' does not entirely apply here. So-called categorical or interest groups provide us with very important points of impact for community work agencies.

The most recent survey mentions as most important groups: youth and young adults, people on the dole, ethnic minorities and women. (Raspe and Vos 1984) But criticising (again) the neighbourhood conception should not, I think, result in the conclusion that the days of the neighbourhood are over. The neighbourhood provides people living in them with an important base and resources.

Recent themes: the example of the living-environment

So how can we summarise the meaning of participation and democratisation today? The following examples shed some light on recent developments.

The Dutch Union of Tenants' Organisations announced at the end of 1985 that the power of the tenants' movement had very much decreased, although not its numbers (1972 ca. 40; 1984 more than 650 organisations). After years of progress the movement has arrived at a dead-end. In the Hague, democratisation is considered a luxury of the 1960s. The cost of living (rent, fuel, and other costs) are more important than participation and democratisation. Therefore these latter issues no longer penetrate the Tweede Kamer (the Dutch House of Commons).

Apparently, we can no longer count on the national government. How about the local authorities? One would expect to have many opportunities for residents to have influence at the local level. For example, urban renewal is decentralised in the new Town and Village Renovation Act. But resident organisations have had well-founded doubts about this new Act. The old regulation still contained separate subsidies for participation, information, guidance and expert support (such as the improvement of the environment of living, information, costs involved in the preparation of plans). These regulations no longer exist in the new Act. An inquiry, carried out in the middle of 1985 among 40 out of the 164 towns with over 20,000 inhabitants showed that only a quarter of these towns have explicitly included extra money in the municipal budget. (Mekel 1985) The 'Centraal Punt Inspraak' (Central Issue Participation) did not appear to be very optimistic about the strength of the position of residents' groups in the new policy of urban renewal. There are various signs that indicate that the existing structures (Local Authorities, Housing Associations and Council Housing) are consolidating their positions at the cost of resident groups. The National Ombudsteam Urban Renewal calculated in 1985 that 19 out of the 35 larger towns – occupying 68% of the urban renewal budget – have hardly anything left of their subsidy (0.47%) for activities of residents' organisations or for expert support. (LOS-magazine 1985) This increases the distance to, and accessibility of, official institutions. However, there are also some bright spots. The 'Centraal Punt Inspraak' recently published an interesting report on the possibilities of neighbourhood control. Thinking about integral neighbourhood-directed management is still very new.

In a very few towns, residents do have a structural influence on the environment situation. Rotterdam is one of those favourable exceptions. Resident organisations and civil servants co-operate in a large-scale programme of urban renewal, a 'historical compromise' (the so-called organisations of project groups in twenty neighbourhoods). The activistic concept of building on behalf of the neighbourhood dating from the 1970s is really applied in these project groups. This co-operation between '*state*' and '*street*' is called the Rotterdam coalition model. Gerard de Kleyn (1985) thoroughly evaluated this model in terms of emancipation.

Meanwhile, 'building on behalf of the neighbourhood' appears to have progressive and regressive sides. The progressive sides become clear from the fact that people with the lowest incomes have fully benefited from renewal! The regressive sides are shown by the increasing social-cultural differences among neighbourhood residents. The neighbourhood is also a seed of disruption. Dutch people tend to blame foreigners for everything that goes wrong. The original residents often depend on the image of the 'respectable neighbourhood'. Therefore, the norms and definitions of norms and values play an important role. The progressive middle groups have made the concept of the neighbourhood too absolute. The principle of solidarity cannot cope with a multinational neighbourhood.

The magazine 'Binnenlands Bestuur' (Interior Administration) reported at the end of September 1985 that Tilburg still experiments with the so-called 'neighbourhood approach'. Inner city residents are given a 'unique right of budget' (*sic*) (what ought to be normal practice is still seen as unique). They had 35 million guilders at their disposal. Within the space of four years they can decide themselves about measures to be taken in the area in which they live. For example, the transfer of a company which is environmentally polluting, total reconstruction of streets, laying out playing facilities and green areas and small changes in the course of the traffic. These are positive development for residents' groups in the direction of neighbourhood control, although the limits within which they can decide for themselves are often tightly determined.

Interpretations for community work

Can we learn something from these developments in community work? During the 1960s, community work was justified because of the crisis in 'democracy'. During the 1970s, a justification was found in the development of solidarity with groups with little power as far as knowledge, income and conditions of living are concerned. During the following years the solidarity at the level of the neighbourhood has been put in a difficult position. Does working under new circumstances also produce new positions? What does all this imply for the role that professional community workers can fulfil? Is the state seeking to discipline and normalise, as some theoreticians propose? In short: how do the movements of the *'state'* relate to the *'street'*, and what justification of community work can result from that? Community workers are situated at the cross-roads of the system and the street, for a societal analysis remains important to their work. So what could their role consist of?

First, they are able to indicate what is important for the 'social actors' who are their clients. Of course the system needs to know what is important for 'clients' (which is, by the way, an indication that the institutions do not function). Liaison officers and manpower are needed for this. Although neighbourhoods have for the most part become technical frameworks of intervention for the system, community workers (and other social workers) can show what norms are at stake. They can have a voice in the redefinition of values such as self-help, law and order, security, neighbourhood development, a fair existence and the finances of daily life.

Second, there will always be locations or areas that need improvement because of the downward spiral of pauperisation and deprivation. Local authorities point these areas out (called 'areas where problems accumulate or areas with education priorities'). Community work can be used to tackle hard social issues such as housing improvement, improvement of education, or rents. By approaching resident-organisations, local government augments its choices. Besides the proposals of civil servants, there are always those residents. (Hillman 1983)

References

Beck, W. (1977) 'Promotion of interests by self-organisation: community work from illusion to concrete utopia', *Marge*.

Blom, M. and Beck, W. (1980) 'A palace of culture for a working class neighbourhood.' *Marge*: Issue 2.

De Kleyn, G. (1985) *The state of urban renewal*. Utrecht: Vakgroep Stadsstudies.

Egas, C. (1970) 'Community work is fundamental democratisation', *NIMO bulletin*. Gastelaars, E. (1985) 'The Netherlands, a mosaic of separate life styles rather than a harmonious community', *Welfare Weekly*, No. 9, March.

Hillman, J. (1983) 'Working together with people in Groningen', In: *Community work in the eighties*, SWP.

Kuypers, P. (1981) 'The end of the beginning', *Marge*: Issue 3, *The Struggle for the Community*: 243.

LOS-magazine, (1985). June-July, No. 6.

Mekel, R. (1985) *Survey of literature*. Central Issue Participation, June.

Peper, (1972) *Formation of social policy*.

Raspe, A. and van Els, H. (1976) *Community work in Urban Situations*, NIMO.

Raspe, A. and Vos, K. (1985) Community work in 1984, *NIMO-brochure*: No. 11.

Schuyt, T. (n.d.) *Community work and local welfare policy*, mimeo.

Van Tienen/Zwanikken (1972) *Community work as a social-agogic method*, 2nd edition: 10.

Ad Raspe teaches community work at the Netherlands Institute for Community Work (NIMO), Hertogenbosch: Vol. 22 No. 4 (1987): 287-293

15

Community Work and the State

Gary Craig

If community work is to be a force for *progressive* social change, community workers – wherever they work – need both a clear understanding of the nature of the state, the changing ways in which conflicts in society have been played out through the state, and of the opportunities presented by their own position for pursuing progressive action. In Britain now, these issues are made all the more salient by recent changes in local-central government relations which have brought the two levels of government in some areas into more or less open conflict. This poses significant dilemmas for theory and practice.

Early history

British community work's antecedents lie in two areas of activity, one domestic, the other overseas. In the domestic context, at the end of the Victorian era (which brought large-scale urban industrial development but little social improvement), a number of charitable paternalistic organisations developed such as the Charity Organisation Society and university settlements (essentially buildings located in working-class urban areas). Whilst there is no doubt that many in poverty benefited materially from these organisations' activities, it is also clear that the concern of the upper class was prompted as much by growing unease at the possibilities of social unrest as by a philanthropic desire to improve the lot of the poor. Early social legislation – particularly in the areas of health and housing – strongly reflected a fear of the spread of disease and a recognition of the need for a workforce fit to run the growing industries. (Benwell CDP 1978)

These organisations didn't see their role as helping to develop independent working class organisations: their 'community' work was highly conservative, reflecting a predominant concern with social control – although there were some notable exceptions. One London settlement actively supported strikes, encouraging trade union organisation amongst low-paid and dock labourers. Wider political developments were significant, such as the emergence of autonomous working class organisations, presaging the establishment of the

176

Labour Party, the major expression of working class demands in Parliament, and the growth of a new tier of government – local councils – which were to become the institutional context within which conflicts between the drive for social control and pressure for social reform were acted out. During the First World War, rent strikes led by women in cities such as Glasgow, linked poor housing conditions with the exploitation of workers.

Overseas, in the context of imperial economic exploitation, activity recognisable as community development emerged only in the 1930s. Following the end of the First World War, the League of Nations established the concept of self-determination for all people which generated growing interest in the role of education: '… the Colonial Office … over the years pursued research and field study with the constant aim of improving education … (This revealed) the swing away from a preoccupation with schools to concern for education for life in the wider community … educationalists turned to examine the school as an agent to assist community improvement.' (NCSS 1962: 32) Whilst, again, material and educational gains were made, the political context was one of control: gains were made *for* the inhabitants of the Colonies, not *by* them. The role of educationalists, extension workers and district officers was as agents for a colonial power concerned with maintaining political and economic power and not with promoting political and social change beyond that necessary to support the economic development of those colonies. In the Cameroon, for example, 'comprehensive programmes (were) introduced in schools to enhance collaboration between education, agriculture and health education. This collaboration was probably emphasised to enable the dependencies to increase production of raw materials in view of the world economic recession of the 1930s.' (Kwo 1984: 204) Even in those areas where extension workers could promote community development with local people, choices available concerning priorities and political direction were constrained by the colonial political context, a context increasingly challenged by the emergence of independent nationalist organisations, particularly after the Second World War.

In inter-war Britain, independent working class organisation suffered major setbacks. The capitulation of the trade union movement in the 1926 General Strike, collaboration between most of the Parliamentary Labour Party with the Tory Party in a National Government, and the effects of the 1930s world recession left progressive political forces divided. One interesting development of this time, a precursor both of the 1970s community action movement and of attempts to link struggles within the community and those at the workplace, was the growth of unemployed workers movements, comprising militant self-help organisations, active around economic and social issues.

After the Second World War

From 1945 onwards, the colonial political context changed rapidly. The growing movement for independence dominated and a range of activities concerned with social and political change occurred as it became clear that self-government would rapidly be attainable. By 1948, the United Nations offered a definition of community development which recognised the possibility of change emerging from within communities, rather than being imposed from outside. It pointed to the growth of 'community' organisations separate from government agencies: 'a movement to promote better living for the whole community, with active participation and if possible on the initiative of the community, (or) by the use of techniques for ... stimulating it ... It includes the whole range of development activities ... whether these are undertaken by government or unofficial bodies'. (UN 1953: 33)

One of the then-leading British theorists of community work, Batten, whose writing up to the 1960s was based extensively on colonial experience, developed the distinction between what he termed 'directive' and 'non-directive' methods of practice. Whilst this distinction is a real one in terms of community work methodology, his analysis was limited. In the context of the colonies, what was significant were the political auspices under which community workers were operating. All community development programmes overseas had been overseen by a colonial government. Thus the theory, as Batten (1967: v) put it, that: 'Workers who adopt this (non-directive) approach no longer try to guide or persuade. They stimulate people to think about their needs, feed in information about ways of meeting them, and encourage them to decide for themselves what they will do to meet them'. The theory underlying this approach, that people are far more likely to act on what they themselves have freely decided to do than on what a worker has tried to convince them they ought to do, soon ran up against a political and economic system based on coercion and control, however disguised. As one African leader put it:

... any humanitarian act of any colonial power towards the 'ward' is merely to enhance its primary objective: economic exploitation ... The attitude of Britain ... towards what they call 'participation' by colonial peoples in colonial government and public affairs are half-way measures ... to throttle their aspirations for complete independence ... social projects, agricultural planning, facilities for 'full participation' in government ... serve as means to ... the perpetuation of foreign rule upon colonial peoples and the economic exploitation of their material resources. (Nkrumah 1962: 27-8)

Batten's theories were nevertheless influential, as an early British attempt to construct a community work theory and methodology. As many colonial expatriates returned to join the growing British community work movement, these theories gained wide currency.

After the Second World War, the major British political event was the election of a Labour Government with, for the first time, an effective majority. This briefly heralded a period of large-scale gains for working people, particularly in the shape of the welfare state, a series of linked social programmes (education, housing, social welfare and income maintenance), representing a major shift towards the demands for social reform made by an increasingly well-organised working class alongside a recognition by the state that it needed to maintain basic welfare provision as a necessary condition for economic growth. The welfare state has a major significance for community work since it provides the context within which most community work has subsequently emerged, and around which the sharpest ideological struggles have developed.

Immediately after the war, direct community action developed around housing issues, with activists squatting in government-owned premises to protest against the lack of adequate state housing. The major type of community work undertaken in the 1940s and 1950s was, however, exemplified by councils of social service (voluntary organisations funded with grants from local councils) and community centre wardens in new housing developments who sought to stimulate the growth of social and welfare facilities. Apart from the influence of Batten and his colonial contemporaries, the major contribution to community work theory then came from social anthropologists whose findings suggested that the role of community workers should be to establish a sense of 'community spirit' where it was lacking. Community was seen as a homogeneous entity, and not, as a later writer put it, also 'belonging to capital'. The task of community work however remained incorporation. In the view of the

National Council of Social Service (the national umbrella body) in 1950, community carried 'undertones of order, cooperation, the harmonious working and development of an established system.' (Baldock 1977: 68)

By the early 1960s, a considerable volume of writing about community work (described as community organisation) had emerged from the United States, influencing British thinking and practice. The origins of US community work were shaped by different forces, particularly the impact of the immigration of workers from many different countries and cultures to a country rapidly industrializing in the early part of the 20th century. Much early American theory thus saw community work as a social welfare intervention necessary to deal with the 'unfortunate side-effects of economic development.' It was a Canadian writer, Murray Ross (1955:39), who expressed the contemporary essence of community development:

> a process by which a community identifies its needs or objectives, orders (or ranks) them, develops the confidence and will to work at them, finds the resources (internal and/or external) to deal with them, takes action in respect of them, and in so doing extends and develops cooperative and collaborative attitudes and practices in the community.

This definition, and those of other American writers who continued to fill the void in UK community work theory, continued to stress a class-less view of society, the community and, by extension, community work. Together with Batten's writings they were seized upon by the community workers of the day because they 'suggested there was a theoretical basis for their work and it set up a debate about community work as neighbourhood work and ... as ... inter-agency work.' (Smith 1979: 152)

Even the later, more sophisticated, American 1960s community organisers such as Alinsky continued, despite their growing emphasis on conflict as a tactic, to operate within a broadly consensual and pluralist view of society. (see Hanmer 1979) Notwithstanding the attraction of Alinsky's tactics to more radical organisers, and the growing influence of radical American organisers of civil rights, Black and student movements, or, at a more conventional level, the U.S. War on Poverty programmes, British community work in the 1960s was dominated by the American view that it represented a third method of social work intervention, alongside social casework and groupwork. Community workers continued to be employed largely by voluntary organisations concerned with the organisation and delivery of services and social facilities, rather than with explicitly political forms of action, although there were a few innovative community development projects such as work with London housing estates tenants by community workers which led to the formation of the Association of London Housing Estates, an autonomous tenant-controlled organisation. The form of this organisation suggested a first clear challenge to the local state from community work although much of the content of the work continued to be located within the theoretical traditions of Batten, Ross and American writers such as the Biddles.

1968: a turning point

Community work in Britain was transformed from the end of the 1960s with 1968 regarded as a key milestone. The influences which began to shape community work from that time are outlined below. By the mid-1960s, Britain had experienced 20 years of the welfare state, the system of taxation-financed universal social provision based, in theory at least, on need rather than the ability to pay. However, and notwithstanding a period generally of economic growth, it began to be clear that an increasing number of people were not only not getting the services they needed but were in increasing poverty relative to the mainstream. This recognition (in some quarters, alarm) prompted the growth of social programmes designed to reach further 'into the community'. This meant, though it was rarely stated, working class neighbourhoods, echoing the concern of the Victorian upper classes about the possibility of social unrest amongst a disenfranchised minority. At the same time, self-help organisations also emerged such as claimants' unions, autonomous groups of unemployed with a programme of demands related to securing adequate incomes.

There was a growing view that the Labour Party in Government could not be the vehicle for the far-reaching social and economic reforms required by large sections of the working class. The signs were already clear when the Labour Government, in 1948, abandoned much of its wide-ranging social programmes as a condition for receiving aid from the U.S.A. to support its policies of economic reconstruction and military expenditure. This pattern was repeated when Labour governed again in the later 1960s. Many supporters felt betrayed by the unwillingness of the Labour Party to adopt a policy of nuclear disarmament, and turned again to direct action, a strategy carried over into pioneer community projects such as the Notting Hill Community Workshop.

At a local level, considerable gains had been made by the working class, particularly in areas controlled by Labour councils. However, the experience of growing numbers of tenants, particularly in council housing, was that Labour local councils were not effectively confronting problems of urban decay in ways which responded to their (the tenants') needs. There often seemed indeed little difference between their policies and those of the Tory Party.

> Once again Labour-controlled councils trying to represent the interests of the poorly-housed found themselves building houses described as slums from when they were built ... Council housing, (in 1964), continuing the Tory tradition, was now only for those in special need, and then hit by economic crises ... public spending cuts shifted priorities not, as before, toward slum clearance policies, but away from council housing altogether ...' (CDP 1976b: 79)

In areas where Labour had generally not been in political control, the frustration of local activists was more marked. Disillusioned Labour supporters turned to other channels as a means of political expression. One activist commented: 'It was because the local Labour Party had not provided a real channel through which people could effectively challenge the controlling class interests of the Council and private capital, that a political vacuum had developed in the 20 years of the post-war period, which was a necessary condition for the growth of a strong political life outside the traditional party structure.' (O'Malley 1977: 21)

The local state came slowly to be seen not as the munificent provider of services but as an obstacle to progress. This 'strong political life' was expressed in the form of thousands of independent tenants' associations, residents' groups and independent community action organisations throughout the country, many with demands which went beyond calls for social amenities to more explicitly political statements such as programmes for the nationalisation of land or of private housing. Whilst this self-directed community action movement was rapidly expanding, there was a further set of responses, as it were, from the top-down.

> ... new approaches were needed to deal with defects in the welfare state. While much had been achieved since the war in terms of physical well-being, it was evident that state bureaucracy was often daunting and that in

its face, people often fell into an apathy that generated new problems. The immediate obvious answer to this diagnosis was that of the laissez-faire Right: there should be less of the welfare state. For many who had contributed in their political or professional life to the creation of the welfare state this was intolerable. They looked for a way out of the dilemma that ... clustered around a few key words or phrases of which the most popular was 'participation' [which] could be brought about by changes in laws and structures. But it also required that the public be educated to participate and this education could be achieved to some extent by community work. (Baldock 1977: 69)

Participation became a key concept within a wide range of state-sponsored services and the term 'community', as one commentator noted, was used as a 'spray-on additive'. Social work, youth work, adult education, planning, the law, were all encouraged to develop a 'community' dimension to their work. For a while, the interests of the state in engaging the potentially dispossessed and disaffected seemed to accord with those who were attracted by the political possibilities offered by working more directly with working class activists at a neighbourhood level. Significant numbers of new jobs were created or redefined for community work, particularly within the new unified local authority social services departments, formed from a sweeping reorganisation of local government welfare services. Just as the local state began to come under attack from community activists for its failure to deliver, it became itself a major employer of community workers as well as indirectly sponsoring the growth of community work in other ways by providing grant aid to semi-autonomous community projects. At the same time, central government also began to indirectly fund an increasing number of programmes with an explicit community work orientation, such as the Community Projects Foundation[1] which sponsored neighbourhood projects in collaboration with local councils, or law centres which adopted a community-based approach to the delivery of legal services in working class neighbourhoods.

The growth of the community work industry, as it came to be viewed, in Britain at this time was encapsulated in two milestone publications. These retained community work firmly within a pluralist view of society and attempted to reconcile the contradictions beginning to emerge at that time within community work theory by endorsing all forms of community work as equally valid including (with some difficulty) the more conflict-oriented stance of community action. Another significant development during the 1960s was the growth of race relations programmes. Black immigration to Britain after the Second World War had been accelerated by the recruitment of many Asian and Afro-Caribbean workers to keep British industry operating at a time of labour shortages. Successive British governments, however, failed to accept any major responsibility for properly meeting the needs of these minority communities: when, as one observer put it, laissez-faire discrimination gave way to overt racialism which was then institutionalised in the discriminatory provision of jobs, housing and social services, Britain's black population increasingly protested. Governments of both parties sought both to buy off dissent from the right by rapidly limiting immigration (though only of black immigrants), thus implicitly placing the blame for deteriorating conditions in many parts of the inner city areas on the black population, and to co-opt black protest by the creation of a series of organisational forms (finally emerging as Community Relations Committees), designed to contain the energy of black militants. However, conflict continued to be barely suppressed and in an attempt to resolve the growing tension between black dissent and right-wing calls for immigration control and repatriation, the Labour Government abruptly launched another major series of social programmes. These were fundamentally to affect the nature of the debates about British community work.

CDP: and after

In 1968, the Government established its own Community Development Project (CDP).

> Politicians of all colours were under pressure to meet the major threat to *social stability* which many people, drawing particularly on American experience, saw in terms of the collapse of the inner city areas. When Enoch Powell in April 1968 chose to translate this into a vision of 'rivers of blood' and linked the social threat clearly with growing coloured (sic) immigration, the Government felt it had to act. Two weeks later, the Urban Programme was announced by the Prime Minister, a programme of which CDP was to form a significant part. (Corkey and Craig 1978: 146)

There were other influences shaping this package, in particular government concern with cost-effectiveness, presaging massive cuts in welfare provision to follow within a few years and a concern which has been disguised frequently under the rhetoric of 'community care'.

The need for ever-more effective forms of social control were highlighted by the prospect of 'race riots' within the USA and the UK and open insurrection on the streets of Paris and, to a lesser extent, London. The significance of the Home Office-sponsored CDP lay in the fact that for the first time, the state (in the form of the government Ministry of Law and Order) attempted to use community work as an instrument of social control. However, the complicated set of institutional arrangements within which the local CDP projects operated offered a degree of freedom for thought and action which the Government had not anticipated. The CDP emerged as the 'largest and most controversial of all Government-sponsored priority programmes.' (Henderson 1983:7). Most controversy centred around the developing structural analysis of a group of local CDPs, which focused attention on the changing industrial and economic processes within the inner city rather than on the social pathology of the poor. It was '… an analysis of the inner city as not only the creation of a capitalist system, but also functional to it as the inner city provides an area of changing land use and value with a population who can be used as a reserve army of labour.' (Hanmer 1979: 206)

This analysis fundamentally challenged the dominant pluralist view of community work maintained throughout the whole of the post-war period and located the community worker as, as a later book was to characterise all welfare workers to differing degrees, in and against the state. (LEWRG 1979) The state's response was predictable: often with the collaboration of disgruntled local councils who had seen CDP as helping them deal with the growing problems of urban management, the CDPs were dismantled almost as rapidly as they had been established. Most local projects were closed by 1975 by which time CDP had become an arena within which two further significant debates began to emerge. The first was the increasing interest shown by community workers in linking industrial and economic struggles with those within the community; links of a theoretical and practical nature began to be drawn between conflict at the workplace, the point of production, and within the 'community', at the point of reproduction. The CDP experience sought to demonstrate that neighbourhood-based community action, set within a pluralist framework, could only achieve limited gains (often at the expense of other 'communities') particularly if it were not to be linked to wider organisations of the working class such as progressive sections of the trades union movement and political organisations. Community struggles were an important focus for change in their own right but they were also to be seen as one dimension of a broader struggle:

> ... mass action at the community level has limitations because people outside the workplace are merely consumers, not producers of goods and services provided by the state. Withholding rent, the occupation of buildings and demonstrations, do not attack the capitalist state at a local level where it hurts most – the process of capital accumulation. However such activity does put pressure upon the allocation of the surplus extracted from the working class and thus is a vital element in challenging capitalism. (North Tyneside CDP 1978: 80)

The second debate focused on the developing influence of feminist perspectives. One woman CDP worker summarised the impact that this dimension had on community work debates:

> Our concentration on the economic and class analysis of the problems of the area in which we worked allowed us to ignore important aspects of what was going on around us in the neighbourhood and in groups with which we worked - that is, at the theoretical level, the sexual division of labour and at the practical level, its implications for the way we worked with people. We talked about the people we worked with as *'tenants'* but this obscured an important reality – that they were for the most part *women*. (Remfry 1979: 188)

From the mid-1970s, community debates have reflected the ideological confusions apparent in wider political discussion, and the growing crisis of confidence in liberal democratic forms. Central government sought not to repeat the mistakes of the CDP experiment and successive 'poverty programmes' were designed to preclude any opportunities for innovative community work. At the same time, the growing economic crisis in Britain – a crisis of capital accumulation – led to further moves to cut back on welfare expenditure. Governments, both Labour and Tory, have argued that the share of Gross National Product spent on public services threatened future economic growth. Social services, housing, education and income maintenance programmes all suffered as governments sought to rechannel public investment towards private industry. This process reached a climax with the election in 1979 of a Tory government committed to 'rolling back the state', dismantling virtually all the services which comprised the welfare state. From a position in the early 1970s, where community workers frequently helped to organise and work with groups to press for improvements in housing and other public services, the situation moved rapidly to one of defensive struggle to maintain levels of service which had already been identified as inadequate.

The regulation of economic activity by the state to achieve certain social ideals has now given way to the regulation of social expectations to achieve economic goals. However, despite the threat to employment possibilities posed by the contraction of public expenditure on welfare and by rapidly growing levels of unemployment, which reached numbers unsurpassed since 50 years earlier, community work as a profession seemed to offer more and more opportunities. A survey of UK community workers undertaken in the early 1980s indicated that nearly 6,000 community workers were employed at that time as compared with probably no more than 1,000 ten years earlier. (Francis *et al.* 1984) Part of the explanation for this lay in the fact that many agencies had redesignated jobs, using the 'spray-on additive', involving little actual change in job content. A further reason was that, as the state has sought cuts in public expenditure, and stressed the savings to be gained by pursuing policies of 'community care', it has simultaneously required a layer of (low-paid) workers to implement its strategy of shifting the burden of welfare work from public collective to private individual shoulders. And also, just as the CDP experience highlighted for government and local councils the dangers of community work being allowed to operate in ways that were relatively uncontrolled by the state apparatus, so a more subtle use of community work could continue to offer opportunities for the wider task of managing deprivation and social dissent. In a prophetic piece of writing, one writer observed: 'People called "community workers" or something similar will be paid to service and in many ways to create this new system. It will be their task to manage the multiplicity of new groups and organisations which will have to be brought into being to engage the long-term structurally unemployed and to provide the new community-based social services.' (Waddington 1979: 230)

The same writer noted however that contradictions continued to be posed by the community worker's situation:

> It would be simplistic to suppose that the new system could be operated in a monolithic line-management way and its inevitable contradictions will provide locations for new forms of struggle. Alongside the quest for control from the centre, there will be struggles for control from the periphery and the grassroots. Many organisations will struggle to maintain maximum autonomy. (*Ibid.*)

These contradictions have emerged more sharply still in recent years in the context of conflict between central and local government.

Working in and against the state

The many publications emerging from the CDP experiment – and its own conflict with the governments of the early 1970s – alerted community workers most sharply to the need for a clearer understanding of the state and the implications of their own position within it. In *Local Government Becomes Big Business*, for example, CDP showed how local government, by adopting the allegedly 'value-free' principles of corporate management, had come to operate more and more *like* big business and increasingly in favour of its interests. *The Costs of Industrial Change* analysed the process of industrial restructuring throughout the 20th century, pointing to the role of the state, at local and central levels, in facilitating the reorganisation and rationalisation of private industry in the interests of private capital. *Gilding the Ghetto* provided an account of the many government-promoted social and economic 'poverty programmes', CDP itself included, which attempted to marry the conflict between 'responding to the needs of capitalism on one hand and maintaining the consent of the working class on the other.' (CDP 1976a: 63)

The central role that community struggles had to play in challenging capital, and the contradictory position of all welfare workers in those struggles was highlighted by other contemporary research.

> Since many of the issues arising in communities arise in the state services, there is a case for defining our action as anti-state struggles. But to do so deflects attention away from the mode of production, which is the real cause of exploitation. It tends to give the state too much importance and apparent detachment from the economic base. What ... we are involved in is struggle *in the field of capitalist reproduction* ... there is struggle at the point of reproduction, in schools, on housing estates, in the street, in the family ... it identifies the significance of the action of *women in the home*, in privatised reproduction ... (Cockburn, 1977: 163)
>
> The state is not neutral. It does provide services and resources which most of us need – education, health care, social security. But it does not do so primarily for the good of the working class. It does it to maintain the capitalist system ... Those of us who work for the state are inevitably part of the state. We must find ways to oppose it from within our daily activity, which means breaking out of the social relations in which the state involves us ... If we do not ... we are perpetuating a capitalist society – one which is exploitative, sexist and racist.' (LEWRG 1979: 2-3)

Community workers in the state were to be faced with even more contradictory demands in the years to follow. The Labour Government which lost power in 1979 had continued the recent relative decline of spending on social programmes, setting the stage for the most radical right-wing government of recent years, one with a commitment to rapid and massive cuts in social expenditure, and to a concerted attack on the civil liberties of the organised left in Britain. Its response to liberation movements – amongst the black dispossessed of Britain's inner cities, for example – was one of repression. Social control was now more overt through vastly increased policing as well as through the economic instrument of record unemployment levels.

By the early 1980s, it became clear that the Government's social and economic policies were not only responsible for a rapidly deteriorating situation within the urban centres, but that the legal and financial ability of local government to respond to this situation was becoming severely curtailed. By increasing financial and legal constraints on local councils, government diminished the scope of their collective services. The reaction of some progressive councils was to develop a strategy of opposition, both individually and through new alliances with other councils and progressive organisations, including sections of the public sector trades union movement, community groups and local political organisations. At the time of writing, the balance in this struggle has tilted in favour of Government, with other arms of the central state, notably the judiciary, consistently undermining the policy strategies of these councils. Levels of social and economic distress in Britain's urban centres are now greater than at any time since the 1930s, undermining the possibilities for effective collective responses.

In this rapidly changing position, community workers – in common with all welfare professions – have had to be alive to the possibilities of progressive change in increasingly complex and discouraging situations. Despite government hostility to the politics of collectively-financed public provision, there have continued to be opportunities for practising community work.

> ... the Thatcher Government has to rely on (personal social service workers), however reluctantly, as the specific effects of cuts and general economic policy work their way through to the individual crises experienced in working class people's lives. (Bennington and Leonard 1983: 30)

New temporary jobs have been creatively used to promote community organisations, in various government make-work schemes, established to obscure the true impact of unemployment; many long-standing local organisations such as the Councils for Social Service and Settlements have continued to employ community workers as have national bodies receiving significant state funding such as the Community Projects Foundation. The single largest employer of community workers continues to be local councils with perhaps as much as 40 per cent of all community workers, though very few community workers do not have part of their wage bill met directly or indirectly by the state. The 'radical revolution' of Thatcherism is, however, gradually constraining these opportunities.

Many community workers now have a heightened consciousness of the state as the arena, both at central and local levels, within which struggle continues between the interests of capital and labour (now more broadly defined to include autonomous black groups, women's organisations, community groups and movements concerned with the liberation of other oppressed groups such as gays and people with disability), and as the vehicle – dependent on the shifting political context – both for programmes by which government attempts to suppress dissent or, in recent years, for progressive action. Within the labour movement, the emergence of strong autonomous black and women's organisations has posed a challenge to the dominance of the white male leadership in all forms of political activity. Community workers have been forced to reassess their work in the light of these developments. The women's movement, for example, has not only widened the parameters of political debate by insisting on the importance of personal politics but has 'questioned the social security system's reinforcement of women's dependent status, both within the family and at work, and raised the necessity for [taking] account of women's rights to financial and legal independence.' (Lees and Mayo 1984: 192) Black organisations have led the struggle against racism in the delivery of key services such as housing, social security and the police.

By the early 1980s, many radical workers and professionals, including some community workers, took leadership roles in the local state, as councillors, senior officers and welfare workers of various kinds. The political logic of this seemed clear: that of taking control of the local state and reshaping it to service the interests of the working class. Many interesting and important initiatives were developed which reflected a more open form of community emphasis across the range of council services (the Greater London Council being the example *par excellence* with its women's campaigns, police monitoring unit and anti-racist and anti-sexist policies). These initiatives were developed in the face of open hostility from central government. Where the central state failed effectively to control such oppositional activities, it went one step further and abolished the councils altogether or ruled that their activities were illegal. Despite this opposition from government and, occasionally, from conservative town hall trade unions or professional welfare interests, sufficient interesting work around the decentralisation and community-based management or delivery of services, and community control of resources, has been achieved to ensure that these issues will remain high on local political agendas. Once again, the role of community workers will come under close scrutiny. (Gregory and Smith 1986)

A further dimension to this debate concerns the relationship between the voluntary sector as a whole and local councils. Many local councils have effectively used the provision of resources to voluntary groups (many of which are only concerned with the direct delivery of services) as a means of avoiding developing their own community development strategy. Community workers are in the position of having both to encourage independent community action as well as promote demands for these councils to develop such a strategy.

Community work theory and practice, in the light of these developments, is forced to develop more subtle understandings of the possibilities for action. One major theoretical contribution towards understanding the changing nature of the state came from European neo-Marxists.

> ... (their) sophisticated analysis of the modern state makes it no longer possible to refer crudely to the needs of capitalism nor to the working class but to recognise conflicting interests and fractions within capital and layers and fragments of a working class. The state apparatus is not a smooth, effectively controlling machine masterminded by lackeys of capitalism. Policies are inconsistent and contradictory reflecting the crisis-torn and competitive nature of capitalist economics. (Fleetwood and Lambert 1982: 53)

In situations where the local state, dependent on central government for more than half of its expenditure, is in conflict over cuts in that expenditure; where local councillors are debarred from office for pursuing policies on which they were elected; where services are reduced directly as a result of central government intervention in the face of organised opposition from local councils, it is misleading to view the state either as a homogeneous entity single-mindedly opposing the interests of the working class at central and local levels, or on the other hand as the benevolent dispenser of welfare. Nor is it adequate to regard independent community action as the only kind of community work which can properly advance progressive working class action. Recent experience of work within local councils has shown that it is possible to make gains, however marginal, through working in the local state apparatus at the same time as defending the autonomy of community groups. These gains currently appear transitory: the progressive 'municipal socialism' of a few left local councils has all but collapsed under the weight of central government attacks. But the dangers of co-optation have also become clear; increased levels of co-operation between some councils and community organisations can lead to those organisations themselves becoming part of the state apparatus.

A pluralist political framework where the state is believed even-handedly to respond to demands from different sections of the community, is insufficient for informing theory and practice. In times of economic growth, it was possible to believe that the state could meet demands from many quarters for a greater share of the public cake; at a time of deep economic crisis, the class-based nature of the state is more clearly revealed and community workers, as front-line workers engaged particularly in organising around aspects of the welfare state, are faced with ever more difficult questions of strategy and tactics and are forced to recognise that the role of the state confronts them at every turn. (Blagg and Derricourt 1982)

What opportunities can state-sponsored programmes offer for real gains to be made? What specific constraints are placed on community work by the nature of different employing agencies? What possibilities are there for new alliances between community and workplace groups, black groups, women's organisations, single-issue groups (such as anti-nuclear organisations) and so on? In what ways can the apparatus of the local state be used as an oppositional base to central government? What is the most effective kind of relationship between community action and progressive political parties? To what extent can the local state, in the hands of the Labour Party, be used as a vehicle for social reform of a progressive kind? How can community workers work with sections of local councils pursuing progressive policies when other sections are facilitating the interests of private capital? How can demands for community control of resources be reconciled with centralised mechanisms for planning the allocation of resources? These are the sort of questions which community workers need to be asking: the future of UK community work lies in a direction inexorably tied up with questions of the role of the state. These questions, for most community workers, have yet to be translated into effective action 'in and against the State'.

References

Baldock, P. (1977) 'Why Community Action?' *Community Development Journal*, 12 (2), April.

Batten, T.R. with the collaboration of Batten, M. (1967) *The Non-Directive Approach in Group and Community Work*, Oxford: Oxford University Press.

Bennington, N. and Leonard, P. (1983) 'The Personal Social Services' In: Special issue of Critical Social Policy, *Parties, Policy and the Election*, Summer.

Benwell CDP (1978) *Private Housing and the Working Class*, Newcastle upon Tyne, especially Ch.1.

Blagg, H. and Derricourt, N., (1982) 'Why we need to reconstruct a theory of the State for a radical community work': In G. Craig, N. Derricourt and M. Loney (eds) *Community Work and the State*, London: Routledge Kegan Paul.

CDP (1976a) *Gilding the Ghetto: The State and the Poverty Experiments*, London: Community Development Project.

CDP (1976b) *Whatever Happened to Council Housing?* London: Community Development Project.

Cockburn, C. (1977) *The Local State*, London: Pluto Press.

Corkey, D. and Craig, G. (1978) 'CDP: Community Work or Class Politics?' In: P. Curno (ed.) *Political Issues and Community Work*, London: Routledge Kegan Paul.

Fleetwood, M. and Lambert, J. (1982) 'Bringing socialism home: Theory and practice for a radical community action' In: G. Craig *et al.* (eds), *op. cit.*

Francis, D., Henderson, P. and Thomas, D.N. (1984) *A Survey of Community Workers in the United Kingdom*, London: NISW.

Gregory, S. and Smith, J. (1986) 'Decentralisation Now' *Community Development Journal*, 21 (2).

Hanmer, J. (1979) 'Theories and Ideologies in British Community Work' *Community Development Journal*, 14 (3).

Henderson, P. (1983) 'The contribution of CDP to the Development of Community Work' In: D.N. Thomas (ed.) *Community Work in the Eighties*, London: NISW.

Kwo, E.M. (1984) 'Community Education and Community Development in Cameroon', *Community Development Journal*, 19 (4).

Lees, R. and Mayo, M. (1984) *Community Action for Change*, London: Routledge Kegan Paul.

LEWRG (1979) *In and Against the State*, London: Pluto Press.

NCSS (1962) *Community Organisation, An Introduction*, London: NCSS.

Nkrumah, K. (1963) *Towards Colonial Freedom*, London: Heinemann.

North Tyneside CDP (1978) *Organising for Change in a Working Class Area*, Final Report No. 3.

O'Malley, J. (1977) *The Politics of Community Action*, Nottingham: Spokesman.

Remfry, P. (1979) 'North Tyneside Community Development Project', *Community Development Journal*, 14 (3).

Ross, M. (1955) *Community Organisation*, New York: Harper and Brothers.

Smith, M. (1979) 'Concepts of community work; a British view' In: D.A. Chekki (ed.) *Community Development: Theory and Method of Planned Change*, New Delhi: Vikas Publishing House.

(UN) United Nations (1953) *Report of the Mission on Rural Community Organisation and Development in the Caribbean Area and Mexico*, New York: United Nations.

Waddington, P. (1979) 'Looking Ahead – Community Work into the 1980s', *Community Development Journal*, 14 (3).

Notes

1. Originally known as the Young Volunteer Force Foundation, formed in 1968 as a voluntary service scheme for young people; a group of key staff shifted it quickly to become a community development agency.

Gary Craig is Editor of the *Community Development Journal*: Vol. 24 No. 1 (1989): 3-18

16

The Grass Is Always Greener: Political Structure and Economic Development in the United States

Peter B. Meyer and Robert Kraushaar

Introduction

The United States has served as the model for many of the economic and political policies of British government since the 1960s. Frequently, US policies appear to have been reproduced in Britain, sometimes in modified form. (Miller and Kraushaar 1979) However, the locus of control over the programmes and policies has been fundamentally altered in the trans-Atlantic conversions. Whereas in the U.S. the control over resources and their uses – if not the source of the resources themselves – is *local*, the British, especially during the Thatcher Government, use these policies and programmes to reaffirm *national* conformity. Mrs. Thatcher's claim that she has followed her 'leader', President Reagan, with regard to local economic development policy is simply false.

A review of US policies and their British analogues can thus provide a basis for exploration into the factors shaping the potential for local actions. We focus here on cities and urban centres in industrially advanced and economically powerful nations. The situations faced by smaller nations and cities and regions elsewhere on the globe are, however, analogous, especially relative to non-local (generally centralized) economic power.

Three current major British programmes have clear links to US policy. Urban Development Corporations have been primarily waterfront land re-use efforts, and are conscious imitations of such US models as the Baltimore Inner Harbor, Boston Waterfront, and Pittsburgh Golden Triangle projects. The Urban Development Grant (UDG) programme is a direct adaptation of US Urban Development Action Grants (UDAG), albeit a net improvement since it incorporates a stronger requirement that developers *justify* their requests for grants: no audit provisions such as those in the UDGs exist for US UDAGs. Industrial and Commercial Improvement Areas reflect the logic which led to massive Federal provision of funds to cities for

195

Urban Renewal in the United States in the 1950s and early 1960s. (Fainstein and Fainstein 1986)

This article first outlines US national initiatives for local governments over the last few decades. It then offers a picture of what the implications of these policies would be if carried out in full in Britain. The final issue discussed is whether the US system for addressing local economic development concerns offers a better model and what really are the requirements for its implementation.

The American model of local economic development

One of the lynchpins of Reaganite domestic economic policy has been downsizing the Federal non-defence budget. Thus the Federal role in all domestic programmes, including economic development, has decreased over time, both in real dollars spent and relative to state and local expenditures. (Stein 1986) This recent development merely highlights, however, the U.S. political structure in that the power over local public policy implementation is vested in the smallest political units in the US Federal system, and, within them, in voluntary groups.

The early Urban Renewal programmes infused Federal dollars to cities, but local governments decided on the projects they wished to pursue, subject to broad national guidelines. When these programmes fell into disrepute in the 1960s, the Model Cities and Demonstration Neighbourhoods Act combined social services and neighbourhood support with physical development, gradually weakening the restrictive government guidelines dictating local policies over time. The emergence of Federally-supported Community Development Corporations completed this aspect of devolution, as neighbourhood and ethnic organizations were granted funds for local business development, training and other efforts which only required very broad justification as to their benefit to low-income residents.

The same pattern of devolution is evident in the programmes of the U.S. Department of Housing and Urban Development. Federal funds were originally provided for specific tasks: project design, site acquisition and preparation, construction, etc. Under the Nixon administration, these categorical programmes were replaced by Community Development Block Grants (CDBG), but the funds provided to any given locality depended on its ability to propose projects satisfying central government's priorities. CDBGs have not become 'entitlement' grants for major cities: specific amounts of money are provided on the basis of a needs formula; accountability to the central Federal government is minimal.

In manpower and training areas, the Federal government has long relied on the individual counties to identify training needs and characteristics of job vacancies, and to initiate training programmes. The counties themselves have devolved powers to individual municipalities and to neighbourhood groups. Under the latest revision of manpower programmes, the Reagan Administration's Job Training Partnership Act (1981), control over employment and training powers for the poor and long-term unemployed was moved towards 'private industry councils', which include a majority of private sector (typically business) members. Private control does, however, remain local as council members must be residents of the service area for which they develop policy and programmes.

Another response to the decline in Federal dollars and direction is that the fifty states in the United States have replaced the Federal government as the major source of new initiatives for economic development. Community development finance agencies have been created to support local economic development efforts, other financial institutions set up to channel public sector capital to new business start-ups and otherwise fill gaps in the availability of business capital, and innovation support and technology transfer networks created with state support and matching funds for university-business joint efforts. (Perry *et al.*1985) These and many other new approaches have come into being as the funding for the Federal Economic Development Administration and Housing and Urban Development programmes have been cut in the 1980s.

A good illustration of this is the concept of Enterprise Zones (EZ), one of the few British ideas to have taken root in the United States. (Butler 1981) Whilst no Federal Enterprise Zone programme exists, thirty of the states have EZ legislation in place. Each programme is different, tailored to political priorities and economic needs in the individual state. Further, designation of the zones has been, for the most part, a *local* function, exercised by individual 'minor civil divisions' (MCD), the lowest level of government in the United States – which can be an area with a population in the hundreds! The devolution does not necessarily result in balkanization of efforts: the Louisville, Kentucky, Enterprise Zone, the nation's largest, spreads from the city of Louisville through a half a dozen smaller MCDs in the county, all of which co-ordinate their tax incentives and other special treatments of in-migrant and expanding businesses. Still, all decisions on the zone area and mix of incentives offered are made by local governments, within broad guidelines laid down by Kentucky state.

Local powers and programmes

Every MCD in the United States, regardless of how small it is, has full 'general government' powers. There are no non-statutory functions, and each unit has the power to implement whatever programmes it wishes, providing it can finance the activity. Taxation powers are generally broad, including some powers to tax incomes and/or sales in addition to property in most states.

State economic development programmes provide legal and financial tools for local governments to use, rather than dictating specific policies. Most states allow local governments the right to adjust sale prices on public lands, abate taxes on private property, and raise subsidized capital through independent bond issues for loans to individual businesses in efforts to attract new businesses.

The shape of public sector participation in economic development is thus determined by local government. In turn, the local governments rely on voluntary organizations and neighbourhood groups for much of their programme implementation. This reliance on non-governmental organizations can lead either towards increased democratic control over development efforts, to the extent that neighbourhood groups and community development corporations are provided access and resources, or towards greater business control over the economic development agenda, if voluntary organizations from the for-profit sector are used as the planning resource.

Americanised Britain?

What would the American model look like if transposed onto Britain? The details of local actions taken on the basis of broadened powers cannot be predicted, but the environment in which local authorities would operate would look very different:

1. At the broadest, local authorities would get full general powers to tax and spend. At the very least, local economic development would become a statutory function, and would include both business support and development *and* job training programming.

2. Expenditure limits (rate caps) would be abolished, or at least weakened with respect to economic development. In fact, the taxing

powers of counties, regions and local authorities might well be broadened to include more than the rates. Grants from Government would include minimal restrictions on their uses and would frequently require no local match or share.

3. Local authorities would have powers to borrow as they saw fit for capital expenditures, floating their own bonds on the open market. (Thus the 'big bang' would apply to public, as well as private, capital).

4. Local authorities would have discretionary control over the uses of their resources either to provide services publicly or contract with community groups, other voluntary organizations or the private sector to provide those services.

5. The Government and its agents (including the Scottish and Welsh Offices) would have minimal power to impose projects on any local authority or district, and could not override the land use and zoning controls of the local authority. Instead of the current 'stick' approach to local government compliance, Westminster would be forced to offer inducements, the 'carrot' approach, in order to implement unpopular national policies.

A solution? Some observations

This picture may look rosy indeed to local authorities whose powers have been systematically undermined by successive Local Government Acts under the Thatcher Government. (Blackburn 1984; Boddy 1984; Department of the Environment 1986) However, the US experience has demonstrated at least three major constraints to the use of such devolution of power to democratise the economy:

1. Local elites and local capital tend to dominate economic development decision-making through greater participation and 'expertise' in economics. Thus US local efforts continue to restructure in favour of capital more than in the interests of labour. (Fainstein and Fainstein 1986)

2. Often, even the local capitalists cannot control economic change processes. On the one had, this is a matter of the internationalisation of capital, which is a problem facing even the national state. On the other hand, the small size of many US MCDs and their limited financial resources and staff complements means that planning and policy implementations for economic development are unrealistic and inadequate.

3. Cities, and even states, in the United States frequently fight among themselves in attempts to lure capital to their political jurisdiction.

The result is often the underselling of public resources for private benefit.

Despite these problems, many cities and states in the United States continue to expand the range of local economic development interventions. The more activist ones use their financial powers, moving their accounts and banking activities to those banks which are committed to retaining more capital in the city. Some use their control over their own pension funds to make capital available to local firms or businesses in a manner akin to the investment decision processes in British Enterprise Boards. Others continue to explore the boundaries of how they can use Community Development Block Grants and other Federal resources, as well as their own land use control powers, to alter the relationship of commercial and industrial capital to their cities. (Clavel 1985) Boston, Chicago and Santa Monica, California are examples of cities that have linked office-building construction permissions and co-operation with UDAG applications to developer 'donations' of land or capital for other, more social, purposes within the city. (e.g. City of Chicago 1984)

In Britain, the US problems could become issues if an American system were introduced. First, on the positive side, is the very existence of Labour-controlled local authorities (and of the Labour Party itself, which has no similar presence in the United States), which increases the likelihood that local capital interests will not completely dominate economic development efforts. Secondly, the fact that local authorities have larger population bases than most US MCDs would imply more staff capacity and financial resources to define *public* economic development goals and to implement a programme to pursue them. There are severe limitations, however, to any strategy which seeks to address wider economic issues at the local, or even regional, levels. One strength of UK policy development, as opposed to in the United States, has been its focus on national initiatives and concerns over local conditions. Some of the ambivalence towards municipal socialism in Britain by elements of the Labour Party is due to differing perceptions i.e. whether these local policies are 'oppositional' or 'alternative' in nature, and, more specifically, the value of concentrating significant resources and energies at the local level. An American-style decentralized political system would only exacerbate these concerns.

Thirdly, the focus on local initiatives in the United States has the side-effect of putting significant pressure on local officials to 'solve' local economic problems. The variety of responses usually ensures that economic conflicts are redefined as local political concerns. Hence the continuing competitive efforts of states and MCDs to undercut other localities and bribe private capital into locating within their jurisdictions. (Goodman 1979) Devolution in Britain could lead to the same results.

Devolution of economic development powers is therefore most assuredly *not* a panacea. Depressed cities and local economies persist throughout the United States, despite decades of local efforts. While the grass may seem greener, a close examination of the turf reveals just as many weeds, so to speak.

Conclusion

Lessons from the American experience *are* salient to national and local policies in other economic and political contexts. First, there is the clear issue of the actual extent of local power. A nation state has capacities which even the US MCDs cannot garner, notwithstanding the real power of international firms and capital flows. The power to respond differently even within a global capitalist economic order is present.

Secondly, the hegemony of the capitalist ethos may mean that the professionals and decision-makers may be minimally inclined towards challenging the system. The clear contrast between the politics of local Labour-dominated councils and the British Parliament draws the lines well for local authority officers and others advising on economic policy. In the US, without clearly defined political differences, even those MCDs with professional staff cannot always identify their best interests and act on them.

Thirdly, the reality of external control over availability of capital remains a constraint on local initiative under the American or the British models. Given the limited national capacity to generate and control capital in many countries, the dangers of devolution within the nation-state rise above all because of the inability to exercise any meaningful control over the relations of production within the local area and the terms of trade between that area and the rest of the nation – and the world.

Politically, the American experience and structure does provide some promise, and could permit activist cities and nations to take specifically-designed local actions on behalf of their constituencies. An important benefit is that the American system has historically allowed for the evolution of new ideas that can, if successful, be implemented more broadly. Another advantage of a decentralised approach, which is of particular importance in multi-ethnic nations, is that the American model permits somewhat easier access into the local political system by disadvantaged and minority groups.

Perhaps internal conflicts within nation-states may be muted by planning for *both* diversity and unity. The political formula might involve devolving powers while constraining economic weapons available for intra-locality competition. Within a world context, implementation of this feature of the American model would require the provision of scarce resources for local 'experimentation'. The irony of this is that it would necessitate different criteria for provision of funds by international lending bodies or a willingness to 'go it alone' by some nation-states.[1]

References

Blackburn, P. (1984) 'Towards the unitary state: Tory attacks on local government', *Critical Social Policy*, 6(4).

Boddy, M. (1984) 'Local Councils and the Financial Squeeze', in Boddy, M. and Fudge, C. (eds.) *Local Socialism?: Labour Councils and New Left Alternatives*, Basingstoke: MacMillan.

Butler, S.M. (1981) 'Enterprise Zones: Pioneering in the Inner City', in Sternlieb, G. and Listokin, D. (eds.) *New Tools for Economic Development: The Enterprise Zone, Development Bank, and RFC*, Piscataway, NJ: Rutgers Center for Urban Policy Research.

City of Chicago (1984) *Chicago Development Plan*, Office of the Mayor: Chicago.

Clavel, P. (1985) 'The Local State: Hartford, Cleveland, and Berkeley under Populist Rule in the 1970s', *Community Development Journal*, 20(2).

Department of the Environment (1986) *The Conduct of Local Authority Business: Report of the Committee of Inquiry into the Conduct of Local Authority Business*, (Widdecombe Report), London: HMSO.

Fainstein, N.I. and Fainstein, S.S. (1986) 'Regime Strategies, Communal Resistance, and Economic Forces', in Fainstein, S. *et al.*, *Restructuring the City: The Political Economy of Urban Redevelopment*, London: Longman.

Goodman, R. (1979) *The Last Entrepreneurs: America's Regional Wars for Jobs and Dollars*, New York: Simon & Schuster.

Miller, T. and Kraushaar, R. (1979) 'The Emergence of Participatory Policies for Community Development: Anglo-American Experiences and their Influence on Sweden', *Acta Sociologica*, 22(2).

Perry, D.C., Kraushaar, R., Lines, J.J. and Parker, E.L. (1985) 'Ending Regional Economic Dependency: Economic Development Policy for Distressed Regions', SUNY-Buffalo Center for Regional Studies.

Stein, J.M. (1986) 'Militarism as a domestic planning issue', *International Journal of Urban and Regional Research*.

Notes
1. In reality, the independence of the U.S. state governments exceeds the degree of flexibility World Bank and IMF client states now have in the design of their own national development policies.

Peter Meyer is at the School of Urban Policy, University of Louisville, Kentucky and Robert Kraushaar was, at the time of writing this article, at the State University of New York, Buffalo: Vol. 24 No. 2 (1989): 95-100.

17

Critical Issues in Community Participation in Self-Help Housing Programmes: The Experience of FUNDASAL*

Alfredo Stein

Introduction

This paper examines the role of community involvement in FUNDASAL's site-and-service projects. It contends that it is possible to achieve efficient and effective post-project maintenance if participation is conceived as a means to empower participants. (Paul 1986; Moser 1989)[1] It starts by describing the nature and goals of FUNDASAL's community development approach, emphasising the issues by which empowerment was meant to be obtained. It illustrates how community participation was implemented during the period 1968-1985, pointing out four basic constraints to the process: the national political crisis; the conditions of the loans; the internal administrative limitations originated by the national context and the nature of the projects; and the logic and philosophy of the model itself.

There are two reasons for choosing this period. First, it is during this period that FUNDASAL conceptualized and set in action its physical and social model of non-conventional housing programmes, to be financed by the World Bank. Secondly, since 1985, this model has been revised and assessed by FUNDASAL itself and new methods of community participation are now being tested. The paper concludes that a community development model that is basically induced diminishes the scope of issue by which effective post-project maintenance can be achieved.

FUNDASAL's experience[2]

FUNDASAL is a non-governmental organization (NGO) originating in 1968 as a humanitarian response to a natural disaster that left homeless 30 families living in one of the poorest squatter areas of San Salvador. (FUNDASAL 1985a) This first pilot project of reconstruction showed the possibilities of developing a more significant and complex work which would contribute to the integral development of the community directly involved, and to support the efforts of the poor to improve their housing and living conditions. (*Ibid.*) Yet, the institution endeavoured to achieve wider social goals. It attempted to contribute to promoting structural changes in Salvadorean society through the articulation of a social force that could lobby for those changes, and through the generation of alternative models of community development. These were intended to inspire the poor and homeless to seek similar models which could be replicated by those institutions responsible for finding solutions to the problems of popular urban shelter. (Sevilla 1987)

Housing was viewed not as an end in itself but as a means for social change, providing institutional legitimacy, financial resources, and an issue which could integrate the immediate economic and broader social concerns of the communities involved. (Hart and Silva 1982: 234) Moreover, FUNDASAL never accepted the assumption that within the prevailing structure of El Salvador, the acquisition of a housing unit, whether or not by assisted self-help techniques, represented social change. The idea was to integrate housing into an action programme designed to promote greater awareness of social needs, collective responsibility and a democratic practice. (*Ibid.*: 246)

In an internal document, FUNDASAL (1980) systemized and outlined the methodology by which this process was to be achieved. Although it considered its social programme part of the general framework of urban movement demanding from the State 'a redistribution of the means of collective consumption', it pointed out that it differed from the latter in terms of the process which produced it. 'Community Development', as it was called, was an 'induced' practice which 'clearly' designed stages and not a process dictated by the urgency of the demands posed by these movements. (*Ibid.*: 19)

The following scheme was used in the majority of sites and services projects implemented from 1968 to 1985. Communities were built on undeveloped land, according to projects made by FUNDASAL, using private construction companies for the initial stages. The core housing units were completed using the mutual-help process. Communities had open spaces and areas for future community services that would be provided by the respective national and local authorities. (Hart and Silva 1982: 242) The first major phase of activity with the families was the process of participants' selection and the formation of groups for the mutual-help stage.[3] Basic information about the institution and the financial, technical and social aspects of each project was shared with the beneficiaries. (FUNDASAL 1980: 40)

Mutual-help is a social and technical process in which families work together in groups building their own houses. FUNDASAL has used it to incorporate low-income urban sectors into housing programmes and to use the experience of working in construction groups to initiate a process of communal organization. The group size varied from project to project but usually had between 25-30 families. The groups were heterogeneous in composition (i.e. female-headed households were combined with construction workers; people with different leadership characteristics and skills were put together and participants from different places were mixed). The idea was to close any possible socio-economic gap between participants from different squatter areas and tenements so that the building and educational process of all groups would have a similar pace. Before they started working, families signed a collective contract of participation in which their rights and obligations during the mutual-help process were stipulated. Participants would determine different penalties to treat those who breached the contract. (*Ibid.*)

During the mutual-help stage, families were trained for different building, organizational and social tasks. By working in groups together, without knowing which house would be assigned to each family, the future neighbours got to know each other and developed an organizational structure that would permit them to carry out the building tasks and to start a collective reflection process about broader social issues.

Once the housing units were constructed, the team of social workers, one for every 150 families (or around 5 grass-root groups), remained to work with the community to develop a viable organizational structure to assist the community and its leaders to respond to felt needs. (Hart and Silver 1982: 247)[4]

Each grass-root group would elect internally its own directive body, and their representatives to the general assembly of the community. The general assembly itself divided into working commissions and would elect an upper, coordinating body. The commissions would deal with issues such as health, education, sport, culture, finance, physical improvement, social and productive activities. (FUNDASAL 1986) At this grass-root level, a democratic practice was expected to be generated after the community settled down. It is partially through this communal organization and participative structure that FUNDASAL hoped that participants would be able to take more initiatives in terms of actions and decisions pertaining to the community, including project maintenance, and their relations with FUNDASAL and the established structures of power (i.e. government agencies and the State in general). The emphasis would be in petitions for urgently-needed services (i.e. water, electricity, garbage collection) as well as education in citizens' rights, identification of possible available resources for them (i.e. loans and credits for productive activities), and the rallying of support and solidarity for their demands amongst similar communities. (FUNDASAL 1980)

These demanding actions would be done within the 'room for manoeuvre' tolerated by the administrative bodies of the State and the political circumstances surrounding the evolution of the projects. Thus it was expected that families, on the one hand, would improve their living conditions and that of the community, and on the other hand, raise their consciousness and enlarge their negotiating power vis-à-vis the State. (*Ibid.*: 21) At this point FUNDASAL hoped to withdraw from the community, playing an occasional advisory role only at the request of the community. (Hart and Silver 1982)

Constraints to the model

According to Sevilla (1987), the implementation of these aims and methodology required finding the right balance between the following set of dilemmas, given the nature and work of the institution, and the unequal and unjust structure of the Salvadorean society. First, the short-run objective of improving the living conditions of the poor versus the long-run objective of empowering them. Secondly, developing efficient and relevant models that addressed the problem of popular housing versus assuming the responsibility for solving the problem of housing for the poor. Thirdly, finding proper ways to build beneficiary capacity versus establishing paternalistic and dependency links between the communities and the institution.

Since the first projects developed during the period 1968-1974, and then through the sites-and-services programme developed from 1974 to 1985 under a series of loan agreements with the World Bank,[5] there has been an ongoing debate within FUNDASAL about the nature of the housing projects and the role of community participation. For some, it was evident that it was possible to produce low-income housing on a scale that could help to decrease the housing deficit of the country. For others, the effectiveness of housing as a means to produce psycho-social change among the urban poor was evident. For all the potential, risks and dangers posed to the institution were clear, as the scale of the operations was expanded, not only in terms of modifying the housing problem but also the socio-political equilibrium. (Sevilla 1987)

Institutional performance during this period suggests the following. First, it showed that the model of mutual-help and progressive development was replicable at a scale that made it relevant and significant to the overall housing problem of the country. This was more evident when compared to the performance of governmental institutions devoted to low-income housing.

Secondly, it showed that it was possible for an NGO to have an impact on the provision of low-income housing.[6] However, this was misunderstood by the Salvadorean government, which was never interested in delegating responsibility of solving the housing problem to an NGO. Nor was the government interested in promoting the model itself, thus reducing FUNDASAL to the role of a government executing agency. (FUNDASAL 1980) This sometimes created confusion, especially among these project participants who saw FUNDASAL as part of the state apparatus, and an instance where it was possible to direct their demands to government.

Thirdly, by expanding its operations, FUNDASAL contributed to social change not only by transferring resources to the urban poor but also by organizing them and raising their consciousness. The experience confirmed that self-help programmes could lead to forms of social organization that could put pressure upon the state for the redistribution of resources.[7] Lastly, the increase in the volume of operations made the institution vulnerable to unpredictable financial and political changes in the environment. (Sevilla 1987) As of 1979, a process of social, political and economic deterioration has unfolded at an ever-increasing pace. This process had a substantial impact on the popular sectors and on the institutional capacity to carry out its work and survive.

The initial political changes that occurred with the October, 1979 *coup d'état*, and the ensuing closure of 'political space' and repression which occurred as of 1980 generated a brain drain in FUNDASAL that affected the highest levels of management and administration. The most experienced staff members left or were forced to leave the institution and the country. The government and other powerful political and economical sectors saw with suspicion, and faced with hostility, the work of those NGOs who, through their methods and philosophy, attempted to go beyond the mere supply of a service (i.e. housing in the case of FUNDASAL) and were pressured to abandon their long-run objectives. One area especially affected was that of social promotion, both in terms of staff and communities attended. (Silva and Altschul 1986; Sevilla 1987)

In spite of the increasing decline in the executive capacity to implement projects, and the reduction of political space to do so, personnel was maintained and, at some points during the crisis, expanded. The lack of leadership, the polarized environment, and the rapid rate of personnel turnover, led to different and contradictory conceptions as to the nature of the problem of popular urban shelter and the role of FUNDASAL's community development model. (Sevilla 1987)[8]

As Moser (1989) suggests, community development projects tend to make explicit the fundamental contradiction, at the staff level, between the technical and non-technical aspects of projects, with the economic as against the 'social', including community participation, identified as the determining project component. That is why, she argues, it is necessary to try to find a proper combination of technical expertise with social commitment.

However, in the circumstances described above, the issue at stake went beyond this contradiction. For some, the question was whether or not the moment was ripe to support the 'constitution of the social basis for other organizations that were seeking social change and the ideological neutralization of the established powers'. (FUNDASAL 1980: 18) In other words, the institution ran the danger of trespassing the delicate border that existed between a committed social action programme and political militancy. (Sevilla 1987)

In addition, labour instability generated difficulties and eventually paralyzed the execution of on-going projects, precisely the largest ones included in the World Bank's loans agreements. From a total of 1,246 units built in 1979, in 1981 FUNDASAL built only 27, a total that dropped to 14 in 1982. (FUNDASAL 1985b) This in turn led to financial problems that resulted in the exclusion of the poorest from participation in the benefits of the projects. Labour instability affected not only the projects but also the administrative staff, to the point of forcing the institution to close its entire operations in July, 1984 and to start a restructuring process in September of the same year.

The last 3,900 units of the projects financed by the World Bank were completed in 1984-1985. In total, during the period 1968-1985, FUNDASAL established 22 communities with 10,500 housing units.[9]

An assessment of the social programme of FUNDASAL

In trying to provide the criteria for the assessment of community participation, Paul (1986) and Moser (1989) propose that the fundamental issue to deal with is if the approach includes an element of empowerment or not. Although this poses the question of what empowerment means, Moser suggests that a distinction be made between participation as a means and participation as an end. Moreover, the important thing to identify is if and how projects which include objectives of participation as a means move towards participation as an end, and to identify the consequences of empowerment in the context of specific projects.

From the above mentioned experience of FUNDASAL, it is possible to add another element to the dilemma of means and ends in projects with a sound component of community participation. It is clear that housing was viewed by the majority of project participants as an end to be achieved by means of participation. Nevertheless, for FUNDASAL, housing was viewed as a means to achieve broader social goals that went beyond the mere provision of shelter.

According to an evaluation done by the World Bank (Bamberger *et al.* 1982: 180) the participants' basic aim was to obtain proper housing. At the beginning they showed no evidence of collective attitudes, and perceived the new community as a result of their own efforts, and not as a result of group's work. As the work went on, they realized the importance of organization and of working in groups for the solution of problems, while maintaining their orientation towards immediate goals – the construction of their housing. Once the mutual-help process finished, a change in attitude became apparent; most participants perceived it as a process which made it possible for them to form relationships with other persons, to solve group problems and in general felt the need to continue working in groups.

Undoubtedly, the basic educational problem of the whole process was how to make compatible the ends of the participants with the ends of the institution. The fact that objectives of empowerment were enunciated was not enough. Thus, the process of transforming the participants' ends into means became the real challenge of the whole educational process and the key to assure community involvement in post-project maintenance.

The question was, however, whether the stage-by-stage model of community participation was sustainable after years of such political, social and institutional unrest? By 1985, all the 22 communities established by FUNDASAL had gone through an organizational experience of community development. Yet, only five of them were well-consolidated in terms of their participative, administrative and post-project maintenance process. (FUNDASAL 1986)

Basically, these five communities had their central commissions functioning and the communal leadership at all levels was recognized as representative of the interests of the grass-root groups. Community leaders were able to plan and evaluate their own work and had the power and ability to negotiate with different state agencies. It was possible to identify high levels of commitment and solidarity by representatives and grass-root groups, especially regarding the installation of new infrastructure and basic services, as well as road and internal path maintenance, self-help housing consolidation, garbage collection, new projects of income-generation, the introduction of self-managed health clinics and a continuous programme of sport and cultural events. FUNDASAL's role was to provide collateral, giving guidance and technical and social assistance only in those areas demanded by the community commissions. As a rule, it was possible to identify in these communities an existing relationship between efficient post-project maintenance and an active process of functioning of the representative bodies and an effective intra-and inter-communal process of discussion.

The other seventeen communities, however, showed regressive symptoms in terms of this process or were starting more slowly than expected to consolidate their communal structures after the mutual-help stage. There was little consciousness among community leaders about the need of an autonomous organizational structure capable of being responsible for negotiations with governmental institutions for the provision of the missing infrastructure and services (especially water, health and schools). In general, the leading communal commissions, although active, did not have clear plans of activities and forms of self-evaluation. The majority of administrative chores related to the collection of payments or decisions about rental or transfer of property titles authorizations were done by FUNDASAL's staff without communal involvement. Moreover, communities were still very much dependent on the institution and its resources, and not once did FUNDASAL become the target of their demands when it was very clear that the state was responsible for fulfilling them. (FUNDASAL 1987)

An evaluation of the social programme pointed out that massive projects implemented under a fixed framework of financial and implementation timetables as required by the World Bank, were ineffective to achieve broader social goals, especially the ones related to empowering participants. This, combined with the community development model sometimes adamantly induced, created a scheme not flexible enough to meet the changing political context, and reduced therefore, the issues by which participation could actually affect urban policies.

Moreover, the role assumed by the social workers in this type of projects amid the ongoing social crisis in El Salvador, contributed to exacerbate the problem. On the one hand, the close coexistence of social workers with the projects allowed them a better understanding of the general and specific problems of the communities, but on the other, it created very strong unilateral ties of dependency between the communal structures and the institution.

To a large extent, through the social worker, FUNDASAL controlled, and was present at, almost any important decision the community took in terms of its consolidation and post-project maintenance. The fact that social workers accompanied the whole project process, from the participants' selection, to the later stages of communal consolidation, forced it to increase the number of workers with every new project. In spite of the growing difficulties of doing field-work due to the closure of 'political space', no real mechanisms of follow-up were established.

In addition, the process of selection, training and evaluation of the social workers became very lax. A clear distinction between what were the administrative and educational chores of the social worker was not always clearly made. The educational process which was meant to train project participants to acquire new skills and abilities at the material and organizational levels, and to raise their consciousness about the social reality, was not fully comprehended by the social worker.

On the one hand, education was understood as a process of transmitting mere information to participants about the administrative and bureaucratic steps necessary to obtain resources or other technical services from FUNDASAL. On the other, some social workers were more interested in responding to the necessities of the political process, and did not take into consideration the conditions, readiness and needs of the participants themselves. (FUNDASAL 1985b) Some social workers were reluctant to conciliate elements of effectiveness and efficiency with broader socio-political goals. Others regarded the efforts of improving the housing and material conditions of the urban poor in the context of a civil war, as a demobilizing factor that impeded the radicalization of the *status quo*, rather than as a means for social change. (FUNDASAL 1979) These perceptions were exacerbated by the above-mentioned fact that not once did the government attempt to change FUNDASAL's role to a sort of efficient semi-autonomous executing agency of low-income housing.

Accordingly, empowerment was confused with the ability of the communal organizations to handle resources and efficiently execute the building time-tables, or simply as to how much participants were willing to act on political issues, not necessarily related to settlers' needs.

Even though the institution had a different theoretical approach to the problem, the educational experience carried out during the period 1979-1985 lacked the critical elements that could lead to more appropriate self-managed communities. By the end of 1984 it was clear that FUNDASAL needed to update its notion and conception of the poor so that the concepts of mutual help and community development could be applied in the new conditions created by the national crisis. (Sevilla 1987)

From the beginning of 1985 to the end of 1987, FUNDASAL went through an administrative restructuring process aimed at redefining its social and managerial models of work. It became evident that it was necessary to adopt a modern and flexible management system capable of reading and understanding the changing environment of the Salvadorean society. New participative techniques and projects were started with the displaced population affected by the civil war, and victims of the earthquake that shook San Salvador in 1986. Slum and squatter settlements' upgrading and renewals were initiated although the site and service scheme was maintained. During the period 1985-1987, the institution started to develop a total of 7,000 housing units and established relations with more than 350 communities in the main cities of El Salvador. All these activities were undertaken with only one third of the staff it had during 1979. The establishment of a community leadership training school in fields such as health, productive programmes and community administration strengthened the relations with the communities and gave FUNDASAL the possibility to multiply the impact of its work without increasing the number of staff.

It is still early to assess the impact of this new methodology, but it has confirmed that empowerment is not necessary a linear and stage-by-stage induced process, to be replicated automatically without any thorough analysis of the national and institutional context, and more important, without a careful examination of the needs, characteristics and readiness of participant families to engage in this type of project.

Conclusions

FUNDASAL's practice shows that it is possible for an NGO to replicate self-help housing programmes on a large scale, and to make them affordable for urban poor families, while maintaining as Turner (1988) seeks, its 'community enabler character'. It confirms that it is possible to generate models of participation that help to achieve high levels of cost-recovery, project efficiency, and effective post-project maintenance. Yet, it simultaneously illustrates the dilemmas, contradictions and constraints that an NGO has when it uses non-conventional housing programmes with a strong component of community participation, as a means to achieve broader social goals in unjust societies and repressive regimes.

The experience confirms, on the one hand, the need for greater caution in the design of large high-profile participatory projects, especially under these types of regime. (Moser 1987) On the other hand, it implies that a working model, to be successful, requires a minimum of internal institutional cohesion and coherence, as well as of political space and tolerance. (Sevilla 1987) In this sense, the community development model has to remain within the delicate moving bounds that separate social action from political activism.

Finally, the experience exposes the difficulties of implementing an educational process meant to close the gap between those who 'think' and those who 'execute'; between those responsible for the technical and social advance of development projects and the participants themselves. An induced process used in a rather dogmatic way can become contradictory with the aim of endowing participants with a set of criteria that can help them to discern and choose their goals, methods and ways to improve their living conditions and to struggle for social change. Moreover, the stage-by-stage process of community development, employed rigidly in a moment of social and institutional turmoil, can prevent the articulation of other forms of organization and participation that can allow new experiences in terms of post-project maintenance, the expression of settlers' demands and the possibilities of effective negotiations of the communal bodies vis-à-vis the State and other institutions. This calls for a permanent institutional capacity to read and interpret the reality in which it operates and to train and educate its staff and the communities to do so.

References

Bamberger, M. *et al.* (1982) *Evaluation of Sites and Services Projects: The Evidence from El Salvador,* World Bank Staff Working Papers No. 549, Washington: World Bank.

Bamberger, M. and Hart Deneke, A. (1984) 'Can Shelter Programmes Meet Low-income Needs? The Experience of El Salvador', in G.K. Payne (ed.), *Low-income Housing in the Developing World*, UK: John Wiley & Sons Ltd.

FUNDASAL (1977) *Synthesis of the Results of the Evaluating During the First Two Years, and Definitions of Research Priorities for the Coming Years,* Socio-Economic Evaluation Unit, Report No. 15, San Salvador.

FUNDASAL (1979) *El Desarrollo Comunitario: un mecanismo de integración o un frente de lucha?,* San Salvador: Equipo de Cambio Social.

FUNDASAL (1980) *Hilo Conductor del Trabajo Social qui Realiza la Fundación Salvadoreña de Desarrollo y Vivienda Minima*, San Salvador: División de Acción Social.

FUNDASAL (1985a) *Memoria de Labores, 1984*, San Salvador.

FUNDASAL (1985b) *Lineamientos para la Reestructuracion de la Fundacion Salvadorena de Desarrollo y Vivienda Minima*, San Salvador.

FUNDASAL (1986) *Memoria de Labores, 1985*, San Salvador.

FUNDASAL (1987) *Proyecto de Co-financiamiento para Apoyar y Fortalecer el Trabajo Social de FUNDASAL*, San Salvador.

Hart Deneke, A. and Silva, M. (1982) 'Mutual-help and Progressive Development Housing: for What Purpose? Notes on the Salvadorean Experience in Self-help Housing', in P. Ward (ed.) *Self-help Housing – A Critique*, Oxford: Mansell.

Keare, D.H. and Parris, S. (1982) *Evaluation of Shelter Programs for the Urban Poor, Principle Findings*, World Bank Staff Working Papers No. 547, Washington: World Bank.

Laquian, A. (1983) *Basic Housing: Policies for Urban Sites, Services and Shelter in Developing Countries*, Ottawa: International Development Research Centre.

Moser, C.O.N. (1989) 'Community Participation in Urban Projects in the Third World', *Progress in Planning*, 32 (part 2).

Paul, S. (1986) *Community Participation in Development Projects: The World Bank Experience,* (mimeo), London.

Sevilla, M. (1987) 'The Private NGO's in Institutional Change: Lessons from El Salvador', Presented at the World Bank's meeting *Lessons from the Past and Directions for the Future,* Hot Springs, Virginia, (mimeo), El Salvador.

Silva, M. and Altshul, F. (1986) *Programas de Lotes y Servicios y Desarrollo Comunal, Un Estudio de Caso: FUNDASAL, El Salvador.* (mimeo), Washington.

Stein, A. (1988a) *Monthly Payments and Family Income: its Limitations in the Participants' Selection Process for the Housing Programmes of the Salvadorean Foundation for Development and Low Cost Housing (FUNDASAL): 1968-1985,* Unpublished M.Sc. Seminar Paper, London: DPU.

Stein, A. (1988b) *Critical Issues in Community Participation in Self-Help Housing Programmes Financed by the World Bank: The Experience of FUNDASAL,* Unpublished M.Sc. Seminar Paper, London: DPU.

Stein, A. (1988c) *A Critical Review of the Main Approaches to Self-Help Housing Programmes,* Unpublished M.Sc. Dissertation. London: DPU.

Turner, J. (1988) 'Conclusions' in B. Turner (ed.) *Building Community,* London: Building Community Books.

Notes

* FUNDASAL is the Salvadorean Foundation for the Development and Low-Cost Housing.

1. This paper follows Paul's (1986: i) understanding of empowerment in community development projects as the equitable sharing of power and the process by which weaker groups acquire higher levels of political awareness and strengths. Reviewing more than forty World Bank financed projects with an element of community participation, Paul concluded that only three had empowerment as an objective; two of them were implemented by FUNDASAL in El Salvadore. (Paul 1986)

2. For articles in English about FUNDASAL's housing programmes see FUNDASAL 1977; Bamberger *et al.* 1982; Hart Deneke and Silva 1982; Keare and Parris 1982; Laquian 1983; Bamberger and Hart Deneke 1984; Sevilla 1987; Stein 1988a, 1988b and 1988c.

3. For details about the selection process see Bamberger *et al.* (1982) and Stein (1988a).

4. This number also varied according to the project. In Popotlan I, the last to be financed by the World Bank in 1985, there were about 500 families (17 grass-root groups) for every social worker.

5. In 1974, FUNDASAL, with the support of the Government of El Salvador, entered into a series of loan agreements with the World Bank. The resources provided by the Bank totalled US\$18.7 million, and were conceived to provide 15,000 sites and services with partially-built units.

During 1974-1979, the institution developed a total of 8 housing projects equal to 4,179 units, averaging 786 annually. (FUNDASAL 1985b)

6.From 1975-1985, FUNDASAL produced 75 per cent of the total output of 'formal' low-income housing in El Salvador with costs below US$2,000.00. (Stein 1988a)

7.Silva and Altschul (1986) argue however, that in spite of the success of the site-and-services programmes, they did not achieve any national redistribution of resources due to the fact that the majority of funds came externally from the World Bank or were provided by the community through their participation in the building process.

8.Staff grew from 37 to 195 persons during the period 1974-1980, and from 1979 to 1984, three out of every four persons working in the institution were replaced or forced to abandon it. (FUNDASAL 1985a)

9.Six communities were established with soft funds provided by USA and European private NGOs and internal resources; ten communities with 9,300 families with World Bank loans; and six communities for displace families, victims of the civil war, with grants given by European NGOs. (FUNDASAL 1986)

Alfredo Stein was, from 1985-7, Assistant to the Executive Director and Chief of the Planning Unit of FUNDASAL: Vol. 25 No. 1 (1989): 21-30.

18

Will Politically-Inspired Community Work Be Evident in the 1990s?

Jane Dixon

In this article I briefly review what commentators have said about whether the politics of individual practitioners actually influence the practices they adopt, thereby influencing outcomes. I then describe original research reinforcing the argument that no such congruency exists, at least for radical workers. This finding calls into question the idea that a range of social changes result from community work interventions. On the basis of my and others' empirical work, I argue that the barriers to radical community work are such that community work's major impact is to strengthen pluralism whilst making minimal contributions to more fundamental social change.

Practice and ideology congruency

The proponents of an ideology-practice congruency
In 1975, the Association of Community Workers (ACW) asserted the impact of personal ideologies on methods of community work. In a manual on community work skills and knowledge the Association stated that the ideology of the worker will influence which groups a worker does and does not support and the strategies endorsed by the worker. It suggested that what workers do, as well as what they refused to do, was an indication of their political inclination. Using similar ideological labels to the ACW – conservative, socialist, liberal and anarchist – Lambert (1978: 3) affirmed that 'it should be apparent that different political beliefs or positions provide different justifications for different styles or methods of community work practice'. He argued that radical workers exist and are 'involved in [the] social exposition of capitalism'. (*Ibid.*:14) An Australian academic Rosamund Thorpe (1985) created a model similar to, but more detailed than, that of the ACW. She proposed three major ideological positions: structural, pluralist and consensus, suggesting that certain practices accompanied each position.

The articulation of broad theoretical distinctions behind alleged radical and conservative practices was a feature of another Australian contribution to this debate. In examining the impact of feminist and

218

leftist ideological thought on community work, Creed and Tomlinson (1984) asserted that a difference does indeed exist between leftist and feminist practices and practices of a more liberal persuasion. However, because of their reliance on sweeping generalisations, Creed and Tomlinson's formulation of a politics-practice congruency, like that of the ACW, Lambert and Thorpe, is easy to dispute. First the inclusion, or otherwise, of strategies and practices under the various ideological headings appears to be made on ad hoc bases which are rarely explained. A notable example is Thorpe's omission of self-help from the list of strategies used by feminist/socialists when self-help is a common feature of feminist community work practice descriptions. (Dixon *et al.* 1982; Wannan 1986) However, the most significant problem with each of the cited works is an absence of concrete examples of change-oriented community work. For whilst Thorpe claimed that 'a socialist political strategy within welfare work – be it casework or community work – is quite conceivable' she did not give any evidence of the actual practice of socialist strategies. Similarly whilst Creed and Tomlinson nominated progressive practices, such as 'freeing of creative force and people control' and 'mass mobilisation', they did not attempt to illustrate when and how these practices have been manifested by community workers.

With the case for choosing between, and adopting, particular practices being relatively unproblematic for the ACW, Thorpe, and Creed and Tomlinson, the reader is left with the feeling that practitioners play a key role in social change outcomes. By not being specific about different political orientations and by not undertaking empirical studies of actual practices, a particular vagueness permeates many of the arguments regarding politically-informed community work.

Arguments against the existence of a politics-practice congruency
While most authors agree that so-called liberal community workers adopt consensual strategies and achieve liberal reforms, the disagreement arises in the area of congruency between Marxist and other structuralist analyses and socialist and radical practices. This debate is further complicated by the issues of potential and actual congruency: that is, what workers desire to practice and what they have ended up practising.

Arguments against the existence of a politics-practice congruency generally come from two quarters. The first consists of various groups which have adopted a logico-deductive position. These groups include those who argue that radical community work does not exist because there is no mandate for such work (Thomas 1983), and from socialists who argue that socialist community work practice is a logical impossibility given the nature of 'community' (Repo 1971; Kraushaar 1979) or highly improbable given the class position and training of community workers. (Corrigan 1975; Van Moorst 1983) The other major group comprised researchers who argue that there is no empirical evidence of a unique socialist or radical practice (Specht 1976; Bryant and Bryant 1982; Barr 1987) and from practitioners who describe in case studies the gulf between desired and actual practices and outcomes. (in Craig *et al.* 1982; Falappi *et al.* 1984)

Corrigan's work (1975) was characteristic of the early socialist position which used logico-deductive reasoning to surmise that socialist community work did not exist. Although Corrigan proposed that most community workers in Britain in the early 1970s were 'disaffected left-inclined' he argues that they did not exhibit a socialist practice because they were forced to work in ways contrary to their beliefs. In light of their class analysis being

> *useless to them in terms of their day-to-day activities in the field ... they turn to the tactics taught in community work education: non-intervention; crisis and conflict creation; policy change; group consciousness raising.* (Corrigan 1975: 65)

Equally pessimistic conclusions have been arrived at by many practitioners who analyse the impact of their own work on social change. One useful piece came from Mary Lane (1985) who commented that after six years of community education and development in Western Sydney she was unsure how much residents had gained in terms of resources and power. The reflection upon her practice coupled with her political inclination to 'achieve lasting social change' led her to desire to adopt different practices. However she resigned once the constraints on doing so seemed immovable.

Empirical studies of groups of community workers have depicted much radical rhetoric but a paucity of radical community work practice. For example in the last ten years, Bryant and Bryant (1982), Rigby (1982) and Barr (1987) have all undertaken original research which reveal the tenuous existence of radical and socialist practices.

In a recent article in this Journal, Barr (1987: 14) described the results of interviews with one in two workers employed by the Social Work Department of the Strathclyde Regional Council and found that 20% of workers 'associated themselves with the radical community action' label. Upon analysing their diaries, he reflected that some community workers' 'radical' self-images were misplaced:

in content the work tends toward non-controversial areas of securing material or financial resources for community-based service provision. Though issue-based campaigning work with community groups is being undertaken, its lack of extensiveness is noteworthy. (Barr 1987: 16)

An earlier study in Glasgow described the difficulties of implementing 'radical' strategies from a state-sponsored service and within a context of the agendas of local politicians. The authors concluded that what they found being practised between 1970-1978 was indeed the more radical community action, albeit not of the type supported by the 'radical left'. Rather it was characterised by an emphasis

... on grass-roots organising and intensive neighbourhood work; the uneasy ideological mixture of socialism and libertarianism; the commitment to learning through collective action and a scepticism of abstract theory; the focus on issue-centred groups and the mistrust of political parties and established organizations. (Bryant and Bryant 1982: 209)

According to Bryant and Bryant, the lack of a class-based analysis coupled with the promotion of pluralistic social services endemic in the above description fostered trenchant radical left objections to this type of community action. However, the Bryants reported that 'there were no clear cut examples of community projects which explicitly embodied a radical left approach'. (*Ibid.:* 218).

Barriers to politically-inspired practice

The research background
Western Sydney is a rapidly growing metropolitan region of New South Wales. In recognition of the socio-economic disadvantage of the region's 1,100,000 residents, the State government has since the late 1970s targeted the area with many community-based programmes. In 1986 the organisation Community Workers in the West estimated that two hundred and fifty community workers were employed by these programmes. In that same year I conducted lengthy interviews with nine of these community workers to assess whether they believed that they could undertake politically-motivated community work practices. The workers ranged across the political spectrum and included two self-proclaimed communists and a socialist feminist, one whom I called a radical feminist because of her suspicion of both socialism and capitalism, three workers who espoused a commitment

to social justice and two whom I judged to be liberal democrats.

I found that the desired outcomes of the more radically inclined were circumscribed by a lack of support from constituents for the worker's vision, by bureaucratic interference, inaction due to fear of loss of state sponsorship and an absence of strategy. Certainly my data does not reveal a strong relationship between the practices actually adopted and a practitioner's political inclination. Perhaps because of the paucity of strategically applied practices there appeared to be little relationship between strategy and outcomes.

Three barriers to the exercise of politically-informed practices were isolated. The three factors which are interrelated and which influence practices are the worker's perception of a mandate, the appropriate resources and structures to enact certain strategies and the room to manoeuvre for government-funded organisations and community workers.

Perceived mandate for action
Personal attributes such as political ideology and length of time as a community worker did not appear from the study to play a major role in the practices actually adopted by community workers. Instead, a worker's perception or estimation about what government bureaucrats, the employing body and other constituents, like residents' groups, would and would not tolerate appeared to be important to the practices adopted by community workers.

The more radical workers in the sample attributed their paucity of radical practice to 'conservative' residents, community work professionals and government policies. The less radical workers talked of 'apathetic' residents and the difficulties of encouraging participation. All described the feeling of working in relative isolation from people who supported their particular visions. All but one expressed a desire for greater direction from residents and community interest groups. In short, the inability to practice in desired ways seemed to be attributed to the inactivity or hostile activities of significant others. Most of the workers believed that their mandates were unclear – statements like 'to encourage community development' or 'ensure adequate community services' could mean a variety of strategies and outcomes. In light of this vagueness the community workers suggested that they acted in accordance with their summation of their constituents' predisposition for action. This was frustrating for the majority, including the more liberal workers, because they believed that the constituents' relative deprivation would logically lead them to desire stronger and more purposive actions from community workers.

Peter Marris' work (1987), evaluating a decade of community action in Britain offers a possible explanation for the lack of direction or support for today's community workers. Marris described that during the early 1970s there was a broad consensus from a large constituency about the nature of reforms which were required to counteract the social problems of the day. However, as the decade continued 'the social ideals [the constituency] shared were disintegrating'. (Marris 1987: 3) As the policies which embodied the ideals failed, the ideas tended to be discredited too. This has meant that radical workers, in particular, have lost supportive constituencies over the last decade, thereby creating an unreceptive climate for certain of their practices.

The implications of the demise of a shared vision for community work practice and outcomes are many. The most obvious relates to strategy formulation. There are occasions when the mandate for action can appear to all concerned to be straightforward, the most simple case being where a community group adopts unquestioningly the funding body's guidelines and employs a worker who uncritically, or even critically, adopts the employer's directions. I found three instances of this with the result that the workers were relatively satisfied with outcomes, even though they each wished for more constituent direction and to play less of a leadership role. In other words, they were pleased with the short-term outcomes but desired different long-term outcomes – like enhanced participation and consumer control over services.

Any situation which does not reflect a common understanding of ends and means could result in 'dilemmas of work orientation' – a term taken from Benson's (1983) work on organisations. These are the situations likely to result in community workers, irrespective of political inclination, adopting practice in unstrategic ways with the resulting outcomes either having impacts on social change not desired by the worker or of having conflicting impacts. From the more radical workers it was evident that some of their practices could result in outcomes which contribute to the transition to socialism while others would reinforce capitalism.

Available resources, structures and opportunities

All of the research participants mentioned the centrality of available resources, structures and opportunities to their adoption of particular practices. Hindess (1986) has used the term 'means of action' to denote this idea. One finding from the field research was that no matter what degree of critical analysis a worker brought to the job if 'the means to act' were absent, either because they had not been developed or because of the repercussions of their use, then desired practices and outcomes were curtailed.

The 'means of action' mentioned by the research participants included the existence of a politically progressive umbrella organisation, in this case the Coalition Against Poverty and Unemployment, as a front for their political work; the usefulness of action-research in contacting residents; the relative ease of establishing self-help groups which in turn could empower individuals; the use of community management committees to impart skills and give some control over resources, and community workers' networks for lobbying purposes. An absence of 'means of action', rather than their presence, was more meaningful in shaping practices of the more radical workers and a conservatising force on the practices which were ultimately adopted by them. As a consequence, radical workers' practices resembled the practices of their more conservative peers and sponsors.

Ironically, despite Australia's unique history of union-resident alliances in the late 1960s and early 1970s (Mundey and Craig 1978), one 'means of action' conspicuous by its absence was community work's links with the trade union movement. Both communists stated that their next effort would be in trying to secure such alliances, both as protection for their own actions and as providing a mass movement to defend and extend community services. This is in keeping with the point made by Fleetwood and Lambert (1982) and Jacobs (1984) that community politics, or locality-based power struggles, are relatively ineffectual without links to class-based struggles. Thus when a dialogue between community workers and socialist groups is missing, radical community workers are denied a very valuable 'means of action'. Fleetwood and Lambert (1982) wrote that community politics removed 'from socialism, denied legitimacy by the labour movement … has tended to be small-scale, cautious, uncoordinated and individualistic'.

A good working relationship with state sponsors appears another potent resource. This point was highlighted by comparing the situations of the two communist workers. One worked for an organisation which made use of existing channels of influence and had the support of politically sympathetic bureaucrats. Indeed one of the bureaucrats sought the organisation out when wanting a particular government policy protected. The organisation was able to retain state funding whilst adopting openly a 'social action' role, which allowed the worker to undertake contestual strategies. In contrast, the other worker was part of a collective which had little or no support from any organisation or powerful person. The worker talked of a class analysis and of contestual strategies and alliances with the trade union movement while deriding volunteerism, community management, welfare networks, lobbying and policy consultations. In other words, he saw most community organisations as branches of the state and as not sharing the interests of the working class. However, after several clashes with a senior bureaucrat he had adopted a limited service delivery practice. The organisation and worker had been rendered inactive because of its and his antagonism to the gains able to be secured through existing bureaucratic and resident processes and forums.

In another study of community workers, Rigby (1982: 50) showed that:

> [as] *in most unequal relationships, the exercise of power only becomes manifest when the subordinate transgresses the often unspecified parameters established by the dominant party … the acquisition of such knowledge can, of course, be used as a basis upon which the community worker can proceed to limit his or her activities in accordance with managerial wishes.*

Logically it is possible to deduce that once workers are denied the exercise of certain practices, and their actions conflict with those in more powerful positions, they are likely to react differently to the way identified by Rigby. If the analysis is conducted with politically-aware and supportive others the chance exists that the contradictions inherent in community work positions will become manifest and some may try and develop means to exploit the contradictions. The building of alternative means of action like 'counter hegemonic' institutions or the exercise of processes which prefigure socialism and feminism may result from the reassessment. (LEWRG 1980; Bolger *et al.* 1981)

Room to manoeuvre

The field research confirmed earlier studies highlighting the role of the state in shaping community work practices. (LEWRG 1980; Craig *et al.* 1982; Mowbray 1984, 1985) More specifically, it revealed that government sponsorship operated in a dialectical manner to influence outcomes. Not only did the anticipated reactions of politicians and bureaucrats act as a brake on the adoption of more conflictual strategies but some state policies could be exploited for redistributive purposes.

The concept of 'room to manoeuvre', or the contest between the economy, community groups and the state to win greater concessions and power over one another, was shown to be significant to practice adoption and potential outcomes. Citing Benington's concept of 'carving out a space', Bolger and co-authors defined, at the beginning of this decade, the room to manoeuvre as that 'which will be determined by the politics of the way in which social democracy tries to resolve its contradictions at any particular point in time'. (Bolger *et al.* 1981a) They added that the room to manoeuvre constitutes a set of forces largely outside the control of the community workers and a set of forces which 'greatly determine the possibilities of progressive practice'. (*Ibid.*: 142) Although the authors did not totally dismiss as relevant 'the politics which the community worker brings to the state job and to the locality', they asserted that the relationship of the struggles within the state with class struggles will determine the nature of any progressive practice. (*Ibid.*)

A 1982 report from the Australian Social Welfare Research Centre highlighted the role of bureaucratic interference in relation to the exercise of discretion available to funded groups. When State and Commonwealth public servants were asked their expectations towards funded organisations they responded that accountability was their pre-eminent concern and that funded non-government welfare organisations (NGWOs) should abstain from criticizing the funding body. (Graycar 1982) However, the lack of accountability criteria and procedures meant in effect that little systematic state control was exercised. What this situation did allow for was enormous use of bureaucratic discretion.

Unlike the free hand offered to well-established charities, Graycar (*Ibid.*: 58) found greater bureaucratic interference towards relatively powerless 'community-oriented NGWOs, particularly those which work from an oppositional stance and concern themselves with self-help, consumerism, information and advocacy'. The fear of negative reactions from the funding sponsor in relation to actions by the funded body do seem, from at least three of the research participants, to have weighed heavily in the consideration of which practices they adopted. In other words the threat of withdrawal of patronage is an influence on the mandate given by employers, and adopted by workers.

Liberal eclecticism and pragmatic radicalism: A confusing scenario of pluralism and social change

If, as Marris (1987) asserts, the way social problems are conceived is crucial because conceptions 'give rise to new assumptions and new inhibitions of social action', then the adoption by an increasing number of community workers of no single social change theory, but a range of theories, may have an unfortunate effect. This is not only to render matters of strategy utterly confusing, but to reinforce the pursuit of pluralist solutions. Certainly, confusion over matters of strategy was readily evident in the interviews with more radical community workers in my study. Unlike the liberal community workers, who each could readily nominate 'priorities' for action to achieve their desired reforms, the socialists and feminists mentioned that a major constraint to their achieving desired outcomes was an 'absence of strategy.'

A plethora of social change possibilities has developed since the 1960s' 'time of ferment'. (Brager and Specht 1973) Community work outcomes as diverse as the transition to socialism or a more benign capitalism or a feminist social democracy are all apparently feasible from reading about community work's potential. Moreover, the early practice traditions described in socio-historical accounts (Baldock 1977; Garvin and Cox, 1987) are no longer valid as community development is harnessed for socialism and community struggle adopted to modify capitalism. Whether community work's potential in the former situation can be realised is questionable because of the barriers described earlier. The interrelatedness of the barriers makes then even more difficult to overcome.

Whereas Marris has described the demise of more radical visions over the last decade, Barry Hindess' work (1986) on 'interests' and 'actions' can be used as one explanation for why this demise has occurred. Hindess argues that the actions and potential actions available to groups shape what they perceive to be meaningful, possible and in their best interests. In other words, actions shape visions for change just as particular visions dictate the actions or strategies to adopt. There is a symbiotic relationship between actions and an assessment of benefits. From this point it is possible to argue that given the present limited opportunities for struggle, without incurring punitive state intervention, groups undergo a censorship of what is possible and socially just. The field research certainly supported the proposition that most residents' groups did not subscribe to similar assessments of benefits with community workers, thereby constraining the community workers in the practices which they believed they could adopt.

Searching for evidence of radical workers able to implement radical strategies led Kraushaar (1979: 63) to argue that many activists could best be called 'pragmatic radicals'. They are radical because their '… aims and strategies are geared toward resisting what are seen as the inevitable hardships imposed on the working class by a capitalist economic and political system'. Yet they are pragmatic because they work on feasible strategies whilst recognising the structural constraints to major reforms. Pragmatic radicalism is characterised by an acknowledgement that community action is committed to pluralist solutions, through pressure group activity to advance people's interests. This, according to Kraushaar, is the only logical premise for community work because the very notion of 'community' ignores other social structures thereby creating 'serious contradictions' for community activists.

Indeed, most readily available practitioner case studies are either reflective of Kraushaar's pragmatic radicalism or of Rothman and Tropman's mixing and phasing of methods (1987), perhaps summed up best as liberal eclecticism. Given the adoption of these strategies, a more dynamic and just pluralism is perhaps the best outcome community workers can aspire to. This may lead to the strengthening rather than the weakening of social democracy. There is little evidence however that existing commonly-adopted community work practices can achieve more.

Conclusion

The majority of research which has focussed on the practice-ideology congruency has affirmed its existence for liberal workers but denied its existence for socialist workers. In a small study of NSW community workers, the desired outcomes of the more radically inclined were found to be circumscribed by a lack of support from constituents for the workers' vision, by bureaucratic interference, fear of loss of state sponsorship and an absence of strategy. What does emerge as significant is the interplay between practitioner, the state sponsor, the employer and other constituents.

Not only do theories of action and interests have strategic implications for community workers but they provide the community worker with a constant reminder of the non-directive/directive debate. (Batten and Batten 1967; Jacobs 1984) Directiveness or leadership may be futile in relation to assessments of benefits, but in the area of strategy formulation highly desirable and unavoidable. (Bryant and Bryant 1982) If community workers do not think strategically then the strategies of powerful others, like bureaucrats, will dominate. With confusion over directiveness and strategy evident amongst more radical workers, community work outcomes appear likely to advance pluralist, rather than socialist or radical, solutions for some time to come.

References

ACW (1975) *Knowledge and Skills for Community Work*, London: Association of Community Workers.

Baldock, P. (1977) 'Why Community Action? The Historical Origins of the Radical Trend in British Community Work', *Community Development Journal*, 12 (2).

Barr, A. (1987) 'Inside Practice – researching community workers in Scotland', *Community Development Journal*, 22 (1).

Batten, T. and Batten, M. (1967) *The Non-Directive Approach in Group and Community Work*, London: Oxford University Press.

Benson, J. (1983) A Dialectical Method for the Study of Organisations. In: G. Morgan *Beyond Method. Strategies for Social Research*, Sage: Beverly Hills.

Bolger, S., Corrigan, P., Docking, J., and Frost, N. (1981) *Towards Socialist Welfare Work*. London: MacMillan.

Brager, G. and Specht, H. (1973) *Community Organizing*, New York: Columbia University Press.

Bryant, B. and Bryant, R. (1982) *Change and Conflict. A Study of Community Work in Glasgow*, Aberdeen: Aberdeen University Press.

Corrigan, P. (1975) 'Community Work and Political Struggle', *The Sociological Review Monograph*, 21.

Craig, G., Derricourt, N. and Loney, M. (1982) *Community Work and The State. Towards a Radical Practice*. London: Routledge & Kegan Paul.

Creed, H. and Tomlinson, J. (1984) 'The Role of Ideology in Community Work', *Australian Journal of Social Issues*, 19 (4).

Dixon, G., Johnson, C., Leigh, S. and Turnbull, N., (1982), 'Feminist perspectives and practice', In: G. Craig *et al.* (*op. cit.*)

Falappi, A. *et al.* (1984) *Proofs in the Puddin. Possibilities for local community workers*. Fairfield Community Workers.

Fleetwood, M. and Lambert J. (1982) 'Bringing Socialism Home: theory and practice for a radical community action' In: G. Craig *et al.(op. cit.).*

Garvin, C. and Cox, F. (1987) 'A History of Community Organizing Since The Civil War With Special Reference To Oppressed Communities', in F. Cox *et al. Strategies of Community Organization.* 4th edn. Itasca, Illinois: F.E. Peacock Publishers.

Graycar, A. (1982) 'Government Officers' Expectations of Non-Government Welfare Organisations', A Discussion Paper. Social Welfare Research Centre Reports and Proceedings, No. 28. Sydney: University of New South Wales.

Hindess, B (1986) 'Interests in Political Analysis' in Law, J. (ed.) *Power, Action and Belief. A New Sociology of Knowledge?* London: Routledge & Keegan Paul.

Jacobs, S. (1984) 'Community Action and The Building of Socialism From Below: A Defence of the Non-Directive Approach', *Community Development Journal*, 19 (4).

Kraushaar, R. (1979) 'Pragmatic Radicalism', *International Journal of Urban and Regional Research*, 3.

Lambert, J. (1978) 'Political Values and Community Work Practice' in Curno, P. (ed.) *Political Issues and Community Work*, London: Routledge & Kegan Paul.

Lane, M. (1985) *Community Work or Social Change? An Australian Perspective.* London: Routledge & Kegan Paul.

(LEWRG) London Edinburgh Weekend Return Group (1980) *In and Against the State*, London: Pluto.

Marris, P. (1987) *Meaning and Action. Community Planning and Conceptions of Change.* London: Routledge & Kegan Paul.

Mowbray, A. (1984) 'Localism and Hegemony in Contemporary Australian Social Policy', Paper to the 54th ANZAAS Congress, Canberra.

Mowbray, M.(1985) 'Consensual Practice, Consensual State: Community Work in Australia', *Community Development Journal*, 20 (4).

Mundey, J. and Craig, G., (1982) 'Joint union-resident action' in: P. Curno (ed.) *(op. cit.).*

Repo, M. (1971) 'The Fallacy of Community Control', *Transformation*, 1 (1).

Rigby, A. (1982) 'Managing Management: The exploration of 'nooks and crannies' in community work', *Community Development Journal*, 17 (1).

Rothman, J. and Tropman, J. (1987) 'Models of Community Organization and Macro Practice Perspectives: Their Mixing and Phasing', in: F. Cox *et al. Strategies of Community Organization.* 4th edn. Itasca, Illinois: F.E. Peacock.

Specht, H. (1976) The Community Development Project – National and Local Strategies for Improving the Delivery of Services. London: NISW Papers.

Thomas, D.N. (1973) *The Making of Community Work,* London: George Allen and Unwin.

Thorpe, R. (1985) 'Community Work and Ideology: an Australian Perspective' in: R. Thorpe and J. Petruchenia *Community Work or Social Change? an Australian Perspective*. London: Routledge & Kegan Paul.

Van Moorst, H. (1983) 'Working With Youth. A political process. Occasional Paper No. 8', Melbourne: Footscray Institute of Technology.

Wannan, A. (1986) 'Women, Welfare and the Suburbs' in Marchant, H. and Wearing, B., *Gender Reclaimed. Women in Social Work*. Sydney: Hale and Iremonger.

Jane Dixon lectures in Welfare Studies at Mitchell College of Advanced Education, Bathurst, Australia: Vol. 25 No. 2 (1990): 91-101

19

The Case of the Third World: People's Self-Development

Md. Anisur Rahman

Introduction

During the time I worked with the Bangladesh Planning Commission I learnt two great lessons. One was the utter inadequacy of our professional training as economists to suggest a viable path for the country's development. The other was that the best promise for development lay with the initiatives of the ordinary people.

Our failure as planners may perhaps be summed up as follows. The reasonings and calculations which we had learnt inevitably ended up with a huge resource deficit which could only be met, if at all, by massive foreign assistance. This implied some surrender, at least, of our autonomy as a sovereign nation; the country's economic structure also gets locked into large import-dependence; this, along with the debt burden, would perpetrate the overall continued dependence on foreign assistance; the country's indigenous knowledge, skills and culture would be humiliated in the hands of the alien knowledge and culture embodied in foreign expertise and resources coming in on such a scale; and a beggar mentality rather than a spirit of dignified hard work would dominate the psychology of the society. As economists we were trained mainly in this kind of deficit and dependent 'development' planning. We had not learnt how to plan the mobilisation of the human energy of the people, to plan to develop with what we have, not with what we do not have.

While going through the agonising process of applying the above logic and calculations in our task as 'development' planners, I was also fortunate to have had the opportunity to interact with a number of popular movements in the country in which the people's energy was being mobilised for development activities. Unfortunately such movements sometimes did not last long for reasons which I shall not discuss here. But initiatives like these are being taken in many countries in recent years, either 'spontaneously' or by being 'animated' and assisted by friendly quarters. People's self-development is emerging as a new urgent vision from elements of concerned intelligentsia, social activists and people's own ranks. In

232

this article I propose to discuss the perceptions and premises of this vision, and contrast these with two major trends in development thinking – one to be called the 'liberal' trend, and the other the 'socialist' trend – which have dominated the scene until now.

A central concept in people's self-development is the primacy of human dignity. The Bhoomi Sena movement of *adivasis* in Maharastra, India, for example gave primacy to liberation from bonded labour – a question of human dignity, achieving which was the first step in their self-development. The *adivasis* then fought for land rights and implementation of the minimum wage law. With an intense self-reliant spirit the movement since then has focussed on cultural and political assertion of the *adivasis*, and assertion in particular of their autonomy of action in all spheres, i.e. their self-determination. The movement is avoiding getting into any kind of dependence on outsiders for their 'development', even if this means a slower pace of economic development. To these *adivasis* development is, indeed, the very moving forwards authentically, in the search for their own life.

In a different setting, human dignity has featured as a primary urge in some grass-roots mobilisations in Bangladesh also. Organisations of landless men and women created by the intervention of Nijera Kori, a rural development agency which does not offer any financial assistance to the people and promotes their self-organisation, have not progressed much economically. But these landless groups consider their organisation to be a solid step forward in their lives.

Experiencing human dignity thus is a great leap forward, the first necessary step in anybody's development. But other mobilised people's groups have had better access to economic resources, some with small productive assets of their own, some acquiring rights to economic assets such as land or fishing water by collective struggle after getting mobilised, and some amongst them being also able to mobilise external resources like bank credit or donor finance. With these they have taken initiatives to promote their socio-economic livelihood as well.

Development philosophy

Local development efforts throughout the Third World indicate that the mobilisation of the people's collective energy generates imaginative solutions to the economic problem alone – production, distribution, marketing, skills training, promoting social welfare and social security and, along with all these, the problem of employment

– which are not conceived in or available to professionally-designed and managed economic development projects and programmes. However, my point is not to highlight in particular the economic dimensions of people's self-development. Some of the popular effects which have found ways of significant economic betterment within relatively short periods may be the more fortunate ones, and many countries may not have such possibilities to reduce economic poverty significantly in the short-to-medium run, as discussed below.

The problems of mass poverty

As a Member of the Bangladesh Planning Commission I had made some calculations on the kind of improvement we could most optimistically expect to have in the incomes of the masses of the country's population over a medium-to-long term. I quote below from a submission I made in March 1972 to the then Prime Minister:

> Bangladesh remains one of the world's poorest countries, and will take a long time to meet the aspirations of its people for a decent economic life. Under normal conditions, the income per head in Bangladesh would have been in the order of ... about Rs. 33 a month. The devastation of the economy by the war has brought it down, perhaps somewhere between Rs. 20 and 25 a month. If income per head grows at the rate of 5 per cent per year from now on, it will take close to 20 years for it to reach Rs. 50 per month; for this, total income will have to grow at the rate of 8 per cent or so in view of a high rate of population growth, and such high growth rate of income would be an achievement by any standard ... But even Rs. 50 a month would hardly be a tolerable level of income in absolute terms; in relative terms this would be even less so as international consumption standards would be rising all the time, and hence aspirations all over the world ... As long as some people's incomes remain above the average, rightly or wrongly, it will take longer for the average income of the masses to reach the figure of Rs. 50 a month or whatever else may be postulated, than for the national average to reach the same...In short, the possibility of meeting the aspirations of the people in the short run does not exist, and this is not the problem the government is facing today in any meaningful sense. The problem instead is how to carry the suffering people of Bangladesh through a long and extremely hard journey to the realization of their aspirations within the framework of a stable social order... (Rahman 1972)

The basic problem that we faced was not special to Bangladesh. For many countries in a state of mass economic poverty and unemployment, there may not be an early enough cure, in terms of technological and/or social management possibilities with available resources, except for a specially small country which can be helped quickly by external assistance coupled with its own resources. And for any given country it will be difficult to predict or promise a significant reduction of mass poverty in the near future in view of many factors which are not within the control of the society no matter how mobilised its people are, including internal and external resistances that should be expected to the very effort to promote people's mobilisation and self-determined development.

Viewing the development problem in terms of eradication of (economic) poverty and providing to the population (entitlements to) the basic needs, is liable to raise aspirations more than can be fulfilled for any given generation. And this raises an operational question of social motivation to work constructively for the realisation of such a goal. As suggested above, the first step toward a possible solution of the problem requires a constructive co-operation of those – the 'present generation' – who may hardly be a significant material beneficiary of the solution. But the operational development problem concerns this very generation, which has to be motivated to participate in a social endeavour toward what may be at best a gradual eradication of poverty from which this generation itself may benefit very little. The theoretical economist's answer to this question – and I have myself been a part in this intellectual game-playing – is to conceive an 'inter-temporal social unity function' of 'infinite time horizon', and ask the present generation(s) to feel happy because its sacrifices would maximise this utility function. But we have not considered how precisely the mother will explain this utility function to her hungry and shivering child who is, furthermore, attracted to the toy of the elite's son. Failing this, the mother may have to steal, or try other devious ways of acquiring some privileges for her child at the expense of others. There go the social values, and the society gets into a race for private aggrandisement by depriving others, in which only a minority can win at the expense of the majority.

I suggest that by focussing on economic needs and economic poverty, a culture of development discourse that becomes preoccupied with what the people do not have, gets trapped in the negative thinking and dependence orientation that this generates, rather than motivating the society to become constructively engaged in moving forward. With a constructive engagement, the people show imaginative ways of progressively fulfilling their needs and urges.

This includes, naturally, their need and urge for economic betterment. However, it is the constructive engagement rather than economic achievements *per se*, which is the more universal aspect of popular initiatives; the fact that the people are mobilised, engaged in tasks set by themselves and going about them together, pooling resources and energy whereby they can do better than walking alone, drawing strength and sustaining power from a shared life and effort. Sometimes they succeed and sometimes they fail (in their own terms); but through all this they move forward in the evolution of (search for) their lives. It is such a positive evolution that is possible, and this is important in its own right, both for the involved people themselves a well as for the future generations to whom they can pass on the heritage of constructive social engagement to move through life with all its odds, showing their creativity and a spirit of tackling challenges, developing thereby as a human personality.

The consumerist view of development

Philosophically speaking, there are two opposing views of development. One is a consumerist view, which regards the human being primarily as a consumer of goods and services. Basically, 'development' is seen in this view as an expansion of the flow of consumption. As a means to bring this about, an expansion of the productive capacity of the country is needed, but the primary logic of development remains a progressive increase in consumption. For a time, development was identified with aggregate economic growth to bring about a progressively higher flow of aggregate consumption irrespective of its distribution. Gradually, the interpersonal distribution question was raised, in terms of who benefits from such development as consumers. The development debate then focussed on questions such as growth first or distribution first, or can we have growth with distribution simultaneously, and how can 'entitlements' (command over goods and services) be truly ensured for all. This debate continues to this date; but the basic consumerist view prevails, concerned with who gets what as a consumer, and what are the intertemporal and interpersonal trade-offs. The question that this view does not ask is who in the society are able to take the needed initiative to produce the goods and services, and what happens to the different sections of the population as creative beings i.e. the distribution of the power and opportunity to fulfil oneself by creative acts?

The notion of poverty follows the same viewpoint. The concern here is whether a person has the necessary income or access or entitlement to, the bundle of goods and services postulated to be the needs of human beings as consumers. Poverty in terms of lack of an entitlement to develop as a creative being is, again, not expressed as a concern. The problem of poverty in this sense is a consumer's rather than a creator's problem, focussed on the poor not being able to consume the things desired (or biologically needed) rather than not having the opportunity of producing (or commanding) them through one's creative acts.

These wants and creative urges have become separated as a result of, first, class separation between people by which the control over productive resources was polarised, giving the dominant class the power also over the lives of others. Secondly, the dominant class and its allies (together, the 'elites') developed certain consumption standards and were able to influence by their social power the culture and aspirations of society so that to attain these standards came to be regarded widely as the purpose of life itself. This has resulted in aspirations and urges dissociated from the immediate creative possibilities of the people. In turn this is causing pointless frustration among the masses besides strengthening mass dependence on the elites, and submission to a view of development as the fulfilment of such aspirations, and hence to submission of the initiative for development to the more 'successful' in the hope that such development could possibly be delivered by those who have attained this themselves. Even many 'class struggles', of local as well as of wider scales, retain this consumer consciousness, with material aspirations which are way beyond the creative possibilities of the working class; implicitly, such struggles retain a dependency orientation, cherishing the hope that some other power (class) will deliver the kind of material development needed to satisfy such aspirations.

The creativist view of development

In recent times, the concept of satisfaction of basic needs of the population has emerged as a primary objective of development in liberal development thinking. Interestingly, the five 'basic needs' which have been identified – food, clothing, housing, medical care, education – are in some form or other the needs of animals as well, who typically do not create (materially, socially, culturally) except at a very elementary and static level (e.g. creating the bird's nest). But the distinctive human-ness in us is not in needing these elementary means of survival, but what the combination of our distinctive brain and limbs can do and, therefore, the urge we must have as human beings to fulfil this power. This urge is often for the sake of creation itself, but in the process of satisfying this urge this also creates the means of satisfying whatever other needs, basic or non-basic, that we wish to and can satisfy, according to our own priorities. Through such creation we evolve – develop – as creative beings. This is the basic human need; to fulfil our creative potentials in ever newer ways, although this may not be expressed or asserted by all because of the conditioning resulting from structural social and cultural domination mentioned above.

As opposed to the consumerist view of the liberal school, there exists a creative view of development which regards the human race primarily as a creative being. In recent times this view is explicit in the articulations of activist-intellectuals working directly with the people to promote their self-development. (Fernandez, 1986; Tilakaratna, 1987) But the underlying philosophy is not new. This is, of course, the central message in trends of some major religions. At the level of scientific discourse this view was, perhaps, first suggested in the philosophy of Karl Marx.

Marx viewed the human being primarily as a creator who because of one's class situation either fulfils or becomes alienated from one's creative power. Looking at the development of capitalism, Marx was excited by its spectacular creativity; the central focus of his analysis of capitalism was the revolutionary development of productive forces in this phase of human history. Likewise, the central argument in this theory of revolution was the need, and what he considered the inevitability, of the overthrow of capitalism as its creative phase comes to an end, and as a further development of the productive forces would be possible only in the hands of the working class. While he was thus excited by the creativity of capitalism in its glorious days, Marx saw the working class alienated from its own creative potentials and power, the free exercise of which alone could give it fulfilment as labour. The working class as a producer and not as a consumer must, therefore, revolt and take over the means of production, to fulfil itself as producers. The history of 'Man' (as unalienated worker) would then truly begin. This implied that, through the revolutionary development of the productive forces in its hands, labour would eventually produce (and control) enough for everyone to have according to one's need: but such (material) needs' satisfaction would follow human creativity and does not appear in Marx as the primary motive force for human effort. (Draper, 1977)

Structural change

As I have suggested, people's self-development can start even under conditions of extreme resource shortage; people mobilising themselves for assertion of human dignity and self-determination, and to co-operate to accomplish collectively-determined tasks, in the process developing in capabilities and in human personality. In fact, some conditions of the acutest resource shortage – e.g. under natural calamities – are known to have produced the most impressive popular mobilisations with such self-development elements. The possibilities and pace of self-development, however, are naturally constrained by the availability of physical resources to work with and people's self-mobilisations themselves have often been directed toward achieving greater access to such resources by collective negotiation and struggle. In countries where the bulk of physical resources are controlled by elites, a redistribution of the control over such resources in addition to redistribution of the social power to take development initiatives is, therefore, necessary. This distribution question – rather than the question of distribution of incomes *per se* or benefits from development – is the basic question of equity in the creativist view of development.

While thus calling for radical structural change in societies with polarised control over physical resources, this viewpoint questions the identification of people's ownership with state ownership which, as we have noted, may actually separate the people from the means of production (and thus inhibit rather than promote their self-development). The distribution question is, therefore, one of giving the people (individually and/or collectively) real control over resources to work with to develop their own potentials, not to be dictated to by a state-appointed managerial technocracy. The concept of 'socialist' defined as 'social ownership' of the means of production which has often been identified with state ownership needs, in this light, a thorough re-examination.

There is a need for rethinking also on the tasks before such structural change is accomplished, and on the prerequisite for such change to truly liberate and promote people's creativity rather than stifle it with new forms of domination. Most left activists have been preoccupied with the macro-question of capturing state power to initiate socialist development before action is initiated to animate the people in self-developmental mobilisation. But micro-level initiatives to promote people's self-development show that this need not await a redistribution of resources even for physical resource-poor communities, who can start developing today at least in human personality, social values and social organisation, and who themselves consider such advancement to be a positive gain; on the other hand the question of macro-structural change for most societies where this is desired remains uncertain and often intractable. It is not very convincing to suggest that generations should keep on waiting for the elusive revolution before mobilising themselves to move forward with what they have and what they can acquire through local struggles. There is, furthermore, another profound need, for working to promote micro-level people's self-development right now, to enhance the very possibility that a macro-level social change, if it does occur some day, may truly release and promote people's self-will but not know what this means, nor how this can be animated. This – what a leadership can do after coming into power – is also a question of organic logic resting on what it has done, and hence learnt, previously As a corollary, the hope of a macro-level structural change to promote people's self-development rather than even to suppress the popular initiatives we are witnessing today at local scales, lies in the emergence of an 'organic vanguard' which is rooted in such popular movement and does not claim itself to be above and unaccountable to the people.

Concluding comment

Three years ago I had a four-hour dialogue with about one hundred leaders of landless workers organisations in Bangladesh coming from about thirty contiguous villages. This was one of the most stimulating seminars I have had, surpassing in the intellectual quality of the discussions, in my judgement, many academic seminars I have attended. We discussed questions concerning their immediate environments as well as questions of national policy, politics and social changes. On most of these questions, the landless leaders – not a few but many of them – had well thought-out positions: 'we have discussed this question for the last five years, and our thinking is this...' – this was a typical beginning of the answer to many of my questions.

The point is not whether their position was correct or not. The world's greatest social thinkers and scientists have made mistakes;

sometimes the greater you are, the more profound is the mistake you make. The point is that the ordinary working people are capable of social enquiry and analysis, and that this capability can be enhanced by practice. Anyone's self-development starts, as it must, with one's own action, and is a process in which self-understanding develops as action is taken and reviewed. Formal efforts at social development have, however, been in the hands of elites who have in general considered themselves wiser than the people, and instead of seeking to promote the people's self-inquiry and understanding have sought to impose their own ideas of development. In doing this they have promoted their own self-development in some ways, while bringing the world to the dismal state in which we find it today. In any case this had to be at the cost of people's self-development, for one cannot develop with somebody else's ideas. This has been, I suggest, also the single most important intellectual error in any otherwise committed efforts toward social change for people's liberation, which seek to indoctrinate the people in a vertical relation with them, and give priority to structural change over liberation of the mind. Only with a liberated mind (of the people) which is free to inquire and then conceive and plan what is to be created, can structural change release the creative potentials of the people. In this sense liberation of the mind is the primary task, both before and after structural change.

References

Draper, H. (1977) *Karl Marx's Theory of Revolution*, Vol 1: *State and Bureaucracy*. Monthly Review Press.

Fernandes, M.E. (1986) *Participatory Action-Research and the Farming Systems Approach with Highland Peasants*. Columbia, USA: Department of Rural Sociology, University of Missouri.

Rahman, M. A. (1972). *The First Step*. 8 March, (mimeo).

Tilakaratna, A., (1987). *The Animator in Participatory Rural Development (Concept and Practice)*. Geneva: ILO.

Anisur Rahman is a staff member of the Rural Employment Policies Branch, ILO, Geneva: Vol. 25 No. 4 (1990): 307-314.

20

Reconstruction to Deconstruction: The Transformation of Community Work in Australia

Helen Meekosha and Martin Mowbray

Introduction

Community work seems, at first sight, directionless and fragmented in contemporary Australia. We argue here that this apparent fragmentation reflects the reconstitution of social forces in Australia in the late twentieth century, the decomposition of the welfare state and its replacement with elements of the market on the one hand, and the charitable model of voluntarism and residual family care of the other. What we will show in this overview of the development of Australian community work over recent decades is that, despite the hope of the early 1970s, the practice has never realised the ideals, however questionable they were, behind the immediate post-war flirtation with community development. Instead of a concern with building and with change, community work has become integrated within a contracting and increasingly conservative welfare state.

Community workers have moved away from reformist commitment towards an uncritical acceptance of the precepts of orthodox economics, 'good news' planning, managerialism and community care. The promise of locality-based community work has been challenged by upsurges of identity (disability, gender, age, homosexuality, race) and issues struggles (consumer, environment, peace). This contemporary diversity reflects the signs of the deconstruction of industrial society and the emergence of post-reform community work and community action. Except in fringe or marginal organizations, mostly set within broader social movements rather than professional agencies, there is little evidence of practical concern with challenges to existing race and gender relations or income and wealth differentials. Instead a wishful and relatively mindless commitment to growth prevails. While the number of community work jobs has increased with the growing diversity of employers, there is little space for critical practice or support for critical reflection.

Phases in Australian community work

Immediately following the Second World War there emerged a

period, officially labelled 'post-war reconstruction', in which Federal and State government agencies preoccupied with 'progress' and wanting to reduce political antagonisms fostered voluntary community involvement in local activities, including provision of public infrastructure. A feature of this time was organizations such as the Union of Australian Women, the Kindergarten Union, and the Women's Services Guild, through which women sought to establish local community centres, child care and kindergartens in working class areas. These efforts were largely defeated by resistance from conservative interests, including churches and welfare bodies, keen for women to return to domesticity and to preserve the idealised model of the nuclear family. (Allport 1986)

The two decades from 1948 of Federal conservative government were a period of economic boom, high employment and widespread political alienation in which community-based programs went little beyond charitable activity and privately initiated recreational and youth work. Dissatisfaction with the failure of economic growth to solve the problems of disadvantaged groups, the war in Vietnam and spread of the climate of protest from Europe and North America contributed to a degree of social unrest which was well established by 1970. In the spirit of reform engendered by the tensions of the time, policies under the Whitlam Labour government (1972-75), engaged problems defined in such ways as 'urban decay' and supported various innovative and participatory social programs. Policies centred on local and regional planning became a feature of the Labour regime, particularly of its Department of Urban and Regional Development and the Australian Assistance Plan – a national community development scheme. The labour movement too, took up social causes to an uncustomary extent.

Under the Frazer conservative (Liberal and National Party) government (1972-1983) programs which entailed and even fostered community action strategies, frequently in concert with labour unions, all but disappeared. Governments adopted a considerably narrower view of their responsibilities and took a much firmer grip on the use of public funds. With tighter guide-lines and closer accountability, funded agencies were left with less 'room to manoeuvre'. (Dixon 1990) The ensuing period saw experienced erstwhile community workers and other avowedly radical activists turn themselves into social planners and consultants, promoting a simple belief that better planning and the localization of services were the new hope. Decentralist programs, deinstitutionalization and various government-sponsored community schemes such as community care, community employment and other make-work projects, community enterprise and worker co-operatives became the hope of the future. Where the Federal Labour government's welfare reformers of the early 1970s saw 'community' as a simile for working class development and participation, the neo-conservatist post-socialist Labour social engineers in State and Federal governments of the 1980s saw 'community' as an avenue for cutting back the welfare state and privatising social problems and provision.

Deinstitutionalization and community care were predicted on assumptions that women would be available in the community to carry out the caring as volunteers, or for low wages, in the community services sector. Many programs, which offered short-term relief from economic insecurity to their participants, were promoted by community workers who had entered bureaucracies to avoid the restricted career opportunities of the community sector. By this time, unions too had abandoned oppositional struggles for change and at their most progressive became involved in corporate projects and endorsement of government labour market schemes. Occasionally there were innovative outcomes. Some local projects were directed at minority groups such as immigrants, and they did open the way for women, immigrants, people with disabilities and Aborigines to get employment in local organizations.

By the mid-1980s, as governments exploited the opportunity localist schemes offered for economic austerity, the general failure of such projects to help most of those at whom they were ostensibly directed, was widely understood. Progressive social policy was increasingly seen as about more effective macro-policies. Considerable hope was placed, for example, in the better targeting of social security and tax expenditure and new labour force participation schemes. Faith for the future was accorded to managerialist solutions. Reformist zeal and notions of participatory planning and community management and control were seen as approaches of the past. Peak welfare organizations, like the State and Federal councils of social service, which once supported such approaches, joined the new corporatist bandwagon. Elite decision-making by state managers, often with little or no substantive knowledge of community or social services, based on selective use of the reports of private consultants had become the way forward by 1990. (Meekosha 1989) Effectiveness and efficiency, underpinned by a renewed commitment to economic growth, was the new policy context for community work.

With the exception of some informal enclaves within particular programs, such as public tenants' organizations in Victoria, there is now no discernible radical position in current Australian community work. Moreover, there is very little sense of a distinct community work profession or set of interests, directions or strategies. There does not exist in Australia an organization of community workers, nor any national or State conferences. The closest thing to a distinct left grouping directly relevant to community work is the Australian Social Welfare Union which won a Community Development Workers Award for the State of Victoria in 1988. This award covers persons working with a geographic or other community and addressing 'issues, needs and problems for that community through facilitating collective solutions'. In 1989 the union also won a Social and Community Services Employees Award for New South Wales (NSW). These awards bind community sector employers to ensure minimum industrial standards concerning such matters as payment of wages, leave, allowances, amenities and union rights.

Broad social movements

Progressive community development is more evident in the context of (inter)-national and other broad scale movements, rather than in activities generated at the local level. Next to the women's movement, the most significant of these is the environment movement, made up of numerous groupings tending towards the left of the political spectrum but displaying considerable difference in perspective and strategy. Several of these groups, including the Wilderness Society, the Conservation Foundation and Greenpeace, have become extremely influential in the mainstream political process. Their political sophistication, energy and determination, articulated with increasing public concern about the environment, has given such groups considerable leverage over governments. The peace movement has also become a prominent force in broader scale community development. There has been a recent re-emergence of local community and resident action groups influenced by, and often linked to, the successes of the environment movement. These are opposing such large developments as airport extensions, new freeways and coastal tourist and industrial development. By and large these groups have no paid workers and draw on a usually middle class educated group for leadership and support.

The cause of Aboriginal land rights has maintained momentum for the last two decades. The political heartland of land rights is the Northern Territory, principally because of the continuing presence of the Aboriginal Land Rights (NT) Act and the two powerful (Central and Northern) Land Councils – bodies with strongly defended revenue indexed to royalties for mining on Aboriginal land. Not unnaturally, the land rights movement also has a strong organizational base in the two States (NSW and South Australia) with land rights legislation.

Assimilation, multiculturalism and mainstreaming

Australia's immigrant population is drawn from over seventy nations, and immigration accounts for over half the annual population growth, which is the highest in the industrial capitalist world. The single largest source has been Britain and Ireland, though other European and Asian countries have provided significant numbers. An ethnic rights movement in the mid-1970s played an important part in breaking down prevailing assimilationist policies – the formation of Ethnic Communities Councils in all major Australian cities and a national Federation of Ethnic Communities Councils of Australia provided an institutional base for this movement. Even so government support for community work with immigrants only began with the advent of multicultural policies in the 1980s. (Galbally 1978)

The Galbally report recommended a range of specific services for immigrants, funded by the Commonwealth, in co-operation with the States and local government, and primarily located in the non-government sector, largely dependent on volunteer labour. These services included local Migrant Resource Centres, grants to ethnic organizations to employ welfare, social and community workers, and ethnic Saturday schools. Workers in these organizations rarely had a specific community development focus, but were expected to cover a range of community needs – interpreting, translating, counselling, information, referral, crisis intervention, and community development. In addition these workers, largely women, had poor conditions of work, career expectations, status and opportunities. Government priorities were for these organizations to deliver direct service, rather than organize community action. (Meekosha and Rist 1982) The underlying concern for cultural pluralism identified the issues as problems of immigrant integration, avoiding any action on dominant society racism.

Despite these conditions and constraints, community development with immigrants in the 1980s covered a diversity of needs and activities. In the steel production centre of Wollongong a group of immigrant women, Macedonian, Turkish, South American, successfully took on the Australian industrial giant, BHP, over its refusal to employ women. Their struggle continued for ten years, and received strong support from the Illawarra Migrant Resource Centre. At the other end of the spectrum, many ethnic organizations employed community workers, usually untrained, to carry out direct advice and referral services at a fairly basic level. In addition to welfare services, there was a concentration on cultural activities. By the late 1980s, the 'separate development' or 'ethno-specific' model of funding community work with immigrants, was replaced by a government commitment to 'mainstreaming' – this occurred in a climate of increased racism (particularly against Asians), major cuts to government expenditure and a reassertion of voluntarism and privatization (user pays) as the basis for welfare. (Meekosha and Jakubowicz 1989)

The impact of feminism

The relationship of the Australian women's movement to the state has had a particular impact on the development of women's services and community work. In 1972 a group of women formed the Women's Electoral Lobby (WEL) as a means of achieving equality for women through the parliamentary process. This set the course for feminist involvement with the state. In 1973 Labour appointed a Women's Advisor to the Prime Minister's staff. Federal and State departments followed by establishing women's units and Equal Employment Opportunity and Anti-Discrimination units.

The central thesis of the second wave of feminism, that the 'personal is political', combined with this institutionalization of women's issues within the state to give rise to two important features of community work with women. First, a wide variety of parsimoniously supported women's services was established. The first Women's Health centre (Leichhardt) was established in 1974. By 1989 there were over 50 such centres operating across Australia. (Broom 1989) The growth of women's services supported by government has been the main locus for feminist community work in Australia. The second outcome was the emergence of feminist bureaucrats who have both legitimated some feminist struggles in the community, and at the same time acted as a barrier between less powerful women and government, often with an outcome of controlling anger and dissent.

A tendency of mainstream feminism in the past, which has been to see race and gender issues as separate, has led to Aboriginal and immigrant women setting up separate services. While some feminists in the 1970s initially rejected government support as carrying dangers of co-option, (Dowse 1983; Curthoys 1984) the overall trend has been to demand government delivery of services). This resulted in the establishment of women's health centres, women's refuges, community child care centres, rape crisis (later, sexual assault) services, women's legal centres, working women's centres and women's occupational health action and support groups.

Not all women's services have operated on feminist principles. For example, in 1981, it was estimated that only one-third of women's refuges were feminist. In a 1987 evaluation of the 22 women's refuges operating in Western Australia, only six had aims which referred to improving the status of women and only four translated this into social action aims. (McFerran 1987) Those services that have operated as feminist collectives emphasise the importance of process issues such as collective decision-making, egalitarian conditions of work and skill sharing.

Given the diversity and varied nature of feminism in the 1990s, it would be impossible for it to have had no impact throughout community work practice. Indeed even the most conservative and localized neighbourhood centre is likely to run assertiveness training and discussion groups for women with a focus on encouraging women into further education. Such activities quite happily coexist with traditional, caring, volunteer women's work. This type of neighbourhood work is limited by a perspective which tends to view the state as benevolent, and not necessarily challenging women's dependency on both men and the state.

The scattered community programs servicing the frail, aged and people with disabilities of the 1970s were integrated by the Federal Labour government in joint action with the States in the mid-1980s under the label 'Home and Community Care' (HACC). Community development was increasingly presented as the organising of services and the encouragement of consumer participation in the planning and administration of services. Women were reinforced in roles as carers, while volunteers were represented as one of the more effective avenues for service delivery. Thirty percent of women worked in community services as at August 1987. They made up 56 percent of full-time employees in the industry and 83 percent of part-time employees, yet the level of unionization was the lowest of all industries. (Australia, Department of Employment, Education and Training 1988)

An apparent invulnerability of HACC to feminism is repeated elsewhere in mainstream community work. Men who are employed as community workers in areas such as local government, housing and youth and neighbourhood work, show few signs of responding to the challenges produced by women's services and feminism – for example, there is little evidence of male community workers working on issues of male violence. (Barry 1989)

Progressive community work has been replaced by more authoritarian programs geared to and funded by the market place and/or donations. In an era in which the dominant discourse of state welfare positions itself as post-modern, post-socialist and post-feminist, feminists face a dilemma. The 1990s offer a choice between attempting to engage with and influence governments to move towards social provision for social justice, and thus face dangers of co-option and demobilization, or to withdraw from engagement and seek to develop alternative enclaves. The latter would promote a women's culture, but may be inaccessible to many women.

Local government

Compared to the Commonwealth and State governments, Australian local government has only had a subsidiary role in the provision of welfare services. Historically, local government services have generally concentrated on support for the interests of property owners and business. Local government's most substantial longer-term involvement in social service provision has been in the areas of infant welfare and, especially, services to aged people. The latter services have been mainly in the form of Commonwealth government subsidized senior citizen's centres, welfare officers for the aged, home help and delivered meals. The thrust of such services has been towards maintenance of older people in their own homes.

Over the last twenty years or so, municipalities and shires gradually developed interest in notions of social or community development and social planning. Councils have become major employers of community workers in the form of community service managers, social planners, community project officers, housing development officers, youth, ethnic program, aged and domiciliary care co-ordinators, child care supervisors, and so on. Such positions and related facilities have been partly financed by Federal and State governments.

The enthusiasm of Federal and State governments to devolve welfare responsibilities to local government has been mitigated by the declared reluctance of councils to take up service commitments without guarantees of continuing financial support. Nevertheless, prompted by local demand and growing needs, expansion of local governments in the field of social services is continually expanding. In NSW, for example, the number of council-employed community service staff increased five-fold between 1980 and 1987. (Davis 1987)

Community work personnel have generally seen their roles largely in terms of service development and policies directly related to service provision. Progress has tended to be measured in terms of implementation of new services, rather than in challenges to the inequities in the existing system of local government. Regressive local rating regimes and property development levies or exactions have, for example, been regarded as off-limits for community development and social planning staff. Similarly, council employment policies, explicit gender and race issues, and matters of accountability have not been seen as the business of community service personnel.

Conclusion

Except in isolated programs and within broader social movements, community work and community development practice in Australia has little legitimate claim to progressive directions or politics. Instead, it has been largely consumed within the overall government commitment to the run-down of the welfare state. While this project is unlikely to have the personal support of practitioners themselves, there is at present little base or prospect for resistance. The lack of clear political commitment, leadership and organization has left community workers fragmented and readily co-opted.

We conclude this review with some suggestions which might contribute towards community work practices more capable of countering the increasingly conservative social, economic and political environment in Australia. We canvass three broad areas of concern – the professional orientation and practice of community workers, the industrial organization of community work and its role in the labour movement, and the education of community workers.

The fragmentation of community work can be addressed by the formation of networks in which progressive anti-racist, socialist and non-sexist practices are developed and supported. The need for this is particularly apparent in local government. Directions in local government need to be questioned or challenged and alternative possibilities which offer greater equity need to be examined and advocated. The trade union front needs to be seen as an avenue for not only achieving improved industrial conditions, but as a base for activism over social change in favour of greater social equity and redistribution. This would include improved and more progressive programs.

Community work education in Australia is largely located in Social Work programs, yet many practitioners have come from other backgrounds. Thus community work courses need to be extended, and distanced from the more conservative influences in social work. Current pressure from the social work profession and employers to increase the emphasis on 'hard' skills at the expense of developing students' capacities to challenge current orthodoxies, need to be resisted. Community work education should be made more accessible to practitioners, especially people from social movement backgrounds – Aborigines, immigrants and people with disabilities. Improved accessibility may come about through modifying entry requirements, developing short courses, and providing more support to minority group members entering tertiary education programs.

References

Allport, C. (1986) 'Women and suburban housing: post-war planning in Sydney 1943-1961', in J. McLoughlin and M. Huxley, (eds.), *Urban Planning in Australia: Critical Readings*, Melbourne: Longman Cheshire: 235.

Australia, Department of Employment, Education and Training (1988) 'Women in Community Services', *Women and Work*, 1(1), March: 5-6.

Barry, K. (1989) 'Tootsie Syndrome, or We have met the enemy and they are us', *Women's Studies International Forum*, 12(5): 487-493.

Broom, D. (1989) 'Using the System to Change the System – Contradictions in Women's Health Care', Paper presented at the *Annual Meeting of The Australian Sociological Association*, December.

Curthoys, A. (1984) 'Women's Movement and Social Justice', in D. Broom (ed.), *Unfinished Business*, Sydney: Allen and Unwin.

Davis, L. (1987) *Community Services Review*, Sydney: Local Government and Shires Associations: vii.

Dixon, J. (1990) 'Will Politically-Inspired Community Work be Evident in the 1990s?', *Community Development Journal*, 25(2): 91-101.

Dowse, S. (1983) 'The women's movement fandango with the state', in C. Baldock and B. Cass, (eds.), *Women, Social Welfare and the State*, Sydney: Allen and Unwin.

Galbally, F. (Chair) (1978) *Migrant Services and Programs*, Canberra: AGPS.

McFerran, L. (1987) *Beyond the Image*, Perth: Women's Emergency Services Program of West Australia.

Meekosha, H. (1989) 'Research and the state: dilemmas of feminist practice', *Australian Journal of Social Issues*, November: 249-268.

Meekosha, H. and Jakubowicz, A. (1989) 'Increasing Opportunity or Deepening Disappointment? Access and Equity in the Commonwealth Department of Community Services and Health', *Migration Action*, April.

Meekosha, H. and Rist, L. (1982) 'The Resource Centres: Boom or Bust?', *Migration Action*, vi: 1.

Helen Meekosha and Martin Mowbray work at the University of New South Wales: Vol. 25 No. 4 (1990): 337-344.

21

The Politics of Equality or the Politics of Difference? Locating Black Communities in Western Society

Ranjit Sondhi

Introduction

This article outlines the specific immigration process that ascribes black minority groups to particular social and economic positions within Britain. It examines the extent to which they were excluded from the general struggle for justice and equality. The case for using race and ethnicity as a basis for radical grouping is considered, as are the dangers inherent in a purely ethnic strategy. Shifting notions of community and identity are presented as the source of a contradictory discourse for black politics. New constructions of difference are firmly located in a wider reality, and a strategy is suggested for balancing the fundamental principles of self-determination and equal participation.

Some of the most powerful 'new' social movements of modern times are those that have used race, religion, culture and nationalism as a basis for radical grouping. In Britain, working with black organisations is now regarded an essential consideration for all practitioners in the 'caring professions', and black studies have become an integral part of the training programmes for youth and community workers. Academics continue to examine the meaning of race, while research is regularly commissioned on the nature and extent of racial discrimination. At a popular level, race relations continues to preoccupy the British electorate, even though it is the one issue about which it is kept politically illiterate.

However, the background against which the debate takes place is rapidly shifting. In a world transformed by a micro-chip revolution, a globalized 'post-modern' electronic culture, increasingly sophisticated telecommunication and cheap air travel, and driven by an economic system based on a transnationally integrated finance capital, it is argued that it is difficult to maintain with any deep conviction the idea of discrete national cultures. Not only are social and political boundaries being fundamentally restructured, but it is further suggested that individual identity is itself reduced to a notion of the 'minimal self', a self that is strangely free of race, gender and class – of any specific identifiable political location – and one which appears to be constantly on the move between fragmentation and fundamentalism.

The contours of social and human relations are being redrawn on a grand scale. It may therefore be both timely and judicious to remind ourselves of the manner in which black men, women and young people arrived and settled in Britain before we contemplate formulating concrete strategies of community development in a pluralist society. Detaching the historical process from contemporary analysis would otherwise be fraught with the attendant danger that these strategies do not liberate but further confine black communities to the specific position to which they have been assigned in the social and industrial sphere.

The context of immigration

The pattern of severe and continuing underdevelopment of countries in the Third World immediately after the Second World War, which was the antithesis of overdevelopment in the West and Japan, had laid the grounds for an international movement of labour drawn particularly from those communities that were faced with a declining revenue from their land but which still possessed the ability to travel. The demand for labour after the war was largely in the unskilled and semi-skilled sectors of the British service and manufacturing industries and it was from the villages of India, Pakistan, Bangladesh and the Caribbean countries that the black migrant force was more easily and conveniently recruited.

Black people were brought to post-war Britain from the vast labour reserves of the ex-colonies of the Empire as individual workers, not as communities. They were, first and foremost regarded as 'units of production' during the expansion phase of the British economic cycle. Couples and families rarely came together, and even when they did, as in the case of some men and women from the countries of the Caribbean, they were regarded more as an aggregate of economically active individuals, rather than as social units held together by ties of sentiment, kinship and marriage. Certainly, in the case of those coming from the Indian sub-continent, the family building process was spread out over many years, and in the case of Sylhetis from Bangladesh, sometimes over two decades. In some unusual cases, immigration case workers are still fighting appeals in tribunals and courts on behalf of those who have been denied entry for settlement as dependent wives and children, fifty years after the first arrival of their menfolk in Britain. (Sondhi 1983)

It would be misleading to suggest that the delay in family reunion was entirely due to increasingly restrictive immigration laws, rules and procedures designed specifically to cut down the numbers of black people to an absolute minimum, even though this has been the obsession of every single administration over the last forty years. A substantial proportion of the early migrants regarded their stay in Britain solely as a sojourn that provided the opportunity to remit surplus wages to their families at home. They certainly were not, in the first instance, encouraged to sponsor their dependent relatives even though there were provisions in the earlier immigration control legislation granting the latter an unconditional right to join their sponsors settled in Britain. Not did the earlier settlers themselves wish to expose their close relatives to the unpleasant experience of living in a culturally and socially hostile environment.

After the first phase of migration, older male children were generally brought across to join their fathers, initially to keep house and cook for the working parent and then to be inducted in turn into the workforce. Mothers and younger children then followed to consolidate households and further to increase the capacity of the male member as a wage earner. In some instances, elderly parents were also sponsored, as much to complete the extended family as to child-mind for working mothers. By the 1970s, the locus of the family in most black communities had gradually shifted away from the agrarian hinterlands to the industrial metropolis until finally all intentions of a wholesale return to the mother country were abandoned. As one of the earlier immigrants explains, 'people now return to their villages to sell their lands, not to buy more'.

Now, although fiancées are still sponsored mainly from India, Pakistan and Bangladesh, and the system of immigration control does its best to keep them out, it is undeniably the case that black communities are here to stay. There is also an interesting phenomenon of a small number of black elders taking their pensions out of Britain to retire elsewhere, but this phenomenon is almost entirely restricted to the 'true' immigrant population. The vast majority of black people are now British citizens, either because they have been born here or because they have been registered or naturalised. While their spoken languages and dialects are still to be heard, they accommodate an increasing number of English phrases and words. The ability to write in the vernacular, while it had never been universal among migrant groups, now appears to be in decline among their children. Dress codes and ethnic food and music are without doubt enjoying a revival, while religious beliefs and practices have always been sustained, both in public and in private. But this cultural renaissance does not mask the reality of the break from the homeland, the measure of which is felt and understood most on occasions when the minority culture is directly juxtaposed with the parent group during visits to the homeland.

Black workers, white racism

Any discussion of black politics in relation to community work in modern-day Britain must therefore take into account personal, cultural and structural factors governing their arrival and settlement. Black workers were brought into the country primarily to work with their hands, not as individuals to enrich cultural and social life, and it was initially as industrial workers through their membership of trade unions that they first exercised their political muscle. It should not however be assumed that because they came from agrarian economies they were strangers to the concept of unions. Village communities have historically been based on cooperative methods of functioning and a high level of interdependence is fundamental to their survival and continuity. In addition, no community was immune to the lessons that were being learnt from countries like Russia and China where peasants had been involved in the cataclysmic changes wrought by their revolutions. It was entirely predictable that black workers would become active members of trade unions and play a lead role in the general struggle for a better deal for all workers.

They were to learn however that an allegiance of black and white workers along class lines did not expunge the racism that existed at all levels within the trade union movement. The indigenous working class had for too long benefited from the fruits of colonial exploitation and had been too long steeped in the ideology of superiority that had been deployed to justify it, to support black workers in their struggle against racial discrimination. Indeed, it was precisely at the social and industrial points of contact between black and white people that racism was most keenly felt. Trade unionists had repeatedly lent their voices to the general call for curbs on the immigration of black workers on both social and economic grounds, while at the same time being caught in the invidious position of having to accept them as members of their organisations.

The politics of location: difference and equality

There was another factor that contributed to the early failure of trade unions to provide protection and support for their black members.

The same era that had heralded large-scale black immigration was also one in which it was becoming increasingly obvious that orthodox parliamentary democracy had failed to represent and protect the interests of ordinary working people. During this period, class-based left-wing and trade union politics either became institutionalised or gave way to single issue campaigns around child poverty, nuclear disarmament, homelessness, world hunger, famine relief and racial discrimination. The crucial aspect of this fragmentation was that while a number of activists committed themselves to working for one particular cause or other, very little time and energy was diverted into working across them. There were always exceptions to this rule, notably a number of black workers' associations who maintained that the struggle had to be fought along both class and race lines, but the inexorable trend was to move towards an analysis in which class conflict was never to be mentioned in public. Words like communism, Marxism and socialism have all but disappeared from popular usage, to a point where a quiet reference to these ideologies even in allegedly progressive company invites disapproval and suspicion.

It must now be acknowledged that the drive to maintain a political culture pulls against the desire to create a cultural politics, so that the fight to improve the general quality of life is in tension with the desire to preserve a certain way of life. Nowhere is this more in evidence than in the trajectory of black politics over the last two decades. Being black is now not just politically interpreted, it is being culturally determined to the point that it ceases to have any meaning. 'Black' has gradually been replaced by 'black and Asian' as much in popular language as in the vocabulary of politicians, broadcasters, academics and community activists. This phrase is in turn proving to be inadequate for some who would wish to make a distinction between, say, 'Muslim' and non-'Muslim' communities. They argue that discrimination is based more on religion than on colour. It would seem that the single issue campaign that set out to combat racial discrimination and gain equal treatment for all black groups is being further divided ever more finely along religious, cultural and nationalist lines.

This creates a dilemma for community workers who operate in a modern climate in which the principles of self-determination and participation both hold equal sway. The celebration of ethnic diversity now holds at least as much currency as the principle of equal opportunity in multi-cultural Britain. The inclination is to suggest that the line between self-determination and equal participation should be the line between the public and private – all equal in public and all different in private. In public all are, say, British; in private, some are Christian, some Jews, some Muslims, some Sikh, some Hindus. In public, all are European, in private some are white, some black, some Asian. One does not have to think hard to find some serious difficulties with this tidy approach. Muslims or blacks may not wish to be Muslims or blacks merely in private; they may wish to act on behalf of their minority in the public sphere. Members of minority groups cannot be expected to shed their identity as members of that minority as the price of admission into the public sphere. To require that they never act publicly would render minorities politically impotent which must mean that their private sphere can be threatened with impunity.

But avoiding the relegation of minority identity to the private sphere by no means implies swinging towards the other extreme of expecting public recognition for minority interests or in any way that would grant a special privilege or special right to the minority in question. Sikhs in Britain should not be forced to be Sikhs only in private, but they should also not expect Sikhism to be taught in state schools in any way in which other religions are also not taught. Similarly, Jewish and Roman Catholic schools should not have advantages that are denied to Muslim schools.

At the practical level, these conceptual issues translate into difficult choices about areas of social life that are an inextricable mixture of public and private concerns. Obviously the solution is in striving for an appropriate balance. Educational curricula should, for example, promote no more assimilation than is necessary for active participation, while no minority group should expect any public funds for any of its educational endeavours that it is not willing to see go equally to the similar endeavours of other majority or minority groups – since each group is equally entitled to self-determination and self-development.

Interestingly, a recent European youth campaign, backed by each of the Member states, has been conducted under the banner 'All Different, All Equal'. The serious dilemma for the practitioner is that both the notion of difference and the notion of equality are not only inadequate when considered separately but exist in tension when taken together. The solution can only lie in consciously working with communities to strike an equilibrium, no matter how temporary, between individual freedom and commitment to a wider society, between the desire to hold on to cultural tradition and the need to change, between the struggle for individual rights and the acknowledgement of social obligations.

Perhaps the answer is that individuals should be encouraged to be different in private, but required to be the same in public. In other words their sense of themselves is contingent upon their precise position in relation to others in both space and time. Often, however, the situation is posed as a false dichotomy. Are members of ethnic minorities black first, and then British, or the other way around? These two descriptions are popularly projected as being mutually exclusive to the extent that the construction 'black British' is one which is more hoped-for than realised. In present circumstances, the possibility of multiple identities is difficult to admit or even imagine.

Ethnicity:
the one difference that makes all the difference?

In a world that has no patience with a class analysis, economic determinism gives way to cultural determinism, and ethnicity becomes the one difference that makes all the difference. For white communities, who see this development as a form of self-imposed apartheid, ethnic movements can serve only to emphasise the folly of any social policy that encourages multiculturalism. For black minorities, they can mean a strategic withdrawal into a world where they feel culturally and linguistically at ease before they emerge to operate with more confidence and purpose in wider society. When constructed in this manner, ethnicity becomes a basis of cohesion and a technique of mobilisation, just as nationalism is employed by a subject people to throw off the yoke of imperialism.

Like all such social movements, ethnic movements contain within them the power to question the whole politics of the system in the light of the single issue. But they also contain the seeds of their own destruction. Ethnic consciousness is both a means of dealing with and deflecting issues of discrimination in the same instant. The legitimacy of any black group is judged at the point when it faces a crisis of direction or of internal policy. In their struggle for equal treatment, blacks may find that they have to align themselves with whites, at times against other blacks. There comes a moment when they choose, either to act as a closed group with the ever-present danger of their association becoming a safety valve, or to push the issue to the point when they begin to contradict their own definition and become part of a general campaign for social justice.

There are also great dangers in the use of a purely ethnic strategy, evidenced in recent events in the former Jugoslavia. It has a tendency of becoming an end in itself. An unscrupulous ethnic leader may exploit the ethnic group to sustain power and control to the detriment of the group. But it is when ethnicity is a constituent element of national identity that we must be most on our guard, because it is then that it produces the kind of ethnic chauvinism that leads to the horrors of ethnic cleansing. Ethnicity entails a sense of belonging tied to fixed, permanent, unalterable oppositions – a sense of belonging which, taken in the extreme, can form the basis of the most viciously regressive kind of nationalism leading to the most disastrous consequences.

The test of any group organised along ethnic lines is the extent to which it is inclusive of other ethnicities, or alternatively, the extent to which it armour-plates itself against them. Can it be intimate with members of another ethnic group, cherish and celebrate their differences as much as their own? Does it have an action policy for building staged alliances and allegiances with other groups across the very boundaries that it seeks to preserve? Does it freely grant the freedom to its individual members to move in and out of its ethnic space should they so choose? To what extent is it prepared to fight for the rights of others to self-determination and equal participation even before their own are fully realised?

The construction of difference: inclusion and closure

In post-modern debate it has been suggested that we may not be able to attach ourselves to some fully closed notion of an absolute integrated self, but it does not stop us from drawing boundaries which makes individual identity possible. (Hall 1987) Now I believe this arbitrary closure applies as much to our 'imagined' communities as it does to our 'fictional' selves. In fact, it is what makes their political character – the recognition of difference and the necessity of closure. A political community often embodies a way of life – it is an expression, and a continuing working out of how life ought to be organised. Without closure, no character. And the right of a political community to shape its own character is perhaps one of the most widely- and deeply-held views of our time. Political boundaries, while they may appear incongruous, particularly to those families and communities it dissects, are nevertheless, when it comes down to it, defended by guns and barbed wire.

So black identity is a felt reality. Members of a community are not only bound by a set of common laws and authority, but constitute a group of people united by shared understandings, meanings, interest, values, sentiments, loyalties, affections and collective pride. They feel they have a common history, a shared understanding of their past, collective memories, shared ceremonies and rituals, even common traits of temperament and character, in which and through which these memories are preserved. They form a distinct ethical and cultural unit which they instinctively mark off from other communities in ways they are not always able to articulate clearly. Their sense of the collective 'we' is not simply a sum total of the individual 'I' but something more. (Parekh 1994)

In these new times, the best type of ethnicity is one which defines a new place for identity by insisting on the fact that its difference is something constructed, not simply found. This ethnicity is not tied to fixed unalterable oppositions and, most importantly, is not wholly defined by exclusion. Even where ethnicity is used as a basis of radical grouping, members may draw inwards temporarily only in order eventually to move more effectively outward.

However, let us remember these days, in the heat of ethnic revivalism, that ethnicity should never be complacently accepted. The recent history of Europe should make that abundantly clear. It is incumbent upon us to declare the irrationalities and inherent dangers in ethnic identification. Perhaps, ethnicity is like an act of faith, and ethnicity, like faith, is most attractive when it has lost its recruiting power.

We must however place all this against the concrete reality of contemporary Britain. Whatever we may say about the nature of ethnic identity, we must recognise that we exist in an environment in which prejudice, discrimination, intolerance and xenophobia not only continue unabated but are taking on more entrenched, more virulent forms. We are working against the tide of a white, male, middle-class, middle-aged, heterosexual backlash.

There are still particular sections of the community who are significant as much in terms of their numbers as in their growing tendency to fight back and cause serious damage to a society that they see as having confined them to limbo. I am talking about a whole class of people that is not so much under as out: out of reckoning of mainstream society, out of all the statistics, out of education, out of training, and therefore de-schooled, never-employed, criminalised, locked-up and sectioned off. It is in that one-third society, as Sivanandan (1995) points out, where the poorest sections of our communities – white and black – scrabble over the leftovers of work, the rubble of slum housing and the dwindling share of welfare, that racism is at its most murderous. Here there is no discrimination in employment because there is no employment, no discrimination in services, goods and facilities because these have long been depleted. That is precisely where the challenge lies. To work in the breeding grounds of fascism, with the most disadvantaged, disenfranchised, dispossessed and deprived sections of young people, in areas defaced and defiled by poverty and powerlessness and petty crime – where racism and violence are opposite sides of the same coin.

I mentioned at the beginning that all factors – personal, cultural and structural – should be taken into account in community development. But I am not interested in arguing whether all this is due primarily to individual pathology or a breakdown of family structures or a failure of the social system. The individual, family and society are not separate, or even separable factors. There is an umbilical chord of connection between the position of people within a family and their position in wider society. There is in my mind no point in isolating the home environment from the general mechanisms which fix their position in the urban and industrial environment.

In fact, the same processes that are transforming the relationship between labour and capital are also shifting relationships between young and old, between men and women, between cultural and national boundaries, between those at the centre and those at the margins. What we have to do is to draw out the connections, and stress the underlying philosophy in all strategies whether these are aimed at protecting the right of all individuals to enjoy membership of any cultural group to which they belong as of their right to participate fully as equal citizens in wider society.

The problem for black politics is to hold on to and constantly struggle against, with or without the aid of post-modernist thought, the reality of racial discrimination, harassment and violence. But it must recognise that it is in essence an economic problem born out of a failure of the state to provide fulfilling and remunerative employment and a healthy and safe environment for all its citizens.

Positive action cannot put right the economic ills of the whole of society nor assist in the creation of a classless society with no distinction between the 'haves', 'have-nots' and 'never-will-haves'. Abolishing racial discrimination does not abolish poverty. But it can ensure that any socioeconomic advantage gained by one individual over another, or one ethnic group over another, is not simply determined by any criterion as spurious and irrelevant as the colour of one's skin. The fight for racial equality should not therefore be abandoned just because of the existence of structural inequality. But neither should the struggle for social justice and human rights cease when racial discrimination is eradicated.

The central task of community workers is to create a more just and fair society for all. Their strategies should, I believe, be pitched at every level; at the individual, engaging all people in the struggle to strike the right balance between rights and responsibilities, between freedom and commitment; at the cultural, creating conditions for a truly diverse Britain which openly and positively encourages the survival of different languages, religions and cultural traditions; at the structural, challenging all institutions and organisations, in the public and private sector, to remove all barriers to participation and to minimise the disengagement and disconnection that reduces social cohesion. Only by operating at all these levels simultaneously can we hope to create a society in which all individuals move gradually from a state of dependence through independence to interdependence.

References

Hall, S. (1987) 'Miniminal Selves', in *Identity*, London: ICA Document E, ICA: 44.

Parekh, B. (1994) 'Three Theories of Immigration' in S. Spencer (ed.), *Strangers and Citizens*, London: IPPR: 91.

Sivanandan, A. (1995) 'La trahison des clercs', *New Statesman and Society*, 14th July.

Sondhi, R. (1983) 'Immigration and Citizenship in post-war Britain' in C. Field (ed.), *Minorities: Community and Identity*, Dahlem Konferenzen: 255.

Ranjit Sondhi teaches at Westhill College: Vol. 32 No. 3 (1997): 223-232.

22

The Trajectory of National Liberation and Social Movements: The South African Experience

Viviene Taylor

Goals of national liberation

The anatomy of national liberation movements in South Africa, and Africa generally, and the characteristics which informed them, differed from those that emerged elsewhere. Colonial domination led to different forms of organisation and mobilisation which were self-generated in many instances. Led organically, from the bottom, and acting as pressure to give impetus to a change in direction, generally by intellectual leadership, movements were mobilised to serve collective interests through a process of organised action to take control of state power. National liberation was linked to overcoming conditions of mass-based structural poverty experienced as a conscious policy outcome of the apartheid state. Political, cultural, psychological and economic subordination of black people, dispossession from their land, and unemployment resulted in a deliberate process of under-development. Attaining political power in 1994 was therefore a major advance but not a complete victory because economic power and access to resources are still not a reality for the majority.

Added to this the need to redefine and recast state power into democratic forms has challenged categories of static racial, national and class identity. Political resistance against the apartheid state was part of a resistance of people to the categories assigned to them and according to which their lives were prescribed. Race, class and gender constructs shaped both the political and private spheres of black and white people's lives.

The history and context

Although the anti-colonial struggle goes back many years, since 1948, when the Afrikaner National Party came into power and brought with it the institutionalisation of apartheid and racial capitalism, the resistance of mainly black South Africans against the apartheid state gained new impetus and broad popular mass support. The build-up of mass support against state repression did not, however, arise spontaneously, nor did it occur under a united platform representing common interests. The South African experiences with regard to national liberation struggles and mass movements were historically-specific; they reflected the time, circumstances and material conditions out of which they arose. The struggle for change in South Africa was, therefore, not a uni-linear process but rather a dynamic intersecting process that varied over the last eighty years.

The focus of each liberation movement defined its constituency and distinguished its members within the 'us' from 'them' point of view. The African National Congress (ANC) was grounded on the principle of national unity using non-racialism, democracy, anti-discrimination and non-sexism as its criteria. The Black Consciousness Movement (BCM) also focused on anti-racial domination and attempted to unify all those who were discriminated against on the basis of identity concepts. The South African Communist Party (SACP) based its emphasis on the working classes and used a class-based analysis to appeal to community members and the poorest people who were generally black, rural and industrial labourers. Goals and strategies of these movements emerged from their vision for a just society. All these movements rejected forms of identity that could be divisive. Their ideological focus was to highlight the material, emotional and psychological deprivation caused by apartheid and racial capitalism.

Participatory processes

Movements were characterised by mobilising people from local levels right up to national levels. A chain of communication was fed through from the bottom up and from the top down. This involved two key aspects within these movements. The first had to do with the organising, planning and collective decision-making process on the issue to be addressed: who would be involved, the time factor, the outcomes of mass action, campaigns, events and resources required. The second related to the notion of accountability and evaluation of the overall process, strategy and its successes and failures. Decisions made and the outcomes of action were usually explained to and ratified by the general membership. There were frequent interactions between leaders and members which put into practice the process of accountability to the masses. Processes of organising in the movements took mass democratic form in opposition to the authoritarianism of the state. In action, movements began to do things differently, working with marginalised people within a political approach to spheres usually seen as non-political.

Periodisation

An important feature of the content and form of the democratic struggle was the emergence of distinct phases linked to specific periods and contexts. During the period between 1912 to 1949 the ANC and early political organisations used every political platform to engage in dialogue with successive governments. Since dialogue, petitions, deputations and letters were unsuccessful, strategy changed.

The period from 1949 to 1957 brought great militancy within the ranks of the liberation movements, especially from the youth cadres who radicalised the ANC. They pushed for the development of oppositional structures outside the state apparatus to force a revolutionary tempo to change. (Mandela, 1994) The ANC Youth League was also responsible for leading the liberation movement in the development of its 1949 Programme of Action which led to the most active mass mobilisation campaigns at the time. This period helped to consolidate and broaden the membership, resulted in a cadre of volunteers to help organise various campaigns and, the most significant outcome, produced the Freedom Charter Campaign. The Freedom Charter captured the social, political and economic objectives of the struggle and was the framework within which the movement operated. During 1960 to 1968, state repression, banning, imprisonment and continuous harassment of democratic forces led to the liberation movement going 'underground' and into exile. It also saw the establishment of *Umkonto weSizwe*, the armed wing of the ANC. There was a dearth of open political resistance within the country during this period.

One important development in the late 1960s was the rise of the Black Consciousness Movement (BCM) through students' activities at black tertiary institutions. The formation of the South African Students Organisation (SASO) was a critical factor in unifying black (African, Coloured and Indian) people around their common oppression. It was based on a two-pronged strategy. First, that of increasing the grassroots base by unifying black people across race, class and ethnic divides. Second, it served to affirm the role of black people and their right to take control over their lives. The BCM's strategies to mobilise black people were based on an analysis which showed that the psychological nature of oppression must be addressed for people to overcome their fear and resist their oppressors. For a long time BC activists held their own against oppression because of their psychological assertiveness. They were able to confront the 'enemy' from positions of strength. This emphasis on the psychological nature of oppression and the importance of black people affirming themselves was also influenced by Fanon's (1990) analysis of how colonised people internalise the image of the oppressor and in turn use the same methods of oppression against people. Fanon emphasised that unless oppressed people dealt with the psychological and cultural roots of their oppression they would themselves be likely to replicate patterns of subordination. Colonised people therefore had to decolonise and decondition their minds so that when shifts were made from the body (material needs) to the minds of people the chances of liberation were greater.

The Black Consciousness Movement provided a significant turning point in linking liberation with human development. In analysing black consciousness and the quest for a true humanity Biko (1973) had this to say:

> In order that Black Consciousness can be used to advantage as a philosophy to apply to people in a position like ours, a number of points have to be observed. As people existing in a continuous struggle for truth, we have to examine and question old concepts, values and systems. Having found the right answers we shall then work for consciousness among all people to make it possible for us to proceed towards putting these answers into effect. In this process, we have to evolve our own schemes, forms and strategies to suit the need and situation, always keeping in mind our fundamental beliefs and values.[1]

This statement reflects the strong links made between political liberation, self-liberation and development as a way of achieving full human development.

The period of the state's total strategy against resistance during the 1980s resulted in a massive wave of demonstrations and the build-up of a countervailing force which led to the formation of the United Democratic Front (UDF). The apartheid government was unable to contain protests and resistance within the country which were organised by the civic movements, workers' movements, student movements and a range of other organisations under the banner of UDF. At the same time the economy was in decline, government was utilising its capital reserve for recurrent apartheid expenditure and its loans were being called in by international banks. The state was in crisis both from within and outside. At this stage the base and social composition of the movement expanded with urbanised youth and the working-class coming together to shape a counter-culture of resistance which had materialised in townships after 1976. The techniques of organisation, mobilisation, graphic posters, pamphleteering, films, videos, mass meetings and selective use of the media also corresponded to new skills and the emerging confidence of black activist workers and their allies.

A new cadre of leadership emerged representing different class outlooks: black professionals from the ranks of the clergy, trade unionists, journalists, lawyers and many others. In the community, civil society organisations such as advice offices and NGOs were strengthened. From the spirit of volunteerism in the 1950s, there was a shift to the employment of full-time organisers who worked around the clock on the specific day-to-day struggles of working people to mobilise for mass action. This period could be termed the 'time of the comrades'. There was a convergence between political education, mobilisation and community organisations. In practice the modes of operation played out the strategies of Saul Alinsky (1945) and Paulo Freire (1972). Organised groups moved through the phases of political/social awareness, critical analysis and action for social transformation.

This led to the erosion of state control and an increasing build-up of international pressure. It was followed by a change in strategy of the apartheid government which led to the unbanning of liberation movements and a negotiated settlement during the period 1990 to 1994. It may be said that this change derived not so much from changes in their political ideology or belief in apartheid but rather the effects these had on the economic and political crises of the time.

A significant feature of mobilisation within the ANC and its alliance partners, the SACP, the Congress of South African Trade Unions (COSATU) with the remnants of former UDF organisations[2], the Pan African Congress (PAC) and the BCM, was that mobilisation strategies directly involved the people affected by state repression.

Organisational structures and formations

While national liberation movements had structures and committees within provincial regions, these were usually not small enough to cover the type of wider and more diverse representation needed from the ground. The organic and sometimes planned development of alternative local structures in the form of street committees, advice office forums, youth groups, study groups and sports organisations, burial societies, and the like evolved in response to the need for organisations to support the national movements against repressive and unjust policies and actions of the state.

> There have always been levels of mobilisation in South Africa … of people's involvement in civil society associations, in tenant groups, often very ambivalent and not militant at all urban groupings, many of them attempting to promote democracy. But almost as far back as the history of South African cities, shadowy forerunners to the civic, there was undoubtedly a need for political movements, to actually get involved at all levels to organise a progressive coalition of forces. (Bundy 1996)[3]

Such coalitions did not change the objectives of national liberation but became strategies through which people shifted the sites of struggle against the state, gave the progressive forces a mass character, and challenged the process of governance at all levels.

As repression subdued a generation of leaders, imprisoned hundreds and drove many into exile, popular and open campaigns were replaced by underground political work both in the communities and in the building of new cells/units to pursue armed struggle. At the same time on the industrial front, increasing foreign capital investment stimulated a greater diversification and expansion of the economy. By the end of the 1970s, mining no longer played the leading role of accumulation and was competing with manufacturing and financing as the leading sector. (Marx 1992) Changes brought about by the expansion of industry also resulted in a greater organised working class movement during this period. The changes in the composition, size, skill, stability and social weight of the working class were not accompanied by political and ideological changes in the ruling class however. Labour was still controlled by pass laws and influx control. By the 1980s, more than 60% of workers were permanent residents in poverty-stricken and overcrowded townships. The struggles of the labour movement to improve working conditions saw the establishment of the State's 1979 Wiehan Commission whose brief was to investigate labour relations and the recognition of some conservative and moderate unions and their activities.

It may be said that the rise of unionism during the 1970s, accompanied by nationwide strikes and stayaways in certain industries, also served to maintain a high degree of worker activism linked to mobilisation within the framework of national liberation. This gave rise to what is now being called social movement unionism. Retrospectively, this movement brought about a strong convergence between conditions on the factory floor and conditions experienced by families of workers and others in communities. It resulted in union leaders playing a prominent role in the 1980s in the civic and resident associations to address community issues. It also resulted in these specific movements experiencing a tension, in terms of their membership which ran across political tendencies, and the degree to which they could remain autonomous and still support the liberation struggle. The tensions of maintaining a 'political line' and meeting the needs of a diverse membership are still apparent today.

Social movements

The manner in which social movements respond to forms of exclusion and exploitation within the changing context of new global arrangements provides some useful lessons. The discourse on social movements tends to project a 'trendy' image of them and their potential which does not reflect the reality: 'The new relationships and political participation the develop within contemporary social movements represent efforts to establish an egalitarian practice that is normally implicit in the notion of "community"'. (Cardoso 1992)

This statement reflects the intention of unifying people across various divides (class, colour, religion, gender) under a common objective and in the process they develop a sense of bonding, on community and new ways of relating. Social movements generally tend to maintain a degree of political independence. However, they also have as many organisational, ideological and other problems as other interest groups. The strength of social movements lies in the type of issue that people are mobilised around; identifying the vacuum, the gaps that are not being addressed and what impact these have on the specific group to be targeted. Cardoso and others have emphasised that new forms of relationships and political participation are emerging in new social movements. They are developing a sense of bonding because of what they strive to achieve. The construction of an egalitarian community does not come about because of the possession of common positive attributes but rather through a common deficiency or oppression. In that way, a community can be perceived as an experience of inequality. An identified need can therefore unite people beyond race, class, ethnic and other barriers. Often the terms 'social movements' and 'popular movements' are used interchangeably. While they have common attributes, popular movements also have distinctive elements.

Social movements have generally been single-issue, sector-specific or constituency-led. Their goals focus on improvements in areas which affect a particular group of people, or environment, for instance the trade union movements and the student movements of the 1960s and 1970s. The peace movement was a response to the Vietnam War and the build-up of military power. The green movement, feminist movement and the civil rights movements of the United States of America also reflect this trend. Although many of these movements were influenced by crosscutting issues, spanning political, social, economic and cultural aspects, the selection of issues, processes and strategies of organisation distinguished them.

Further, as in national liberation movements, some social movements (labour for example) have pushed the boundaries of struggle beyond the formal political arena. In South Africa this has resulted in an emphasis on the relative importance given to the processes of organising for change and not only to the structures that exercise power.

Convergence and divergence between national liberation and social, popular and proxy movements

Globally, then, national liberation movements, popular mass movements and social movements have used strategies to mobilise people towards the attainment of specific goals. While these three categories of movements have some common attributes, particularly in the manner in which organisation takes place, they also have distinctive features. These features make it difficult to replicate their strategies without taking into account both the context within which they evolve and their heterogeneity. The struggles of movements and groups of excluded people are too diverse in their origins and outcomes to be seen as a model that can be adopted for all development efforts. As demographic, technological, political, economic and environmental changes influence and reshape the landscape, define current practices and new boundaries, it becomes even more difficult to predict how new struggles will emerge and benefit from past experiences.

Within the emerging global context, different forces from precolonial, post-colonial and neo-colonial periods continue to shape modalities of organising for change by excluded people. To deny this would be to promote a simplistic understanding of the factors, internal and external to countries, that shape the complex social relationships which led to the emergence of movements and the inter/intra movement dynamics themselves. Liberation movements have sought to achieve real gains for the dispossessed majority in their countries through revolutionary mobilisation under the guidance of a vanguard party or enlightened elite. What is common to national liberation movements is that they define oppression in terms of one national group over another. They seek control of the state through the takeover of colonial administration and state power or, as in the case of South Africa, the minority white apartheid regime.

Studies show that social movements emerge in specific national contexts, in response to state or private sector policy initiatives. Some of the gains from social movement activism have benefited people beyond such movements' membership. This has been particularly so of social movement unionism when workers have attempted to mobilise within an industrial sector nationally but where benefits attained go beyond that sector. Social movements which include, for example, workers, residents' associations, health activists or homeless people reflect multiple forms of collective mobilisation of society. This is, in turn, shaped by the plurality of the sites and forms of struggle, and give it a content and character that allows for critical space to express dissent with the *status quo*.

The term 'popular mass movements' refers to those movements that have a membership or following from a wide and varied range of social classes and interests, usually representing people at the local or 'grassroots' levels. 'People' in this sense becomes as problematic a concept as 'community'. When an issue or problem is so fundamental that it cuts across class, race, gender, and geo-political divides it lends itself to the formation of a popular movement. Such movements arise because of extreme disillusionment with the state, alienation from processes of governance and expectations that the state should act in the public, rather than the private, interest and not become guilty of statism or state building. Leadership of these movements is identified with the interests of the membership and usually articulate the demands in language that is understood by its base. Popular movements usually challenge the power structures to respond to the needs, problems and issues of their membership.

Because popular mass movements tend to be 'demand driven' in the sense that they demand rights and space from the state, they are often termed populist. This tends to project an image of an amorphous group of people who are not able to understand the complexity of state and private sector relations and therefore make unreasonable demands on these sectors.

Social movements operating within the objectives of national liberation in the context of apartheid

In the South African context, movements have historically been organised around specific issues affecting workers, youth, women and 'communities'. However, they were located ideologically and in terms of their leadership within the broader national liberation movements. The significant difference between the national liberation movements and movements such as these, which organised around specific constituencies and interests, was that strategies were always aimed at securing concrete physical gains for people. Seldom were the total populations represented in any of these movements and consequently mobilisation for change took place through pressure groups and credible representatives of the specific movement.

Community-led organisations became countervailing forces to the structures of apartheid and also were the conduits through which ordinary men, women, youth and children could plan, reflect and mobilise for action to change their circumstances. The many diverse organisations that came into being at key moments in the history of mass democratic struggles resulted in a vibrant, critical, civil society that positioned itself for democratic, anti-racist and anti-discriminatory practices. Its oppositional style of political activism and mobilisation created critical spaces in society through which the views of excluded people could be voiced.

Diverse and varied organisations therefore can come together to achieve common goals or resolve a conflict that affects the majority if the issue to be addressed is perceived to be legitimate, commands the moral high ground, and does not undermine the integrity of the organisations taking part in it. Further, the history of mass mobilisation indicates that in most cases, strategies for action have involved organisations of people which varied from local civic organisations to national political movements, from shop stewards committees in a factory to a national trade union federation. The strength of most movements (national liberation, popular and social) came from their local character and the location where people were based. They were led by people who represented the interests of members, were aware of the local environment, and who were responsive and responsible.

Organisations in the past were central in constructing democracy and used the process of mobilising for change to do this. A key lesson that has been reinforced from the mass democratic struggle is that the process of forming, maintaining and mobilising organisations is almost more important than the strategies they use to engage in mass action.

Within the broad progressive front, the role played by religious institutions in building democracy reflects that, as with others, these institutions were themselves divided as sites of struggle. Because of their diverse interests and competing claims they were able to play critical roles within the Christian, Islamic, Jewish, Hindu and other faiths. Their contribution to strategies for change was of two kinds. First, progressive religious institutions supported political and economic strategies of the mass democratic movement for change; and second, they provided moral legitimisation of the rights of the oppressed majority to democracy and development. Religious institutions had, and continue to have the support base, usually of the poorest people. Having an effective communication system with their membership and the basis for co-operation between churches and progressive organisations they have been, importantly, able to capture public support and media coverage in less antagonistic ways than organisations that are politically partisan.

Strategies used by organisations in the past to mobilise for change were effective in gaining more control over the development process and were also able to influence government thinking in order to redefine the relationship between the state and civil society. However, the formation of structures and organisations are, in themselves, not sufficient to promote development. Their nature, content, processes and the manner in which these articulate with the needs of their members and the broader society determine their ability to democratise society. In this regard, community sectors and members usually took responsibility for monitoring the processes and helped devise new strategies based on past experiences to remind and pressurise the government to act in the interests of the people.

Proxy movements

A unique feature in mass democratic struggles in South Africa was the formation of 'proxy movements'. While national liberation movements mobilised with people in their own or national interests, social movements mobilised with select representatives of either sectoral groups or categories of the population for the attainment of a specific goal and proxy movements mobilised on behalf of people. While liberation movements and social movements distinguish themselves in terms of their goals and objectives, their membership consists largely of people who are affected by a specific condition, problem or issue. The strategies they use to mobilise are determined by the issue and type of membership. In the South African struggle, the moral and just cause for resistance against apartheid was so compelling that organisations or movements were formed to fight on 'behalf of the oppressed' within and outside of the country. This resulted in a type of proxy movement.

Proxy movements are distinct in their nature, membership and objectives. They are characterised by people who group themselves together to act on behalf of those members/sectors of society who do not have a voice, cannot represent themselves or have no space to mobilise in their own interests. Such movements can be generated by a core group of concerned citizens who act on their own, act together with government or with a coalition of groupings. Since the issue or condition, in many instances, is not one that directly affects them the strength with which they mobilise would be moderate and would not pose a real danger to themselves. The motivating factor which the members respond to is usually the one which is based on morality, social justice, human rights, ethical considerations or the containment of political and social unrest. Using this definition of proxy movements in the South African context, the Black Sash, the National Children's Rights Committee, the Pro-choice and Abolition of the Death Penalty can be identified as more progressive movements in this category. Outside of the country anti-apartheid and other solidarity movements could also be included in this category.

Critical elements and processes in movements: issues for community development

The trajectory of national liberation movements and their relationships with social and popular movements reflect ideological, organisational and interpersonal dimensions in democratising the state. A major dilemma confronting the former liberation movements in South Africa and their allies is how to ensure the objectives of the struggle for democracy are not betrayed. Agents of social transformation need to further the debate on whether the current context can facilitate a socialist transition or popular national reconstruction. Amin (1993) contends that in the changing context, popular national construction combines and conflicts with the tendencies of socialism, capitalism and statism. These tendencies are responsible for different forces and factors in production which collectively are able to respond to the demands and needs of the poorest people. This aspect is a fundamental issue within the field of community development if it is to be seen as a collective holistic process of economic, social and political development of people.

However, South Africa's current transition does not only pose ideological questions but also highlights the internal crises facing the democratic movements and the extent to which they can mediate action for community development. Some of these crises, if not understood and overcome, will not only result in further fragmentation of a deeply-divided society but will make the task of social reconstruction impossible. If community development, as a process and strategy for social transformation which equalises power relations, is to succeed, then those involved need to go beyond seeing new social movements as a panacea for people's struggles from below.

Social movements, when they converge with popular national interests, can play a meaningful role if the identity issues (cultural, social and political) are understood when they move beyond survival issues to the empowerment of people. The form that social and popular movements take in future will largely depend on how national liberation movements transform themselves into political parties. It will also depend on how their allies in the labour, civic, women's, youth and human rights movements, consolidate, realign themselves, grow and capture resources to create the space for critical thinking, struggle and dissent and its expression through political, extra parliamentary and civil society structures. When the goals of liberation and social movements cannot be attained because of political and economic systems that are determined through global arrangements and people at the bottom become alienated, then social and popular movements need to reflect on the extent to which they have become co-opted into these systems and the extent to which they remain anti-systemic. Responses to negative global arrangements should also be dealt with through building solidarity within movements in both national contexts and transnationally. Co-option or conflictual relations might be necessary at different moments, but within the process of community development a key factor is whether the needs, interests and concerns of the majority are being addressed.

Community development practitioners need to understand that an essential precondition for social movement activism is understanding the historical basis of the problem, issue or concerns to be addressed. Further, the issue of clarifying values, ideologies and philosophies on which strategies for action are shaped is important in the promotion of human development. While most movements tend to locate their struggles within a specific set of values and ideologies of development, democracy and social relations, community development workers need to interrogate their own conceptions of democratic development to ensure they themselves are not obstacles in the process of transformation.

The need to construct alternative ways of engaging with the state to address problems within mainstream society can result in a counter-culture that is more people- and environmentally-friendly. How activists, organisations and interest groupings capture and use different forms of power can promote either collective or individual interests.

The challenge that lies ahead for community development and social movements in popular national reconstruction is ensuring that the 'people's will' and aspirations survive. This depends on building forms of solidarity which concentrate people's creative energies on securing, deepening and extending the spaces for democratic and collective action.

The complex nature of the struggle and the changing global context with the realignment of political and economic forces after the end of the Cold War has resulted in both challenges and contradictions for and within democratic formations in South Africa. The contradictions relate largely to how the new democratic political order works closely with private capital, both nationally and internationally, to secure economic stability and growth on the one hand, whilst continuing to advance the class and social interests of its mass-based constituency on the other. The challenge now facing the emerging democratic state is how to link political transformation to the need for social transformation with the active participation of the people on the ground. How to promote this and ensure the socio-economic rights of people are attained is also the challenge facing community development activists who are committed to transforming unequal power relations and ensuring the primacy of people in the development process.

References

Alinsky, S. (1945) *Reveille for Radicals*, Chicago: University of Chicago Press.

Amin, S. (1993) 'Social Movements at the Periphery' In: P. Wignaraja (ed.) *New Social Movements in the South, Empowering People*. London: Zed Books: 76-100.

Cardoso, R.C.L. (1992) 'Popular Movements and Conciliation of Democracy in Brazil' In: A. Escobar and S.E. Alverez (eds.) *The Making of Social Movements in Latin America*. Boulder, Colorado.

Fanon, F. (1990) *The Wretched of the Earth*, Harmondsworth: Penguin Books.

Freire, P. (1972) *Pedagogy of the Oppressed*, Harmondsworth: Penguin Books.

Mandela, N. (1994) *Long Walk to Freedom: The Autobiography of Nelson Mandela*. South Africa: Macdonald Purnell.

Marx, A.W. (1992) *Lessons of Struggle. South African Internal Opposition 1960-90*. Cape Town: Oxford University Press.

Notes

1. This statement is an article written by Steve Biko in 1973 in *Black Theology: The South African Voice* and is quoted in Steve Biko, *I write what I like*, in 1978.
2. A number of organisations aligned themselves with the ANC at various times depending on the issues to be addressed, since the ANC was and is the largest liberation movement in the country. The UDF, formed in the 1980s brought together over 600 civic organisations which also aligned themselves with the objectives of the ANC.
3. Personal interview with Professor Colin Bundy, a historian.

Viviene Taylor is Director of the Southern African Development Education and Policy Research Unit: Vol. 32 No. 3 (1997): 252-265.

23

The Role of NGOs in Democratisation and Education in Peace-Time Rwanda

C. Nungwa Kuzwe

Rwanda is passing through one of the darkest periods in its history and probably one of the greatest tragedies in the history of humankind. Since the beginning of the century, we have witnessed only four real genocides: those of the Armenians, the Jews, the Tziganes (Hungarian gypsies), and the Tutsis in Rwanda. The fact that in Rwanda, one sector of the population massacred more than a million people of another sector, often in atrocious ways, is beyond comprehension or imagination. What makes it even harder to understand is that the different socio-ethnic groups had been living in harmony and symbiosis for decades.

The fact is that the split did occur and that millions of people lost their families, leaving widows, orphans, and cripples. Rwanda has produced the greatest number of refugees in the world, most of whom can be found in neighbouring countries. Many have already been forced to return due to the situation in Zaire.

Several attempts at reconstruction, both of the country and of morale, are underway. Most notably have been the national reconciliation programmes, the victim support programmes, and the resettlement and the socio-economic rehabilitation of refugees. What happened in April-July 1994 in Rwanda cannot and should not be forgotten. We now have to rebuild a nation.

The role of NGOs

Essentially, the NGO movement is a product of the community and it should plant seeds of endogenous and durable development in the basic communities. It is imperative that NGOs participate in the prevention of conflicts and the creation of a culture of peace. NGO members must understand and must make the community understand the true causes of conflicts. They should take part in the eradication of the underlying and indirect causes of these conflicts.

In 'developing' countries, especially in Africa, it has become apparent that the principal cause of conflict is the refusal to share power. In our opinion, if developed countries fail to recognise the tragedies which are the daily lot of many Africans, it is because they have managed to install political systems which favour frequent changeovers of governmental power. Such systems do not exist in African countries. Our NGOs should therefore be actively involved in popular education programmes which promote political and governmental change.

In order to remain in power for as long a time as possible, preferably without sharing it, political leaders invent a whole series of strategies. The recent experience of Rwanda, provides us with examples of a few of these strategies.

It is hardly surprising that in countries divided by chronic conflicts, there is a minute portion of people who are incredibly rich, while the vast majority remain in a state of squalid poverty. This situation is often considered desirable, because a poor and starving person does not think, thus he or she can be manipulated by promises of a crust of bread. In Rwanda people participated in genocide because they were promised the property of their neighbours. However, sooner or later, people revolt. If we truly want to prevent conflicts and create a culture of peace, our community organisations will have to become involved in local programmes which promote the alleviation of poverty and, more specifically, nutritional safely.

The importance of education and the law

There is not a shadow of a doubt that illiteracy and lack of education provide the ideal cultural environment for the propagation of conflict. A population which knows neither how to read nor how to write will accept whatever they are told. So there is a good reason why African leaders put obstacles in the way of national schooling programmes, which could be seen as a source of knowledge and therefore a source of anti-establishment protest. In Rwanda, children begin their primary education at 8 years old and finish at 16. The only language taught in schools is the local language, Kinyarwanda.

Since its creation the National University has only been able to take in 3000 students. We believe that these measures have kept the population under a blanket of ignorance, rendering it incapable of critical analysis and thus susceptible to manipulation. NGOs should thus become more involved in formal and informal education programmes. This would promote a critical spirit which would prevent blind participation in conflicts.

People are often subject to great injustices in poor countries. Injustices which are maintained over a long period of time constitute a potential source of conflict, for sooner or later the injured party will seek justice for itself. It is interesting to note that the judicial system has long been the poor relation of political decision-makers; characterised by the lack of law schools, the shortages of materials and equipment in courts of law, and the blatant mismanagement of legal proceedings. We cannot possibly prevent conflicts without a decent, independent legal system. NGOs should promote training programmes for magistrates, aim to make legal texts available to all, and provide legal representation for those who are unable to arrange it for themselves. Before the modern judiciary system can be fully functional, we therefore have to develop and energise the traditional system of community justice.

Conflicts are born when one is forbidden to think freely or to read and write what you think, freely. Dictators have tried to silence their people but sooner or later the latter always rebel. Given the importance of freedom of speech and education in the process of democratisation, it is imperative that our organisations should invest time and money into the creation and maintenance of autonomous and independent newspapers. Audio-visual means of communication, especially radio, should be given priority due to the fact that a large proportion of the population is illiterate.

Many of us would like to know what our NGOs have done to prevent or to halt the genocide and massacres which have cast a tragic shadow over Rwanda. Certainly we should have done everything in our power to prevent it but could *we* have achieved that? And once it was underway, what could we have done to stop it, when faced with machine guns and machetes and hysterical people? Didn't the UN and the West clear out while they could? However, we must recognise the mistakes we made in the past in order to build a better future.

Providing democratic models

First, we must acknowledge the weakness of our organisations with regard to organisation and planning. The relationship between our organisations and the populations which we are supposed to serve is not as close as it should be. Projects are planned in our offices without any consultation with or participation by those it affects most; the beneficiaries. So, we should review our approach and moreover, encourage communities to resolve their problems themselves.

The management of our NGOs is far from democratic, so how can we continue to criticise our political leaders for being anti-democratic when at the heart of our organisations we don't practice democracy either? Very few decisions are made in meetings and those which are, are rarely enforced. Credibility is an indispensable prerequisite for our organisations if we are to play a determining role in the mobilisation of people and in the creation of a lawful state and a culture of peace. This credibility is threatened by the management of our organisations and by the leaders who abuse their positions so as to make themselves wealthier.

NGOs can only play an active role in the prevention and the management of conflicts if they maintain a politically neutral stance. Overt or covert involvement of a community organisation leader in a conflict can have negative repercussions for his/her organisation. In Rwanda we have seen cases of NGO leaders being won over by politicians. We must establish a code of honour for our leaders so that our credibility and the apolitical stance of our organisations can be safeguarded.

It is also important that we cultivate a culture of peace at the heart of organisations. We can never be considered to be the 'salt of the earth' if we practice exclusion amongst ourselves. If we believe in peace we ought to begin by practising it at home. I personally believe that if all community organisations and their members were to have an absolute faith in the cause of Peace, they would find that their goals would be within easy reach. Think of the numerous religious groups, of the youth and women's associations, of the workers' co-operatives and the consumer co-operatives.

My country has suffered greatly as a consequence of the events of April 1994; peace is still elusive in the Great Lakes region. It is with great difficulty that we forgive the International Community for remaining silent and turning a blind eye to the genocide which threw Rwanda into mourning. But we blame it more for not having helped us to reconstruct our country. Our NGOs, for example, have been crippled by a lack of personnel and equipment. Trust between different socio-ethnic groups has been shattered. We need help to re-establish that trust through constructive dialogue. Thousands of widows and orphans lack food and shelter. You cannot aim for peace without first taking care of these women and children.

Thousands of refugees have returned to their motherland. They continue to sleep under the stars. Women and children are left uncared for and with no schooling. As we have already seen, the absence of peace in Rwanda has been echoed in Burundi, Zaire and other neighbouring countries. Why should our community organisations continue to close their eyes to the foolishness of certain leaders. It is time to wake up! We believe in peace ... so let's defend it! The faith and conviction of Nelson Mandela transformed South Africa; others' faith and conviction in Peace will transform Africa and the World.

Dr. Kuzwe is President of the Forum of Rwanda NGOs: Vol. 33 No. 2 (1998): 174-177.

24

The Environmental Crisis, Greens and Community Development

Crescy Cannan

Introduction

The environmental crisis will be the gravest issue facing the human population in the coming century. I do not need to repeat here the depressing figures about the speed with which the world's natural resources are being consumed, the associated damage caused by burning fossil fuels, the destruction caused to the environment by mining and logging, and the decline in the numbers of species caused by pressure on their habitats through urbanization, intensive farming, pollution and over-fishing. But there is an area that needs stressing, in a community development journal: the environmental crisis intensifies forms of inequality and threatens collective goods – thus it is a human crisis as well as a threat to the entire planet.

The environmental crisis, globalization and social justice

First, something of the big picture. Rees (1999), using UNDP statistics, demonstrates that economic growth, which has increased five-fold since the second world war, has been accompanied by a doubling of the income gaps between poor nations and the rich, with rising gaps within nations. It is, he argues, a fallacy to think that the eco-system could sustain the situation if all of the world's population were to live at the level of the wealthiest twenty per cent – who, in fact, consume nearly eighty per cent of the biophysical output of the planet. Existing levels and forms of production and consumption, driven by artificially created desires and needs, are then associated with global ecological degradation and huge inequalities.

If all the aspects of environmental crisis were tackled together, as greens say they must be (different kinds of energy and materials use, reducing polluting emissions, waste recycling, use of land, air and water, protection of wildlife and the maintenance of genetic diversity), it would involve reductions in existing consumption patterns on a vast scale. We would need to see at least a halving of fossil fuel use and a ten-fold increase in protected lands in Europe to move towards

284

sustainability. (Jacobs 1999a) Social justice would mean proportionately greater reductions of resource used in the developed countries – by up to eighty per cent. (Barrett Brown and Coates 1996) Sustainable development then is a social issue.

Sustainable development is also about the stewardship of environmental goods which are common, collective things – water, landscapes and open spaces, diversity of species, public health and well-being. It is then also a political concept, with growing conflict over water, and over farmers' right to use, share and re-use seeds for the crops of their and their local markets' choice. It is a global issue because the demand for cheap food (and clothes and other goods) in the north is creating injustice in the south (as well as in pockets of the north). What Lang (1999) calls the hypermarket (as opposed to the market) economy is producing cheap food for the north with massive external costs such as energy spent in transporting food, and the reduction of diverse, small scale farming (in north and south) to monocultural production with farmers increasingly dependent on international corporations. For some greens these trends are alarming for spiritual reasons, but we can protest on political grounds. Genetic engineering of crop plants, for instance, is dangerous not because it is tampering with nature or the sacred but 'because it grants big business monopolistic control over the food chain with devastating consequences for both the poor and the eco-system'. (Monbiot 2000)

Community development needs to remind politicians, 'stakeholders' and the general public in the North that their lifestyles rely on damage being done, especially in the South. We can draw on the green argument that the quality of life is not the same as that which is measured by rising income levels, though we are faced with the enormous difficulty of challenging the now dominant ideology of consumerism. (Cahill 1999) However, given that community development is an occupation which eschews such individualistic values, it should have a role in the urgent task of persuading people that consuming and living differently will ultimately benefit us all. To any community developers who suggest that these are middle class issues, I would reply that environmental problems fall most heavily on the poor – they are likely to have the least energy efficient housing, least access to fresh food, least access to transport (public or private), and to live in less desirable and more degraded areas, and among the poor of the north, ethnic minorities are likely to have the kind of housing with the least contact with nature. (Ling Wong 1998) The poor, in North and South, are most likely to suffer from ill-health, and, as a consequence of their poorer housing, to be more vulnerable to the natural disasters which may increasingly be related to climate change and instability. Because community development specialises in mobilizing people in the interests of social justice and in developing social relationships based on co-operation rather than individualism it should have a central role in the processes of confronting the environmental crisis, and in designing more sustainable futures which place people centre-stage without divorcing them from their (ecological) environment.

Community development and varieties of green social thought

Community development has been slow to engage with the environmental crisis, perhaps because, until recently, the green movement in Britain has stressed the threat to the countryside and wild places rather than environmental issues in the urban context. (Worpole 1998) Community development is closer to social democratic traditions which prioritize jobs and urban and economic development as a foundation for welfare. But it is out of tune with much of the wider population if it continues to marginalize environmental issues: two million people in the UK belong to environmental organizations – more than all the political parties put together. (Jacobs 1999b) I want here to show the areas of overlap between community development and environmentalism but also to contrast the rather different paradigm of green theory that underlies environmentalism, considering whether there could be a fruitful synthesis as well as greater clarity about areas of difference.

Over recent years community development has certainly taken on a degree of environmentalism. Local Agenda 21 programmes, one spin-off from the 1992 UN Earth Summit in Rio, have drawn attention to the physical, natural environment and encouraged both education about it and restoration of local open spaces or renewal of habitats, recycling schemes, and the like. All of these are important, but in mainstream political parties, they are often an add-on to existing politics, the tokenistic tidying up around the edges. 'Third way' social democracy in the North talks of markets, business and economic growth, seeking to argue that this can be eco-moderated, with the fruits of growth paying for environmental protection (alongside a degree of social protection). Even if sustainable economic growth were a feasible thing, it is clear that governments are not prepared to risk offending business or their electorates' desires for cars and shopping malls and rising material living standards as greens say they must. (Cahill 1999; Jacobs 1999b)

Much has been written on the definitions and varying strands of 'green' and 'ecological' thought. (e.g. Pepper 1993, 1996; Dobson 1995) I understand 'green' as referring to the uncompromising ecologist tendencies, and 'environmentalism' as a lighter green and reformist tendency, espoused by pressure groups such as Friends of the Earth. The deeper green tendency is eco or bio-centric, refusing to privilege humans over 'nature' and assuming a (lost) 'natural' and balanced system of life on the planet. This perspective views human activity in general as responsible for the degradation of the planet, and therefore takes a pessimistic view of cities and industrialism, whilst romanticizing 'traditional' and indigenous societies which are assumed to be more in harmony with nature. Here, ecological sustainability and social justice do not necessarily go together, indeed, 'it is possible to imagine futures where the price paid for sustainability is a profound social injustice', a social conservatism (Fitzpatrick 1998), a reactionary ecologism in which democracy for humans is secondary to preservation of 'nature'.

On the other hand, social ecologists such as Bookchin have distanced themselves from deep ecology's mysticism, romanticism, and attribution of intelligence and spirituality to the planet. (Pepper 1996) They argue that the exploitation of the environment has its origins in the exploitation of humans by humans, and that it is corporate interests that we need to challenge and confront rather than seeing humankind *per se* as a blight on the planet. Drawing on the anarchist traditions of communalism and mutual aid they have much to offer community development in their insistence that we can prefigure post-capitalist, non-hierarchical environmentally sensitive forms of social economy, and, in practice, there is some overlap with the eco-socialists. Here there is also an anthropocentrism, a humanism which insists that social justice and human rights are the foundation for nature's rights as these are meaningless without people. Eco-socialists tend to place less insistence on the small-scale decentralized community and concomitantly more on planning, on development of environmentally sustainable industries with new technologies, often drawing inspiration from the working class and trade union tradition of co-operatives.

It is only recently that the greening of cities has risen up the agenda – though the Netherlands and Germany have many years experience in this area. This has strengthened the strand that is more humanist and more actively co-operating in local planning and participatory development programmes (rather than urging separatist and direct action). Yet, even here, there are challenges for community development, predominantly in attitudes to work, to welfare benefits, to behaviour (for instance around car use or food consumption), and to what a sense of place really means. Community development has prioritized people over 'nature' and, in general, the urban over the rural. If community development considers 'nature', it is as something to be enjoyed, for holidays or leisure, something to be protected but nevertheless an asset – a commodity rather than something with which we are interdependent. All greens would see this as a spiritually bankrupt attitude which sees the land and all non-human life as there for humans to take and use as they will. But they also argue from the standpoint of science – that biodiversity is necessary for us all. The recent rapid decline in the wild bird population in western Europe is not just regrettable because of the pleasure which birds bring to humans but because the loss of birds threatens the ability of other species and plants to reproduce themselves or to live healthy lives. Greenism and environmentalism therefore force us to look at the common good in a wider context, with useful categories being livelihood, habitat, connectedness, and trust. (Worpole 1998) If any policies are to be sustainable, we need to link rather oppose town and country, formal and informal work, the public and private. Do green ideas of sustainability give a new 'take', then, on community development?

Sustainability and community development

Rather like 'community', the phrase sustainability and community development has a warming sound, so who could be against it? It has crept into community development discourse in the phrase 'sustainable communities' or 'sustainable community development', meaning that certain measures will have more than a temporary effect, that change will bed down. In reaction to the short-termism of regeneration programmes of the 1980s, we see greater awareness that change needs maintenance and takes time, hence the stress on outcome measures like capacity growth, indicated by growth in local groups and activities, take-up of adult education and so forth –

characteristics of a healthy civil society. In community development we find the term 'sustainable' being used in relation to the community development process, but it is a different sense from that which we find among environmentalists.

Sustainable development, as understood by moderate environmentalists, brings together wide and often powerful coalitions of interests – international agencies, multi-national corporations, local authorities, and pressure groups. Whilst in this form it appears to be a way of combining economic development with environmental protection, its underlying green paradigm is never far from the surface, a paradigm which insists that problems cannot be tackled piecemeal, that there needs to be a break with current patterns of economic and social development, of methods of production and consumption and the relations between them. (Jacobs 1999b) Furthermore, environmentalists argue for equality over time – that is between us and future generations – and an equality of place for policies in one region could not be said to be sustainable if they compromised the ability of people in other regions to meet their needs. Much of western life, even of the poor, does compromise both future generations and the lives of those in the third world, but this aspect of sustainability is not usually discussed in relation to community development. Around the fringes that is less so, and some of the most interesting community action comes from beyond the mainstream of community development: recycling and organic food production and distribution co-operatives, for instance, many of which also aim to include marginalized people, such as people with disabilities or who are homeless.

Sustainable communities (and regions) would produce more of the goods and food they consume than is the case today. Food is an example. Describing community-supported agriculture in the USA, Betty Wells *et al.* (1999) write about the pleasure people feel in both seeing where and how their (healthier) food is grown, and how they appreciate the new social networks which emerge from these links between producers and consumers. Sustainability here means enabling local agriculture to regenerate in ways controlled by the re-connected producers and consumers. It means more jobs because organic and small-scale food production is more labour-intensive and it means greater community capacity – more knowledge about food growing, marketing and preparation. It also means more bio-diversity: the families in Wells' research appreciated visiting the farms to see flowers and birds which had increased with small-scale, mainly organic farming. These kinds of projects exemplify the categories of connectedness and of livelihood, within the local habitat. These achievements can also be seen in supported allotment schemes and community gardens in cities in many countries and in the new urban agriculture, all of which begin to correct the current misdistribution of food and which have been crucial to survival in some countries, notably Russia. (Lang 1999)

Convivial communities

Community development has been stronger on process than goals; its expertise, which is now considerable, turns on the means of involving people in decisions which affect their lives and it is especially skilled in working with those who are unused to being listened to. It tends to see some of its processes as goals – participation in both means and end, for the participative society is one in which all can have a voice, where discrimination has been addressed, and where the capacities associated with effective participation continue to develop. But the shape of that future society, beyond being one in which people have access to jobs, to education, to opportunity, are not victims of discrimination or abuse, is fuzzy, partly because community development would not want to be in the position of telling people how they should live their lives (indeed we are rather uncomfortable about those community development forerunners who did just that, such as in the settlement house movement where 'uplift' was a theme).

Greens have given much more thought to the question of the good society – because, they argue, if we do not change our behaviour now, we threaten our (and other species') existence. The need to conserve energy is of course central here: reducing or abandoning car (and aeroplane) use, recycling rubbish, insulating homes to reduce fossil fuel use, supporting local food producers, these are things we all – not just those who are the objects of the development process – should be doing now. Alongside this runs a notion of voluntary simplicity: a self-conscious mission to disengage from the materialistic obsessions created by the global consumerist individualistic culture. This raises differences in attitudes to poverty. The notion of poverty as an inability to live in the ways generally accepted in society would be challenged by greens who would query welfare rights campaigns which seem to acquiesce in western parents' (false) desires for their children to wear expensive brand named clothes and shoes, to have

TVs and videos (with their violent and materialistic values), access to car travel and so forth.

The green stance is, especially in its deepest fringes, that social exclusion becomes an opportunity to move in alternative directions from the mainstream of consumerist society. If households develop self-provisioning abilities, then communities will too. The growing success of LETS across the developed western countries has created a new social economy, social because it includes people and their well-being in the trading nexus. As has been recognized by community development, LETS are a way, like credit unions, of opening services to people who could not pay for them and of connecting people in the process. (Croall 1999) To the community developer these initiatives are mainly a means for the poor to survive their exclusion. In contrast, we should recognize that greens have been important in pioneering new kinds of social enterprise, exchange schemes and co-operatives, which they see as the seedbed of a new, sustainable, community.

There is, however, in this wealth of practical experience, a serious weakness in understanding of 'community'. As we have seen, greens romanticize small-scale communities, assuming that people within them are 'naturally' caring, and that, living closer to nature, are more respectful of it. This naive faith (Pepper 1993) is achieved by confounding the normative and empirical (Kenny 1996), with selective use of examples from traditional societies and from nature to justify the belief in 'natural', benign mutual aid. While 'community' is a core value and the basic organizing principle of green action and policy, it is one of the least analysed in green political discourse. (Kenny 1996) The fact that small-scale and self-reliant communities tend to become hostile to outsiders and to 'deviants' is ignored, and this, combined with a suspicion of the state and 'big government' means that the ability of green to engage with the development of civil life in modern urban, pluralistic and multi-cultural societies (where the rights of minorities and of individuals need protection and cannot be subsumed in the general will) is weak to say the least. Here Kenny (1996) argues, green shortcomings are akin to those of communitarianism, with a lack of sophistication in discussion of power and direct democracy. Most community developers are well aware of the ways in which interests can be promoted or blocked, and of the need both for local action *and* to move beyond the small-scale to engage with national as well as supra-national government and institutions, especially now that the sources of inequality or environmental damage may lie far from the areas affected.

Work and place

Like feminists, greens argue that work is not only that which is paid. Caring and voluntary community action are work. Basic Citizen's income is the means by which greens would release labour into social and ecologically desirable directions for, under this scheme, all would be entitled to a minimum income. This would mean that everyone would have the choice, at any stage of their 'career', either to spend time in paid work or in the informal economy, which, for greens, is the foundation for welfare.

In western regeneration schemes local (paid) job creation is a major aim. Such schemes by their nature are located in areas of higher than average unemployment. Typical aims would be more training, new capacities, new employers attracted to an area with a perceived pool of labour with appropriate skills. Success lies in increasing employability, resulting in large businesses moving to the area as well as local smaller enterprises springing up. We know that to an extent this stress on economic development has been important in community development's renaissance in the West since the 1960s and 1970s. But to a green, some of this is supping with the devil. While community developers have expressed concern that economic objectives crowd out social objectives – or reduce these to a side effect of employment (e.g. Henderson 1997), greens want to know more about the employers, the businesses themselves: do they pollute the environment, what values and ways of life do the products promote, do the firms exploit third world labour or resources?

There are two issues here: one is the green position on growth. The economic development model of community regeneration, so powerful in the USA, is fundamentally unecological and unsustainable. While greens recognize the centrality of work to well-being, there is a split between the deeper greens who would turn their backs entirely on industrial and international forms of production and trade, and the lighter greens and social ecologists who see possibilities for ethical and sustainable enterprise with new, low impact and energy efficient technologies, fair trade and good labour conditions. If community development were to become more green it should make more connections (both in North and South) with this movement arguing for the encouragement of local employment which meets ethical criteria.

Social auditing is making it easier to see which firms do clean up or prevent their own pollution, have adequate labour conditions, adopt a stewardship attitude to natural resources, invest in the local community and so forth. There would also be more encouragement for local alternative social enterprises – community cafés which link with local organic food producers, local self-build and house repair co-operatives, small businesses working on low and alternative technology, and so on – already a growing sector but one which needs much more public support and which could begin to deliver real sustainability to local community development. The issue then becomes less focused on economic growth or no growth, but the kind of growth, the kind of economy and the terms of trade that a democratic world should see.

A sustainable community is of course not just one composed of people relating to one another as they go about their (eco) business, with perhaps jobs and ties far from that locality. Reducing long journeys to work to save fuel, encouraging local employment – these would re-connect the local economy and society. This would mean a closer awareness of locality. Environmentalists' and greens' definitions of locality include dimensions which can be lacking in community development's mentality. Understanding of the local economy, climate and soil, would come from local food production for local needs. If people walked or cycled to work they could know more of their neighbours, and be more likely to work with them. But walking or cycling also means noticing more of your physical and natural surroundings. Common Ground is an English organization which campaigns to save and restore local distinctiveness. Sue Clifford, its founder, argues that agribusiness and supermarkets combined with powerful building firms mean that local crops (such as apple varieties) and building materials and styles (particularly types of stone or brick, of roofing, and decoration) disappear and the landscape becomes dreary and monotonous. (Clifford 1998) Common Ground has been finding lost place names, using local craftsmen to restore small buildings and structures, and, through community orchard schemes, reviving local apple-growing skills, the diversity of plants, and community festivals associated with the agricultural and seasonal cycle.

Conclusion

When I try to discuss green ideas with community developers the reaction is often along the lines 'how can you seriously say that preserving old buildings or protecting animals is as important as helping get people out of poverty?' Community development has tended to think that we should firstly address poverty, that in doing so we create new ties between people and new capacities, at which stage (and not before) the debate about the quality of life takes place. Environmentalism tells us that the ecological crisis makes nonsense of this, it is too serious and too close, that we must (especially in the North) change our ways of living now, avoiding strategies which claim the poor can become like the majority. While environmentalists have offered coherent solutions to the problems, governments including 'third way' social democracies are unwilling really to reduce car use or to impose heavy environmental taxes on industry. Yet, at a local level, in new kinds of sustainable social enterprises, and in new urban and community-based agriculture environmentalists are showing a way ahead.

Community development could make a stronger contribution here with its expertise in the support of participation and of the collaboration of diverse groups and individuals in localities, and with its history of devising less hierarchical and less consumerist ways of living and working. In turn, it could learn from some of the greener approaches to heightening people's sense of place, a sense which extends to an appreciation of local-global interconnections. Environmentalist approaches have real benefits for people's health as well as in the building of trust and companionship in communities and they remind us that the aesthetic is as important as the material. Yet, as Jacobs (1999b) argues, it is important that the ecological crisis is not left to green movements to address. Community development could rise to the challenge of forging associative links for local strategies to address environmental problems and it should work to ensure that as the ecological crisis deepens, public responses, from both top and grassroots are not authoritarian or divisive. Dismissing the environmental crisis because of the romantic, anti-modern and mystical strand in environmentalism is disastrously to miss the point – the ecological crisis concerns us all and we all need to develop our theory and practice consistent with a philosophy of social justice and maximum participation which will mean the goal of sustainable communities becomes more genuinely understood and shared.

References

Barratt Brown, M. and Coates, K. (1996) *The Blair Revolution – Deliverance for Whom?* Nottingham: Spokesman.

Cahill, M. (1999) 'Sustainability – the twenty-first century challenge'. *Social Policy Review*, 11.

Clifford, S. (1998) 'Halcyon days'. In: D. Warburton (ed.) *Community and Sustainable Development – participation in the future*. London: Earthscan.

Croall, J. (1999) 'Local, mutual, voluntary and simple: the power of local exchange trading schemes.' In: K. Worpole (ed.) *Richer Futures – Fashioning a New Politics*. London: Earthscan.

Dobson, A. (1995) *Green Political Thought*. London: Routledge.

Fitzpatrick, T. (1998) 'The implications of ecological thought for social welfare.' *Critical Social Policy*, 54/18 (1): 5-27.

Henderson, P. (1997) 'Community development and children – a contemporary agenda.' In: C. Cannan and C. Warren (eds) *Social Action with Children and Families*. London: Routledge.

Jacobs, M. (1999a) 'Sustainability and markets: on the neo-classical model of environmental models'. In: M. Kenny and J. Meadowcroft (eds) *Planning Sustainability*. London: Routledge.

Jacobs, M. (1999b) *Environmental Modernisation – the new Labour agenda*. London: Fabian Society.

Kenny, M. (1996) 'Paradoxes of community.' In: B. Doherty and M. de Gues (eds) *Democracy and Green Political Thought – Sustainability, Rights and Citizenship*. London: Routledge.

Lang, T. (2000) 'Plots of resistance: food culture and the British.' In: K. Worpole (ed.) *Richer Futures – Fashioning a New Politics*. London: Earthscan.

Ling Wong, J. (1998) 'Ethnic community environmental participation.' In: D. Warburton (ed.) *Community and Sustainable Development – participation in the future*. London: Earthscan.

Monbiot, G. (2000) 'Heaven has nothing to do with it.' In: *The Guardian*. 25th May.

Pepper, D. (1993). *Eco-socialism – From Deep Ecology to Social Justice*. London: Routledge.

Pepper, D., (1996) *Modern Environmentalism – An Introduction*. London: Routledge.

Rees, W., (1999) 'Scale, complexity and the conundrum of sustainability'. In: M. Kenny and J. Meadowcroft (eds) *Planning Sustainability*. London: Routledge.

Wells, B., Gradwell, S. and Yoder, R. (1999) 'Growing food, growing community: community supported agriculture in rural Iowa.' *Community Development Journal*, 34 (1): 38-46.

Worpole, K. (1998) 'Bottle banks in Arcadia? Environmental campaigning and social justice.' In: D. Warburton (ed.) *Community and Sustainable Development – participation in the future*. London: Earthscan.

Crescy Cannan is senior lecturer in social policy at Sussex University: Vol. 35 No. 4 (2000): 365-376

25

Community Work, Citizenship and Democracy: Remaking the Connections

Mae Shaw and Ian Martin

Introduction: time to take stock

In Britain, New Labour has been concerned to promote 'democratic renewal' as one of its big ideas through a variety of new policy initiatives aimed at devolution of decision-making and community involvement. This could be viewed by some as a deepening of democracy – or 'democratizing democracy' in Anthony Giddens' terms; by others, with more scepticism, as a move from formally constituted Local Authority to informally concocted local authority. (Patrick 1999) The question therefore arises as to whether popular participatory initiatives such as these offer real possibilities for a renewal of democracy or whether more governance could, in fact, mean *less* democracy.

Social democracy: the problem of the inactive citizen

The central purpose of community work according to the 1968 Gulbenkian Report, often regarded as a seminal statement in this respect, was to provide a means by which diverse demands could be mediated and managed 'through the application of expertise, promoting universalist social citizenship'. (Clarke 1996) The report was explicit in its advocacy of education for participative democracy in a pluralist society. Essentially, the problem was defined in two ways: there was something deficient in individuals or groups (social pathology) or in the ways institutions and services responded to their needs (institutional deficiency). Either way, certain people were disabled as citizens in relation to the exercise of their democratic rights and/or responsibilities. The solution was two-fold: first, to integrate deficit/disaffected individuals and groups into the mainstream; secondly, to make providers of services more sensitive to their needs, thus bridging the gap between 'distant and anonymous authority' (Calouste Gulbenkian Foundation 1968) and those on the receiving end of services. In short, community work sought, in Seymour Martin Lipsett's celebrated phrase, to 'tidy up the ragged edges of the good society'.

Consequently, as the management of social democracy became both

296

more problematic and critical in the growing fiscal crisis of the state in the 1970s, community workers were well-placed not only to mediate diverse and competing demands but also to regulate and, where necessary, limit them. There is much reference in the literature of the time to 'taking the load off the statutory services'; by voluntary activity and mutual self-help. But, critically for our argument, community work also operated ideologically as a conduit for the transmission and affirmation of particular attitudes and values. (see Mayo 1975) Gulbenkian, for instance, referring to the 'disadvantaged', explicitly advocated the need to 'modify behaviour in the direction of cultural norms'. Community development initiatives would transform the deficient and passive client into the active citizen.

David Thomas (1983) clarifies the construction of citizenship implicit in this model in two ways. First, community development is a distributive process, concerned with the allocation of resources and power to citizens within a pluralist framework. Secondly, it is a developmental process which articulates both 'franchisal' and 'social' dimensions of citizenship. Franchisal development refers to 'enhancing political responsibility', understood principally in terms of exercising both the right and obligation to vote. In this sense, citizenship is conceived in a formally ascribed and institutionalized way. Social development, on the other hand, extends the possibilities to a more active and participative construction of citizenship through:

> ... the promotion and maintenance of communal coherence – the repair of social networks, the awakening of consciousness and responsibility for others and the creation of roles and functions that provide individual significance and social service.

This formation signals a fundamental distinction between *citizenship as a formally-ascribed political status* and *citizenship as a collectively asserted social practice*. (see Lister 1997) It does not, however, adequately acknowledge the wider political and economic context within which citizenship is constructed. It assumes too much 'agency', i.e. the capacity of the subject to act autonomously. Consequently, as Jackson (1995) notes, community development may add a 'confusing gloss' to a process which is 'as much concerned with controlling and determining the direction of change in communities facing crisis as with enabling people to take greater control of their lives'.

What this does is to draw attention to both the ambivalent nature of state policy and the ambivalent positioning of the community worker within it. Community work can thus be argued to take place within the creative space between the intentions and outcomes of policy. Above all, what the social democratic model highlights is the significance of the essentially educational role of the worker. This, in our view, remains particularly relevant to the contemporary task of reconstructing citizenship – not least because it provides us with the settings in which to engage with people in communities around *their* interests.

The structuralist critique: the problem of citizen action

The welfare settlement of the early post-war years was premised on the possibility of successfully managing the inherent contradictions between the interests of capital and labour. Indeed, this has been the essence of the pragmatic compromise at the heart of social democracy. Community development policies, therefore, had a strategic role to play in delivering the benefits of 'welfare capitalism' to working people. However, by the mid-1970s, the emergent critique of what Stuart Hall (1989) subsequently characterized as the 'authoritarian collectivism' of the welfare state had begun to suggest not only that it was failing to meet need but also that it was, in fact, part of the problem.

The 'rediscovery of poverty', dating from the late 1950s and early 1960s, may have been an affront to the 'affluent society', but it could be explained away – for the time being, at any rate – in terms of isolated 'pockets of deprivation' which called for special measures of positive discrimination: 'It was possible to conceive of a society with no losers, if only the "disadvantaged" could be given assistance in making their case'. (Taylor 1995) Thus, despite the first signs of a radical critique, there remained – by and large – a basic confidence in the structure and efficacy of state welfare. The history of the Community Development Project (CDP) typified the ways in which community work came to be incorporated in the management of the wider social welfare system. In fact, it has been argued that the project was established precisely to find new approaches to the emergent crisis in social democracy and the perceived threat of disaffection, dissent and (increasingly racial) conflict. In reality, the CDP embodied the growing tensions inherent in managing the contradictions of state welfare in a period of economic decline and rapid social change. (Loney 1983) On the other hand, with the progressive breakdown of the post-war consensus, there came a new willingness to question old patterns of deference and to challenge – even to take direct action against – duly constituted authority (what Ralph Miliband called 'desubordination').

It was in this somewhat volatile context that space was seized to develop a structuralist and explicitly Marxist/socialist analysis of the crisis and to articulate community work's subversive potential to be both 'in and against' the state. (LEWRG 1980) This analysis exposed the fundamental contradictions of state-sponsored community work, particularly the belief that local solutions could be found to structural problems. (Corkey and Craig 1978) Deprivation and poverty were seen to be structurally created and sustained. Far from redistributing power, the 'community solution' was part of the hegemonic apparatus of the state aimed at organizing consent and managing dissent. This 'counter-insurgency' strategy was neatly encapsulated in the title of one of the best-known CDP publications, *Gilding the Ghetto.* (CDP 1977) Professional community work existed, in effect, to promote and legitimate the interests of the state by 'depoliticising issues and ... reducing the possibilities of tackling them in any serious way'. (Shaw 1997)

Several points need to be made about this analysis in order to take our argument forward. First, in the era of globalization, the structuralist critique of welfare capitalism, particularly in terms of its explanatory force and the coherence of its analysis, remains as convincing as ever. So too is the warning of the medicinal properties of the rhetoric of participation and the rights of citizenship in the absence of greater economic and social equality. Secondly, its redefinition of 'social problems' as the product of unequal socio-economic relations transforms them from pathological traits or merely technical issues into urgent political problems. Thirdly, this analysis significantly extends our understanding of the ambivalence of the state – particularly its role in defining and managing the kind of social problems which community workers set out to address. Fourthly, the problematization of the notion of 'community' itself opens it up as a legitimate site of struggle – a particularly liberating insight for those whose interests have been obscured, such as women (Wilson 1977) or excluded, such as disabled people. (Oliver 1990)

With hindsight, however, we can identify some crucial limitations and deficiencies in the structuralist critique. First, it was simply too reductionist, i.e. based on a relatively crude and overdetermined account of the politics of capital and class. Secondly, and in consequence of this, it was far too dismissive of the possibilities and problems of social democratic reform, the discourse of citizens' rights and the wider cultural politics of what subsequently came to be understood as the politics of 'identity and difference'. (e.g. Dominelli 1990; Green 1992) This helps to explain our third reservation: whilst it is unarguable that this critique was both coherent and convincing, it also proved to be unhelpful (worse, debilitating) to many community workers – even those who accepted its intellectual and political force. (see Cooke 1996) That is to say, its logic was to undermine their willingness and ability to believe in the efficacy and legitimacy of their own work, and they all too easily came to see themselves as the victims rather than the agents of their own marginality.

Most ironically perhaps, the weight given to structure in this analysis ended up reducing those not defined primarily in class terms to passive objects of policy as distinct from active subjects in politics. In this respect, Blagg and Derricourt (1982), writing of community work's 'heroic decade', warned presciently that: 'the labour movement must seek to link its programme with the aspirations of new movements of social protest if it is to become the leading force in society, or even simply to pre-empt "authoritarian populism"'. In the end, given the emphasis on what could be seen as too much structure and not enough agency, radical community work was in danger of becoming trapped in dichotomous rather than dialectical thinking.

In the end, in the discourse of class politics, community work came to be regarded as, at best, marginal and, at worst, an instrument of social control. This was tantamount to a counsel of despair for those who continued to be employed in local neighbourhoods and saw the importance and potential of educational work with people in communities. Furthermore, the force of the structuralist critique did little to enable community workers to see what was coming – and what they were in for. Most of the CDPs were closed down by 1975; four years later Margaret Thatcher was in power. There then followed eighteen years of New Right reconstruction and 'reform' – including that of the infrastructure of local government itself – for which the structuralist critique had done little to help community workers prepare. The final irony was that, in the bleak midwinter of Thatcherism, community workers had rapidly to learn the lessons of the ambivalence of the state – and to defend much of what they had previously attacked.

Marketisation: the problem of the citizen as customer

Throughout the 1970s, the political and theoretical arguments around social policy in general and community work in particular were conducted within a frame of reference in which the central role of the state was assumed. In contrast, throughout the 1980s and 1990s – the New Right offensive continuing under New Labour – the British welfare state was subjected to a systematic process of institutional and ideological restructuring. Of particular significance is the way in which the anti-statism of the New Right project destabilized core assumptions about the welfare state and the role of professional community work within it. Modern community work 'without the state' has no prior reference points in practice or in theory. The new welfare order, therefore, reconfigures the terrain of community work in unique and unprecedented ways.

First, many services have been remodelled as quasi-markets in which consumers – or better, customers – supposedly make choices among competing products. The net effect of this process of marketization has been to make the reality of state power more diffuse and yet, at the same time, more pervasive. Thus, as Clarke (1996) notes: 'What from one angle can be viewed as the diminution of the state's role can be seen from another as the extension of state power, but through new and unfamiliar means'. The result is a system of public welfare – if that is the right word – which has become increasingly under-funded, competitive and unequal. This process has had profound though contradictory implications for community work. At an economic level, community initiatives have been increasingly incorporated in the delivery of 'resource' policies, including the establishment of substantive services. (Butcher 1993) At the same time, growing concern over the rising costs of welfare have made the self-help ethic, institutionalized in the profession of community work, very attractive – yet again – to policy-makers:

> ... community development, underpinned by such concepts as empowerment, participation and partnership, is being 'talked up' as a respectable, indeed essential, process and mechanism for social integration and delivery of public services. Instead of being the sole province of a struggling and insecure occupation, community development has become one of the cornerstones of social welfare intervention strategies. (Miller and Ahmad 1998)

The idea of the 'enabling state' seems to be virtually embodied in professional community work with its emphasis on 'encouraging the helpless to help themselves' – almost tailor-made, it seems, for the task of delivering the community to policy. Furthermore, the self-help ethic performs an ideological function by reinforcing the attack on the 'dependency culture' in ways which have actually facilitated the shifts in policy necessary to transmute 'public issues' into 'personal troubles'. In other words, community work can operate to remoralize communities into the new welfare culture. This is happening in the context of a *re*-mixed economy of welfare in which social purposes have been systematically subordinated to economic objectives, leading to a peculiar and hybrid discourse of welfare:

> In this mixture one is likely to find the conflation of old professional representational systems ('client centred'), new marketised systems ('customer centred') and new managerial systems ('budget centred') in which the last is likely to exercise a constraining, if not decisive, interest ... the bottom line calculation. (Clarke 1996)

Social purposes may continue to dominate the professional discourse of community work practice, but economic objectives are increasingly applied to community development as policy. This is particularly significant when considering the changing relationship between community work, democracy and citizenship – as well as the crucial choices which have to be addressed in seeking to re-make the connections between them. Unless these choices are honestly confronted, community workers may find themselves the unwitting harbingers of the new welfare order – reduced to market researchers, matching supply and demand without regard to the wider political and economic context within which need is generated and resources are allocated.

On the other hand, state policy has also stimulated oppositional forms of politics, consistently demonstrating that its unintended outcomes may be as significant as its intended ones. Thus, as responsibility for welfare has shifted from the public to the private sphere, new oppositional constituencies and sites of struggle have been actively constructed by and through policy. The emergence of community care as a policy issue, for example, has had the ironic effect of redefining the personal as political. In this process, policy has generated new communities of interest whose identities are defined largely by their previous marginalization or exclusion. (Meekosha 1993) This has, in effect, created new constituencies for community work: disabled people, mental health service users, older people and carers – all formerly defined (and individualized) as social work clients. In view of this, we would argue that if the space for progressive community work practice is to be regained, the role of community work itself must shift from that of turning citizens into consumers and customers to that of defining – and defending – democratic citizenship itself.

Democratic renewal: the challenge of active citizenship

> Education for citizenship means above all the nurturing of a capacity and willingness to question, to probe, to ask awkward questions, to see through obfuscation and lies ... the cultivation of an awareness that the quest for individual fulfilment needs to be combined with the larger demands of solidarity and concern for the public good. (Miliband 1994)

As already noted, community work has consistently been deployed to mediate the shifting relationship between the state and civil society. This has traditionally involved the integration of those groups defined as deficient in some critical respect or 'dangerously disengaged' – activating the inactive citizen through regulated forms of participation (and presumably discouraging the over-active citizen who stretches the limits of social democracy too far). For much of the last two decades, however, the politics of policy has been based on the TINA assumption: 'There is no alternative'. Throughout this period many people, in the 'first wave' democracies in particular have experienced representative democracy in terms of what has come to be known as the 'democratic deficit', i.e. the experience of being virtually silenced – and consequently disenfranchized – within the politics of the state. The challenge now, therefore, is to renew democracy by transforming the experience of democratic deficit into a process of democratic renewal. Ultimately, its success is predicated upon two distinct but related things: first, challenging those forces of social exclusion which are systematically at work in contemporary society; secondly, the determined construction of an active and inclusive concept of citizenship.

The global restructuring of capital urgently demands new ways of thinking about democracy and the nature of citizenship in a free society – as distinct from a 'free' market. As capital goes global, it undermines the sovereignty (at any rate, as traditionally understood) of the nation state and simultaneously exerts similar pressures everywhere to maximize profit and cut back on public expenditure. This, in turn, begins to reconfigure the relationship between the state and civil society in complex and often contradictory ways. On the one hand, civil society can become a surrogate state, not least through newly-legitimized mechanisms of governance and participation; on the other hand, new social movements are generated (or old ones resuscitated) in response to policy change. What is distinctive about such movements and groupings is that they are not satisfied with simply being 'added on' to policy and politics as just so many equal opportunities categories. They want – indeed, demand – to contribute their specific experience in ways which challenge and extend the universalism on which so much social democratic welfare policy was originally premised. This raises the fundamental question for democracy today as to whether universal human rights and the principle of difference can be reconciled, moving beyond 'the increasingly monotonous postmodernist celebration of diversity to contemplate how difference can be accommodated politically [within] ... a differentiated universalism'. (Lister 1997)

The crucial point – perhaps for community workers in particular – is that the politics of the state now needs to be reconstructed in ways which strengthen civil society and political life both outside and inside the state. In this respect, it is essential to recognize that the democratic state needs civil society. In a profound sense, it is in civil society that people learn to be the active citizens they become in the democratic state – as many community workers have long understood. Consequently, it is in the relationship between civil society and the state that the process of reconstructing citizenship and democracy must begin. This will require community workers not only to work 'in and against the state' but also (and critically) *for* the state – in the sense of helping to construct a new kind of settlement between the cultural politics of communities and the political culture of the state. In other words, to turn the rhetoric of New Labour's professed interest in democratic renewal into a reality requires that we now reappropriate the idea of the active citizen and make this the dynamic for 'doing politics differently'. This is an intellectual as well as a political challenge.

Democratic renewal must become the means through which a diversity of voices can be conceptualized and articulated. It is a struggle to create a just and egalitarian political culture rather than simply a new set of structures and procedures. In order to 'democratize democracy', therefore, there is an urgent need to politicize politics. The fact that to call something 'political' is almost enough to bring it into instant disrepute is a regrettable, not to say dangerous, reflection on the state of contemporary politics. As David Held (1996) reminds us:

> ... the difficulties of the modern world will not be solved by surrendering politics, but only by the development and transformation of 'politics' in ways that will enable us more effectively to shape and organise human life. We do not have the option of 'no politics.'

This is in sharp contrast to Third Way politics which appears to reduce the political question of what kind of society we want to live in to a managerial one about how to run things (as they are) better. We now need to re-politicise citizenship – as *a process* in which power is something that is claimed, or demanded, through social and political action from below rather than handed down from above. (Cochrane 1996) This also clarifies the distinction between the construction of citizenship as an ascribed individual political status (as in the social democratic model of community work) and the construction of citizenship as a collectively asserted social practice – a necessary precondition of any meaningful form of democratic renewal. Such an active and expansive concept of citizenship requires a politics in which previously excluded voices are heard and respected – in other words, a radically inclusive politics. To put it another way, 'without democracy there can be no politics and without a genuine inclusive politics the claims of the disempowered will not be heard'. (Friedman 1992)

The prospect of democratic renewal offers particular challenges to policy-makers, community workers and communities. The actions of people in communities in pursuit of their own interests (as distinct from the objectives of policy-makers) need to be seen not only as the legitimate expression of active citizenship but also as the essence of democracy itself. This allows the community work role to be about expansion rather than closure: activating 'voice' rather than managing diversity; exposing awkward political problems rather than obscuring them. The real question is whether politicians and policy-makers will grasp the challenge of democratic renewal as a political process in which people in communities are regarded as critical allies and creative actors in the building of a new and inclusive kind of democracy. Community workers are now in a strategic position to foster and sustain such an alliance. In the process, they can become key agents in re-making the vital connections between community work, citizenship and democracy.

Summary Table. Community work, citizenship and democracy: re-making the connections

	Social democracy: the problem of the inactive citizen	Structuralist critique: the problem of citizen action	Marketization: the problem of the citizenas customer	Democratic renewal: the challenge of activecitizenship
Theoretical/ideological perspective	pluralist	Marxist/political economy	neo-liberal/ New Right	differentiated universalism
Priorities	managing change/integration	contradictions of welfare capitalism/emergent conflict of interests	institutional/ hegemonic restructuring	repoliticising citizenship/ democracy
Implicit model of society	social consensus	class consciousness/conflict	possessive individualism	solidarity in diversity
Construction of citizenship	individually ascribed political status	worker/political activist	entrepreneur/ customer	collectively asserted social practice
Definition of democracy	institutionalized participation	working class control/emancipation	market freedom	continuous cultural and political process
Nature of problem	ignorance/apathy/ 'disadvantage'	exploitation/alienation/ false consciousness	dependency culture/exclusion from market	inequality/ democratic deficit
Strategy/prescription	positive discrimination/ compensatory provision	radical socio-economic change	competition/consumer choice/policing poor solidaristic politics	progressive redistribution/
Community work role	promoting self help/selective remedial intervention	obfuscation/regulation OR politicizing	promoting enterprise/ brokeringcontract culture/surveillance	politicization policy/activating citizenship

References

Blagg, H. and Derricourt, N., (1982). 'Why do we need to reconstruct a theory of the state for community work', in G. Craig , N. Derricourt and M. Loney, (eds.), *Community Work and the State*, London: Routledge and Kegan Paul.

Butcher, H. (1993) ' Why community policy? Some explanations for recent trends',. in H. Butcher, A. Glen, P. Henderson and J. Smith, (eds.), *Community and Public Policy*, London: Pluto Press.

Calouste Gulbenkian Foundation (1968) *Community Work and Social Change*, London: Longman.

CDP (1977) *Gilding the Ghetto: The State and the Poverty Experiments*, London: Community Development Project Inter-Project Editorial Team.

Clarke, J. (1996) 'The problem of the state after the welfare state', in M. May, E. Brunsdon and G. Craig (eds.), *Social Policy Review 8*, London: Social Policy Association.

Cochrane, A. (1996) 'From theories to practices: looking for local democracy in Britain', in D. King and G. Stoker, (eds.), *Rethinking Local Democracy*, Basingstoke: Macmillan.

Cooke, I. (1996) 'Whatever happened to the class of '68? The changing context of radical community work', in I. Cooke and M. Shaw (eds.), *Radical Community Work: Perspectives from Practice in Scotland*, Edinburgh: Moray House Publications.

Corkey, D. and Craig, G. (1978) 'CDP: Community Work or Class Politics?' in P. Curno (ed.) *Political Issues and Community Work*, London: Routledge and Kegan Paul.

Dominelli, L. (1990) *Women and Community Action*, Birmingham: Venture Press.

Friedman, J. (1992) *Empowerment: The Politics of Alternative Development*, Blackwell: Oxford.

Green, J. (1992) 'The Community Development Project revisited', in P. Carter, T. Jeffs and M. Smith (eds.), *Changing Social Work and Welfare*, Buckingham: Open University Press.

Hall, S. (1989) 'The meaning of New Times', in S. Hall and M. Jacques, (eds.), *New Times: The Changing Face of Politics in the 1990s*, London: Lawrence and Wishart.

Held, D. (1996) *Models of Democracy*, Cambridge: Polity Press.

Jackson, K. (1995) ' Popular education and the state: A new look at the community debate', in M. Mayo and J. Thompson (eds.), *Adult Learning, Critical Intelligence and Social Change*, Leicester: NIACE.

LEWRG (1980) *In and Against the State*, London: Pluto Press.

Lister, R. (1997) *Citizenship: Feminist Perspectives*, Basingstoke: Macmillan.

Loney, M. (1983) *Community Against Government: The British Community Development Project, 1968-78*, London: Heinemann.

Mayo, M. (1975) 'Community development: a radical alternative?', in R. Bailey and M. Brake, (eds.), *Radical Social Work*, London: Edward Arnold.

Meekosha, H. (1993) 'The bodies politic: equality, difference and community practice', in H. Butcher, A. Glen, P. Henderson and J. Smith (eds.), *op. cit.*

Miliband, R. (1994) *Socialism for a Sceptical Age*,London: Polity Press.

Miller, C. and Ahmad, Y. (1998) 'Community development at the crossroads: a way forward, *Policy and Politics*, 25 (3).

Oliver, M. (1990) *The Politics of Disablement*, Basingstoke: Macmillan.

Patrick, F. (1999) 'The critical, conscious, creative citizen', *Concept*, 9 (3).

Shaw, M. (1997) ' Community work: towards a radical paradigm for practice', *Scottish Journal of Community Work and Development*, 2, Summer.

Taylor, M. (1995) ' Community work and the state: the changing context of UK practice', in G. Craig and M. Mayo (eds.), (eds) *Community Empowerment: A Reader in Participation and Development*, London: Zed Books.

Thomas, D. (1983) *The Making of Community Work*, London: Allen and Unwin.

Wilson, E. (1977) *Women and the Welfare State*, London: Tavistock.

Mae Shaw and Ian Martin teach in the Department of Community Education, University of Edinburgh: Vol. 35 No. 4 (2000): 401-413.

26

Community Development Work in Belgium

Gerard Hautekeur

Introduction

Following regionalization, the national parliament in Belgium is no longer responsible for culture, education and welfare in Flanders; responsibility has now devolved to the Flemish parliament. VIBOSO is a non-governmental organization which, with help of subsidies from the Flemish government, promotes and supports community work in Flanders and in Brussels. The organization is not active in Wallonia, the mainly French-speaking southern part of Belgium, nor does the same structure for community development exist in Wallonia. There are certainly interesting and innovative initiatives with regards to residents' involvement and multicultural projects in the French-speaking part of Wallonia. One striking trend in the French-speaking part of the country is that public authorities have taken the initiative to combat poverty, whereas in Flanders, the private welfare sector and other non-governmental organizations have made a much greater contribution.

This article sketches out some major developments in practice and, on the basis thereof, will try to describe a number of trends in practice. The author's very first experience in writing came at the end of the 1970s and the beginning of the 1980s as editor of the brand new review *Tijdschrift Samenlevingsopbouw* (community development). The early pioneers of community development had launched any number of initiatives under the heading of community development work, an approach typified by blazing enthusiasm. The society-related involvement of the social and community workers left their mark on everything. In the areas in which they were active, they identified with the local residents. Their socio-critical points of view led them to be seen, by the government and the local authorities, as opponents, and vice versa. Nevertheless, in the 1980s, many community development workers were in at the beginnings of local consultative platforms which, together with various partners in the rural areas, worked together to find appropriate services in rural areas and in the deprived neighbourhoods in the city. In this pioneer phase, all sorts of initiatives

309

flourished; the Flemish government made room for a variety of initiatives in the area of community development work, category-based community work and territorial-based community work.

Social approach

The social approach was central. At that time, little was said with regard to a methodical or strategic approach, never mind personnel management. The latter was in fact unheard of. Some staff went unpaid for months by the bodies which employed them. Many community workers were, in fact, their own employers. A great many social workers and community workers worked for years in a situation of insecurity and with temporary contracts, which were simply renewed year after year.

In 1982, the Flemish authorities providing the subsidies brought about a basic change in the face of community development, although the new decree/law with regard to community development work was not finalized until 1992. Since 1983, the Flemish government no longer provides subsidies to the fifty to sixty small associations of community development but provides subsidies for one institute for the support of community development work in Flanders and in Brussels (VIBOSO), and eight regional institutes for community development work (RISOs). RISOs have been set up in the three major cities, Antwerp, Ghent and Brussels and, in addition, in the five Flemish provinces. The RISOs are thus now the employers of the community development workers in their cities or provinces.

Changes

The first change is the bigger scale of the organization and the second is the importance of strategic planning. In order to obtain subsidies, VIBOSO and the RISOs have to provide the Flemish government with a five- to six-year budget/plan, covering the major options and priorities for the coming years. Moreover, each year, an annual report has to be presented for approval to the Ministry for Social Affairs. Thirdly, the community development work has to be result-oriented. The Flemish government which provides the subsidies decided that it would no longer provide these for basic services such as neighbourhood work, but that the RISOs would get a budget to initiate and support short-term projects – for two to four years – to help the deprived. From the RISOs, community development workers were sent into areas with social problems. The community development work was aimed at the whole area, but the participation methods aimed primarily at mobilizing and involving the least vocal residents.

The principal issues of community development work are local quality of life, housing and environmental well-being, welfare and services, work and education, and the integration of newcomers and community life of different communities in the area. Community development work is developed at the level of the neighbourhood, the whole community and the wider society (a region).

Community development projects

In total we are now dealing with some 120 community development work projects in Flanders and in Brussels, directed by seventy-one professional community development workers. These community development workers are supported by the eight co-ordinators of the RISOs and their various administrative personnel. For Flanders and Brussels, with a total of seven million inhabitants, the community development work sector is indeed small, some would say 'peanuts'. In addition to this, however, the RISOs are investigating other sources of finance, for example, the Social Impulse Fund set up by the Flemish government, European sources, contracts with provinces or projects promoted by local authorities. As a result, the total personnel of the whole community development sector is now some 300 workers.

Present community development work in Flanders and Brussels is typified by a range of important characteristics:

● Growing professionalism: community development workers pay great attention to the methodical and planned approach to residents' participation.

● The sector (and principally VIBOSO) makes a major contribution to the training of community development workers, research, documentation and the publication of its own review on local policy and community development work.

● Community development work also often lies at the basis of the building-up of networks bringing together partners focusing on a given problem.

● Many community development workers work closely or even at the behest of local authorities, for example, in the framework of the Social Impulse Fund, 60 of the 308 Flemish local authorities called on the help of the community development network in planning their policy for combating poverty and not only as advisors but as leading figures in the consultations between all the local partners as 'animators' to activate the local residents. In this, community development work creates a bridge between residents and the authorities.

● Thanks to this new professional approach on the part of the community development workers and, at the same time, the changed attitude of the authorities themselves, mutual prejudices have become a thing of the past.

● Thanks also to the pooling of community development workers in the Regional Institutes for Community Development (RISOs), employees in the sector have greater security.

● There is a contrast between the older generation of staff members, many of whom have been employed for fifteen to twenty years, and the more rapid turnover amongst younger community development workers.

● The Flemish government provides subsidies, but it leaves enough room for autonomy on the part of the local community development initiatives.

Some major issues

First, the issue of the growing multicultural nature of society is a major one, and is related to the ability of different societies and cultures to live together in one neighbourhood. How does one deal with diversity, what are the repercussions on the content of neighbourhood work and the methodological approach on staff management?

Secondly, the Flemish government now wishes to play a more steering and managerial role; they are pressing for greater cooperation between community development work and the integration sector, which is seeking to integrate ethnic-cultural minorities into the community in a more participatory fashion. Very often both are equally active in the same neighbourhood. The Flemish Minister responsible for the subsidies is looking, in the long run, for a fusion of community development work and work driven by the integration sector.

Thirdly, consultation is growing from the grass roots up, and our hope is that we can determine the contours of the growing co-operation, rather than being confronted with a ready-made merger.

Community development work recently came under the authority of the Flemish Minister for Welfare. This Minister increasingly stresses the role of community development work in combating poverty, whereas community development work itself has no wish to limit itself to combating poverty but rather wishes to be a pioneer in improving the process of participation and networking with regard to the environment in a given neighbourhood or an area.

One further hot issue at present is the decentralization of authority. Flemish community development workers are fully involved in the debate with regard to the different levels of decision-making. What is at issue is which managerial level is best suited to carry out certain tasks within the framework of the principle of subsidiarity. Within the present majority in the Flemish government there is a trend to hand over an increasing number of tasks and powers to the local authorities. In this scenario the local authorities would, in the long term, become responsible for community development work, youth work and integration work. Community development workers fear that, as a result, the greater autonomy of community development work would be threatened. And what would happen with regard to support for the third and second tier of agencies which support community development, VIBOSO and the RISOs? What then would be the role of a Regional Institute for Community Development Work and a Flemish Institute for Community Development Work?

In the framework of these basic debates we hear ever more clearly a call for the primacy of policy and the question of what the government itself should do, and what can be turned over or left to the private sector and its partners. Even the community development work at present subsidized by the Flemish government is in danger of falling into this arena of tension between the public and private sector. A number of politicians nevertheless stress that the local authorities must cease doing so many things themselves, but should instead become responsible solely for strategic direction, bringing together the relevant partners to make strategic choices.

Meanwhile, the Flemish government is establishing a great number of requirements in the framework of a quality decree which, to a growing extent, will measure and evaluate the results of community development work. At present the whole sector is working on a quality-control manual.

The present 'purple' coalition of red, green and Liberal members of the Flemish and the national government, stresses (largely due to the pressure of the Liberal partner) the relationship with the individual citizen. Key terms are 'client-friendliness' with regard to the individual citizen and 'effective management'. The so-called social-centred mid-field (trade unions, socio-cultural associations, advisory committees, etc.) is increasingly neglected. In itself, client-friendliness is positive, but at present little attention is paid to the other dimension, namely the citizen as 'le citoyen' – whom the authorities address as a resident of a given neighbourhood or a local community – or to working in the interests of the group or collective interest.

Broader role

Nevertheless, the broader societal role of community development work is undoubtedly recognized in the organization and participation of the disadvantaged social groups and neighbourhoods in society. The expectations are sometimes even exaggerated, as has been common in the history of community development work everywhere. It is said, for example, that community development work has failed to stop the advance of extreme rightist groups.

There is a growing call for a professional and methodical approach towards the full participation of all residents, not only in deprived areas but in all – even suburban or well-to-do – areas of a city. But there is still a future for community development work and workers in Flanders and in Brussels.

Gerard Hautekeur is an employee of the Vlaams instituut ter bevordering en ondersteuning van de samenlevingsopbouw (VIBOSO – Flemish Institute for the promotion and support of community development work) in Flanders and in Brussels. VIBOSO is a member of the Combined European Bureau for Social Development (CEBSD): Vol 38 No. 1 (2003): 26-31.

27

Gendered Micro-Lending Schemes and Sustainable Women's Empowerment in Nigeria

C. Otutubikey Izugbara

Abstract

Micro-lending to poor women has burst upon the development scene to offer a veritable strategy for *women's empowerment* in developing countries. Despite the powerful logic of this strategy and donors' commitment to it, there is lack of field-based data regarding whether the strategy really supports the sustainable empowerment of poor women. Relying specifically on definitions of women's empowerment offered by Keller and Mbwewe (1991) and Ashford (2001), and data emerging from my fieldwork in *Nigeria*, I argue there is little evidence that the strategy promotes the goal of sustainable women's empowerment. Whilst *micro-credit* schemes increase *poor women's* access to incomes, they often fail to help women step out of their culturally-defined boundaries. Rather, the strategy merely supports the kind of empowerment that never goes beyond marginal improvements in small areas of poor local women's life, leaving unchallenged the critical issues of women subordination and gender inequality.

Introduction

The incorporation of gender-sensitive approaches in current development research and action has pushed the gender-related dimensions of poverty to the threshold of public consciousness, bringing the issue of women's empowerment more sharply into focus worldwide. There is persuasive evidence that women are disproportionately represented among the poorest sections of the world's population and female-headed households tend, on balance, to be worse off than male-headed households do. (Agarwal 1990; Alarape 1992; Kabeer 1999; GTD 2001; Rankin 2001; Sarin 2001)

Although poverty and sustainable women's empowerment are current buzzwords in development action and discourse globally, it is largely in the global south that the critical issues which they raise remain most alarming and evident. (Ekong 1991; Mortimore *et al.* 2000; Izugbara and

Ukwayi 2002) Many developing countries continue to face a growing crisis in ensuring that the socio-economic and political marginalization of women is halted. George and Jawsell (1994) report that in Asia, poverty continues to drive an increasingly great number of women into unprotected sex with slumlords in order to meet immediate economic and housing needs. Consequent upon this, HIV/AIDS infection levels among urban slum women have reportedly spun out of control. Tamale (2001) also reports that a major obstacle to the consolidation of sustainable development in Africa is the appalling level of gender inequality in access to and control of the key resources of society. Yet, for several years, national and international efforts have been made to promote sustainable women's empowerment in the global south.

McWhirter (1991) defines empowerment as the process by which people, organisations, or groups who are powerless (a) become aware of the power dynamics at work in their life context; (b) develop the skills and capacity for gaining some reasonable control over their lives; (c) exercise this control without infringing upon the rights of others; and (d) support the empowerment of others in the community. Keller and Mbwewe (1991) view women's empowerment as a process whereby women become able to organize themselves to increase their own self-reliance, to acquire independent right to make choices and to control resources which will assist in challenging and eliminating their own subordination.

Ashford (2001) implies that the sustainable empowerment of women is the surest key or avenue for reducing the differences between the sexes that exist in nearly all societies. She contends that empowerment is sustainable if it enables the powerless gain control over their lives. It means not only greater control over resources but also greater self-confidence and the ability to make decision on an equal basis with men.

As a Southern country, Nigeria presents a particularly interesting case for interrogating the dynamics of women's empowerment. Nearly half of Nigeria's population of 120 million are women. It has been reported that the majority of these women live below the poverty line and possess little or no education, capital base or institutional connection to extricate themselves from the claws of poverty. (Okeke 1998; Udoh 1998; FOS 1999; World Bank 1999; Izugbara and Ukawayi 2002). Substantial investments have, however, gone into supporting the empowerment of Nigerian women. Apart from many well-intentioned efforts to fill the gaps between female and male achievements in the sphere of education, economic activity and political participation, Nigeria has also recorded impressive strides with respect to reducing gender-based violence, sexism and enhancing women's rights. There has also been greater discussion and awareness of gender issues and of the socially constructed differences between men and women in Nigeria. (Ike-Mark-Odu 1994; Mama 1996; Okeke 1999; Ezumah 2000; Igbuzor 2000; Pereira 2000)

One of the ways women's empowerment is currently being pursued in Nigeria is through the provision of gender-specific micro-credit interventions. Currently, diverse organizations in Nigeria have stated a commitment to using the micro-credit strategy to empower women. These include government ministries, international development agencies and development NGOs. But despite the powerful logic of the gender-specific micro-lending strategy and donors' commitment, there is little field-based information regarding its actual impact on the goal of women's empowerment, indicating a critical area for further research.

The present formulation addresses the following questions in the search for concrete lessons for the future: what is the rationale of the gender-specific micro-credit strategy? What scope does micro-lending to poor rural women offer for their empowerment? And what constraints face this project strategy and what scope exists for addressing them? Answers to such questions have much broader development implications and could offer critical scope for practices and policy efforts to address all forms of marginalization and inequality.

Cases and methodology

The fieldwork focused on three micro-credit schemes in south-eastern Nigeria. Two of the schemes, the Genderlift Foundation Project (GFP) and the Rural Women's Economic Aid (RUWEAP) programmes, are in Abia State, launched in 1998 and 1999 respectively.

At the time of fieldwork, eighty-one and sixty-four rural women were individually benefiting from GFP and RUWEAP. The two organizations provide micro-credits to women through women-only organizations in rural areas of Abia State. The third scheme, in Akaw Ibom State, is a UNDP (Nigeria) South-South Office-funded project. The UNDP-funded scheme which became operational in 1998 has provided interest-free micro-credits to over 200 rural women as at January 2001. These three schemes were selected because of their popularity in southeastern Nigeria. They are also well-known in government and donor quarters, recent assessments also lauding them as 'success stories'. (Ibanga 2002) Further, the number of women participating in these schemes was also large enough to allow sampling and generalization.

Six trained research assistants were employed to collect data between August 2000 and January 2001. The main focus of data collection was on the relationship between women's participation in micro-credits and their ability to: organize themselves; increase their own self-reliance; make independent choices; challenge their own subordination at the household, community and other levels; have greater control over resources; and have greater confidence and ability to make decisions on an equal basis with men in their society. Data collection involved in-depth individual and group interviews with sixty-three benefiting women, ten field officials of implementing organizations, twenty-six non-benefiting women, and eighteen men, including husbands of benefiting women.

Theorizing modern micro-credits

What is now strikingly clear among development scholars and practitioners is that most formal socio-economic institutions fail the poor, particularly poor women. (Eade and Ligteringen 2001) The performance of formal financial institutions with respect to the livelihood realities of poor people provides sound support for this contention.

Discourse on micro-credits has its origins specifically in a 1970s action-research project that countered mainstream misconceptions about the rural poor and focused on issues such as improving their livelihood conditions through a variety of activities. The important findings of the particular action-research as Kabeer (1999) puts it, were that the rural poor earned their livelihood from a variety of activities, rather than relying on waged labour; that they were women as well as men and that their major constraint was perceived not as the lack of agricultural wage labour, but lack of access to mainstream financial resources. The Grameen Bank responded to this need by setting up a poverty-reduction scheme to deliver credits to this excluded group focusing most of its initial efforts on landless poor women, whom it found to be a better credit risk. The Bank now enjoys higher repayment rates than most official credit schemes for poor people. (*Ibid.*)

This is the background against which current responses to women's lack of funds have emphasized credit schemes that are sensitive to the needs, positions and unique concerns of poor women. Micro-lending to poor women has thus emerged to offer solutions to the more specific issues which poor women face in accessing formal credit services by compensating for the lack of material collateral; subsidizing access to credit facilities; and simplifying the procedures for obtaining credits.

In the Grameen Bank case, as in most other current initiatives, the primary need identified was an economic one, dealing with the inadequacy of financial entitlements. However, since the early 1990s, other issues have gained topicality in the discourse on micro-credits. Taken together, these more recent issues represent a concern with the political biases that underpin critical development interventions. This is especially the case within the decisive shifting development policy context from state-led to market-led approaches that are lauded as favouring political freedom, social justice and mass empowerment. The prevailing neo-liberal orthodoxy (Rankin 2001) has also assumed a distinctively feminized character, as development interventions increasingly target women as expected beneficiaries.

Within this context, the inter-penetration of development action and financial orthodoxy has been questioned, not least because it represents something of a backlash against the goal of sustainable grass-roots empowerment. The emerging debates generate important questions that call for different understandings of the objective impacts of development initiatives on the empowerment of marginalized groups. The very language of mainstream discourse on micro-credits and their role in the empowerment process ('strengthening', 'capacity-building', 'capital formation', 'participation', 'well-being') has tended to betray a normative view of the purpose and goal of development action. This has obscured a potentially more fruitful engagement with the ways in which micro-credit initiatives perform and operate outside the boardrooms of donors and implementers. A critical gaze at the implications of micro-credits for women's empowerment is thus urgent in order to sharpen current understanding and broaden debates beyond what anecdotal evidence presently allows.

Findings

Micro-credits and women's livelihood conditions
Do micro-credits support the empowerment of women? Emerging from interview data is evidence that participation in micro-credit schemes enhance women's economic independence and livelihood conditions. On balance, the monthly net income of sampled benefiting women averaged N11,000 Nigerian (naira), while that of non-benefiting women stood at N6,000. Benefiting women reported that being in micro-credit schemes had enabled them to 'expand farm sizes', 'have access to improved agro-inputs', 'employ more labour', 'increase the size of goods and merchandise', 'buy and rear more

domestic animals', 'rent stalls in local markets', 'build their own stalls' and 'begin their own trade'. Many non-beneficiaries were also aware of the differences micro-credits were making in the lives of beneficiaries in their communities.

Both beneficiaries and non-beneficiaries reported that the economic gains of the loans also trickled down to others in the community. As beneficiaries expanded the sizes of the farms and livestock diversified into non-agrobusinesses and adopted improved agro-inputs, a need was created for more labour, with the effect that real rises in rural incomes were reported for farmhands, labourers, relatives of beneficiaries and many other categories of people.

Data shows also that the households of those women in micro-credit schemes had more children in school. The average number of school-age children in households of benefiting women stood roughly at five, while for non-benefiting women it stood at three. Benefiting households also reported enjoying reduced poverty-related stress, improved nutrition, higher net income and better health status than non-benefiting ones.

There is also evidence that being in micro-credits has tended to enhance women's freedom of association, involvement in household decision-making, self-worth and esteem. Benefiting women generally reported that their husbands accorded them more say in household decision-making. Most of the beneficiaries spoke of attending meetings regularly with other beneficiaries and project staff. Such occasions added to women's sense of freedom and were important in developing and sustaining social networks.

In rural south-eastern Nigeria, participation in micro-credit schemes also tends to make women less vulnerable to domestic violence. Husbands of benefiting women reported beating their wives less often than those of non-benefiting women in the past six months. Benefiting women themselves confirmed this, linking it to their increasingly important contribution to household upkeep and management. However, we found that benefiting women were ever more cautious not to allow their successes to affect their relationship with their husbands. Some of the women confessed that they avoided situations and behaviours that made their husbands feel like they (women) were using their resources to challenge them or seek equality with them.

Micro-credits, gender equality and empowerment

Interviews with credit field staff and implementers suggest that benefiting women were often explicitly dissuaded from thinking that the purpose of credit schemes was to promote gender equality or make women challenge male authority and domination. Implementers maintained that the schemes were not aimed at challenging male headship of families, patriarchal structures and women's subordinate position in the family. They tended to view micro-credits as primarily aimed at improving women's 'economic status, 'income potentials' and 'self-reliance'.

Most of the benefiting women thought similarly. They were agreed that the purpose of the scheme was not for them to challenge or seek equality with men. Some of them argued that male headship and household control was natural and that women who seek equality with their husbands are wayward. This suggests that micro-credits merely hit feebly on the boundaries of what is considered permissible for women to do in Nigerian local cultures, offering little scope for women to step out of their culturally-defined boundaries. One benefiting woman thus said: 'The money cannot fool us into demanding equality with our husbands.'

Women benefiting from micro-lending schemes showed little readiness to challenge gender inequality, patriarchy and lack of control over their person circumstances and community resources. Thus the 'empowerment' that the scheme promotes rarely goes beyond marginal improvements in small areas of women's life with limited resources and within the conditions permitted by local patriarchal structures and institutions. The control and subordination of poor rural women by men persists in the form of overt and covert violence sustained by the implicit and explicit invocation of traditional male-privileging ideologies. In the communities surveyed, political authority continues to reside in men, and women continue to see it as the natural order of things. There was also little or no sign of readiness among benefiting women to question or challenge male dominance and leadership. Female autonomy and leadership remain taboo while the discursive practice surrounding these issues in local communities continues to reflect constructions of gender relations that support male dominance. One man thus reflected:

> *My wife may be making money...but I am still the one who married her. She still has to take orders from me. She still has to respect me. She can't challenge me because she now makes her own money...she knows the implications of this in this community.*

Constraints on micro-credits

Emerging responses on a number of issues such as how micro-credits relate to gender relations, equality and structural change gave us insights on some of the constraints on micro-credits with respect to women's empowerment and gender equality. For instance, micro-credit field staff and implementers were explicit that they do not aim to challenge or change gender relations in society.

Evidently, implementers of the surveyed schemes conceived empowerment primarily as a process of increasing women's access to incomes or participation in income-generating activities. Also, we found no evidence that the schemes had any real linkage with the wider livelihood realities of women. For instance, none of the schemes studied had a health, political, literacy or numeracy training component. The absence of literacy and numeracy training in the schemes, for instance, often resulted among other things, in the reliance of benefiting women on their husbands to keep the accounts, which is most likely to perpetuate rather than challenge the basis of women's subordination. The schemes' lack of linkage with the broader social realities of local women contradicts the good practice of gender mainstreaming and integration, which is central to current development action planning and implementation. Further, we also found evidence that micro-credits only supported women's investment in areas that offer little or no critical scope and leverage for local women to begin to challenge male dominance and authority.

The type of investments supported by the schemes included pottery, livestock husbandry, leatherwork, trading, farming, etc. Most of these were operated at small scales. They were thus unlikely to provide the women sufficient income and capital base with which to organize themselves and others towards challenging and eliminating their own subordination, even if they were to be aware of the power dynamics at work in their life contexts.

Conclusions and policy implications

The findings of the present study draw attention to the inability of micro-credits to support women's sustainable empowerment. Findings show that gendered micro-lending schemes in south-eastern Nigeria merely supported women's access to incomes and not their ability to challenge and overcome the more complex set of constraints that mediate women's access to resources, power and opportunities in society or their breakout from culturally-defined boundaries and positions. Yet herein lies the critical goal of true empowerment. If gendered micro-lending is not to slip back into the impotent maze of development policy rhetoric, the strategy needs to be rethought to:

● adopt a critical, inter-sectoral, and comprehensive definition of women's empowerment and not merely limit it to women's access to money. This will guarantee that women's credit schemes have training and educational components, relating with women's health needs and leadership concerns etc.

● focus more on supporting investments in areas that will give women substantial political and economic leverage successfully to challenge male domination and hegemony.

● adopt culturally-sensitive implementation designs that will facilitate the schemes' acceptability among rural men and women and guarantee that schemes are not misinterpreted by either.

● develop culturally-responsive programmes of action, channels of delivery and mechanisms to identify and reveal the actual and potential constraints to be fed back into planning and implementation as well as monitoring options and principles for accommodating on-field contingencies.

References

Agarwal, B. (1990) 'Social Security and the family in rural India: coping with seasonality and calamity', *Journal of Peasant Studies*, 17 (3): 341-412.

Alarape, N. (1992) *The Nigerian Woman: Dawn of a New Era: The Better Life Programme of Maryam Babangida*. Nigeria: Jeeson International Ltd.

Ashford, L.S. (2001) 'New population policies: advancing women's health and rights', *Population Bulletin*, 54 (4).

Eade, D. and Ligeringen, E. (2001) 'NGOs and the future: taking stock, shaping debates, changing practice' In: D. Eade and E. Ligteringen (eds.) *Debating Development*, London: Oxfam: 11-18.

Ekong, E.E. (1991) *Rural Development and the Persistence of Poverty in Nigeria*. Inaugural Lecture Series No. 1, University of Cross River State, Uyo.

Ezumah, N. (2000) 'Integrating feminist perspective into sociological research in Nigeria: problems and prospects' *The Nigerian Social Scientist*, 3 (1), 20-25.

Federal Office of Statistics (1999) *Facts and Figures: Ten Years of Women's Empowerment in Nigeria (1988-1998)*, Lagos: FOS.

George, A. and Jaswell, S. (1994) *Understanding Sexuality: Ethnographic Study of Poor Women in Bombay*, Washington, D.C.: Women's & AIDS Programme.

GTD (2001) 'Nijeri Kori: organizing the landless and powerless in Bangladesh' *Gender, Technology, & Development*, 5 (3): 477-481.

Ibanga, S. (2002) 'Microcredits and Women's Challenging Status in Nigeria', mimeo.

Igbuzor, O. (2000) 'Methodological issues in gender studies in Nigeria', *Nigerian Social Scientist*, 3 (10): 14-20.

Ike-Mark-Odu, E. (1994) *Women on the Move: A Course to Remember*, Lagos:

Princess Communication.

Izugbara, C.O. and Ukwayi, J., (2002). Conceptual issues in Nigeria's gender-specific rural poverty alleviation strategy. *Development in Practice*, 12 (1), 81-85.

Kabeer, N. (1999) *Reversal Realities: Gender Hierarchies in Development Thought*, London: Verso.

Keller, B. and Mbwewe, D.C. (1991) 'Policy and planning for the empowerment of Zambia's women farmers', *Canadian Journal of Development Studies*, 12 (1): 75-88.

Mama (1996) *Setting an Agenda for Gender and Women's Studies in Nigeria*. Report of the Network for Women's Studies in Nigeria, No. 1.

McWhirter, E.H. (1991) 'Empowerment in counselling', *Journal of Counselling and Development*, 69: 222-227.

Mortimore, M., Adams, W. and Harris, F. (2000) *Poverty and Systems Research in the Dry Lands*, Gatekeeper Series No. 94.

Okeke, P.E. (1998) 'First lady syndrome: the (en) gendering of bureaucratic corruption in Nigeria', *CODESRIA Bulletin*, 3 and 4: 16-19.

Pereira, C. (2000) 'Feminist knowledge – alternative visions, new questions for the social sciences in Nigeria' *The Nigerian Social Scientist*, 3 (1): 1-14.

Rankin, N. (2001) 'Governing development: neoliberalism, microcredits and the rational economic woman', *Economy and Society*, 30 (1): 18-37.

Sarin, N.S. (2001) 'Empowerment and disempowerment of forest women in Uttarakhand, India', *Gender, Technology and Development*, 5 (3): 341-364.

Tamale, S. (2000) 'Point of order, Mr Speaker: African women claiming their space in parliament', *Gender and Development*, 8 (3): 8-15.

Udoh, A.J. (1995) 'Personal, socio-economic and infrastructural indices for poverty alleviation in Akwa Ibom State of Nigeria', *South-South Journal of Culture and Development*, 1 (2): 110-117.

World Bank (1999) *Nigeria: Poverty in the Midst of Plenty, The Challenge of Growth with Inclusion*, Washington D.C.: World Bank.

C. Otutubikey Izugbara teaches and researches in gender, health, and environmental anthropology: Vol. 39 (2004), No. 1, 72-84.

28

Left to Their Own Devices? Community Self-Help between Alternative Development and Neo-Liberalism

Erhard Berner and Benedict Phillips

… If you teach a poor man how to fish you will feed him for a lifetime. (But who will make sure that he has access to waters? And how many poor people cannot fish, anyway?)

Introduction: from participation to self-help

It is now widely agreed that the poor are not passive in the development process. Participation, once radical and controversial, has become mainstream management theory. Together with the related concepts of decentralization, good governance and empowerment, it has become the buzzword in the development debate. Phillips (2000: 10f) has summarized the main assumptions that underlie participatory approaches: compared to professionals, beneficiaries have important and complementary *information* on their needs and capacities, are *competent*, and *reliable*. These three factors become causes of improved effectiveness of participatory projects, the more so if participation goes beyond 'listening to beneficiaries' toward their active role in decision-making. That legitimacy and acceptance of interventions is enhanced by the process is a welcome side effect. Participation is argued for on three further grounds, as:
– an end in itself. According to Sen's work (most pronounced 1999) the *freedom* to make meaningful choices between various options is the essence of development and a precondition for personal well-being.
– a means to ensure quality, appropriateness and durability of improvements. The key word here is *ownership:* by being involved in the design and production of facilities poor people would feel (more) responsible for their maintenance.
– a means to increase *efficiency* and cut costs by mobilizing communities' own contributions in terms of time, effort, and often money.

All three rationales, most obviously the last, make tough additional assumptions about both underutilized resources and capacities of the poor, and skills and capacities of intervening agencies. Little attention is paid to the requirements and costs of organizing, itself a precondition of *community* participation. Considerable time is required to reach a consensus on issues vital to a community, and time in turn is the most scarce and precious asset for poor people, especially women. Critics have long argued that there is little willingness on the part of development agencies to really share decision-making power, and that the cost-cutting effect is the real reason for the popularity of participation. (Mayo and Craig 1995; Cleaver 1999) Indeed the donors' and policy-makers' frame of reference (fixed timeframe, tangible results, output indicators known in advance) is not compatible with any real influence of beneficiaries on relevant decisions. In Indonesia for instance, *partisipasi* is generally known to signify a burden in terms of extracted labour.

Self-help, finally, can be seen as participation squared. The poor have completed their journey from being recipients, via beneficiaries and stakeholders, to become champions of development. In the process the focus has shifted from *deficiencies* (that would require some redistribution as a remedy) to *obstacles* (that can be removed without others having to sacrifice). The best-known protagonist of this line of thinking, de Soto, has gained tremendous influence on the thinking of international development institutions, notably the World Bank, identifying state action as the crucial *cause* (not potential remedy) of poverty. In *The Other Path* (1989) he portrayed the poor's external struggle against incompetent and predatory governments. Now he offers nothing less than a solution to the 'mystery of capital' (2000): by simply legalizing assets worth trillions and allegedly under the factual control of the poor, markets can be made to work in the interests of all.

The shift towards self-help can be seen as a masking defence against calls for redistribution. Without altogether denying the validity of the self-help approach, our paper scrutinizes both its practical assumptions and ideological underpinnings. Does it work for all poor communities, and critically, for all people in such communities? And is it its efficiency, or rather the implicit justification of cutting subsidies and transfers, which make it so popular with the international financial institutions? While we focus on urban communities and habitat issues in particular, we believe that the findings are relevant for all policies aiming at community development.

The case for community self-help: a focus on habitat

Community self-help as such is of course nothing new but rather the default strategy of the poor. As documented by their very survival, poor people are experts in making the most of scarce resources under adverse circumstances, and have always used institutions of mutual support and risk-sharing in order to do so. To acknowledge and attempt to strengthen these capacities and institutions is a both obvious and sensible approach to community development. In their review of seven successful programmes of urban poverty alleviation, Anzorena *et al.* sum up the rationale: by 'rooting the initiative on the capacities, skills and knowledge of low-income communities' it is possible to reduce dependency and outside control, fine-tune policies according to people's needs, reduce costs and improve cost recovery. (1998: 171ff) Particular attention is paid to credit as a non-redistributive means of making capital available for poor people to invest in housing, infrastructure and productive ventures. Another strategy – though stressed in rhetoric far more often than put into practice – is the reform of unrealistic standards and cumbersome procedures that force small entrepreneurs underground, increase their transaction costs and deny them the protection of the law; de Soto is right at least so far.

Self-help capacity of the poor is nowhere as clearly to be seen as in the field of housing. It is estimated that between 30% and 70% of urban populations live in 'irregular' settlements, with a growing tendency (Durand-Lasserve and Royston 2002: 3); according to UNCHS (1996: 200), 64% of the housing stock in low-income countries, and up to 85% of newly produced housing, is unauthorized. In the last two decades, self-help housing (*vulgo* squatting) is increasingly recognized as the only means available to fulfil the immense demand for mass housing, and thus a solution rather than a problem. John Turner's influential book *Housing by People* (1976) and the first Habitat conference in Vancouver 1976 are markers of this paradigm shift towards an 'enabling approach'. Recent literature on urban housing widely agrees that self-help housing is still the only 'architecture that works' (Turner 1968) in sheltering the poor. On a cautionary note, Berner insists that policy-makers still fail to understand the functioning of informal housing markets, and consequently 'little progress has been made in translating the new paradigm into practical and sustainable policies'. (2001: 292) The crucial issue is whether it is indeed just 'proper guidance and encouragement' (Abatena 1995: 5) without a net transfer of resources that poor communities need to improve their situation, and whether governments and development agencies are well-equipped to provide such guidance.

At least in rhetoric what was visionary in Turner's time is now standard. Slum clearance is no longer defended but is condemned (rightly) as plain 'mass deportation' (Berner 2000: 555); 'top-down solutions to housing' are said to have 'contributed as much to the problem as the solution' (Aldrich and Sandhu 1995: 21); the 'ways, plans, designs and building materials' of the poor are said to be 'often far better suited to local needs, local incomes, local climatic conditions, and local resources than the official, legal standards demanded by governments'. (Hardoy and Satterthwaite 1989: 16) Government solutions have often been inappropriate – incompetent, mis-targeted, insouciant and even brutal. The strategies of the poor have often been imaginative and cost-effective. Nevertheless, there is a risk that the current 'autonomous development' orthodoxy may fail adequately to serve the needs of the poor, succumbing to a neo-liberal wolf dressed up as a populist sheep. Autonomy must be distinguished from autarky. Most notably, the community self-help paradigm needs to be refined by a recognition that the poor cannot be self-sufficient in escaping poverty, that 'communities' are systems of conflict as well as co-operation, and that the social, political and economic macro-structure cannot be side-stepped.

Poverty and self-sufficiency

If history is a fair judge, the case against government and market-led solutions is a strong one. Slum clearances of the 1970s were so severe that UN officials estimated that governments were destroying more low-income housing than they were building, in a decade when the urban population in developing countries increased by 70%. (Werlin 1999: 1524) Just as governments have a poor record, market solutions too have systematically failed to serve the needs of the poor. (Baken and van der Linden 1993; Jones 1996) In addition, self-help solutions have the advantage of building on the already considerable investment that poor residents have put into their dwellings (Berner 2000) – probably the largest investment they have every made. To be mistrustful of those who have so frequently failed, and to seek to build on rather than waste considerable sunk costs seems a sensible approach. It is, however, an approach born of necessity, and attempt to turn its strategy of 'do-it-yourself' into its chief virtue and selling point are severely flawed, both ethically and practically.

The case for self-sufficient solution is too often infused with a Reaganite rhetoric concerning redistribution: 'The less subsidy a poverty reduction programme provides, and the more cost recovery it generates, the less it is seen to be a 'welfare' or 'charity' programme.' (Anzorena *et al.* 1998: 172) Transfers of resources are degrading, goes the argument, so let's boost the self-esteem of the poor by 'letting' them take care of themselves. Anzorena *et al.* claim that their model projects 'achieved partial or total cost recovery for some (or all) of their intervention.' (1998: 167) Siddiqui and Khan declare proudly that the Hyderabad Incremental Development Scheme is 'fully self-financing, without any element of subsidy on the government's part ... Speed and standard of development depend on payment of deposits.' (1994: 281) 'The approaches that work', argues Werlin, 'are generally 'tough-minded' ... in Lusaka water is supplied to groups of households on the understanding that, after a given level of default, supply will be cut off for the entire group.' (1999: 1530) And what if some *cannot* pay?

The self-help campaign risks being transformed from a survival strategy in the face of government unconcern into a *defence* of such unconcern. Seeking to avoid this trap, Taylor points to an important distinction in asking how to 'release people's energies without exploiting and exhausting them.' (1995: 108) Anzorena *et al.* admit that it 'seems unfair to seek the least-cost solutions for poorer groups' but insist that 'there are important reasons' for doing so. (1998: 171) Thus, in the rhetoric of the new orthodoxy, the supposedly hard realism of the seasoned practitioners is contrasted with what is portrayed as the soft moralism of the naïve welfarists. In fact, however, the extreme self-help ethic of some of the new populists may not even be *practical*. Cleaver's reprimand is simply put and very apt:

> *'Development practitioners excel in perpetuating the myth that communities are capable of anything, that all is required is sufficient mobilisation and the latent and unlimited capacities of the community will be unleashed in the interests of development ...* [In fact, however,] *there is significant evidence of very real structural and resource constraints operational on communities, most severely impacting on those who may need development the most.'* (1999: 604)

Aldrich and Sandhu point out that the common shortcoming in all policy approaches to housing – from relocation, to sites-and-services, to 'autonomous housing' – is that none have been 'substantial enough, ie ... supported with enough resources and time to rehouse entire populations.' (1995: 28) Earlier, overly interventionist approaches may have been doomed to fail for expecting *too much* from governments. Self-help campaigners may be making the opposite mistake. Community-led development may be a cheaper option but it is not a costless one, and the rhetoric of 'no subsidy' may prevent the securing of necessary resources to reach the poorest of the poor. Programmes and projects that aim at full cost recovery *have* to exclude the poorest either deliberately or implicitly; mechanisms include self-selection in group-credit schemes, incentives for well-endowed people in entrepreneurship development and benefits for homeowners in upgrading.

Tackling poverty generally requires some form of redistribution, and the seductiveness of cost-free poverty reduction should make us suspicious. Community participation itself, admit Pathirana and Sheng, 'brings additional costs, in particular overhead costs, and is time-consuming .... [it is not] a short-cut to successful project implementation but needs to be embedded in other supporting activities.' (1992: 13)

The self-help approach recognizes, rightly, that many of the best strategies in tackling poverty come from members of poor communities. This should not mean, however, that outsiders should withdraw to a minimal role. Although Turner's scepticism against governmental activities was well-founded, his plea for a minimalist state has not stood the test of time. (Werlin 1999) Governments and NGOs need to make themselves responsive to, not absent from, poorer communities, and especially the poorest of the poor. They need to encourage initiative not by walking away but by offering stable, long-term, targeted financial and technical support. Such support should increase people's security, widen their opportunities, and strengthen their demand-making power vis-à-vis other, wealthier, groups. To misquote Marx: the point is not to escape from society; the point is to change it. Self-sufficiency, the idea that 'left to their own devices' (and their current resources) poor communities would lift themselves out from poverty just fine, makes for an attractive myth but a regressive policy.

Communities and co-operation

The concept of 'the' community is fashionable to the point of ubiquity, but remains deeply problematic. It merges the administrative, the spatial and the social, it oversimplifies reality, and it can act as an obstacle to the proper examination of local power systems. When NGO activists and social scientists talk of how 'a community' lobbied local government, built a well, borrowed money or decided on a development strategy, who are they talking about? Do they mean *everyone* in the community, or just the majority, or just the older ones, just the richer ones, just the men? Is the will of 'the community' the same as the will of the community leadership?

The organizers of the Hyderabad Development Authority found that 'self-styled leaders have posed the most serious problem to the execution of the Incremental Development Scheme.' (Siddiqui and Khan 1994: 285) Even elected block representatives exploited their position to cancel plots 'mainly for financial gain'. (1994: 287) Slum leaders tend to seek vertical links with politicians, administrators and other power brokers to 'position themselves for patronage'. (Friedmann 1993: 29) 'The peculiar dynamics of informal settlements often lend themselves to an autocratic style of leadership based on patronage, which reinforce the prevailing inequality of the existing social structure.' (Botes and van Rendsburg 2000: 49; cf. Nientied *et al.* 1990: 45) In addition to issues of outright corruption, most projects have also found significant inequalities along gender and other lines. (Pathirana and Sheng 1992: 8) Community solidarity cannot be automatically assumed: in Seevaleepura, the community contracts were successful, *because* an NGO undertook community development work for several years.' (1992: 13, emphasis added)

It is not just an issue of the development techniques, however. There may be structural obstacles to community co-operation, based not on 'false consciousness' or petty snobbery but on real divergent interests. Rural development strategists have been more cognisant of this than some of their urban counterparts. The Bangladesh Rural Advancement Committee, having failed to establish an all-embracing rural community organization, realized that there was a need for separate groups to represent the divergent interests of landless and landed. So too, it has long been recognized, those living upstream and those living downstream will have different interests in water usage. (Korten 1983: 193) Comparable issues arise in tackling urban housing poverty, yet most policy approaches have not yet been properly adjusted to deal with this. The Community Mortgage Programme in the Philippines, for example, requires beneficiaries 'to be organized as the land titles are transferred to associations rather than individuals'. (Berner 2000: 560) It treats the neighbourhood association as synonymous with the community, and yet 'by agreeing to a selling price acceptable to the landowner, the association [and thus the CMP] willingly or unwillingly excludes a substantial part of the residents'.

(*Ibid.*:12) The CMP 'leads to – or rather uncovers – divisions and conflicts among the apparently homogenous group of the urban poor'. (*Ibid.*: 2)

Ironically, the community idealism so beloved by the new populists is a creation of *outsiders*. Only outsiders would see homogeneity and harmony where there is complexity and conflict. Bottom-up approaches to development need to start from the recognition that exploitation and marginalization also take place inside the slum. Including structurally disadvantaged groups – be they women, children, ethnic or religious minorities, disabled people, renters, or the poorest of the poor – requires NGOs and governments actively to reach out for them: 'Selective participatory practices can be avoided when development workers seek out various sets of interests, rather than listening only to a few community leaders and prominent figures'. (Botes and van Rendsburg 2000: 53)

Local solutions and macro-structures

The notion that those seeking to tackle poverty can ignore the very power systems that generate and perpetuate poverty is an attractive one. It would make things much easier. It is, however, ultimately unsustainable. No development strategy can 'opt out' of the realities of power. Thus the developers of the Sri Lankan Community Contract System had to deal with opposition from government departments: 'The Finance Department objected to the payment of money to communities without the guarantee that they would spend it correctly. The Engineering Department questioned the ability of communities to construct infrastructure of acceptable quality'. (Pathirana and Sheng 1992: 5) Even the least confrontational approaches need to deal with macro-power issues sooner or later.

Let us say that all a programme asked from the government was for land, for which the government would be paid in full. Such a programme, inadequate as it would clearly be for serving the needs of the poor, would still have problems if that government was corrupt or cronyist – as far too many still are, to the detriment of housing programmes in Indonesia, Pakistan and elsewhere. (Siddiqui and Khan 1994; Werlin 1999) Let us then say that the government was neither corrupt nor cronyist. Even then, they would still suffer from what Allende's former Secretary to the Ministry of Justice called 'the contradiction between government programmes which aim to improve the living conditions of poorer groups but which must operate within a legislative structure designed to serve the interests of middle and upper groups.' (Hardoy and Satterthwaite 1989: 24) The failure of states to grant legal recognition to community organizations (like the Sri Lankan CDCs), or even to women's rights to property, hinders the effectiveness of programmes to tackle housing poverty. In addition, housing rules inherited from the colonial powers serve to criminalize the autonomous solutions of the poor. And this is only to talk of legal and administrative solutions – economic structures can represent an even more formidable constraint to policies to increase the power of the poor.

There are some problems, too, that are too big for anyone except governments to solve. A 1989 survey found that about 40% of Jakarta's population depended on groundwater, and that 93% of the city's shallow wells appeared to be faecally contaminated. (Werlin 1999: 1525) Issues like this lead Werlin to call for 'a very powerful as well as humanistic bureaucracy' (*Ibid.*: 1526), 'a strong administration to combine 'development from above' with 'development from below.' (*Ibid.*: 1533) A positive role for civil society, note Mayo and Craig in somewhat softer language than Werlin's, 'necessitates positive support and resourcing from the public sector'. (1995: 9) Self-help should not mean 'don't help'.

No community is an island, and macro-systems act to structure local choices. Anzorena *et al.* may insist on the importance of 'addressing dependency' (1998: 172), but we are all *interdependent* – and Hardoy and Satterthwaite (1989), Aldrich and Sandhu (1995) and Berner (1997) all note the important role of squatting as an essential subsidy for the urban economy. Those calling for 'autonomous development' make a mistake if they start by accepting hugely inequitable wealth distributions as God-given, if they privilege a pseudo-independence for the 'respectable poor' over a changed social structure. The big issue in urban housing poverty, note Hardoy and Satterthwaite, is that 'governments refuse to recognise that they [squatters] are citizens with right and needs for government services.' (1989: 15) On a similar line, Vandergeest (1991) calls for public support for self-help efforts as a 'democratic right' rather than a 'gift' which can be discontinued at will. Even Anzorena *et al.*, despite much of their 'autonomous development' romanticism, accept that 'in most instances, external agencies would be far more effective in reducing poverty in urban areas if their actions strengthened the capacity of low-income groups to *negotiate* with local authorities and to reach agreement on *partnerships to address poverty.*' (1998: 176, emphasis added) The purpose of empowerment is not to make beneficiaries 'independent' but to make them more powerful. The new populists are right to be critical of mere social *inclusion* (the poor are already included – just on bad terms), but voluntary *exclusion* as a 'solution' is equally problematic. Empowerment means *changing* the relationship between rich and poor, not the false option of 'breaking' it.

Self-help can be *part* of a movement for empowerment – by, for example, improving the negotiating strength of the poor – but it can also be a mere cost-cutting and socially regressive approach. Strengthening the power of the poor requires the targeted use of co-operation with wealthy 'allies' and confrontation with wealthy 'opponents': either way, macro-structures cannot be avoided. Self-help can be an excellent *tool* – and collective (or 'community') self-help can be an effective (if imperfect) way of pooling resources for mutual benefit. It should, however, be the start, not the end, of a co-ordinated movement to tackle urban poverty. Empowerment cannot be depoliticized.

Conclusion

The self-help debate does have its merits in creating respect for poor people's capability and creativity, and modesty on the side of development 'experts'. Evidence on the futility of top-down interventions is overwhelming, and a return to government-led development would not help the poor. The opposite extreme, namely relying completely on their own latent capacities, will likely prove to be just as futile. The idea that poor communities can 'develop themselves' – if it means that they require no redistribution of resources, if it means that heterogeneity and inequity *within* communities can be glossed over, if it means that the macro-structures of wealth and power distribution can be ignored – is flawed to the point of being harmful. It harms calls for realistic levels of funding for tackling poverty; it blurs the divergent needs of the heterogeneous poor, and masks those of the poorest; and it risks legitimizing inequity, reinforcing the complacent view that the poor are poor because they have not helped themselves. To knock all resource transfers as 'welfare' or 'charity' is to accept unquestioningly the current distribution of wealth as both optimal and fair. The powerful, Gramsci taught us, maintain their power not just through force and wealth but through ideological hegemony too. In recognizing, as the populists do, the capabilities of poor people to act as 'agents' in their own empowerment, we should not fall into the neo-liberal trap of seeing all assistance to that process as both undeserved and demeaning.

To expect poor people to lead the autonomous lives unattained by the middle-classes is both cruel and unrealistic. To expect 'communities' to be havens of co-operation is utterly naïve; to treat them as homogeneous will further marginalize those most in need. Poverty and wealth are opposite sides of the same coin. The wealthy cannot withdraw from the lives of the poor, and the poor cannot withdraw from the lives of the wealthy – sustainable solutions will require either partnership or confrontation. Self-help approaches can and should be part of strategies to tackle exploitation and marginalization, but should be considered as complements, not as alternatives, to accessible public services and the redistribution of income and wealth. If and where poverty will be reduced is a question of the poor's own demand-making power. If and where power-holders have no price to pay for neglecting the needs of the poor, they will very likely do precisely that.

References

Abatena, H. (1995) 'The significance of community self-help activities in promoting social development', *Journal of Social Development in Africa,* 10 (1): 5-24.

Aldrich, B. C. and Sandhu, R. (1995) 'The global context of housing poverty' in B. C. Aldrich and R. Sandhu (eds.), *Housing the Urban Poor: Policy and Practice in Developing Countries,* London: Zed Books.

Anzorena, J., Bolnick, J., Boonyabancha, S., Cabannes, Y., Hardoy, A., Hasan, A., Levy, C., Mitlin, D., Murphy, D., Patel, S., Saborido, M., Satterthwaite, D. and Stein, A. (1998) 'Reducing urban poverty: some lessons from experience', *Environment and Urbanization,* 10 (1): 167-186.

Baken, R.-J. and van der Linden, J. (1993) 'Getting the incentives right': banking on the formal private sector, *Third World Planning Review,* 15(1): 1-22.

Berner, E. (1997) 'Opportunities and insecurities: globalisation, localities and the struggle for urban land in Manila', *European Journal of Development Research,* 9 (1): 167-182.

Berner, E. (2000) 'Poverty alleviation and the eviction of the poorest: towards urban land reform in the Philippines', *International Journal of Urban and Regional Research,* 24 (3): 554-566.

Berner, E. (2001) 'Learning from informal markets: innovative approaches to land and housing provision',*Development in Practice,* 11(2&3): 292-307.

Botes, L. and van Rensburg, D. (2000) 'Community participation in development: nine plagues and twelve commandments', *Community Development Journal,* 35 (1): 41-58.

Cleaver, F. (1999) 'Paradoxes of participation: questioning participatory approaches to development', *Journal of International Development,* 111(4): 597-612.

De Soto, H. (1989) *The Other Path,* London: Taurus.

De Soto, H. (2000) *The Mystery of Capital: Why Capitalism Triumphs in the West and Fails Elsewhere,* New York: Basic Books.

Durand-Lasserve, A. and Royston, L. (2002) *'Holding Their Ground: Secure Land Tenure for the Urban Poor in Developing Countries',* London: Earthscan.

Friedmann, S. (1993) *The Elusive 'Community: The Dynamics of Negotiated Development,* Cape Town, South Africa: Centre for Policy Studies (Social Contract Series, No. 28).

Hardoy, J.E. and Satterthwaite, D. (1989) *Squatter Citizen: Life in the Urban Third World,* London: Earthscan.

Jones, G. A. (1996) 'The difference between truth and adequacy: (re)joining Baken, van der linden and Malpezzi', *Third World Panning Review,* 18(2): 243-256.

Korten, F. (1993) 'Community participation: a management perspective on obstacles and options', in D. C. Korten and F. B. Alfonso (eds.) *Bureaucracy and the Poor: Closing the Gap,* West Hartford, CT: Kumarian Press.

Mayo, M. and Craig, G. (1995) 'Community participation and empowerment: the human face of adjustment or tools for democratic transformation, in G. Craig and M. Mayo (eds.) *Community Empowerment: A Reader in Participation and Development.* London: Zed Books.

Nientied, P., Mhenni, B. and Wit, J. D. (1990) 'Community participation in low-income housing: potential and paradox', *Community Development Journal,* 25(1): 42-55.

Pathirana, V. and Sheng, Y. K. (1992) 'The Community Contract System in Sri Lanka: an innovative approach for the delivery of basic services to the urban poor, *Habitat International,* 16 (4): 3-14.

Phillips, B. (2000) *The End of Paternalism: Child Beneficiary Participation and Project Effectiveness,* The Hague: Institute of Social Studies (MA Research Paper).

Sen, A. (1999) *Development as Freedom.* New York: Oxford University Press.

Siddiqui, T. A. and Khan, M. (1994) 'The Incremental Development Scheme', *Third World Planning Review,* 16 (3): 277-291.

Taylor, M. (1995) 'Community work and the state: the changing context of UK practice, in G. Craig and M. Mayo (eds.) *Community Empowerment: A Reader in Participation and Development,* London: Zed Books.

Turner, J. C. (1968) 'The squatter settlement: an architecture that works, *Architectural Design,* 38 (4): 357-360.

Turner, J. F. C. (1976) *Housing by People: Towards Autonomy in Building*

Environments, London: Boyars.
UNCHS (United Nations Centre for Human Settlements) (1996) *An Urbanizing World: Global Report on Human Settlements 1996,* Oxford: Oxford University Press.
Vandergeest, P. (1991) 'Gifts and rights: cautionary notes on community self-help in Thailand', *Development and Change,* 22 (3): 421-443.
Werlin, H. (1999) 'The slum upgrading myth', *Urban Studies,* 36, (9): 1523-1534.

Erhard Berner is a Senior Lecturer in Local and Regional Development at the Institute of Social Studies, The Hague, Netherlands. Ben Phillips is an Education Campaign Officer, Oxfam, Oxford, UK: Vol. 40 No. 1 (2005): 17-29.

29

Conceptualizing Community Development in War-Affected Populations: Illustrations from Tigray

Alastair Ager, Alison Strang and Behailu Abebe

Competing discourses of support to war-affected communities

Over the last thirty years, development assistance support to refugee and other war-affected communities has increasingly addressed social and psychological aspects of community recovery in addition to economic factors. Harrell-Bond's classic 1986 text 'Imposing Aid' is principally respected as a searing critique of an assistance regime negligent of the resources, perspectives and capacities of refugee populations. However, in arguing that the conceptualization of refugees upon which such strategies were based was also essentially 'over-socialized', the book was also amongst the first actively to promote consideration of the psychosocial needs of refugee populations. While local culture and community mechanisms are to be respected, argued Harrell-Bond, with the strain placed upon them by conflict and displacement it should not be assumed that such resources are adequate to address the suffering of all, particularly those vulnerable through social or economic position.

In the last three decades there has been a steady increase in programme interventions seeking to address such dimensions of the refugee experience. Media coverage and, arguably, the engagement of European populations in conflict in the course of wars in the Balkans have brought the human dimensions of suffering in war into sharp profile. Humanitarian and development assistance strategy is inevitably shaped by such globalized public sentiment. (Adelman 1999)

Programmes explicitly addressing the broader social and psychological experience of communities impacted by conflict have generally been presented under the 'psychological' banner. But this term has obscured huge variance in terms of goals, strategy and approach. Mental health programmes, particularly those addressing issues of traumatization, have been a significant area of intervention in many settings. (de Jong 2002) Others, particularly those focusing on the needs of children, have targeted support to key agents of socialization within war-affected communities, notably families and schools. (Ahearn *et al.* 1999) Others have adopted a rights-based approach to address the position of vulnerable groups, such as single women. (Lorentzen and Turpin 1998) Others have adopted a broader community development approach, mobilizing communities to address locally defined needs. (Wessells and Monteiro 2001)

More significant than this diversity of approach is the tension in the overall discourse of such interventions. (Ager 1997) Such tension typically stems from the varying status given to 'external' and local knowledge in formulating programmes. Several authors have been critical of the imposition of 'western' concepts and expectations in the course of implementation of such projects. (Bracken *et al.* 1995; Summerfield 1996; Pupavac 2001) While the 'trauma' discourse has come in for particular criticism, the critique of the impact of 'western' discourse on local – often traditional – communities potentially holds as much for the concepts of universal human rights and local participation. Few have responded to such critiques with an assertion of the pre-eminence of western concepts as the fruits of modernity. Rather there has been an attempt to accommodate such critiques by integrating – and valuing – local knowledge within programmatic responses still largely structured around modernistic notions of community well-being. (Ager 2001; Wessells and Monteiro 2001; van de Put and Eisenbruch 2002)

Such attempts at coherent integration of perspective and expertise from local communities and external agencies show a diversity of approach, but inevitably are required to face a consistent set of conceptual and practical issues. The Psychosocial Working Group (2005) was established in 2000 to bring together five international NGOs (Save the Children US, International Rescue Committee, Medecins sans Frontieres – Holland, Christian Children's Fund and Mercy Corps) and five research groups (from QMUC Edinburgh, Oxford, Columbia, Harvard and U. Penn) to formulate a framework for coherent action, evaluation and development for this developing field. The resulting framework addresses a broad range of issues of relevance for community development work in refugee communities.

A conceptual framework for psychosocial intervention in complex emergencies

The framework begins with the assumption that in the context of most initiatives, the needs of individuals are generally appropriately conceptualized within the context of a family or household which, in turn, is located within an 'affected community'. (Hobfoll 1998) The community is considered to be 'affected' by some particular series of events, related to war and displacement, which has disrupted or diminished the resources available to that community. In terms of the 'psychosocial well-being' of the community, three particular domains are recognized as significant: human capacity, social ecology, culture and values.

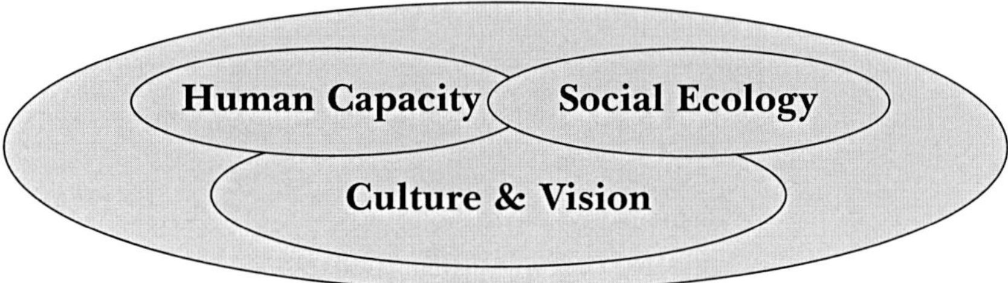

Figure 1: The key domains that determine psychosocial well-being within a community

Conflict and displacement can lead to a loss of 'human capacity' within the community. This domain is taken to constitute such resources as the physical and mental health of community members and the skills and knowledge of people (which can be referred to as the 'human capital' of the community). Events can clearly reduce such human capacity by many means. Physical disability, loss of skilled labour, social withdrawal and depression all serve to degrade human capacity, as do less tangible impacts such as a reduced sense of control over events and circumstances.

The circumstances of war and seeking refuge also frequently lead to a disruption of the 'social ecology' of a community, involving social relations within families, peer groups, religious and cultural institutions, links with civic and political authorities etc. (that can be referred to as the 'social capital' of the community). Targeted disruption of such structures and networks is often the central focus of contemporary political and military conflict. (Summerfield 1999) Impacts on the social ecology of an affected community frequently include changes in power relations between ethnic groups and shifts in gender relations. (Lorentzen and Turpin 1998)

Events may also disrupt the 'culture and values' of community, challenging human rights, and cultural values and mores (that can be referred to as the 'cultural capital' of the community). Conflict can threaten cultural traditions of meaning that have served to unite and give identity to a community. (Wessells 1999) Conflict can also serve to reinforce hardened images of other political or ethnic groups, encouraging escalation of violence and hatred. (Kostorova-Unkovska and Pankovska 1992)

Whilst psychosocial well-being is appropriately defined with respect to these three core domains of human capacity, social ecology and culture and values, loss of physical, economic and environmental resources clearly have major impacts in many refugee settings. Availability – and depletion – of such resources define the broader context within which individuals, families and communities seek to protect their well-being.

The framework has recently been used to map the resources depleted within communities displaced by the Ethiopian-Eritrean war of the late 1990s. In the border town of Zalanbesa – and across rural villages of Northern Tigray – it identified significant loss of human capacity in terms of knowledge and livelihoods (particularly those related to cross-border trade), major disruption to social networks which had previously spanned the border, and challenge to culture and values both through the desecration of places of worship and the disruption of processes of identity. (Abebe, 2004) Perhaps far more usefully, however, the framework also identifies the resources that are being deployed by communities in engaging with the events and aftermath of the conflict, resources which can again be mapped across the identified domains. In terms of human capacity and livelihoods, women have been particularly successful in developing small trading enterprises. Historically-grounded social connections are being utilized to rebuild wider community networks, and capitalized upon for social support and economic development. Cultural traditions of religious associations have re-emerged, providing a key platform of shared analysis of challenges and co-ordinated action. Mythico-history and personal identification with saints and angels are being used as key sources of sense-making and resilience, drawn from across communities.

The framework thus serves not simply as a means of mapping the disruption and depletion of community resources in the context of war and displacement but, most crucially, as a means of mapping emerging *engagement* by communities in protecting and promoting well-being. This notion of local engagement is crucial to the use of the framework, as the model supports the view that community development should seek to bolster existing community processes. The resources that a project or intervention brings to the community should be matched to the existing, emergent processes of engagement, rather than used to promote coping or development processes 'alien' to that community.

The process by which the community assents the receipt of external resources (that again can be mapped as involving human, social or cultural capital) is one of *negotiation*. This interaction between (powerful) external agencies and local (weakened) communities clearly relates to the conceptual tensions of the field identified earlier, and must be seen as the key to effective, sustainable intervention.

Finally, it is tempting in working with war-affected communities to think of the process of community engagement as one with the goal of 'restoration' of the situation existing before the impact of events, a perspective emphasized by a number of authors. (Ager 1999) The goal of intervention would thus be to restore human, social and cultural capital – and the interaction between them – to a situation as before the conflict. Settings such as Rwanda and East Timor, where elements of a pre-conflict situation have contributed directly to the onset of violence, suggest that it may be more helpful to think of this process as one of *transformation*, involving new relationships between the capacities, linkages, values and resources of that community. In Zalanbesa, despite the importance given to tradition and history in the current recovery period, changes in the broader political landscape – notably state development processes within Eritrea and Ethiopia – require that there is a degree of transformation in community processes and values. (Abebe 2004)

Social capital: the role of bonds, bridges and links in community development

There is a range of implications of the above framework for the theorizing of community development work with refugee communities post-conflict. Those selected for further consideration here relate to particular challenges in such work. In the next section, process issues of community development support are considered, structured around a consideration of the processes identified above of engagement, negotiation and transformation. In this section, aspects of the domain of social ecology are particularly highlighted, addressing the various forms of social connection that may usefully be fostered post-conflict.

The domain of social ecology can be elaborated with respect to a number of concepts, but the language of social capital is gaining increasing prominence as an explanatory and organizing tool. (Field 2003) Although particularly promoted by the World Bank (2003), acknowledging the value of the social resources of relationship and trust has found wide acceptance, particularly in work in post-conflict settings, where issues of inter-group conflict and exclusion may be seen to have contributed to the onset of war and displacement. (Colletta and Cullen 2000)

Although there are many approaches to understanding resources available through social connection, a structure of clear relevance to such environments is one that distinguishes between bonding, bridging and linking forms of social capital. (Woolcock 1998) Social bonds are seen as 'strong ties' (generally held with kin and wider co-ethnic or co-faith members of a group), social bridges are comparatively 'weak ties' (with other communities) and social links indicate the connection with 'vertical' structures of the state.

Using this template to consider the situation in Zalenbesa, the social ecology of the war – and displacement-impacted areas – reflected the resilience of social bonds defined by various means (eg lineage, shared mythico-history, etc). However, community development initiatives in the area have frequently been implemented without a keen awareness of the huge resource represented by such bonds. (Abebe 2004) Rotational shared meals such as *Sewasanbat* provided a powerful indigenous structure onto which initiatives could have been grafted. Further, the strengthening of governance in Northern Tigray following the conflict represented a positive means of exploiting social linkage to deliver food aid and emergency humanitarian assistance, but at the cost of weakening cross-border bridging ties that had been a crucial social, cultural and economic resource for the area for decades. Strengthening social linkage – promoting identification with national agendas – compromised investment in social bridging capital.

Such analysis is of particular interest if one asks what form of social capital should be the focus of community development efforts. Clearly, this will depend upon context. There may be occasions when citizenship, rights and governance education programmes – strengthening social links through participation in local democracy and the working of the state – will be a key priority. In others, perhaps where inter-ethnic conflict has played a contributory role to current circumstances, developing bridging capital across community groups will be the relevant priority. In others, where social fabric has been devastated by war, exploiting social bonds for protection and support may be primary. While such prioritization will be context dependent, it is worth noting the distinctive role of bonding and bridging capital in formulations such as that of Woolcock. (1998) Social bonds can be seen to be principally defensive and protective in function, a key element in enhancing wellbeing. In contrast, social bridges are required for economic and political development. Such ideas prompt a 'phased approach' to fostering the development of social capital in refugee settings: social bonds provide the initial focus as a basis for security; once these are established social bridges may be strengthened to support broader social and economic development. Such principles have, for instance, informed recent work on supporting processes of refugee integration in the UK. (Ager and Strang 2004)

The key processes of engagement negotiation and transformation

Earlier, the Psychosocial Working Group framework was used to highlight the distinctive processes of engagement, negotiation and transformation. Working coherently to support these processes is an important foundation of community development work with refugee communities, as can again be illustrated with respect to the war-affected area of Northern Tigray.

Detailed study of these communities – that have received little attention by way of international development assistance – reveals the intense level of *engagement* by these communities with post-war circumstances. In terms of the framework, such engagement involved the deployment of human, social and cultural capital available to communities. While such responses have not redressed all social and material needs of these areas, they have achieved huge recovery of well-being and livelihood. While it can appear to be in communities' interests to 'under-report' such resilience and coping to mobilize more external assistance (Abebe 2004), effective deployment of such external resources must build upon existing processes of community engagement. Such engagement is often 'invisible' to external agencies (PWG 2003), but surfacing such capacity is a crucial first step in developing effective partnership working.

This leads to consideration of the second key process of *negotiation*.

The power differentials between local Tigrayan communities and potential intervening agencies were so great – and the need for mobilizing addition resources so pressing – that (somewhat complicitly, as noted above) the agendas of the latter largely dictated to the former. What is required is an approach – prompted by the conceptualization presented in *Figure 2* – that acknowledges the distinctive agendas of engagement of affected and intervening external communities, but also the areas of their potential complementarity. In short, the domains of human capacity, social ecology and culture and values can serve as a framework to evaluate the mandate and resources of potential intervening agencies with respect to the depletion of resources across such domains within a war-affected community.

Community of external intervention

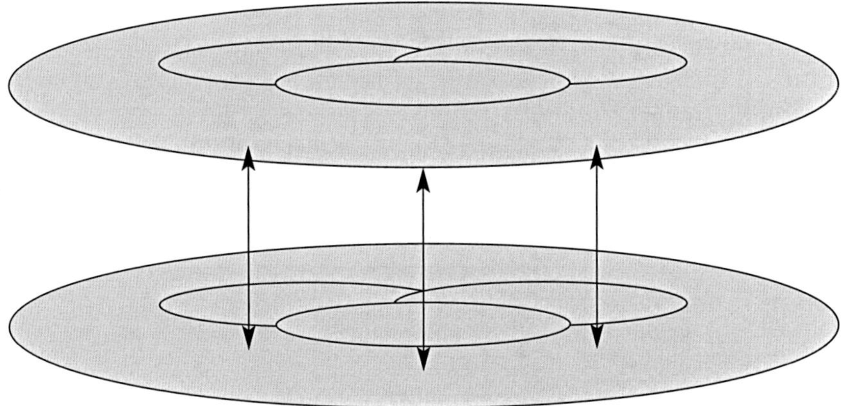

War-affected community

Figure 2: External resources can be mobilized to complement the engagement of human, social and cultural capital by affected communities

Such explicit examination of what intervening agencies 'have to offer' with respect to local coping strategies and needs promises to protect against the worst distortions of assistance in war-affected populations, where resources offered do not match requirements, but are accepted as they nonetheless boost local resource availability. (Eyber 2001)

Finally, the fact that communities generally seek not a restoration of their human, social and cultural capital but a *transformation* of the deployment of such resources provides a third process challenge. Transformation inevitably unleashes divergent visions across a community. External agencies entering with modernistic notions of 'awareness raising', 'rights' and 'empowerment' may inevitably be drawn into driving or privileging certain of these visions at the expense of others. Processes of 'good governance' or 'democratization' are not value-free policy goals. External actors need again, therefore, to explicitly consider their mandate for intervention, this time with respect to processes of community transformation.

The framework suggests that 'unlocking' resources within communities that have been under-deployed (due to marginalization, for instance) provides one technical basis for intervention. What voices and agendas have been muted by pre-existing structures, whose surfacing can benefit the community as a whole? Within Tigray, continuity with the past provided rich resources for post-conflict recovery. But many social groups and structures did not seek restoration of a past order. Social bonds, bridges and links began to accommodate to not only the new political context, but to new economic and gender relations shaped by the conflict. (Abebe 2004) In many such developments, history could serve as a foundation for the future, far more than a constraint upon it.

References

Abebe, D. (2004) 'Coping and Resilience in War-affected Areas of Tigray, Ethiopia'. Queen Margaret University College, Edinburgh: unpublished doctoral dissertation.

Adelman, H. (1999) 'Modernity, globalization, refugees and displacement' In: A. Ager (ed.) *Refugees: Perspectives on the Experience of Forced Migration,* London: Cassell.

Ager, A. (1997) 'Tensions in the psychosocial discourse', *Development in Practice,* 7(4): 402-407.

Ager, A. (1999) 'Perspectives on the refugee experience' In: A. Ager (ed.) *Refugees: Perspectives on the Experience of Forced Migration.* London: Cassell.

Ager, A. and Strang, A., (2004). *Indicators of Integration.* London: Home Office.

Ager, A. (2001) 'The problem of the wool' In: M. Loughry and A. Ager (eds) *The Refugee Experience: A Psychosocial Training Module,* Revised edition, Oxford: Refugee Studies Centre.

Ahearn, F., Loughry, M. and Ager, A. (1999) 'The experience of refugee children' In: A. Ager (ed.) *Refugees: Perspectives on the Experience of Forced Migration,* London: Cassell.

Bracken, P., Giller, J. E. and Summerfield, D. (1995) 'Psychological responses to war and atrocity: the limitations of current concepts' *Social Sciences and Medicine*, 40(8): 1073-1082.

Colletta, N. J. and Cullen, M. L. (2000) *Violent Conflict and the Transformation of Social Capital*, New York: World Bank.

De Jong, J. (2002) *Trauma, War and Violence: Public Mental Health in Socio-Cultural Context*, New York: Kluwer/Plenum.

Eyber, C. (2001) 'Alleviating Psychosocial Suffering: An Analysis of Approaches to Coping with War-related Distress in Angola'. Unpublished doctoral dissertation. Edinburgh: Queen Margaret University College.

Field, I. (2003) *Social Capital*, London: Routledge.

Harrell-Bond, B. (1986) *Imposing Aid: Emergency Assistance to Refugees*. Oxford: Oxford University Press.

Hobfoll, S. (1998) *Stress, Culture & Community: The Psychology and Philosophy of Stress*. New York Plenum.

Kostorova-Unkovska, L. and Pankovska, V. (1992) *Children Hurt by War.* Skopje, Macedonia: General Children's Consulate of the Republic of Macedonia.

Lorentzen, L. and Turpin, J. (1998) *The Women and War Reader,* New York: New York University Press.

Pupavac, V. (2001) 'Therapeutic governance: psycho-social intervention and trauma risk management', *Disasters,* 25(4): 358-372.

PWG (2003) *Psychosocial Intervention in Complex Emergencies: A Conceptual Framework*. Edinburgh: IIHD, QMUC.

Summerfield, D. (1996) *The Impact of War and Atrocity on Civilian Populations: Basic Principles for NGO Interventions and a Critique of Psychosocial Trauma Projects*. London: Relief and Rehabilitation Network Paper 14, Overseas Development Institute.

Summerfield, D. (1999) 'Sociocultural dimensions of war, displacement and conflict, in A. Ager (ed.) *Refugees: Perspectives on the Experience of Forced Migration*. London: Cassell.

Van de Put, W. and Eisenbruch, M. (2002) 'The Cambodian Experience' In: J. de Jong (ed.) *Trauma, War and Violence: Public Mental Health in Socio-Cultural Context,* New York: Kluwer/Plenum.

Wessells, M. (1999) 'Culture, power and community: intercultural approaches to psychosocial assistance and healing', In: K. Nader, N. Dubrow and D. Stamm (eds) *Honouring Differences: Cultural Issues in the Treatment of Trauma and Loss,* New York: Taylor and Francis.

Wessells, M. and Monteiro, C. (2001). 'Psychosocial interventions and post-war reconstruction in Angola: interweaving Western and traditional approaches', In: D. Christie, R. V. Wagner, and D. Winter (eds) *Peace, Conflict and Violence: Peace Psychology for the 21st Century,* Upper Saddle River, NJ: Prentice Hall,.

World Bank (2003) *Social Capital for Development,* Washington DC: World

Bank, 18 December 2003 accessed at:
http://www.worldbank.org/poverty/scapital/whatsc.htm.
Woolcock, M. (1998) 'Social capital and economic development: towards a theoretical synthesis and policy framework', *Theory and Society*, 27(2): 151-208.

Professor Alastair Ager, Dr Alison Strang and Dr Behailu Abebe work in the Institute for International Health & Development in Edinburgh: Vol. 40 No. 2 (2005): 158-168, Special issue on Community Development with Refugees.

COMMUNITY WORK

in the 1990s

Edited by

Sidney Jacobs

&

Keith Popple

COMMUNITY work needs to recapture its radical traditions. During the 1980s, the very survival of community work demanded considerable flexibility and innovation. Such adaptability is reflected in a diversity of initiatives spread throughout the country, some of which are represented here.

This textbook was conceived as a tribute to Phil Bashford, a community worker in Birmingham. His was essentially a humane response to society's ills, and his vision was of a collectivist and democratic future. He believed passionately in the ability of the exploited and oppressed everywhere to organise themselves, under their own leadership, against injustice. It is these values that this book seeks to keep alive within community work.

Available from Spokesman Books

Price: £11.99
ISBN: 978 0 85124 569 0

www.spokesmanbooks.com

Community Development Journal

Community Development Journal
is a forum for the international
exchange of contemporary debates
and topics in community development
theory and practice. For more
information about the journal,
including forthcoming issues and
submission instructions, visit the
journal homepage.

www.cdj.oxfordjournals.org